Open access edition supported by the National Endowment for the Humanities / Andrew W. Mellon Foundation Humanities Open Book Program.

© 2019 Johns Hopkins University Press
Published 2019

Johns Hopkins University Press
2715 North Charles Street
Baltimore, Maryland 21218-4363
www.press.jhu.edu

The text of this book is licensed under a Creative Commons Attribution-NonCommercial-NoDerivatives 4.0 International License: https://creativecommons.org/licenses/by-nc-nd/4.0/.
CC BY-NC-ND

ISBN-13: 978-1-4214-3607-4 (open access)
ISBN-10: 1-4214-3607-8 (open access)

ISBN-13: 978-1-4214-3605-0 (pbk. : alk. paper)
ISBN-10: 1-4214-3605-1 (pbk. : alk. paper)

ISBN-13: 978-1-4214-3606-7 (electronic)
ISBN-10: 1-4214-3606-X (electronic)

This page supersedes the copyright page included in the original publication of this work.

*Making Furniture in
Preindustrial America*

Studies in Industry and Society
PHILIP B. SCRANTON, SERIES EDITOR

Published with the assistance of the Hagley Museum and Library

1. BURTON W. FOLSOM, JR.
   Urban Capitalists: Entrepreneurs and City Growth in Pennsylvania's Lackawanna and Lehigh Regions, 1800–1920

2. JOHN BODNAR
   Workers' World: Kinship, Community, and Protest in an Industrial Society, 1900–1940

3. PAUL F. PASKOFF
   Industrial Evolution: Organization, Structure, and Growth of the Pennsylvania Iron Industry, 1750–1860

4. DAVID A. HOUNSHELL
   From the American System to Mass Production, 1800–1932: The Development of Manufacturing Technology in the United States

5. CYNTHIA J. SHELTON
   The Mills of Manayunk: Industrialization and Social Conflict in the Philadelphia Region, 1787–1837

6. JOANNE YATES
   Control through Communication: The Rise of System in American Management

7. CHARLES W. CHEAPE
   Strictly Business: Walter Carpenter at Du Pont and General Motors

8. JOHN K. BROWN
   The Baldwin Locomotive Works, 1831–1915: A Study in American Industrial Practice

9. JAMES P. KRAFT
   Stage to Studio: Musicians and the Sound Revolution, 1890–1950

10. EDWARD S. COOKE JR.
    Making Furniture in Preindustrial America: The Social Economy of Newtown and Woodbury, Connecticut

EDWARD S. COOKE JR.

Making Furniture in Preindustrial America

The Social Economy of Newtown and Woodbury, Connecticut

The Johns Hopkins University Press
BALTIMORE AND LONDON

This book has been brought to publication with the generous assistance of the Frederick W. Hilles Publication Fund of Yale University.

© 1996 The Johns Hopkins University Press
All rights reserved. Published 1996

05 04 03 02 01 00 99 98 97 96   5 4 3 2 1

The Johns Hopkins University Press
2715 North Charles Street, Baltimore, Maryland 21218-4319
The Johns Hopkins Press Ltd., London

Library of Congress Cataloging-in-Publication Data will be found at the end of this book
A catalog record for this book is available from the British Library.

ISBN 0-8018-5253-6

For Charles F. Montgomery, who provided the initial direction, and Carol, Ben, and Rachel, who have supported and enriched that direction

Contents

	List of Tables and Charts	ix
	Acknowledgments	xi
INTRODUCTION	The Need for the Artisanal Voice	3
ONE	The Preindustrial Joiner in Western Connecticut, 1760–1820	13
TWO	The Social Economy of the Preindustrial Joiner	33
THREE	The Joiners of Newtown and Woodbury	49
FOUR	Socioeconomic Structure in Newtown and Woodbury	69
FIVE	Consumer Behavior in Newtown and Woodbury	91
SIX	Workmanship of Habit: The Furniture of Newtown	118
SEVEN	Workmanship of Competition: The Furniture of Woodbury	151
CONCLUSION	The Response to Market Capitalism	190
APPENDIX A	Biographies of Newtown Joiners, 1760–1820	201
APPENDIX B	Biographies of Woodbury Joiners, 1760–1820	217
	Notes	233
	Glossary of Furniture Terms	273
	Note on Sources and Methods	277
	Index	285

Tables and Charts

Tables

1. Wagon and spinning wheel ownership	16
2. Newtown joiners	50
3. Woodbury joiners	51
4. Population of Newtown and Woodbury	70
5. Gross rates of persistence	71
6. Grains	72
7. Animal ownership	72
8. Packed meat and dairy products	73
9. Cowhouses and horsehouses	76
10. Cider and clothmaking	77
11. Ownership of artisanal equipment	77
12. Tax list 1798	79
13. Raw frequencies of selected household goods	95
14. Chairs	97
15. Storage forms	100
16. Table	102
17. Woods and colors of seating furniture	103
18. Mahogany and cherry tables and case furniture	104
19. Raw frequencies of selected artifacts	105
20. Distribution of furniture by four value categories	106
21. Book ownership	113

Charts

1. Mean value of consumer goods	92
2. Mean/median values of household goods	94
3. Mean/median values of furniture	95

Acknowledgments

I have incurred numerous debts in the course of developing, researching, and writing this book on the context of furnituremaking in preindustrial America. In honing the multidisciplinary nature of this study, I benefited greatly from the comments and suggestions of numerous colleagues, especially Abbott Lowell Cummings, John Demos, David Hall, Patricia Kane, John Kirk, Myron Stachiw, Robert Trent, and Electa Kane Tritsch. I am particularly pleased to recognize the contributions of two other individuals. James Henretta, who served as my advisor for the dissertation that forms the core of this book, was tireless in his close readings of the manuscript, provided extensive, insightful comments, and demanded that the study of material culture meet the highest standards of social history. Ann Smith, director of the Mattatuck Museum, hired me as a guest curator to research and mount an exhibition of Newtown and Woodbury furniture. Throughout planning the project, conducting research on local manuscripts and furniture, the exhibit's installation, and preparation of the catalogue, Ann supported my endeavors with energy, enthusiasm, and commitment. Her insistence on the accessibility of public history kept my efforts grounded.

Most of my research involved months of extensive fieldwork in Connecticut. For help in locating examples of Newtown and Woodbury furniture and building an appropriate object pool, I would like to thank Harold Cole, Joel Finn, the late Ken Hammett, the late Frank Johnson, Dan Shied, Linda Stamm, William Warren, and many other private individuals whose homes I visited to examine furniture. One of the true joys of fieldwork is the opportunity to share information and to feel part of the process of maintaining historical memory. The staffs of many libraries, museums, historical societies, and town clerk's offices also willingly provided assistance: Connecticut State Library, Yale University Library, Cyraneus Booth Library, Old

Sturbridge Village, Yale University Art Gallery, Winterthur Museum, Colonial Williamsburg, Historic Deerfield, Mattatuck Historical Society, New Haven Colony Historical Society, Scott-Fanton House, Newtown Historical Society, Newtown Town Hall, Southbury Town Hall, and Woodbury Town Hall. During my time in Connecticut, many people offered hospitality and friendship: Woody and Beverly Mosch; Ken, Connie, and Matt Minor; Peter and Linda Nelson; David and Jacky Corrigan; Gene Leach; and Elizabeth Baker.

Several colleagues provided constant support, encouragement, and advice throughout the writing of this book and have read drafts of the manuscript. It is my hope that Bill Cotton, Adrienne Hood, Bill Hosley, and Barbara and Gerry Ward realize the important role they have played in shaping this publication.

In the course of research and writing, I have been very fortunate to receive several grants and fellowships. Costs of some of the early research were subsidized in part by the Mattatuck Museum during the planning stages for the 1982 exhibition "Fiddlebacks and Crooked-backs: Elijah Booth and Other Joiners in Newtown and Woodbury, Connecticut, 1750–1820." That show and the accompanying catalogue attracted great interest in the area and brought many additional objects and account books to my attention. Through a Forman Fellowship at the Winterthur Museum, I was able to read the account books of many different New England joiners, draft the first two chapters of the book, and present my work to colleagues there. While working at the Museum of Fine Arts, Boston, I received a Lamb-Mellon Grant to undertake further documentation of the furniture of Newtown and Woodbury. I greatly appreciate the support and confidence of Alan Shestack and Jonathan Fairbanks in awarding me that grant. A senior faculty fellowship from Yale University made it possible to concentrate on preparation of the final manuscript.

Daniel Tenney and Celine Larkin willingly offered their considerable drafting skills, knowledge of graphics, and encouraging friendship. Luke Beckerdite, editor of *American Furniture 1995*, helped by commenting on part of the manuscript and procuring many of the photographs in this volume; an article condensed from chapters 1 and 2 appears in that journal. I would like to thank the Chipstone Foundation, publishers of *American Furniture*, for providing another forum in which to present my ideas. My editor at the Johns Hopkins University Press, Robert J. Brugger, and copyeditor Julie McCarthy provided excellent counsel and comments.

Personal thanks are owed to my parents, Ted and Barbara Cooke, and my sisters and their husbands, Allison and Blake Brown and Cate and Chip Lux, for their interest in my work. My greatest debt is to my wife, Carol, and our children, Ben and Rachel. Carol watched over this book for more than a decade and was indefatigable in her encouragement, support, and willingness to help see the publication to print. Ben and Rachel have provided important perspective and energy to the final product.

Making Furniture in Preindustrial America

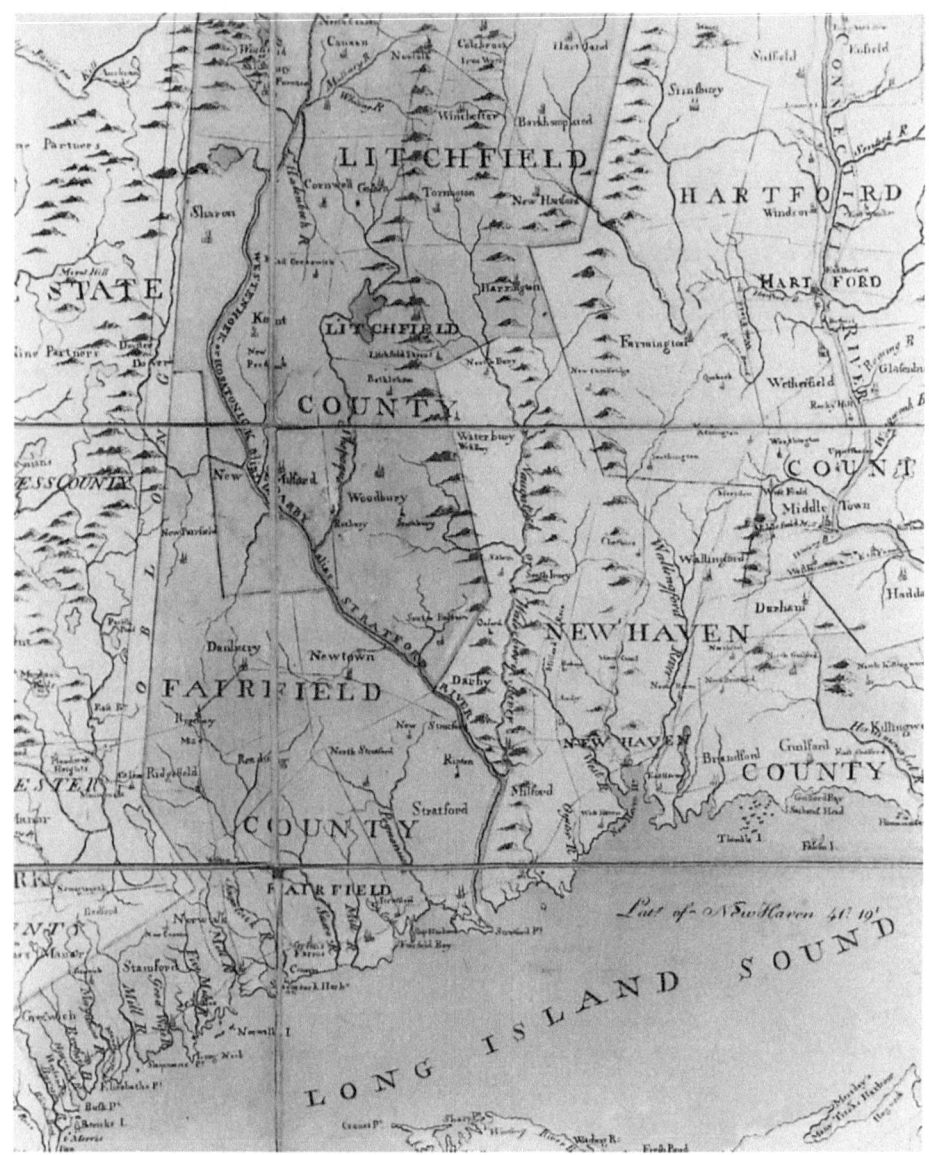

Fig. 1. Detail of Bernard Romans's map, *Connecticut and Parts Adjacent*, 1777. Beinecke Rare Book and Manuscript Library, Yale University.

INTRODUCTION

The Need for the Artisanal Voice

Samuel Goodrich, author of the many Peter Parley stories published in the second quarter of the nineteenth century, grew up in the southwestern Connecticut hill town of Ridgefield during the late eighteenth and early nineteenth centuries. Reflecting on his childhood home several decades later, Goodrich commented on the local agrarian economy, the role of yeomen-craftsmen, and the "simple character" of domestic furnishings. "Nearly all the inhabitants of Ridgefield were farmers, with the few mechanics that were necessary to carry on society in a somewhat primeval state," he wrote. "Even the person not professionally devoted to agriculture had each his own farm, or least his garden and home lot, with his pigs, poultry, and cattle. . . . The household, as well as political, economy of those days lay in this,—that every family lived as much as possible within itself."[1] Among those not professionally devoted solely to farming were the blacksmith David Olmstead and the joiner, or furnituremaker, Elisha Hawley. These craftsmen served both economic and cultural roles. Their "articles of use" were important items of exchange in the specie-poor economy. On a deeper level, the artifacts they produced "expressly" for their fellow townspeople became cherished possessions. Goodrich fondly recalled the identity of the local craftsmen who helped to create his family's domestic environment.[2]

Goodrich's reminiscences draw attention to an important segment of the New England preindustrial population, yet his commentary reveals how difficult it can be to integrate the study of craftsmen and farmers with analysis of artifacts and economics. In spite of his perceptive suggestion that craftsmen such as joiners played an important economic and cultural role in the network of independent households in Ridgefield, Goodrich was not able to explicate fully the meaning of yeomen-craftsmen and their work in preindustrial western Connecticut. His recollections reveal a distance from the artisanal world. Goodrich had considerable knowledge of agricultural practices and rhythms that enabled him to comment on the agricultural economy of Ridgefield, but he lacked familiarity with the craftsman's practices and rhythms. Activities and decisions of the joiner's shop remained obscure and mysterious, and Goodrich consequently could not link completely the artisanal to the agricultural economy. Goodrich also seemed unable to understand the full dimensions of the craftsman's products, lumping Elisha Hawley's furniture under the rubric "simple" or "primeval." Such comments reveal both Goodrich's limited experience—he was a user or owner of only a certain set of products made in Hawley's shop—and his perspective as someone who gained abundant domestic refinement in his later years. Generalizations drawn from a few pieces of furniture precluded a full grasp of the range of choices and possibilities within that shop or the alternatives offered by other shops. Goodrich could not understand the artifactual language on its own terms or within the context of its production and use; he merely compared the furnishings of his youth with those of his later life.

The limitations of Goodrich's observations about the fit of artisanal work in the mixed agricultural economy of Connecticut in the late colonial and early national period indicate the need to look more closely and analytically at craftwork during this time, understand its integral role in a community's economic and cultural activity, probe artisans' values and decisions in a period of economic intensification and diversification, uncover the multiple meanings of craft products, and develop a more complete sense of preindustrial production and its links to industrial manufacture. Examination of craftwork's economic context builds upon the studies of many social historians who have focused considerable attention on the agricultural elements of household economies—interdependence of a community's farms, the dense network of service transactions that drew a neighborhood or community together and permitted an even distribution of work, and the cognate structure of kinship and transmission that ensured the establishment of new households within the existing structure.[3]

During the sixty-year period between 1760 and 1820, New Englanders experienced many significant changes that included war for independence, creation of a new federal government, growth of commercial and manufacturing interests, and a steadily increasing and more mobile population. New forms of economic relationships—greater availability of cash, increasing reliance on credit, institution of interest payments, job specialization, and closer connections with external markets—began to transform the New England countryside into a capitalist economy. Many New Englanders sought to preserve familial autonomy and local exchange value while adapting to the various changes around them. In describing the coping strategies of rural New England farmers living in the capitalist world but not of it, the historian Christopher Clark coined the term *involution*. Rather than simply adopting a new form of society, rural New Englanders intensified or specialized their production to grapple with demographic growth, social inequalities, and land shortages. This permitted rural farmers to blend a traditional *mentalité* with market awareness. The structures or institutions for concentration and control of production were nascent and weak, so involution's form and rate took on a very local and regional character.[4]

The uneven spread of capitalist systems and the ability and willingness of New Englanders to adopt involution strategies raise the question of an appropriate term to describe the constantly changing social and production relations of New Englanders during this period. What existing structures, habits, and values were the foundation for the varied intensification of agricultural and craft activity in the early nineteenth century? The term *social economy* is an appropriate one for New England because it refers to a particularized web of relations and activities that preceded a capitalist political economy. Since markets were created in, derived from, and responded to social circumstances, the locus of power remained rooted in communities and regions during this transformation. Social economy affirms the conscious decisions of households or of a series of households about resource allocation for production and exchange. The demands of craft processes and the demand for the craft product often guided decisions about household activities and relations, consumption, and involvement with the market. An analysis of the social economy thus allows consideration of craftwork and manufacturing as equals to agriculture rather than as only supplemental to it.[5]

Social economy provides a particularly valuable paradigm with which to probe the craftsman's role and product in a specie-poor, preindustrial economy. The period under study was a time when the value of work and objects was gauged more by social standards than by monetary ones. The product both emerged from and helped to shape a specific set of social relationships. In such an integrated community, *skill* took on meanings far different from today's notions of quality. The act of making a domestic object or farm implement was much more than the competent creation of a functional or utilitarian thing. Making an object could be a favor, a service, an obligation, or a payment. The craftsman chose from a wide variety of locally acceptable forms and details to match the intention or social or economic credit of his client. Notions of design concept and work performance were defined through dynamic local social relations.[6]

Unfortunately the artisanal voice has not been an integral part of recent scholarship on New England society during the late colonial and early national periods. Most of the new historical scholarship has focused on agrarian production and exchange with local storekeepers or merchants. Few historians have considered the true diversity of by-employment in the mixed agricultural economy of colonial New England. Their analytic energies are devoted to the types and extent of crops, the species and uses of animals, and the merchant's increased power in determining farmers' decisions. By ignoring artisans or viewing craftwork as a new occupation, historians leave unexamined the true mixed agricultural economy of the region, an economy that incorporates grains, animals, and crafts.[7]

Lack of historical interest in premechanized production, even in textiles, has hindered full interpretation of early craft production as an economic and cultural process. Rural artisans rarely have been the focus of analytic research. One of two standard secondary works that continue to be cited is Rolla Tryon's 1917 publication *Household Manufactures in the United States, 1684–1860*, in which the author falsely separates the "system of family manufacturing" from the "handicraft system." Concentrating almost exclusively on textiles and wearing apparel, Tryon seeks to demonstrate that home industry made people virtuous citizens. Most rural families produced their own material necessities or patronized itinerant or part-time craftsmen for those items beyond their capabilities. Implicit in Tryon's argument is that part-time craftsmen were semiskilled or unskilled artisans. Romanticism, inadequate analysis of shop-floor practices and technology, and no consideration of the relationship between imported work and locally produced work call Tryon's analysis into question.[8]

Carl Bridenbaugh's *The Colonial Craftsman*, a 1950 publication that is the other most frequently cited book, suffers from similar shortcomings. Bridenbaugh contrasted the rural craftsman with his urban counterpart, who sharpened his skills through competition and followed fashion closely. In setting up this polarized framework, Bridenbaugh overlooked the potential competence of rural craftsmen—part-time does not necessarily mean part-skilled—and their access to a variety of styles. Competition among urban craftsmen easily could have resulted in shoddy workmanship or a concentration on cheap, conservative furniture for export. Ignoring craft processes and products, the historian removed craftsmen from their particular work and its context. The broad strokes of Bridenbaugh's impressionistic overview obscure the realities of the artisans' varied experiences and preclude any understanding of their actual fit in local economies.[9]

The study of preindustrial craftsmen has been the focus of decorative arts scholars, most of whom have written object-centered descriptive biographies or compiled long lists of craftsmen with genealogical information or skeletal biographies. Such publications, which have their origins in antiquarianism and are perpetuated by the predominant collector/dealer mentality of the field, require merely the gathering of new data to prove who made a specific object and when. The genealogical approach has overemphasized the visible master craftsmen who signed their work or who advertised, with less attention paid to craftsmen who appear rarely in the more accessible historical records. Such biases preclude gaining information about artisanal hierarchies and the context of production and use.[10] Furthermore, most artisanal studies have concentrated on craftsmen working in major urban areas; objects made elsewhere often are viewed as generic New England examples. Works from the rural Northeast have been interpreted as slavish imitative works, eccentric creations, or simple wares, all produced by anonymous craftsmen. As a result we understand little about the material culture in specific rural areas, why certain patterns of production and use gained acceptance, and how the artifacts reveal broader issues of social and economic activity.[11]

Clearly there is a need to reassess craftwork on two concurrent fronts. First, we need to integrate information drawn from account books, inventories and wills, tax lists, census records, town and church records, land deeds, genealogies, diaries, and other pertinent material in a more sophisticated manner. Scholars of preindustrial crafts typically use these records to chronicle the forms made by a single artisan or to demonstrate the time he devoted to making his wares. Most of these studies also analyze the works' monetary value and the tax ratings of craftsmen and their clients. There is little attempt to reconstruct the local economy and customers' status beyond these criteria.[12] Along with such basic issues as seasonal rhythms, sources of tools and materials, clients, and identification of the workforce, we should explore the initiation of transactions, locations of different productive tasks, how work was organized, how tasks were altered when demand fluctuated, how the craftsman's age affected the organization of the shop and the type of work, and how the shop related to others in the town or region. In short we need to ask deeper questions to allow us to reconstruct the craftsman's world of relationships, the choices or influences that affected him, and the reasons behind behavioral patterns. In this way historians would apply questions to craftwork similar to those they already apply to agricultural work.[13]

Woodworkers of the preindustrial "age of wood" are a particularly promising artisanal group for in-depth analysis. In the eighteenth century, wood possessed a psychological as well as a sociotechnic meaning. New England settlers viewed the howling wilderness of the native forests as dangerous and believed that their mission was to clear, cultivate, and occupy the land. The progress of cultivation was tied inextricably to an agricultural economy and to subjugation of the forest. The woods remained part of the frontier where economic, social, and political life were wild and lacked all rules. Toward the end of the seventeenth century, however, New Englanders' attitudes about the forest began to change. The colonists came to recognize that cultivation of the land could be accompanied by cultivation of the forest, with the resources of the woods adding immeasurably to their quality of life and to commercial activity. Thus the processing and manipulation of wood took on an important role in the New England psyche. Leaders of New England society sought to distinguish themselves through possession of time-consuming, material-consuming, or style-consuming craftsmanship such as rusticated architectural details, complex hipped or gambrel roofing systems, elaborately carved decoration, or elaborately shaped blockfront or bombé furniture made in a wasteful manner from imported mahogany.[14]

On a sociotechnic level, the extensive stands of hard and soft wood that covered the landscape provided an enormous source of raw material, which was supplemented by walnut and mahogany brought to New England ports through coastal trade. The greater cultural value placed upon wood that had been improved through artifice, an increased awareness of the economic opportunities in forest cultivation, and the intensified commerce in forest products provided additional opportunities for woodworking craftsmen in the eighteenth century. In the tax lists of rural New England communities from this period, craftsmen working with wood consistently represented the greatest number of artisans. Their impact was not merely in numbers but also in their products. Housewrights, carpenters, furnituremakers, wheelwrights, coopers, and similar craftsmen built the physical community —its meetinghouses and churches, houses, bridges, and fences. They also constructed components of its economy—barns, vehicles, storage containers, and tools—and provided social props for its inhabitants, such as domestic interiors and furniture. They shaped the community and gave it a particular feel or look. The number of woodworkers and their widespread influence warrants close analysis.¹⁵

At the same time we need to examine surviving objects more closely. Rather than consider an individual object solely from an idealized stylistic point of view, it is necessary to examine as many surviving objects from a single shop or community as possible and to understand the full range of choices available to a shop or a client. Casting such a wide net helps in two ways. First it encourages detailed analysis of conventions and techniques that might shed light on the world of the maker. Evidence of habits or idiosyncrasies helps to establish the shop practices of the period. A large object pool also makes it possible to evaluate the original meaning of an object's form, decoration, and use, permitting recovery of the local parameters of production and patronage. What was possible but not used or what was not even a possibility often can be as important as what was chosen in creating the surviving object. Analysis of objects within what the anthropologist Grant McCracken calls "a system of goods" and "a system of cultural categories" demonstrates that the creation and use of objects are integral parts of a dynamic social process, not just static events or ends unto themselves. Artifacts evolve out of and in turn shape cultural values and social relationships. In a period of limited advertising and fluctuating exposure to several fashion systems, the local arena was where the meanings of goods were invested, adapted, or divested.¹⁶

Furniture possesses particular significance. It can provide functional enjoyment or comfort for a person or household; indicate surplus exchange power; signify recognition or rejection of fashion; manifest memories of past experiences and social relationships; unify or differentiate people; embody abstract ideals such as accomplishment or achievement, social power, and stability; and serve as an owner's legacy. Too often in the study of historical furniture we focus only on the name, rank, and serial number of a surviving example—its attribution to a maker, style of the object, its date and origin, and its genealogy. All of this information is used to address issues of style and fashion in a formal and superficial way. The study of the object instead should be a departure point to uncover the multiple meanings and uses of furniture. The decision to make or purchase a piece of furniture, the variety of formal and decorative choices, and the context in which the artifact is used arise from a localized social economy and sustain or alter that social economy.¹⁷

How does the study of furnituremakers, who played an active role as agents and recipients of new ideas and fashion, shed light on the early stages of the transformation of rural life? The supply of furniture, evident in the number of makers and the types of shops, and the demand for furniture (the increase in the number of furniture pieces per household, sets of furniture, new forms, or new decorative conventions) help to chart the penetration of the external market and a local community's response. Making furniture, like many other craft skills, was not merely a supplemental pursuit during the colonial period or a new strategy to provide for a household during a phase of involution in the early national period. Rather, it was an integral part of a community's economic and cultural life.

Changing agricultural opportunities always played a role in the decisions of rural joiners. During good harvest seasons, the demand for furniture might grow, yet the craftsman had to weigh the social and economic value of agricultural work against that of craftwork. A healthy agricultural economy could lead to a variety of responses: intensification of existing shops, more decentralized production, or the emergence of larger full-time shops or specialists. When natural disasters or the declining size of farms affected agricultural opportunities, craftsmen had to balance their productive time with local demand. Similarly, population growth in a town could fuel demand for new furniture, meaning that more inhabitants had to intensify their craftwork. New furnituremakers might appear, competing with existing local shops through further division of the local market and the introduction of new forms or decoration. Growing demands of external markets and the appearance in the early national period of urban warehouses that sold furniture made in nearby rural communities also provided increased opportunities for joiners and necessitated the more frequent or more intense application of skills. Some furnituremakers embraced the opportunities of a larger market, while others resigned themselves to outwork for other firms.[18]

Furnituremakers, whose products combined enduring utility and changing fashion, worked at the interface of traditional household values and modern market forces in production and consumption of domestic goods. Thus increased opportunities for furnituremakers may also be attributed to the effect of the consumer revolution in the last half of the eighteenth century. As English and American merchants employed more efficient and aggressive distribution systems and as American society's expansion and mobility placed additional emphasis on the role of personal possessions to provide status, a greater demand for and supply of domestic goods may have fueled an increase in quantity and quality of furniture. The increasing artifactual literacy of New Englanders resulted in a class of consumers who demonstrated greater interest in the fashion of furniture, its uses in social behavior, and its meaning as a symbol of accomplishment or aspiration. Within each community the nature of local exchange networks and the extent of contact with the external market, as well as the dynamic balance between the two, forced the local craft system to respond according to local parameters.[19]

This book, which examines furnituremakers, community social structure, domestic possessions, and surviving pieces of furniture, demonstrates the value of revising Tryon's and Bridenbaugh's views of the rural craftsman, underscores the importance of localized studies of social economy, and provides important insights about rural western Connecticut during the late colonial and early national periods. A two-pronged research strategy guided the study: analysis of local records to identify joiners, become familiar with clients, and reveal patterns of economic change and material consumption; and establishment of an object pool containing furniture pieces with local histories of ownership and containing related examples without provenance. A synergism exists between joiners, their furniture, and the environments in which they lived and worked; analysis of each generates ideas, provides proof, and sheds light upon the others. The resulting study blends the contextual richness of social history, the artifactual analysis of material culture studies, and the interest in shop-floor practices of labor history.

The community parameters of this analysis permit a sound explication of the social economy of the joiner. I begin with a discussion of the joiners' technical system, then examine their active economic and cultural role in the community. Much of the discussion in chapters 1 and 2 is based on information drawn from southwestern Connecticut, particularly northern and eastern Fairfield County and southern Litchfield County (see fig. 1). During the late eighteenth century this region, which featured fertile hilly land along Long Island Sound and the Housatonic River and less fertile upland, supported a moderate population and diversified economy. Towns such as Fairfield, Stratford, and Derby were ports for schooners and ships engaged in coastal trade with Boston, New York, and the West Indies. Danbury, New Milford, and Woodbury formed a ring of northern towns settled at the turn of the eighteenth century and served as important links to the northwestern hill towns that were laid out and settled from the 1730s to the 1770s. The lack of high-quality farmland in the region contributed to a diverse economy including coastal trade, fishing, and grain and fruit harvesting along the coast and rivers; animal husbandry for salted meat, wool, and dairy products in the hilly regions; small shop craftwork in all of the communities; and even iron mining in the Roxbury and New Milford area.

After talking about woodworking and joiners in the larger region, I turn to adjacent, seemingly similar communities: the "yeoman town" of Newtown and the "gentry town" of Woodbury. Chapter 3 provides information on the towns' joiners, while chapters 4 and 5 discuss the socioeconomic structure and consumer behavior in the towns. Chapters 6 and 7 analyze the actual products of the joiners. Careful analysis and linking of manuscript and artifactual sources reveal that each town's social economy was actually quite different and responded in a separate manner to changes of the period. A final chapter emphasizes the importance of artifact-driven studies in understanding the transformation of the rural New England countryside, especially in showing that artisans as well as merchants and capitalists played active and important roles in the early phases of industrial production.

Intense analysis of a specific artisanal activity in a restricted geographical area is not an isolated case study incapable of generating new lines of inquiry about the American past. Rather, careful documentation and assessment of the activities and products of a local social economy, undertaken with full awareness of larger events and patterns of the period, underscore the necessity of conceiving broad lines of historical inquiry. Such inquiry informs and in turn is shaped by documentation and re-creation of specific local activities. The study of a community is the means, not the end, of the examination of social economy. Mastery of local events and values can lead to greater understanding of the nuances and shape of larger issues. In Newtown and Woodbury, as well as myriad other communities in New England, shifts in joinery practices, furniture design, and productivity took place in the context of community development, social stratification, economic opportunity, and consumer behavior. Analysis of consumer behavior, so popular at the present, must be conducted alongside the analysis of production. There is an inextricable link between the two activities, and the best place to observe them is at the local level.

Returning to Samuel Goodrich's Ridgefield, we need to probe the activities and understand the perspective of the local rural craftsman. How did the craftsman view changing economic opportunities? How did he allocate household resources and his time to earn a livelihood for his family? How did he develop a common understanding with patrons about designs and performance? In short, we need to restore a voice to silent craftsmen like the joiner Elisha Hawley.

ONE

The Preindustrial Joiner in Western Connecticut, 1760–1820

In preindustrial America, wood was the dominant material for construction, as well as the main fuel for heating and cooking. Wood by-products included maple syrup to sweeten the diet and bark-based tannin to tan leather. Wood's ubiquity, low cost, and relative workability all contributed to its primacy. Therefore it is not surprising that woodworkers were the most numerous and active craftsmen, using the products of forests that had been cleared to permit cultivation and creating various parts of the built environment. Furniture was just one of the many items made from wood, so it is important to begin the study of furnituremakers in late eighteenth-century western Connecticut by explaining their position among all the woodworking trades at the time.

During the late seventeenth and early eighteenth centuries, the various woodworking trades often overlapped. Distinctions among carpenters, housewrights, furnituremakers, coopers, and wheelwrights blurred, giving way to the "ambidextrous" woodworker throughout rural New England.[1] Toward the middle of the eighteenth century, such ambiguity among woodworkers in western Connecticut began to change. Although trades never reached guild-like exclusivity, certain lines of demarcation became firmer. Rather than try to isolate very specialized trades or to lump them together arbitrarily, it is more helpful and accurate to consider a range of woodworkers, based upon training, tools, and task difficulty.[2]

The Spectrum of Woodworkers

At one end of the spectrum were menial jobs that almost anyone could undertake, even villagers who were not woodworkers. Such tasks included felling, scoring, sledding, splitting, and sawing timber. Ownership of the necessary tools—axes, saws, hammers—by a large number of inhabitants and the basic nature of these jobs permitted such widespread involvement. Another low-end, semiskilled type of work included framing outbuildings, laying floors, rending (splitting and dressing) shingles and clapboards, covering roofs and sides, splitting rails and making fences, and making and repairing wooden agricultural tools. This part of the spectrum was the domain of the general handyman carpenter. On rare occasions, nonwoodworkers or woodworkers from the upper end of the spectrum performed such tasks. Closer to the upper end of the spectrum were the coopers, wheelwrights, and house joiners, each of whom tended to specialize in a particular skill. Of these three groups, house joiners were more likely to cross task boundaries because the demand for new building or extensive renovations fluctuated. At the highest end of the spectrum were the shop joiners, or furniture builders, whose products required the greatest amount of fastidious work.

Over the last half of the eighteenth century, a group of general-purpose handymen carpenters was restricted to certain basic jobs at the lower end of the woodworking spectrum. Such yeomen-handymen as Daniel Bishop of Bethlehem and Joseph Curtiss of Southbury spent most of their time chopping and sawing wood, sledding wood, mending or making agricultural tools, splitting rails and making fences, or riving shingles. Only in a few cases did such woodworkers make a cart, lay a floor, or cut rafters. Handymen carpenters were excluded from furniture production and house building even though they occasionally painted furniture or bottomed chairs.[3]

Coopers were another group of woodworkers to specialize in the last half of the eighteenth century. As farmers in western Connecticut started to pack their surplus meat and pork for the New York City and West Indies markets during the 1760s, a steady demand for barrels and hogsheads arose every year during the slaughtering months of November through February. Consequently a number of coopers could make a living in each town.[4] The inventory of Stephen Sperry, a cooper in Bethlehem, Connecticut, whose estate was appraised in 1776, documents the emergence of cooperage as a distinct craft. He had a large, active shop devoted to making wooden containers: his shop was valued at £13, and his stock included 1,850 staves and 400 headings.[5] The local cooperage business kept growing during the Revolution as Truman Hinman and Shadrach Osborn, prominent Southbury merchants, organized the region's collection of supplies for the Continental army. Crucial to their meat and pork shipping were the thousands of barrels supplied by local coopers in New Milford, Roxbury, Woodbury, and Bethlehem.[6]

In the early nineteenth century, many farmers in western Connecticut began to produce and export greater quantities of butter and cheese. This intensification of dairying further solidified the coopers as a separate group. Pails, tubs, churns, presses, and firkins were essential equipment for processing and storing dairy products, which took place during the summer months, between planting and harvesting. The dairy and meat trade ensured year-round activity for the leading coopers in rural western Connecticut.[7] Coopers would build barrels for meat in the fall, sell the barrels during the winter slaughtering months, build firkins for dairy products in the spring, market the firkins in the summer months, and supply churns and pails as the demand arose. The only other service coopers provided was the riving and dressing of shingles and clapboards. Their tools and techniques suited them to this task—they were accustomed to riving or splitting oak or chestnut into roughly shaped staves and finishing them with shaves and drawknives. This process was considerably quicker than sawing and planing. The same woods and techniques were used for clapboards and shingles.

Coopers' specialization also can be seen in the increasing quantity of tools they owned. For example, the 1782 inventory of Benjamin Dunning of Newtown listed a bung bill, cooper's adze, and a cooper's howel in addition to other, more general woodworking tools, whose total value was £4.2.0. In 1801 the estate of Henry Glover included a greater quantity of tools, many of which were more specialized: a heading jointer, stave jointer, cooper's croze, crooked shaves, and a stack shave in addition to many other tools, extra heading, and oak boards.[8]

A second woodworking trade that became differentiated from the others was that of the wheelwright. By the end of the eighteenth century, craftsmen such as James Kasson of Bethlehem, Thomas Stedman of Newtown, and John Leavenworth of Woodbury specialized in making wagons and spinning wheels.[9] Shaping and fitting wheel hubs, spokes, and rims necessitated great skill in turning and bending wood and in creating extremely strong joints. Wheelwrights often owned several lathes and cauls to accomplish these tasks. The growing external market for meat and dairy products was a catalyst for the wheelwright's specialization. Demand for wagons grew as local farmers shipped more meat and dairy products and as transportation improvements facilitated longer travel (table 1).

Developments in cloth production provided a greater need for compe-

TABLE I
Wagon and Spinning Wheel Ownership in Newtown and Woodbury, 1760–1824
(percentage of estates with specified item)

	1760–64	1770–74	1780–84	1790–94	1800–1804	1810–14	1820–24
NEWTOWN							
Number of estates	15	17	18	17	29	26	48
Spinning wheels (%)	67	88	100	76	83	77	90
Wagons/carts (%)	13	41	67	47	38	73	56
WOODBURY							
Number of estates	16	13	20	17	20	24	29
Spinning wheels (%)	62	77	70	76	85	83	86
Wagons/carts (%)	50	38	45	59	55	63	59

SOURCES: Estate inventories for Woodbury, Danbury, and Newtown probate court districts (microfilm of the original record books is held by the Connecticut State Library, Hartford).

tent wheelwrights. Clothing the Continental army and local producers' subsequent involvement in an external market increasingly drew on the labor of families that spun wool and flax at home. This reliance on outwork contributed to a steady demand for great and Dutch wheels, used for wool and flax spinning, respectively. Later, as local spinning and weaving manufactories were established in the 1810s, the need for wooden power wheels and bobbins created additional work for wheelwrights.[10]

As a result of these economic changes, wheelwrights such as John Sturdevant of New Milford, who had made chairs earlier in his career, eventually shifted their output to concentrate on the wheelwright business. The inventory of Sturdevant's estate in 1825 included three turning lathes, numerous turning chisels and augers, twenty-seven cranks and spindles, and eleven wheel forms.[11] Nevertheless, a few wheelwrights and wagonmakers continued to devote a small portion of their time to producing inexpensive furniture, either because demand for wheels and wagons did not require full-time work or because demand for chairs had occasionally exceeded the technical and temporal limits of normal production. An 1828 mortgage by Charles Glover of Newtown lists the contents of his shop for the manufacture of wagons. In addition to partly finished wagons, sawed wagon tills, cart axletrees, wagon spokes and hubs, cart spokes, bending blocks, and other wheelwright tools, the deed listed field bedsteads (light, portable bed frames) and high bedsteads (more elaborate fourposters with headboard and tester) and posts for kitchen chairs. Glover used his spare time and turning skills to provide parts for other furnituremaking craftsmen.[12]

Although wheelwrights sometimes used their turning equipment and skills to produce inexpensive chair and bedstead parts, joiners performed most furnituremaking tasks in rural western Connecticut at the end of the eighteenth century. Such furniture craftsmen were often specified as either a house joiner or shop joiner.[13] House joiners mainly framed houses, produced window sashes and doors, and finished interiors, but they also made furniture. For example, Charles Prindle, a Woodbury house joiner, made four inexpensive kitchen chairs for Reuben Mitchell in 1803 and a built-in cupboard for Luman Ovit in 1805. Nehemiah Pray of Huntington and Brookfield, Connecticut, devoted most of his time to framing, making sashes and window frames, and other house joiner's work, but occasionally made a chest, a chest of drawers, or a stand.[14]

Several characteristics distinguish house joiners from shop joiners: tools, approach to work, and mobility, among others. Owing to the scale of work and the necessary technology, house joiners needed a different chest of tools. Preparing and dressing large beams for sills and posts called for broadaxes and adzes. To assemble these large-dimensioned frames, the house joiner had to use large augers, socket chisels, and slicks to cut appropriately sized mortises and tenons. The joiner erecting a house constantly used large squares and chalk lines to create accurate right-angle joints and plumb lines. Such tools restricted the range of the house joiner's tasks. Many house joiners rent, sawed, or dressed shingles and clapboards but lacked the smaller precision tools to produce furniture other than plain chairs, built-in architectural furniture, or simple case furniture such as board chests, which consisted of five boards nailed together.[15]

Contemporary writers made similar observations about house joiners. In 1703 in *Mechanick exercises*, the Englishman Joseph Moxon pointed out the differences between joinery and house carpentry. Although noting that the trades employed similar tools and technology, Moxon wrote that carpenter's tools were "somewhat stronger for Carpenter's Use than they need be for Joiner's." Moxon also drew a distinction between the trades on the basis of the practitioners' respective attitudes toward work: "Joiners work more curiously, and observe the Rules more exactly than Carpenters need do." To demonstrate this point, Moxon compared a joiner's table and a carpenter's floor, both of which are flat and true. To him, the floor is "not so exactly flat and smooth as a Table." Furthermore, joiners found it easier to "work slightly," unlike carpenters who, taught to work "more roughly, do with greater difficulty perform the curious and nice work."[16]

Another distinguishing feature of the house joiner was the need to move from town to town according to demand. During periods of extensive new building or rebuilding, these woodworkers could remain in their hometown, but if demand were sporadic they would have to work in adjacent areas. Charles Prindle worked in Poughkeepsie, New York, during the spring, summer, and fall of 1799, in Bethlehem in 1801, and in Southbury in the fall of 1801. David Fabrique, a house joiner born in Newtown, lived and worked during the last quarter of the eighteenth century first in Newtown, Derby, Southbury, Roxbury, and then in Newtown again. New building contracts precipitated each move. Equally peripatetic was Nehemiah Pray, who worked in Huntington from 1810 until 1815, undertook work in Weston and Trumbull between 1814 and 1816, and then moved to Brookfield in 1817. The accounts and mobility of these house joiners demonstrate the early existence in rural Connecticut of tramping artisans, who worked in regional teams in response to the growing need for dwelling houses, meetinghouses, and mills in the early national period.[17]

Technical Aspects of Joiner's Work

In sixteenth-century England and early seventeenth-century New England, a joiner was a craftsman who exclusively used paneled construction to assemble furniture. In eighteenth-century western Connecticut, the term took on a more general meaning, representative of broader responsibility. It described a craftsman who made, finished, and repaired furniture. The occupational label of "cabinetmaker" was not used in western Connecticut until the end of the eighteenth century.[18] At that time, shop joiners produced most of the furniture, regardless of its value.

As a descendent of the seventeenth-century joiner and the ambidextrous woodworker of the late seventeeth and early eighteenth centuries, the rural joiner of the late eighteenth century could draw on a number of different techniques to conceive and construct furniture.[19] In one technique, as implied by the term *joiner*, entire storage forms, tables, or chairs were treated as framed structures. The seventeenth-century joiner would make panels and fit them into grooved horizontal rails and vertical stiles. These grooved framing members, in turn, were fastened at each corner with pinned mortise and tenon joints. To this basic structure the joiner could attach a hinged chest top, nail a tabletop or chair seat, or nail a bottom board for a chest.

The eighteenth-century joiner retained only parts of this technology rather than the whole system. In certain situations he continued to favor the mortise and tenon joint. The most common use of this joint was in fastening carcass boards to the legs of dressing tables and cases of drawers (fig. 2; see also figs. 17–21, 23–24) and fastening seat rails and stretchers to the legs of

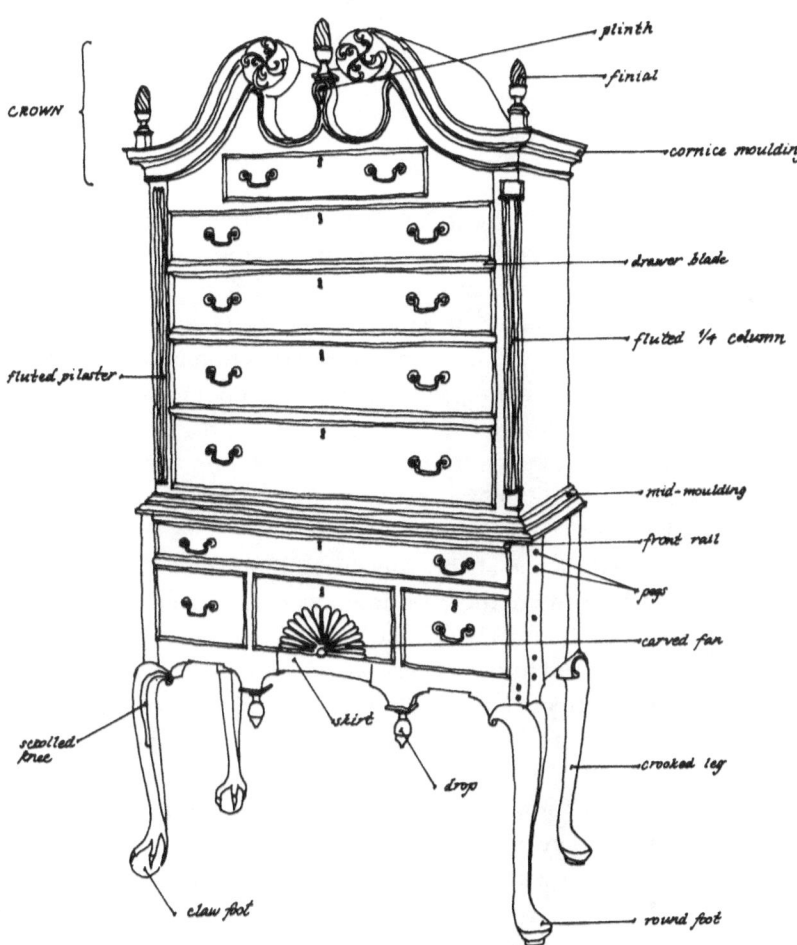

Fig. 2. Case furniture nomenclature. Drawing by Larkin/Tenney.

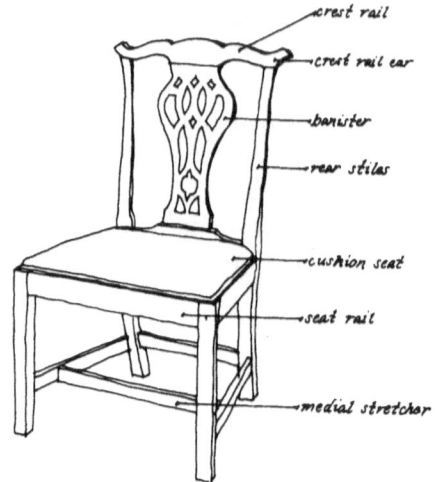

Fig. 3. Joiner's chair nomenclature. Drawing by Larkin/Tenney.

joiner's chairs (fig. 3; see also fig. 37). A mortise and tenon joint also secured chair banisters (a vertical back support, or splat) to the crest rails and shoes (fig. 4; see also figs. 8–15) and secured chair slats (horizontal back supports used in groups of two, three, or four) to the rear posts (see fig. 7). Vestiges of joined-panel construction can be found in the preferred method of drawer construction. The drawer bottom, slightly beveled under its front and side edges, was fitted into a groove cut along the inside of the drawer front and sides. However, the drawer bottom did not float within this groove like a true panel because the bottom was nailed along its rear edge to the bottom of the drawer back (see fig. 5).[20]

Although both house and shop joiners used mortise and tenon joinery, differences in scale between the final products necessitated the shop joiner's use of finer tools. To dress wood, the shop joiner used a series of bench planes—fore, jointer, and trying planes—to produce a very square and even board or stick. He then cut a protruding tenon with a ripsaw and crosscut handsaw and cleaned up this projecting tab with a straight-edge chisel. Unlike the house joiner, who used augers and socket chisels to make mortise holes, the shop joiner worked with a brace and bits and smaller chisels to achieve a smaller, more precise hole for the tenon.

The second construction technique in the eighteenth-century joiner's repertoire was turning. After shaping wood parts on a lathe, the artisan assembled them using round mortise and tenon joints. This method, also

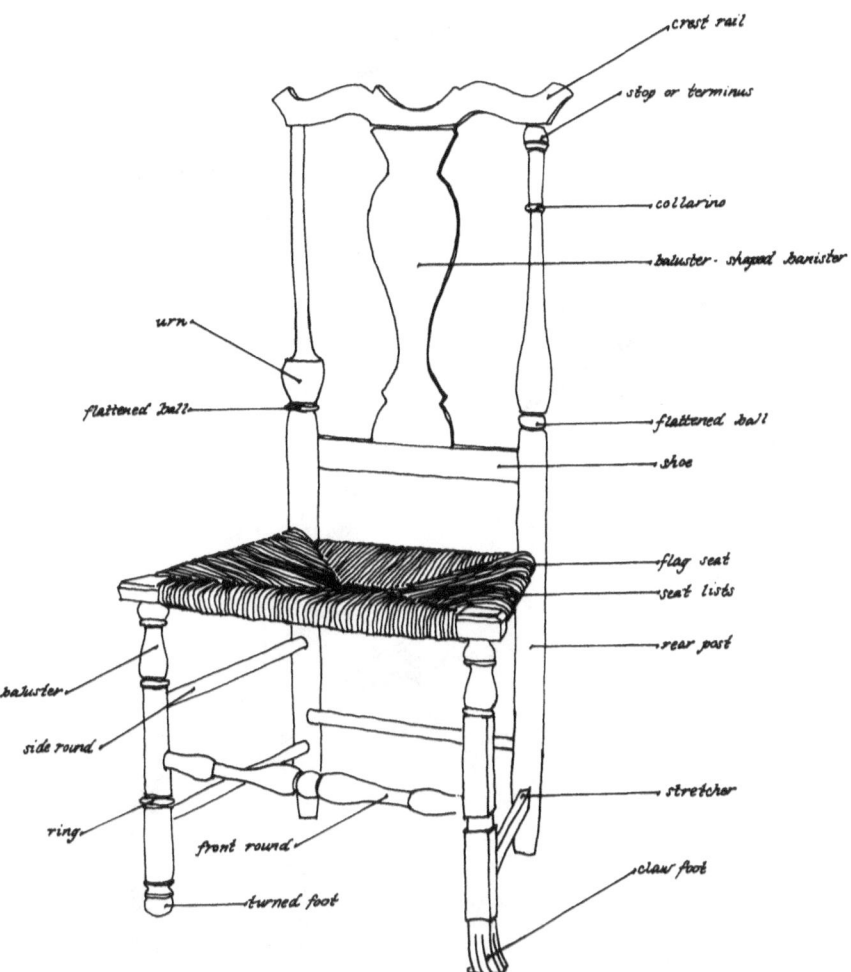

Fig. 4. Turned chair nomenclature. Drawing by Larkin/Tenney.

known as post-and-rung construction, was applied most often in building chairs. Entire chairs or specific parts of chairs and tables such as posts or rounds featured turned construction (see figs. 4, 7–15). The joiner also used the lathe and turning tools to shape the round feet on case furniture (see figs. 2, 16–19). That the lathe became part of the joiner's realm rather than being used exclusively by a specialized turner is explicitly revealed in the 1778 inventory of Hezekiah Porter, which listed "a joiners lathe."[21]

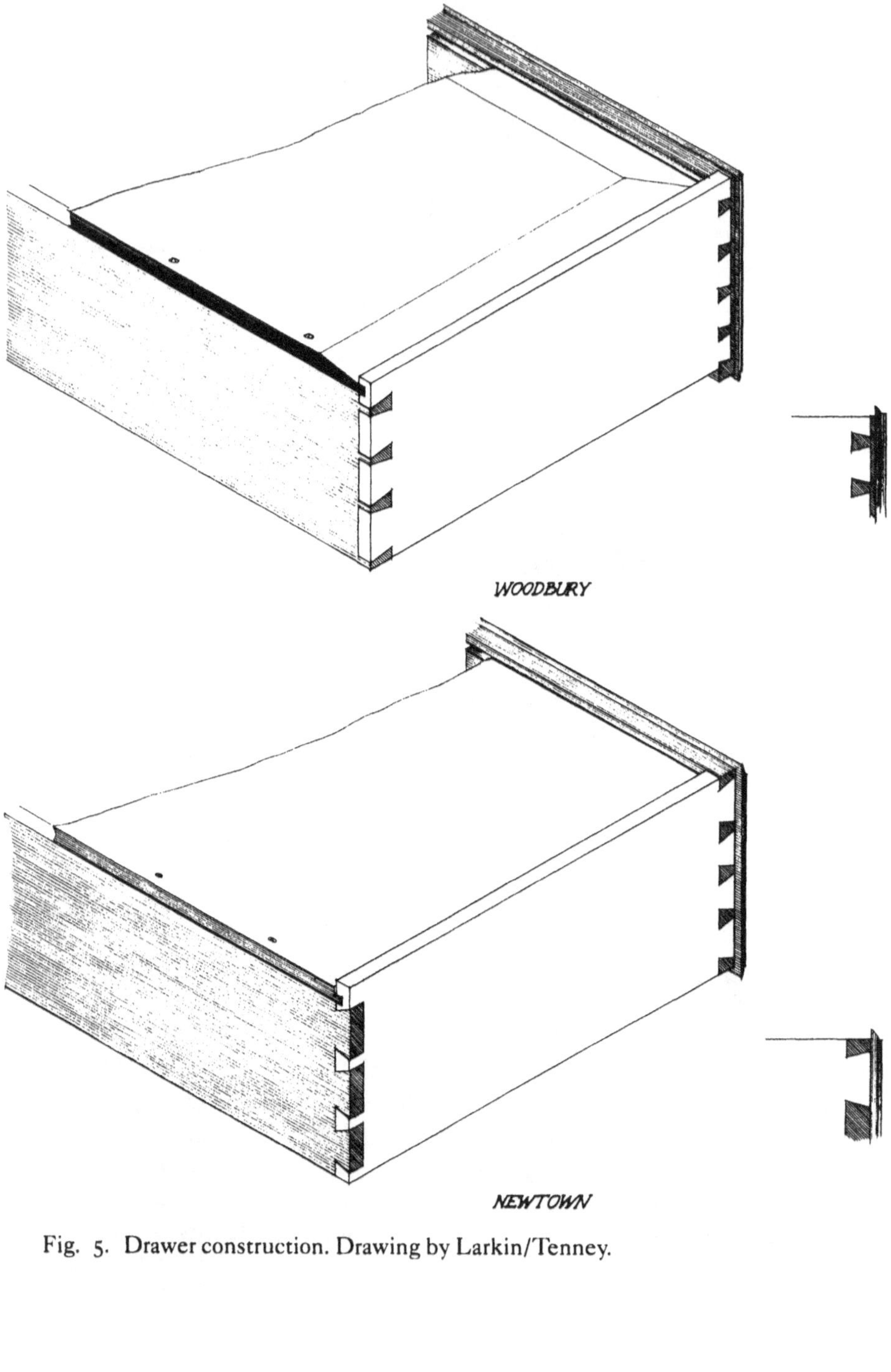

WOODBURY

NEWTOWN

Fig. 5. Drawer construction. Drawing by Larkin/Tenney.

The third method of furniture assembly was dovetailing. The joiner cut interlocking, wedge-shaped fingers at the ends of butted boards, applied glue to the touching surfaces of the fingers, and fit the two boards together (see fig. 5). The lock of the fingers and the larger long-grain surface for gluing gave this joint great strength, which resulted in its widespread use in a variety of circumstances. In making chests and the upper sections of cases of drawers, the joiner dovetailed the bottom and top boards to the sides. Similarly the long boards in the frame of a fall leaf table were dovetailed to the end boards at the corners where the swing legs retract (see fig. 41). The joiner also used dovetail joints to attach drawer sides to their fronts and backs, to secure drawer blades, to fasten battens to the underside of tea table tops (see fig. 40, left), and to secure medial stretchers in joiner's chairs. Among the tools necessary to cut dovetails were marking and bevel gauges to lay out the desired joint; a fine handsaw, often referred to as a dovetail saw, to cut the fingers; a range of straight-edge chisels to clean up the fit; and a gluepot and glue to bond the joint.

A final construction technique, nailing, found greater favor among house joiners, although seventeenth-century shop joiners had used it. Carpenters relied on nails to lay floors, cover roofs and sides, and sheathe interior walls. For shop joiners, inexpensive board chests represented the most extensive use of nailing techniques. The joiner fit the sides into small rabbets cut along the inside corners of the front boards and backboards and then nailed these joints from the front and back. With the perimeter established, he dropped a bottom within these sides and nailed it in place. Finally, he attached a top with hinges. On other pieces of furniture, the joiner used nails only in areas that were not visible. For the backs of case furniture, the joiner devised a fast and easy technique not unlike flooring. Using a series of horizontal or vertical boards, he butted or shiplapped these boards against one another, set the outer edges into rabbets cut along the back of the sides, and then nailed the backboards to the sides, bottom, and top. Another common use of nails was to fasten the rear edge of a drawer bottom to the drawer back. Some shop joiners also used nails to secure drawer supports or to fasten moldings to carcasses.

Other skills related to furniture production involved decorating, finishing, and chair bottoming. Sawn profiles, moldings, turned ornament, carving, and inlay were the available options for surface ornamentation in order of complexity and required time, and therefore of expense. The joiner effectively used sawn decoration on the skirts of dressing tables and cases of drawers and on the backs of chairs. Simply by the way the joiner sawed out the front boards and sideboards of case furniture or the crest rail and banister of a chair, he could alter the design.

Molding planes provided another relatively easy way to embellish a piece of furniture. Joiners often owned extensive sets of these tools, whose soles and blades allowed a regular result with minimal effort. Used individually, molding planes provided a decorative edge on drawer fronts or on the straight legs of joiner's chairs and fall leaf tables. The joiner also used combinations of molding planes to execute intricate base molding, midmolding, and cornice molding that could be applied to case furniture.

The lathe, owned by nearly all joiners in late eighteenth-century Connecticut, provided an easy but riskier decorative option. While turning chair posts and rounds, the joiner worked with turning chisels and gouges to form ball-, ring-, urn-, and baluster-shaped elements (see figs. 4, 7–15). He also could use the lathe to fashion finials and drops for cases of drawers and dressing tables.

For carving, the joiner employed many of the same tools that he worked with in furniture construction. With a compass, he laid out a fan, shell, or rosette, which he then carved using a series of gouges and chisels. Gouges were also used to execute relief carving and scrolls on the knees of the crooked legs that supported case furniture (see figs. 20–21). A third carving technique can be found in rope-twist quarter-columns (see fig. 44) and flame finials (see fig. 24). To achieve this spiraled, or rope, effect, the joiner laid out the line of the spiral while the wood was set in the lathe. Then he took a fine handsaw and sawed a kerf along the marked line. Finally he used a file to smooth the ridges left by the kerf.

The least common form of decoration was inlay. Although inventories of joiners did not list strips of inlay or veneering tools such as veneering saws or weights, surviving artifacts document limited use of stringing, patterned inlays, and pictorial inlay (see figs. 49–50). The time and precision necessary to cut an inset, compose an inlay from several pieces of wood, and set it snugly in place may have made such decoration prohibitively expensive for most customers.[22]

Finishes for furniture depended on the type of wood used. Maple, pine, or yellow poplar furniture was often painted red using Spanish brown or black using lampblack. These two colors retained their popularity into the early nineteenth century, even though green Windsor chairs began to be made in the 1780s, and blue or yellow chairs in the first decade of the nineteenth century. For cherry or mahogany, western Connecticut joiners did not stain the wood to resemble mahogany or walnut but rather used linseed oil or varnish for a finish. James Briscoe Jr. of Newtown listed jugs of oil, jugs of varnish, Spanish brown, red ochre, and lampblack among his shop contents in 1765. According to a recipe recorded by the Woodbury house joiner Charles Prindle, varnish consisted of "Rosum red led and oil," which had been boiled together.[23]

Most chair bottoms were constructed of flag or rush. The maker quickly rounded seat lists with a drawknife and fit the lists into holes drilled into the vertical posts. He or a bottomer then wove the flag seat over the lists. The Housatonic River area apparently was renowned for the quality of its rushes for chair bottoms. This material's availability made it appropriate for all chair types, as Ezra Slason, a chairmaker in Stamford, Connecticut, informed the public in 1792: "Flags of the best kind and quality—Likewise Rushes of various Kinds . . . are transported from Derby, or the Ferry a little below, and are supposed to be some of the best in the State or County for handsome genteel gentlemen's parlor chairs—also, a course kind for kitchen chairs may be had." Chair bottoming, however, was not the exclusive domain of the joiner. Handymen carpenters, older joiners who had passed along control of their shop, and even nonwoodworking villagers occasionally rebottomed chairs.[24]

The 1759 inventory of Jacob Leavitt, a shop joiner from Fairfield, provides a clear picture of the joiner's chest of tools for furniture production in the late eighteenth century (fig. 6).[25] To prepare boards for assembly, Leavitt used two fore planes, two long planes, and a smoothing plane. A fourth bench plane, the glue jointer, was specifically the tool of the shop joiner, who used it to "shoot" the edge on long boards to ensure a tight fit when glued together edge to edge. The shop joiner's careful gluing of boards contrasted with the house joiner's tendency to butt boards edge to edge or to use a shiplap joint. After planing the wood, Leavitt laid out mortises and tenons or dovetails using scribing gauges and squares. He cut tenons with steelplate and crosscut saws, mortises with a stock and bits and chisels, and dovetails with a dovetail saw and chisels. Or, if making a turned chair, Leavitt shaped the individual parts on the lathe with seven turning tools and then used a stock and bits to drill holes. After fitting the members together and gluing them, he used a scraper to achieve the smoothest surface possible. Like the glue jointer, the scraper, with its implicit concern with surface, was distinctive among the shop joiner's tools. To provide decoration, Leavitt relied upon nineteen molding planes and six chisels and gouges.

With the product in final form, Leavitt then would have turned to its

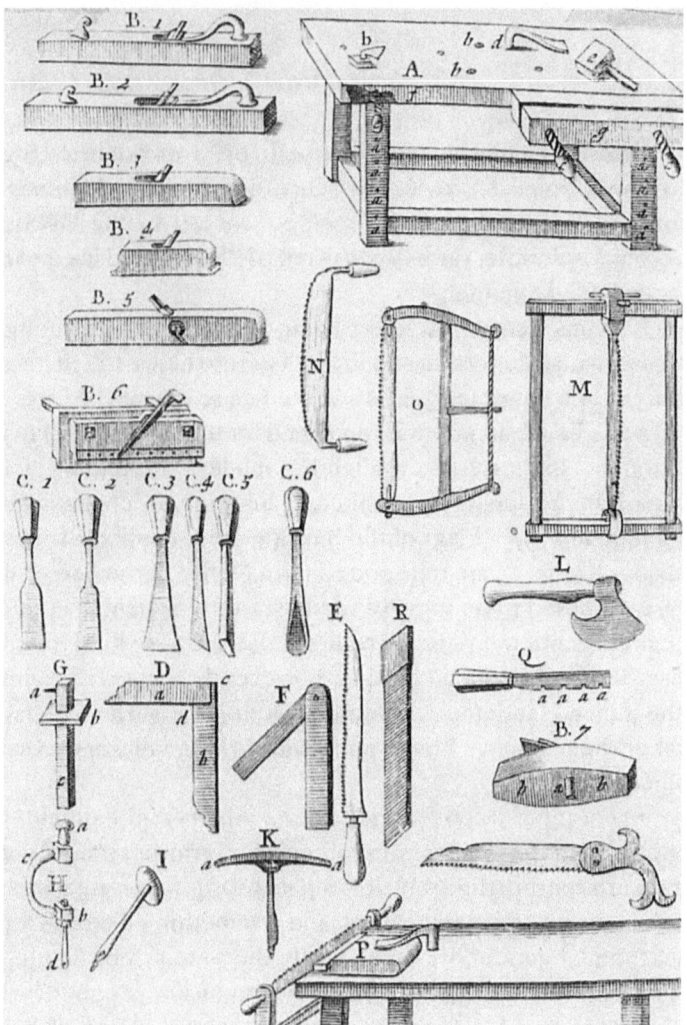

Fig. 6. Joyner's work. Joseph Moxon, *Mechanick exercises: or, The doctrine of handy-works* (London, 1703), pl. 4. Photograph courtesy of the Winterthur Library: Printed Book and Periodical Collection.

Moxon used these labels in the text:
A. *Work-bench*: a. *Holes* for pins;
   b. *Hook*; b. *Holes* for *Hold-fast*; c. *Bench-Screw*; d. *Holdfast*; e. *Mallet*; f. *Table*;
   g. *Bench-Screw* [or vise]
B. [Planes]: 1. *Fore Plane*; 2. *Joynter*;
   3. *Strike-Block*; 4. *Smoothing-Plane*;
   5. *Rabbet-Plane*; 6. *Plow*; 7. *Block-Plane* (a. *Mouth*; b. *Tongue*;
   b-a-b. *Sole*)
C. [Chisels]: 1. *Former Chissel*; 2. *Paring-Chissel*; 3. *Former Chissel*; 4. *Skew-Former*; 5. *Mortess-Chissel*; 6. *Gouge*
D. *Square*: a. *Handle*; b. *Tongue*;
   c. *Outer Square*; d. *Inner Square*
E. *Compass Saw*
F. *Bevil*
G. *Gage*: a. *Tooth*; b. *Oval*; c. *Staff*
H. *Piercer*: a. *Head*; b. *Pad*; c.*Stock*;
   d. *Bitt*
I. *Gimlet*
K. *Augre*. a-a. *Handle*
L. *Hatchet*
M. *Pit-Saw*
N. *Whip-Saw*
O. *Bow-Saw*
P. *Whetting Block* or *Rub Stone*
Q. *Saw Wrest*
R. *Mitre Square*
[S]. *Tennant Saw* [above lower table]

finish. Unlike the estates of many other joiners in the area, Leavitt's inventory does not list flags, Spanish brown, lampblack, varnish, or oil. Although he owned a small bit of beeswax, an alternative finish to oil, it is impossible to determine his favored finish. As a final step, Leavitt attached brass escutcheons, handles, knobs, and hinges, which he had in stock.

The shop joiner's woodworking tools and skills did not restrict him to furniture production. Gouges, carving skills, and a working knowledge of steel acquired through repeated sharpening and honing of edge tools enabled Lewis Prindle and Ebenezer Booth to stock guns. Familiarity with precision joinery allowed Joel Booth and Cyrus Prindle to make and repair the wood parts of such musical instruments as spinets, violins, and flutes. In slack times or when expediency was required, shop joiners applied their skills to other woodworking tasks. William H. Peabody repaired farm tools and turned a roll for a map; Harvey J. Linsley turned two rolling pins; Cyrus Prindle made sashes and doors and helved axes; and Lewis Prindle mended a table, fixed a saw, made a lathe, and turned bobbins.[26] However, house joiners and handymen carpenters performed most of these tasks. The woodworking spectrum was more flexible at the top. Most shop joiner's work involved furniture production and maintenance even though they also performed other jobs. On the other hand, handymen carpenters made no furniture and were confined to work associated with agricultural equipment and agricultural buildings.

Organization of the Joiner's Work

With this knowledge of the shop joiner's basic skills and tools, one can examine his shop operations without the misperceptions that have arisen in the past century and a half. Specifically, the early twentieth-century Arts and Crafts ideal of the solitary craftsman using simple tools to create individual products must be dismissed. One also has to look beyond the large-scale, mechanized, and specialized furniture industry of the last half of the nineteenth century. It is very important to understand the scale of the rural joiner's work, his mode of production, and his materials. The largest joiner's shops in rural western Connecticut contained two benches; most shops probably operated with only one. A joiner relied on the bench, with its vise and holdfasts, to hold the boards or assembled parts on which he worked. The use of only one or two benches, therefore, greatly influenced the pace of work. Brewster Dayton's Stratford shop, which contained two benches, was engaged in work on twelve chairs, one case of drawers, two stands, and one bedstead when he died in the late spring of 1796. Fewer pieces of furniture in progress appeared in those shop inventories that listed only a single bench.[27]

Although no shops in western Connecticut are known to have survived, they probably were similar in size and layout to the shop of the Dominy family, formerly located in East Hampton, Long Island. Measuring between 300 and 400 square feet, shops of this type were attached to the home or located in a separate small building. Extra boards and timber were stored in the garret or chamber above the shop, while some tools hung on the walls or from the joists in the ceiling. Other tools lay on the bench or benches, which were placed in front of a window (most joinery, especially cutting dovetails and carving, required good natural light).[28]

Not only was the physical size of the rural joiner's shop small but so was the workforce. Even as late as 1820, the Ridgefield shop of Samuel Hawley was considered large, and it operated with only two men and four boys.[29] This scale fostered easy interaction among the workers and allowed, even encouraged, apprentices to learn most aspects of the trade. The size of the shop and workforce, relatively low cost of tools and basic materials, and variety of techniques permitted the preindustrial joiner a great deal of technical flexibility. He could respond quickly to a client's demands or to new fashion without drastic retooling.

Probate inventories and account books provide glimpses into the seasonal rhythms of furniture production. Inventories that listed partially assembled furniture were usually appraised between November and March, a pattern that suggests that the bulk of production took place during the winter months when agricultural duties slacked off. With the arrival of spring, the joiner may have been engaged more often in agricultural endeavors, in assembling work begun in the winter, and in making occasional pieces of furniture as demand occurred.[30] Unlike John Dunlap, a New Hampshire joiner in the late eighteenth century, Connecticut joiners do not appear to have alternated between shop joinery and house joinery according to the seasons. Connecticut's denser population allowed joiners to focus on one craft in addition to their agricultural demands. Yet, like Dunlap, they tended to work within the warmth of their shop in the winter months.[31]

Contrary to popular belief, not all joiner's work was custom work, which represented individual designs and solutions to every demand. Concern with efficient production and the desirability of predictable, polished products did not begin only with industrialization, or even just in urban areas during the preindustrial period. Rather, it already was a major part of the rural joiner's values during the preindustrial period. The joiner recognized the waste of redrawing the profile of a chair crest rail, crooked leg, chair banister, or bracket foot every time one was needed, so he used patterns to save time, ensure compatibility of products made *en suite*, and ease his work. Templates, probably made from thin wood, appeared in the inventories of Ezekiel Hawley of Norwalk, Ebenezer and Joel Booth of Newtown, Thomas Kimberly of Southbury, and Hezekiah Porter of Waterbury. Hawley must have used many templates, for his "number of patterns" were valued at twelve shillings, the same as four molding planes. Ebenezer Booth's estate listed "a set of patterns" valued at thirty shillings, the equivalent of three new round fall leaf tables or two calves.[32]

Rural joiners applied their knowledge of the properties of wood to organize efficient production and to ensure predictable results. During the slow winter months the craftsman would turn large quantities of "chair stuff." Wood was easily cut and sledded in December and January, after which the joiner would turn posts and rounds, shave seat lists, and rive and bend slats while the wood was still relatively moist and easy to work and turn. Using one set of tools at a time to fabricate and stockpile parts always in demand was much more efficient than constantly juggling different sets of tools to produce individual parts as needed. Many inventories document the custom of stockpiling seasoned chair rounds. Such examples range from Hezekiah Porter's five dozen chair rounds in 1778 to Joseph Foot's forty-three dozen chair rounds of various sorts in 1801 and William Adee's seventy dozen in 1765. The listing of rounds, posts, and partially assembled chairs in inventories appraised in the summer and fall demonstrates that joiners assembled these parts only as time permitted or demand necessitated.[33]

The power source for the woodworking process was another important aspect of joiners' labor in eighteenth-century rural Connecticut. Throughout the process, nonhuman power was applied only to the basic preparation of wood. Water-powered sawmills, which had been established early in seventeenth-century New England, provided great quantities of sawn lumber. Nevertheless, water-powered machinery had many drawbacks: high capital investment in machinery and power drive, inefficient operation, dependence on variable water level and velocity, and vulnerability to flood damage.[34] Whereas some felt that the widespread demand for boards and the hard and time-consuming labor of pit sawing outweighed these shortcomings, similar reasoning was not applied to tasks other than basic sawing.

Most rural Connecticut joiners took advantage of the moderate population density as a source of power. Craftsmen relied on young apprentice labor to turn great lathes, foot power to turn smaller pole lathes, mallets to drive chisels, and plenty of muscle. Even when their shops had a prime location for using water power, joiners consistently rejected this option for driving their lathes or other equipment. The Newtown shop of Ebenezer and Joel Booth, for example, was located right on the Pootatuck Brook, where a gristmill operated and a satinet factory, rubber hose factory, and other water-powered businesses prospered in the 1820s and 1830s. Yet the Booths chose not to harness that power.

Apparently the town's social economy, in which a truly mixed agricultural system accommodated the population and balanced production and consumption, made human power more appropriate than the costly, erratic harnessing of water power for furniture production. Not until the market demanded increased production in the late 1810s did rural Connecticut joiners feel that the market possibilities outweighed continued use of their traditional power source. They turned to the abundant natural advantage of their hilly upland environment and began to use water power to drive lathes.

In Newtown during the 1820s, Abijah and George Bradley began to purchase land with water rights to ensure a reliable power source for their machinery. The inventory of Nehemiah Gray of Huntington, appraised in 1827, contained the first explicit reference to such a shift. In addition to a large stock of table, chair, and bedstead parts, he owned a "shop & machinery & pond" valued at $125. In the following year, a Woodbury deed included a water-powered saw, lathe, and boring machine among the equipment in William Hurlbut's shop. By the 1830s, water-powered manufacturing provided the Housatonic Valley with its distinctive industrial identity, ranging from papermaking and iron furnaces near the Connecticut-Massachusetts border, to clockmaking and brass buttons around Waterbury, to textiles around Derby.[35]

The joiner acquired wood and materials from a wide variety of sources, which meant involvement in both local economic exchange and commercial relations with external economies. If the joiner owned woodland, he would cut timber and sled it during the colder months. He then faced a number of options. If it was oak or chestnut to be used for shingles, clapboards, rails, slats, or rounds, he or another woodworker would split it. He might saw some timber himself if he owned a whipsaw or frame saw. More likely he would take the logs to a nearby sawmill. Although David Miles of Woodbury and Elijah Sherman of Newtown owned sawmills, most joiners did not. Of the twenty-eight owners or part-owners of sawmills in Newtown in 1820, only three were woodworkers. Elijah Booth sledded his timber, or contracted a handyman to sled it, to the sawmill owned by his neighbor David Stiles. At the mill, Stiles or Booth himself sawed the logs into boards and, sometimes, into bedstead posts.[36]

For the most part the joiner purchased the bulk of his boards directly from the sawmill or from a lumber merchant. Charles Prindle relied on a local sawmill in Bethlehem, but he often traveled as far as Norfolk or Derby to acquire boards from sawmills or from traders who dealt in timber. The reliance on mills and lumber merchants indicates that local wood lots no longer provided sufficient material. Lumbering in the region had become more intensive, and craftsmen relied on whatever might be available locally or sought good-quality primary woods elsewhere. Surviving objects from western Connecticut reveal inconsistent uses of different types of woods for interior structural elements (e.g., some Woodbury case furniture features drawer linings—the sides and back of a drawer—of oak and yellow poplar in the same object) or use of poor-quality knotty or slab-cut boards for interior elements (case furniture from Canaan, where the iron industry also used great quantities of wood, often has low-grade white pine as drawer linings and backboards).[37]

A third source of wood was the joiner's clientele. Customers could supply the craftsman directly with boards intended for a specific piece of furniture or indirectly with boards as a medium of exchange. While the latter occurrence is recorded throughout surviving account books, the former appears to have been less common. Thomas Tousey, a minister-turned-doctor in Newtown, supplied Alexander Bryan with boards for a two-drawer chest and two tables in 1747. In 1803 Dennis Bradley of Woodbury made a chest for Matthew Minor with poplar boards provided by the customer. These two examples are the only clear-cut cases in which the client provided specific boards to be used in the construction of his furniture.[38]

For tools and hardware, the joiner relied on local and urban sources. Although a joiner was skilled with both wood and metal, he usually did not make his own tools. Even when creating a tool for a specific purpose, he merely altered existing tools.[39] Local blacksmiths usually provided nails, iron hinges, snipebill hinges, and such basic tools as axes and large chisels. John Hubbell, a Newtown blacksmith, provided Joel Booth with nails, bench hooks, hammers, and chisels. In Woodbury, blacksmiths such as Samuel Moody and Hezekiah Cole used their nail molds and nailing tools to provide local shop and house joiners with plentiful supplies of nails. For the most precise edge tools (planes, gouges, and chisels), saws, and brass hardware, the joiners depended on those local storekeepers who imported goods from hardware merchants in New York City. Shadrach Osborn bought tools from Ustick & Hartshorn and brass hinges, locks, escutcheons, and knobs from John Broome and Rogers & Murray. Merchants such as Osborn and John Botsford of Newtown sold these tools and fixtures to local craftsmen.[40]

In the late eighteenth century, joiners in western Connecticut ranked at the upper end of the woodworking spectrum. During this period of "low technology" craft production, reliance on human skill rather than on sophisticated specialized equipment permitted considerable flexibility.[41] Drawing upon a broad technical repertoire and a shop tradition that stressed economy, the joiner worked skillfully and efficiently to create a wide range of furniture, from simple to intricate. The local economic context provided the broad parameters of shop rhythms, and the interaction between makers' traditions and patrons' needs established the acceptable standards of performance and degree of elaboration.

TWO

The Social Economy of the Preindustrial Joiner

Despite joiners' use of similar tools, technologies, and workspaces, considerable variety prevailed among the furniture made and owned in western Connecticut from 1760 to 1820. There are differences in furniture forms and decoration not only between towns but also within towns. We thus need to identify what determined the artisan's choice of form, technique, or decoration. The specific context in which a joiner worked is crucial to any understanding of these selections and adaptations. A web of social and economic relations determined the joiner's composition, tool selection, techniques, work rhythms, and levels of production, as well as the look of the final product. The craftsman's choices were grounded in a specific set of learning experiences, economic systems, and social norms and obligations. By focusing on how the joiner first learned his trade and then refined or expanded these skills and attitudes, we can begin to analyze the details of the region's social economy.

Acquisition of Skills

Apprenticeship, a very clear example of the social basis for the joiner's trade during the preindustrial period, was the primary method for learning the craft. In the eighteenth century, apprenticeship differed significantly from its present form. Today, a person voluntarily enters into an apprenticeship with a company to learn a specific aspect of the trade. The company pays the apprentice a minimal wage during the learning process and defines the entire relationship with that person in terms of wage rate and working hours. The company essentially cares only about the apprentice's performance on the job and how quickly he or she will pay back the investment. Room, board, and life outside of work are the apprentice's own responsibilities.[1]

By contrast, preindustrial apprenticeship was fundamentally a social contract in which mutual obligations and expectations bound the two parties. A young lad followed certain prescribed rules of living in return for instruction in a trade. Like the son of a farmer, the apprentice was willing to give up certain personal freedoms and perform specific tasks for a paternal figure with little direct recompense because he expected to become a master himself. The master willingly took the youth into his household and taught him because the apprentice's commitment permitted the master to increase the variety and scale of operations and maximize opportunities during the master's peak years of physical activity. Apprenticeship ensured the availability of extra human power for preparatory tasks such as sawing and dressing stock as well as the ability to undertake larger, more logistically complicated tasks such as fabricating large case furniture, paneling interiors, or hauling boards.

Young apprentices also served as a form of human credit. During slack periods in the shop, the master "rented out" his apprentices to others in the community for simple woodworking tasks or even for agricultural labor. In such a case, the youth was not working on his own time but rather as a member of the master's household. The apprentice's labor thus built up indebtedness within the community, which the master could draw on as the need arose.

Even apprenticeship selection was based upon the social network. A young craftsman in his twenties took on the sons of neighbors or relatives; a joiner in his thirties turned to his adolescent sons. Those with daughters but no sons often arranged for a daughter to marry an apprentice or a member of another shop, thereby consolidating the trade for the next generation. Once the elder craftsman had set up his children as independent adults, he had less interest in his own production and earning power. At this later point in his career, the joiner became an individual craftsman, helping out in local shops when needed or undertaking light work or repair work.[2]

The apprenticeship agreement between Lazarus Prindle and Joseph Peck Jr., both of Newtown, sheds light on this training process in a time when life and work were interwoven and work was arranged along household lines. On June 5, 1793, Peck, then fifteen years old and with his father as witness, bound himself to Prindle for a two-year training period. In return for instruction, Peck promised to serve faithfully, keep his master's secrets, waste none of his master's goods, avoid unexcused absences, and obey his master's lawful commands. In addition, Peck pledged not to commit fornication, contract matrimony, play at dice or other illegal games, haunt taverns or playhouses, or buy or sell anything on his own during the term of his apprenticeship. In short, Peck completely resigned himself to Prindle's authority.

For his part, Prindle, thirty years old and without a son ready to apprentice, swore to teach and instruct the apprentice in the trade and mystery of a joiner. Furthermore, Prindle provided Peck with lodging, food, and laundry services by treating him as a surrogate son within the household. On completion of his training, Peck would receive a good suit of clothes and take his place as a productive member of the community in good standing.[3]

The "art, trade, and mystery" of the joiner's craft encompassed a wide range of attitudes, responsibilities, and activities. In an era before specialization drew lines of distinction between design, workmanship, decoration, and marketing, the rural joiner oversaw and participated in the entire furnituremaking process from conception through sale. The apprentice acquired these values and skills through a process that combined observation and imitation. Because of the casual interaction that took place in the small shop, a boy could see the decisions, actions, and results of the master or of any other craftsmen who worked there. In this manner the apprentice internalized his master's approaches and techniques. Less consciously the apprentice also adopted certain attitudes about working wood. From a broad range of possibilities, the apprentice therefore learned and practiced the solutions favored and used by his master. In a time of human power and relatively low technology, a reliance on internalized solutions to structural problems, systematic and habitual motions, and familiar sequences helped to ensure efficient, satisfactory work. This workmanship of habit made craftwork economically viable. As a result, reflexive actions acquired and developed during training became an integral part of the joiner's chest of tools. These conventions serve as diagnostic features that help to group surviving furniture and identify it as the work of a particular shop tradition.[4]

A joiner's later experiences supplemented the basic technical foundation acquired during his time as an apprentice. His performance, however, was not entirely confined to mere replication of his master's work. Rather, working within a dynamic tradition of furnituremaking, he selectively gathered ideas about new techniques or approaches from the products of other shops in the same town or nearby, from observations made during travel, or from the challenge of replicating imported furniture, meeting a client's demands, or repairing a piece of furniture made in another shop.[5] These new ideas, inevitable in a New England society far more mobile than has been perceived, were grafted onto existing structural habits or reinterpreted through local standards of performance and design.

In Stratford, for example, two shops dominated the local furniture market: Brewster Dayton's and that of the Hubbell family. Dayton (working in Stratford c. 1762–96) was born across Long Island Sound in Brookhaven, New York, and apprenticed with an English-trained immigrant joiner in Stratford. His early experiences exposed him to the Anglo-Dutch work of Long Island joiners and the vernacular Georgian work of his master. Ebenezer Hubbell (1726–1812), master of the Hubbell shop in the last half of the eighteenth century, probably trained with his father Josiah, a joiner who helped to build the side galleries for the town's meetinghouse in 1715. Ebenezer's training thus took place entirely within Stratford.

Case furniture that is documented or attributed to the Dayton and Hubbell shops reveals a specific set of Stratford features: carved feet with square pads, central toes flanked by two smaller toes on each side, and a tightly curved crooked leg; deeply carved shells in the lower drawers of desks and chests; blocks of wood nailed to the inside surface of these drawer fronts to provide extra depth for the shell carving; and extensive use of wooden trunnels rather than iron nails to secure drawer bottoms, moldings, and drawer supports. The work of each shop, however, is distinctive in its individual workmanship and forms. Slight differences in decorative work also distinguish the two shops: Dayton's carved feet feature a central spade-shaped toe and are blockier than the Hubbell's more modeled feet; Dayton's legs are slightly taller and therefore less sinuous; Dayton's shells are rather flat with simple ribs while Hubbell's are deeper with more undulating ribs; and Dayton's base moldings tend to be thicker than the more complex cymas by Hubbell. Dayton also developed certain conventions for his construction: He often smoothed the inside surfaces of a carcass side with a toothing plane, added a butterfly key to strengthen the glued butt joint of a carcass side consisting of two boards, and chamfered the top edges of his drawer sides and backs. None of these features are found on furniture from the Hubbell shop. Clearly, contemporaries in the same town could draw from different training to develop a related language with distinct dialects.[6]

A similar relationship is evident in the work of Bates How of Canaan and Reuben Beeman of Kent. Signed work by these joiners bears a strong resemblance: squat carved ball-and-claw feet, extensive reliance on rope carving along base moldings and quarter-columns, similar dovetailing of drawers, and backboards dovetailed to the back edges of the carcass sides. In spite of these shared idiosyncrasies, there are noticeable differences. How's signed chest features extensive use of screws to attach the moldings and quarter-columns and an abundance of knotty, second-grade white pine boards. Beeman's work does not rely on screws and scrap pine and has a distinctive drawer detail: the sides taper toward the upper edge, thereby permitting more material where the groove for the bottom drawers is run. The variations between the How and Beeman shops suggest that craftsmen with different training, revealed in their particular structural logic and conventions, could respond to the market in similar ways, especially in regard to decoration, in the hill towns of northwestern Connecticut.[7]

Rhythms of Work

Under apprenticeship, young joiners learned to organize their tasks and rhythms in accordance with local custom. A master subtly schooled his apprentice in local economic cycles, labor conventions, and sources of materials and credit. Although most rural New England communities followed some sort of mixed agricultural economy, the mixture varied based on the town's location, time of founding, size, and social structure, and on local materials. From the time of the earliest settlements, making chests, chairs, and tables was one facet of the agricultural cycle and fit neatly with the responsibilities of animal and grain husbandry and fishing.

In the older coastal communities of western Connecticut, stretching from Milford to Norwalk, limited coastal trade made imported products and materials available. Several Stratford storekeepers imported chairs made by Edward Larkin of Charlestown, Massachusetts, in the 1740s and 1750s, and the 1763 probate inventory of Captain Joseph Squier of Fairfield lists "6 Chairs boston make."[8] Inventory references also make clear the increased availability of black walnut from the Middle Atlantic and southern regions and mahogany from the West Indies during the second half of the eighteenth century. Although Captain John Brooks of Stratford, who conducted trade with the Caribbean in the 1770s and 1780s, shipped six chairs made by Henry Beardslee to St. Croix in 1785, joiners' work along the Long Island Sound was not as dependent upon maritime and shipbuilding rhythms as in maritime centers such as Marblehead, Massachusetts. Coastal trade was only a small part of an economy based on agriculture, animals, fishing, and small shop craftwork. Lewis Burritt (1772–1839), an accomplished joiner who made inlaid mahogany case furniture, also participated in the varied Stratford economy of the 1790s and early 1800s. Besides making furniture, he hayed and pulled flax, made and mended oyster rakes, and made hat blocks and farming tools.[9]

Shop joiners in the recently settled lands of western Connecticut also organized their work in accordance with local agricultural rhythms. Widespread local use of such tools as axes, saws, broadaxes, and the like enabled the professional joiner to draw on a number of neighbors during the slack farming months of December, January, and February to fell, score, sled, split, and saw the locally available cherry, maple, yellow poplar, oak, and white pine. Winter was the ideal time for such activity: farmers had more free time and eagerly accepted such occasional work, the wood cut best at that time, and logs were easily sledded on the snowy ground.

Most preparation and assembly of furniture took place between harvest and spring planting. Joiners could count on uninterrupted time, so the workmanship of habit and the setup of lathes or bench clamps in the small shops could be used to efficient advantage. One task was the production of great quantities of turned chair parts when the lathe was set up and slightly green wood was available. Case furniture could be produced throughout the year, but the work seems to have been concentrated in two periods of heightened activity: February to April and August to November. The first period followed the cutting of new wood and allowed the joiner to work the wood while it was slightly green, an advantage in turning and in some types of carving. The second period was when the farmer clientele were able to calculate their harvest yield and therefore gauge what they could afford to spend on furniture.[10]

The seasonal rhythms and local economies affected the types of furniture produced. Turned chairs often were produced and exported by urban craftsmen such as Edward Larkin, but they also were the ideal chair type to be produced in a rural-based mixed agricultural community. There always was a market for chairs—they tended to get knocked about a fair amount, were more affordable than more complicated furniture forms, possessed visual flair, and enjoyed greater demand because of changing social customs. In addition they were easier to design and make than case furniture. Owing to practical considerations such as seat height and other dimensions, the maker worked in a more circumscribed habitual manner when making chairs and tables than when making storage furniture. Standard dimensions provided the general parameters of design. Variations tended to be in degree rather than in kind and often were concentrated in the appearance of the legs and back.

Rural joiners, who had the winter months free, could produce considerable quantities of turned chairs. They set up their lathes and turned parts efficiently and quickly by using a strike pole, or marking stick, to lay out the sections of turned elements and by maximizing the rhythm of their turning tools and lathe. They could rive out large quantities of wood for the slats or use a template to cut out the banisters and crest rails. It was thus possible and advantageous to stockpile certain parts such as rounds, posts, and slats. Several jobs, like bottoming and painting, could be subcontracted to others within the community. Joiners in western Connecticut often delegated such irregular work to young joiners who were just establishing themselves, older joiners in the twilight of their careers, or other members of the community. Subcontracting was not simply a means of reducing price but also of distributing work during the slack months, providing work for aging craftsmen, drawing tighter the web of local exchange, and allowing a craftsman to organize his work so as to focus on furnituremaking during the winter months and other opportune times.[11]

Turned chair production was not a specialized task but rather was standard output for a largely local market. Because of the speed of producing chairs and the use of local labor and materials, craftsmen could also make case furniture in the winter months. Unlike chairs, case furniture was a complex, open-ended product: Per capita ownership of case furniture in comparison with the sets of chairs listed in accounts and inventories indicates that there was relatively limited demand for large storage forms. Most households had several pieces of storage furniture, but consistently there were many more chairs and tables. There were also a great number of options for form, size, and configuration of drawers and compartments. Finally, large drawered or doored furniture required a lot of material and labor. Limited demand and the high cost of labor contributed to certain patterns of production in rural shops. A plentiful supply of butted and nailed chests—easily assembled from boards sawed at the local sawmill—has survived, but so has a variety of joined case furniture such as high chests, dressing tables, and chests of drawers.[12]

The number of complex storage forms listed in written documents and the evidence of the many surviving examples suggest that western Connecticut joiners employed various strategies to produce case furniture efficiently. Foremost was their reliance on local sawmills to provide boards with desired dimensions, thereby precluding the need to resaw or plane the boards to usable thicknesses. In Newtown and Woodbury, surviving artifacts reveal the joiners' use of blanks, which required only light planing before use. Some boards that were used for drawer linings or backboards still retain their water-powered-saw marks. In Newtown, most cherry boards were sawn ¾-inch thick, and yellow poplar and oak, ½-inch thick. In Woodbury, cherry tended to be ⅞-inch thick; yellow poplar, ½- or ⅞-inch; oak, ½-inch; and white pine, ⅜-inch. With boards delivered in the proper thickness, a joiner could readily lay out and cut joints. Preparations also were made easy by jigs such as a marking gauge to mark mortise and tenon joints and a bevel gauge to lay out consistent pins and tails for dovetails. Workmanship of habit made cutting tenons or dovetails proceed quickly. We tend to romanticize the cutting of dovetails, but joiners of this period could perform like machines in turning out these items.[13]

Probate inventories indicate widespread ownership of templates and patterns. Although many scholars believe that template use was an urban phenomenon typical of large-scale production, patterns also proved worthwhile in a rural shop with infrequent or seasonal production. Using templates to lay out crooked legs, bracket feet, and skirt profiles saved considerable time and, combined with the mental templates of rote structural work, enabled the small-shop joiner to make a desk in about a week and a half and a case of drawers in about three weeks.[14]

The organizational structure of the joiner's shop was critical to its successful operation. Written records identify two coexisting approaches to furniture production in western Connecticut during the last half of the eighteenth century: the family-based shop and the individual shop. In the family shop, a master craftsman took on neighbors or kin and then his own sons, as they matured, to staff his shop. These shops were part of a household economy that included improved land for crops and pasturage for animals. Acreage varied, but usually there were one to five acres of improved land and five to thirty acres of unimproved land. The historical evidence of such family dynasties as the Durands of Milford, the Hubbells and Beardslees of Stratford, and the Prindles and Fabriques of Newtown attest to the success of this approach.

For other joiners, continuing in the community was not desirable or possible. Drawn by the promise of a newly developing area or pushed out of a stagnant or overcrowded center, some joiners lacked the means or connections to purchase sufficient land to establish their own mixed agricultural–craft household. Many bought or rented small lots of one acre or less. To compensate for their lack of productive land, such craftsmen were under more pressure to make a living from their services. They thus concentrated more on craftwork and irregular handyman work. The instability of their lifestyles meant that their families often lasted less than a generation in a town and then moved along.[15]

Social Aspects of Composition

With the exception of shops in commercial centers such as Boston and Newport, furniture production in eighteenth-century New England was essentially a face-to-face negotiation between the joiner and his customers. The customer purchased a piece already assembled or specified an assemblage of features. In the latter case the patron had a more active role in the craftsman-client relationship, but the joiner still selected the form, decoration, and trim from his repertoire or through his own understanding of the desired style. The artisan controlled the "nature of work"—the physical knowledge of materials and techniques and its application—whereas the community controlled the "context of work." A joiner allocated his time and skills among the members of the community as he saw fit, while the community constantly judged his performance and bestowed him with a reputation. It was therefore important for the craftsman to understand and respond to the community. After all, the local clientele ultimately determined the success of a single joiner or the viability of several joiners.[16]

Apprenticeship introduced boys to the role of the joiner within that particular community and directly exposed them to the town's opinions and expectations of the master and his shop. Schooled in social as well as technical skills and conventions, the young artisan developed a personal expression that blended empirical craft techniques and local aesthetics. A joiner's cultural acumen and market judgment allowed him to practice a dynamic craft, but this dynamism was dependent on his patrons. Just as a kit of tools and learned techniques shaped the craftsman's range of possibilities, so did the needs, aspirations, and expectations of his clientele.[17]

Owing to the social basis of the craft, most joiners found it easiest to remain in the town in which they were trained. Established accounts with neighbors or relatives and familiarity with the available labor and materials certainly gave such a joiner an edge. A less tangible advantage was his internalization of local aesthetics. Within a familiar context of work, he continued to apply learned attitudes and techniques for design and fabrication. His training conditioned him to recognize that particular community's needs and provided him with the skills currently in demand. If techniques were introduced by a newly arrived craftsman, the locally trained joiner would perceive these options from a viewpoint similar to that of the majority of his customers. Work performed in such a context tended to be traditional but not unchanging and can be characterized as cumulatively adaptive.

On the other hand, a joiner trained in one community but active in another often had different experiences. Some clients may have sought his work as different or the latest fashion, but his learned techniques and the customers' demands did not always align so neatly. To continue his trade, such a joiner had to be willing to alter his internalized approaches, especially with respect to decoration and forms. He had to embrace and elaborate on chosen techniques rather than rely on learned methods. To survive he incorporated different techniques seen in work by other craftsmen, paid more attention to new forms produced elsewhere, or gave greater weight to his customers' requests. If he worked in a community with joiners trained in a number of different traditions, he had many techniques from which to draw.[18]

To understand the social context of furnituremaking, it is essential to reconstruct the social and economic structure of the community over time and identify the joiners' backgrounds. Particular attention should be paid to periods of dynamic growth or internal stasis and to turning points in these trends. For example, the prosperous coastal town of Stratford experienced considerable cultural flux during the 1710s and 1720s: the Anglican church established its first Connecticut parish there; several teachers at Yale College who converted to Anglicanism in 1722 had close ties with the community; there was trade with Boston merchants and with Anglo-Dutch traders on Long Island; and two immigrant English joiners, Thomas Salmon and Samuel French, settled in the town. French and Salmon introduced a British vernacular tradition that blended with Boston and New York work to become a distinctive Stratford Georgian style. This style became the standard for much of the century as an Anglican–Old Light coalition established cultural hegemony in the 1740s.[19]

Stratford's selective conservatism affected clients and makers alike. Inventory references after 1750 to new fashionable and expensive furniture forms, such as sideboards, breakfast tables, and easy chairs, signified the availability of these products and an awareness of them. These forms appeared infrequently in household inventories, however. People of all income levels did own substantial quantities of furniture, but they favored traditional forms. They purchased expensive case furniture, particularly cases of drawers, dressing tables, and desks, and large quantities of chairs, especially turned and crookedback chairs. For much of the last half of the century, the conservatism even influenced younger households, which acquired traditional furniture. During the first decade of the nineteenth century the joiner Lewis Burritt made several inlaid mahogany tables—decorative features and materials typical of the neoclassical style—but he still satisfied the traditional demands. He made chests, cherry chests of drawers or desks, and even fiddleback and York chairs; these chairs had been fashionable forms in the 1740s.[20]

Brewster Dayton, who trained with an English joiner and had access to many sophisticated forms and techniques, restricted his performance in Stratford. Much of his work had its roots in a vocabulary established before 1750. The proportions, tympanums, and crowns of two signed cases of drawers from 1784 resemble those found on Long Island examples of the 1740s. To this Anglo-Dutch work, Dayton blended the carved feet and scrolled knees introduced by his master. Dayton's probate inventory and various account book references also indicate that he made slat-back, fiddleback, and crookedback chairs, all of which are based on traditional chair forms. Even his furniture's primary woods, which include sycamore as well as subgrade cherry heartwood, reflect his reliance on local networks. The artifactual evidence points to the selective conservatism of the local clientele.[21]

The Hubbell shop evidently enjoyed a slightly greater latitude. Whereas the surviving Dayton work features only pad or carved versions of feet for case furniture, the Hubbells offered a variety: pad feet, bracket feet, carved feet, and ball-and-claw feet. The Hubbell shop is also distinguished by a greater variety of primary woods. Of all the identifiable Stratford shops, it is the only one in the last half of the century to use walnut and mahogany. Ebenezer Hubbell's brother-in-law Captain John Brooks, a merchant who was the "principal inhabitant of Stratford," provided the Hubbell shop with access to these imported woods. The handling of the ball-and-claw foot also suggests an external influence—the Hubbell feet closely resemble the squat plumpness of Philadelphia work. A set of joiner's chairs that might have been made in the Hubbell shop also manifest the influence of Philadelphia furniture. Chairs of this type were listed in John Brooks's probate inventory of 1777, which included "New furniture at Hubbells"—"1 Case Black Walnut Draws £8.10.0, 6 Cringle Back do Chairs @ 20/ £6, 1 great

Chair £1.5.0." Although the Hubbell shop could make high-style case furniture and joiner's chairs, the bulk of their work was executed in a simpler fashion. Most surviving chairs that relate to the single set of joiner's chairs are fiddleback and crookedback versions.[22]

Contrasting with the stylistic cohesion of Stratford was the stylistic frenzy of the New London County region between 1770 and 1800. In eastern Connecticut, an entrepreneurial merchant class orchestrated a vast export trade of beef and pork for the West Indies market. Reliant on elaborate credit connections with colonial and British merchants and constantly vulnerable to local and extralocal economic changes, these traders suffered from status anxiety. Through military supply contracts and privateering profits, the regional elite amassed significant fortunes during the Revolution. After the conflict, they sought to display their rank in their furnishings: joined chairs and elaborately conceived and decorated case furniture. Within a fairly closed community, they competed with one another, a competition aided by the diversity of joiners active in the region. Joiners who had trained in Philadelphia or Boston, and even an English prisoner of war captured during the Revolution, offered a rich variety of possible techniques and conventions. Exposure to New York and Newport furniture also provided ingredients for a stew of chosen traditions that was constantly remixed in towns such as Colchester, Norwich, or New London.[23]

Samuel Loomis of Colchester (1748–1814), who apprenticed with the Philadelphia-trained Benjamin Burnham, blended elements from many regional traditions and added extra shells, multiplied moldings, and developed new carved decoration to produce elaborate variations for clients who were closely related by familial or business ties. In southeastern Connecticut, the size of case furniture and any carved, molded detail on it were most highly valued. Felix Huntington of Norwich (1749–1822) developed a line of plain joiner's chairs made of rich, dense imported mahogany and upholstered by his brother Jonathan. Huntington drew his designs from imported English and Boston examples, but eliminated expensive carved details in order to provide a more affordable alternative to the carved Boston chairs. For seating, the number, upholstery, and type of wood seemed paramount to clients.

Even though permanence and learned techniques often resulted in traditional but evolving styles, and mobility and chosen techniques often resulted in rapid stylistic change, we need to be careful not to suggest simple polarities. All furniture blends the familiar and the new; what is different is the proportion of each and where change is permitted. Similarly we should be careful in studying Connecticut not to automatically draw a distinction between the traditional, Old Light western part of the colony and the cosmopolitan, New Light eastern section. Analysis of specific craftsmen-community relationships is essential to understand the nuances of differences in social economy.

The Cultural Significance of Joiners

In eighteenth-century rural New England, a world characterized by increasing population density, flourishing coastal trade, and chronic agricultural underemployment, a craft skill such as furnituremaking served an increasingly important function. Possession of craft skills had always been an integral part of estate settlement strategies, but certain trends in the eighteenth century endowed it with new importance. The expanding population, shrinking supply of unsettled land, increasing quantity and quality of English products, and rising accumulation and consumption of household goods shifted the balance of craftwork and farming. Whereas earlier craft by-employment was subordinate to agriculture, by the end of the eighteenth century craft activity was primary. As many household farms became smaller and the increased population demanded and produced more goods, the transmission of craft skills gained stature. Whether in a stagnant or dynamic rural area, furnituremakers personified the adaptive resiliency that became a fundamental trait of the New England character in the late eighteenth century. Making furniture embodied the prevalent values of the period: the familial priority of permanence and stability and the pragmatic need to conduct some entrepreneurial activity with the external market.[24]

Many New Englanders placed particular emphasis on stability. By the mid eighteenth century, subdivision of family lands throughout several generations had taxed the limited land resources and was creating impractically sized farms. To preserve stability, agrarian families sought to keep their children on the family land or within a community of kin. Fathers provided sons with craft training, thereby enabling them to earn a living with a smaller plot of arable land. Part-time artisan work thus provided the means to subdivide family lands further while maintaining economic viability and preserving the family identity in town. Combining craftwork and farming allowed a particular family to balance numbers and resources and to strengthen ties within the community. Craft shops produced needed goods for the expanding population and drew on the services of other community members.[25]

In families with several generations of woodworkers, joiner's skills provided both a livelihood and a legacy. Craft skills and tools, like land for sons of farmers and furnishings for their daughters, became another form of "property" that could be transmitted through the family network. Like real and personal estate, skills and tools allowed the succeeding generation to establish its own productive household unit while maintaining cross-generational rights and responsibilities. The success of this artisan strategy can be seen in the families who produced several generations of joiners within each town: the Durands in Milford, Hubbells in Stratford, and Prindles in Newtown.[26]

Other New Englanders placed slightly less emphasis on geographic permanence. If pressure for land continued unabated, the father could acquire land in a nearby town or on the frontier. Then the father assisted his son's migration by deeding him the land. Sons with joiner's skills probably found such relocation easier. Demand for joiner's work permitted some sons to establish themselves in a nearby community, close to kin support. For instance, John Fabrique, a Newtown cordwainer, provided two sons with woodworking skills. David and Bartimeus Fabrique were then able to practice the house joiner's trade in Newtown and the adjacent communities of Derby, Southbury, Woodbury, Roxbury, and New Milford. Other families provided a number of house and shop joiners who formed a regional network of related woodworkers. Among the many examples of such families in western Connecticut were the Beardslees, Prindles, and Booths.[27]

Those who moved farther away often moved with other kin or people from the same town. Such joiners preserved the group's cultural identity by providing familiar products. Like the English joiner who emigrated to New England in the 1630s, the rural Connecticut joiner who moved north or west in the early nineteenth century created physical and psychological comfort for others in a new environment. Lemuel Porter, a Waterbury joiner, moved west to Tallmedge in the Western Reserve in 1818 and built a church and several houses that re-created the appearance of Litchfield, Connecticut.[28]

Craft skills could be used in more innovative ways. Instead of being pushed into the joiner's trade by familial pressures, some sons were pulled into it. The growing population fostered a growing need for furniture, and such structural shifts gradually and unevenly affected cultural values. Some sons of farmers took advantage of available opportunities. Lacking the strength of family tradition, farmers' sons like Arcillus Hamlin may have been less tied to tradition and therefore more innovative in their work. Hamlin, the son of a Sharon farmer, worked as a joiner in Newtown. His 1827 inventory listed many items that were unique or rare for Newtown joiners: trunks, sheets of veneer, and bureaus. Such free agent joiners were also more willing to migrate as individuals. William H. Peabody, born in Norwich, worked for a few years in Stratford, sold his shop and moved to Woodbury, worked in Woodbury for twelve years, and then returned to Stratford. Joiners like Hamlin and Peabody may have perceived their skills as a marketable commodity for an individual rather than as an adaptive strategy for family continuity and identity.[29]

Woodworkers' sons who inherited skills and tools sometimes made different uses of these traditions as economic patterns changed and altered their attitudes. Justin Hobart Jr., the son of a Fairfield shop joiner, received his father's home and shop in 1797 but preferred to seek his fortune as a journeyman cabinetmaker in New York City. His entrepreneurial attitude was expressed in several letters to his sister Mary. In some of the early letters from 1797, Hobart reported constant work and good earnings. Within three years, however, he lamented: "I dont think that I shall work Journey work any longer their is no profit in it I dont Earn but Just Enough to pay my Expenses and I believe I can doe that in the Country. . . . I have work on hand that will take me about 6 weeks to finish and then I intend to quit working Journey work for a Spell . . . if their is going to Bee so many traders in Fairfield it will Doe for me to Carry on the Cabinet Business their they Cant get that away from me." Nevertheless, Hobart remained in New York a while longer, for in 1804 he took on John Jackson as an apprentice.[30]

Silas Cheney, a member of another woodworking family from Manchester, Connecticut, moved to Litchfield in 1799, probably with the intent to exploit the growing economy in northwestern Connecticut. He established a rural manufactory for the production of furniture, employing several journeymen and apprentices at one time and drawing on woodworkers in nearby Connecticut and Massachusetts towns for outwork. A Lenox, Massachusetts, woodworking shop, West & Hatch, provided Cheney with parts for kitchen and Windsor chairs. One of Cheney's journeymen, Lambert Hitchcock, went on to refine some of these practices in the large-scale production of turned, flag-seated fancy chairs.[31]

In the eighteenth century, similarities in technical repertoires, tool ownership, and shop layout linked the joiners of western Connecticut. However, these artisans made different uses of the same processes and equipment according to the traditions in which they were trained and the context of their mature work. By identifying the diagnostic details of craft traditions, it is possible to follow the flow and confluence of ideas and people over the New England landscape. Changes in consumption patterns or production rhythms often coincided with shifting commercial relations and increased involvement with external markets. Documentary evidence of craftsmen and communities, used in conjunction with artifactual evidence, offers explanations why different towns supported both different types of joiners and contrasting taste for furniture in the late eighteenth century.

THREE

The Joiners of Newtown and Woodbury

Located approximately eighteen miles apart and separated by the Housatonic River, the neighboring eighteenth-century towns of Newtown and Woodbury shared many topographical features (see fig. 1).[1] Both areas were characterized by relatively fertile loamy soil that covered an undulating, hilly terrain crisscrossed by several streams and brooks. Such upland determined similar mixed agricultural economies, whose products included grains, beef, pork, cheese, butter, wool, and cider. The plentiful streams afforded each town a comparable number of sites for the gristmills and sawmills necessary to process their natural resources. The Housatonic River provided each community with equal transportation and communication access to northwestern Connecticut, western Massachusetts, Long Island Sound, and New York City.[2]

Within these shared geographic and economic parameters evolved different cultural and social textures, to which the contrasting experiences of joiners in the two communities provide a valuable entrée. As a group, joiners tended to be rather ephemeral actors on the historical stage. They usually left little written record other than the occasional account book; few signed and dated their work and many left no inventories. Even some of those with surviving probate inventories had already retired or passed their tools along to others before their estates were appraised. To identify all possible shop and house joiners who worked in Newtown or Woodbury between 1760 and 1820, it was necessary to cull biographical information from a wide variety of sources, including inventories, wills, tax lists, land deeds, account books, manuscripts in private hands, published genealogies, and town histories. The data on birthplace, mobility, type of work performed, and length of working career within that town form collective biographies that facilitate comparison within and between towns over time.

For each town, the sixty-year period of this study was broken into three twenty-year segments.[3] This comparison (tables 2 and 3) indicates that stability and long careers as yeomen-craftsmen best characterized the joiners of Newtown. Woodbury joiners, on the other hand, experienced greater fluctuations.

Joiners of Newtown: Native Traditionalists

Of the twenty-one joiners active in Newtown between 1760 and 1780, almost two-thirds had been born in Newtown even though the town had been founded only in the second decade of the eighteenth century. Five other joiners immigrated from Stratford and Milford, coastal towns to the south that provided most of Newtown's first-generation inhabitants. Town of birth, in turn, affected the number of different places in which each joiner lived. More than half resided solely in Newtown, whereas only a third

TABLE 2
Newtown Joiners, 1760–1820

	1760–80	1780–1800	1800–1820
Number of active joiners	21	40	39
Number of joiners with sufficient data for analysis	20	38	37
Town of birth			
Newtown	12 (60%)	32 (84%)	29 (78%)
Stratford	3 (15%)	3 (8%)	2 (5%)
Milford	2 (10%)	0	0
Unknown	2 (10%)	0	0
New Haven	1 (5%)	0	0
Weston	0	1 (3%)	1 (3%)
Redding	0	1 (3%)	0
Maryland	0	1 (3%)	1 (3%)
Derby	0	0	2 (5%)
Fairfield	0	0	1 (3%)
Sharon	0	0	1 (3%)
Mean number of years working in Newtown	30	28	29
Other residences			
Newtown only	10 (53%)	25 (66%)	23 (62%)
Elsewhere before Newtown	6 (32%)	8 (21%)	9 (24%)
Elsewhere after Newtown	2 (11%)	7 (18%)	5 (14%)
Town of death			
Newtown	19 (95%)	30 (79%)	30 (81%)
Elsewhere	1 (5%)	4 (11%)	3 (8%)
Unknown	0	4 (11%)	4 (11%)

SOURCES: See appendixes A and B.

TABLE 3
Woodbury Joiners, 1760–1820

	1760–80	1780–1800	1800–1820
Number of active joiners	23	31	30
Number of joiners with sufficient data for analysis	22	30	29
Town of birth			
Woodbury	7 (32%)	11 (37%)	15 (52%)
New Haven	2 (9%)	2 (7%)	1 (3%)
Newtown	2 (9%)	4 (13%)	3 (10%)
Farmington	2 (9%)	2 (7%)	1 (3%)
Roxbury	2 (9%)	2 (7%)	1 (3%)
Stratford	1 (5%)	3 (10%)	0
Milford	1 (5%)	0	0
Branford	1 (5%)	0	1 (3%)
Goshen	1 (5%)	0	0
Hartford	1 (5%)	0	0
Edgartown	1 (5%)	0	0
Acadia	1 (5%)	1 (3%)	1 (3%)
Huntington	0	2 (7%)	2 (7%)
Weston	0	1 (3%)	1 (3%)
Norwalk	0	1 (3%)	1 (3%)
Wallingford	0	1 (3%)	1 (3%)
Norwich	0	0	1 (3%)
Mean number of years working in Woodbury	23	27	29
Other residences			
Woodbury only	7 (32%)	8 (27%)	13 (45%)
Elsewhere before Woodbury	15 (68%)	20 (67%)	15 (52%)
Elsewhere after Woodbury	3 (14%)	7 (23%)	5 (17%)
Town of death			
Woodbury	19 (90%)	16 (53%)	20 (69%)
Elsewhere	1 (5%)	8 (27%)	5 (17%)
Unknown	2 (10%)	6 (20%)	4 (14%)

SOURCES: See appendixes A and B.

lived elsewhere before working in Newtown. Once settled in Newtown, these joiners remained. Joseph Ferris left town for several years to join the Loyalist cause during the Revolutionary War, but he returned in 1783. Only Amos Sanford left town to follow his trade. Sanford worked in his hometown for eleven years, and then migrated north to Sharon, where he worked as a joiner for fifteen years.[4]

Another significant characteristic of this first group is the length of their careers in Newtown. The Newtown joiners of this period averaged thirty years of work in town. Such length of service had several interrelated ramifications. The long life spans of this cohort, the need for apprentices to provide power and permit efficient production, and the increasing local recruitment of joiners enabled older joiners to train great numbers of local youths in the established conventions. Most of these approaches originated in the compatible furnituremaking traditions of the coastal towns.[5] As a result, only a limited number of local shop traditions were established but many inhabitants possessed skill in joinery.

In the period between 1780 and 1800, the number of active joiners almost doubled from that of the previous period. This increase followed rapid population growth in town.[6] Yet the greater demand for furniture and houses was met by local artisans. Eighty-four percent of the joiners active in this twenty-year period were born in Newtown, and two-thirds of all the joiners spent their entire lives there. In short, there was a direct correlation between an increase in population and an increase in the number of craftsmen, especially native ones. Population growth provided a greater number of tradesmen to satisfy the growing demand for products.

The familial connections among woodworkers demonstrate the custom of local recruitment. Daniel, Edward, George, and Joseph Foot represent three different branches of the Foot family. George was a first cousin to the brothers Daniel and Edward, and Joseph was a second cousin to the other three. Furthermore, Edward's wife was a first cousin to the Prindles. Enos (1703–1724) and Ephraim Prindle (1707–1756) of Milford were among the first "carpenters" active in Newtown during the first decade of settlement. Their nephew Joseph became one of the most prominent Newtown joiners during the last half of the eighteenth century. Joseph drew on the familial labor pool by training two sons, Cyrus and Lazarus, a nephew, and a grandson. Thomas Skidmore, a Newtown carpenter of the 1720s and 1730s, was the progenitor of three generations of woodworking Skidmores active between 1780 and 1800. A third familial dynasty, the Booths, will be covered in detail later in this chapter.[7]

Families like the Prindles, Skidmores, and Booths recognized the advantages of an intergenerational labor force. They used family members as cheap labor, who in return could expect eventual inheritance of the shop, tools, and customers. Similar skills and aspirations for continuity linked generations.[8] Other Newtown families used craft-training as a one-time, immediate solution to the problem of providing for children during a time of population growth and increased strain on resources, especially land. The sons of Ebenezer and Sarah Fairchild included two joiners, a blacksmith, and a tailor. Their first cousins included masons, sawmill owners, and millers. With these craft skills, each Fairchild was able to live on a smaller plot of land and to combine craft and agricultural work. Consequently, a greater number of Fairchilds in this generation remained in Newtown.[9]

Only eight joiners working in Newtown during the last twenty years of the eighteenth century are known to have lived or worked in some other town before working in Newtown. Two of these eight, David Fabrique and Abner Judson, were born in Newtown, worked elsewhere for a time, and then returned to Newtown. Of the other six, three were born in Stratford and one each was born in the neighboring towns of Redding and Weston. The last of the six and the most atypical joiner was John Boyer, who is thought to have come from Maryland. Boyer was also distinguished from the other craftsmen because he owned only one acre of land, barely enough for a house, shop, and garden. Unlike the other Newtown joiners, therefore, he was unable to combine his artisanal activity with some farming or husbandry. However, his marriage to Mehitable Briscoe, daughter of the joiner James Briscoe Jr., established him within the larger Newtown community and the smaller extended family of joiners.[10]

The craft-training strategy of Newtown families was so attractive and successful that it resulted in an overabundance of native joiners by the end of the eighteenth century and, therefore, many moved elsewhere after working in Newtown. Most of these craftsmen left only in the twilight of their careers. The northern and western frontiers acted as a type of pressure valve that balanced the supply and demand of joiners. Mature artisans ready to retire moved away from town, creating openings for younger, locally trained youths. For example, Ebenezer Mallery moved to Catherine, New York, in 1807 after operating a highly valued shop in Newtown for twenty-four years, and Zardis Skidmore left for Patterson, New York, in 1815 after twenty years of service in his hometown.

The group biographies of joiners who worked in the third twenty-year period resemble those of the second group and further corroborate the existence of certain cultural values that guided the adaptive choices of Newtown inhabitants. The continued vitality of a mixed agricultural economy in which many individuals undertook part-time furnituremaking allowed sons to remain in their hometown among kin. The remarkable consistency in town of birth, mean number of years at work in Newtown, gross mobility, and town of death emphasizes the strength and stability of this effective form of resource management. Immigrant craftsmen were not attracted to or perhaps not even welcomed in Newtown. Whether intergenerational or intragenerational, the emphasis on continuity is well documented in the careers of Newtown joiners active between 1780 and 1820.

The careers of Cyrus Prindle, Alanson Northrop, and John Beardslee provide specific details. Cyrus continued to perform the same sorts of tasks carried out by his father, Joseph. He made furniture, produced window sashes and doors, and even performed such basic work as helving axes and bottoming chairs. Moreover, his father deeded him the family shop and part of the family farm in 1795. One of Cyrus's cousins married Alanson Northrop, another joiner who spent his entire life in Newtown. Northrop worked in a single-bench shop and balanced part-time artisanal work with farming. On his eighty-seven acres, he grew grain and flax, tended an apple orchard, and kept four oxen, fourteen cows, and fifteen sheep. Upon his death in 1812, Northrop's shop, tools, and half his house were distributed to his son Oliver, thereby permitting familial continuity within the craft.

John Beardslee owned only twenty acres, three cows, twelve sheep, and two pigs. He did, however, own a full complement of agricultural tools and processing equipment, a joiner's shop, and half a sawmill. The variety of tools and products in Beardslee's inventory indicates that he performed the work of a joiner, wheelwright, and cooper. His estate included cherry and butternut boards, jointer planes, a lathe and turning tools, many augers, broad chisels, cart and wagon spokes, oak timber, staves, heading, and window sashes. Birth in town, continuation of the yeoman-craftsman identity, and participation in several levels of the woodworking spectrum characterized the typical Newtown joiner of this period.

Arcillus Hamlin and Abijah and George Bradley, all of whom settled in Newtown by 1816, are the notable exceptions to this pattern and indicate the changing nature of the joiners' community in the late 1810s. Hamlin's birth in Sharon, Connecticut, and his association with William Chappell, a Danbury cabinetmaker, may have imbued him with a set of values and expectations that differed from those of his native Newtown counterparts. His estate, appraised in 1827, explicitly reveals these differences. Hamlin's home contained such stylish items as a new mahogany tea table, a bureau, a toilet table, a work stand, and four window blinds. The products and materials of his shop included unfinished trunks, an unfinished bureau, a dining table frame, three benches, twenty-five feet of veneering, and mahogany planks. His large shop, use of mahogany and veneers, and collaboration with the urban cabinetmaker Chappell distinguish Hamlin from other Newtown joiners.

Different attitudes toward furniture production also characterized the careers of the Bradleys, who grew up in the nearby commercial town of Derby. The Bradleys purchased land, a dwelling, and shop and machinery on the Halfway River in 1816. In the late 1810s and 1820s, they purchased water rights to ensure reliable power for their sawmill and other machinery and acquired sixty-six acres of woodland to provide the needed raw material for their shop. To finance expansion they mortgaged their property to merchants in nearby commercial towns. The Bradleys' sole concern was furniture production, particularly turned work such as chairs and bedsteads. In 1819 they entered into a formal partnership, under the name of A & G Bradley, as manufacturers of furniture.

Joiners of Woodbury: Immigrant Innovators

The analysis of joiners who worked in Woodbury presents a very different picture (see table 3). Patterns evident in their lives are not as coherent as those in the lives of Newtown joiners. Some craftsmen were born in Woodbury, but almost half were born elsewhere. High rates of migration into and out of town resulted in a high turnover rate, which permitted no single or even compatible shop traditions to dominate. The variety of careers reflects the fluid openness of the joiner's world in Woodbury.

In the period between 1760 and 1780, only about a third of the twenty-two joiners active in Woodbury for whom there were sufficient biographical data had been born and lived their entire lives there, even though the town had been settled for approximately one hundred years. In some ways, these seven joiners resembled their Newtown counterparts. Land records, probate inventories, and tax lists indicate that these native joiners owned more than five acres of land and continued to combine mixed husbandry and craftwork. The native Woodbury joiners followed production rhythms similar to those in Newtown. Simeon King's inventory of 1776 reveals that he made black chairs, white chairs, and cases of drawers in addition to window frames and sashes. Like Cyrus, Joseph, and Lazarus Prindle, King was a shop joiner who made window sashes during slack time. However, none of the native Woodbury craftsmen passed along the craft identity to his children. King had only a daughter, so his widow sold his shop and tools. Joiners with sons apparently did not train or encourage them to continue in the trade. Samuel Munn distributed his joiner's tools to his daughters, Ruth and Patty, and deeded land, farming tools, and shoemaking tools to his sons, Daniel and Benjamin. Either the joiner's trade was sluggish or the town lacked an internal cultural system that provided the needed supply of joiners. The former explanation seems inadequate because Woodbury's population growth during this period must have fueled a great demand for joiner's work in Woodbury. Furthermore, the continued migration of woodworkers into Woodbury implies a certain vitality in the furnituremaking trade.[11]

Joiners born elsewhere represented two-thirds of the total workforce and performed the greater part of the needed joiner's work. Not only were there more immigrant craftsmen in Woodbury than in Newtown but a greater variety of Connecticut regions were represented. Eighteen percent came from the neighboring towns of Newtown and Roxbury; 24 percent from the coastal communities of Branford, New Haven, Stratford, and Milford; and 10 percent from the Hartford and Goshen areas. Such varied origins and an average working life in town seven years shorter than that in Newtown resulted in a greater variety of shop traditions in Woodbury.

Joiners came to Woodbury for various reasons and in various ways. Artisans such as Samuel Curtiss, Truman Hurlbut, and Amos Leavenworth trained and married at young ages in their hometowns. Often related to Woodbury families, they would then move to Woodbury to begin work on their own. Such career patterns suggest either that their farming fathers had specifically apprenticed them to assist their settlement in a neighboring town or among relatives or that the fathers or sons had recognized the existence of sufficient work in Woodbury. Placing children in neighboring communities or among kin was a more open-ended variation of familial continuity than that favored in Newtown. These sons' desire and ability to remain and work in Woodbury suggests an inadequate supply of local apprentices and underscores the difference between Newtown's and Woodbury's craft structure.

Other joiners came to Woodbury of their own volition in the prime of their careers. Some of these craftsmen migrated from the crowded, oldest settlements of the colony. Like David Miles, for example, they may have recognized the greater opportunities to work and provide for their children. Miles came from Milford at the age of thirty-eight and within three years accumulated one hundred and two acres of land, a sawmill and gristmill, and a joiner's shop. Not having sons, Miles divided his estate equally among four daughters. Neither he, Eldad Spencer, Zimri Moody, nor William Adee passed along a woodworking identity to their children. Instead the shops and tools were treated simply as another form of personal estate. They were distributed equally without consideration that such dispersal diminished their intended function as a set. Other craftsmen who moved to Woodbury as mature joiners fared less well than did Miles. They either did not accumulate sufficient estate or became restless, so they moved along. Typical was Billious Hill, who hailed from Goshen, worked in Woodbury from the age of thirty to forty-four, and then moved to Lenox, Massachusetts.

The openness of the joiner's craft in Woodbury presents a sharp contrast to the closed nature of the Newtown artisan community. Newtown inhabitants viewed craftwork as an important means of conserving local resources and achieving continuity. Craftwork in Woodbury represented a different strategy designed to achieve immediate stability. Immigrant craftsmen established themselves in the community without reliance on family. A few joiners, such as Elijah Booth and Zimri Moody, received small plots of land when they married the daughter of a Woodbury resident. A greater number of joiners like William Adee, Ebenezer Bull, and David Miles purchased their home lots and brought their families with them. Economic involvement served as their only connection to the Woodbury community.

John Gould, an orphaned mariner's son from Branford, followed the most impersonal approach. He bought his land and remained a single man. Save for his craftwork, he was not involved with the community. According to his sister, his appraisers even took advantage of his isolation by tampering with his estate. Moreover, immigrant craftsmen such as Adee, Gould, Hill, and Naboth Candee were likely to own less than two acres of arable land. As a result they relied more on their craftwork than did their Newtown counterparts and were unable to distribute sufficient real estate to their children. These joiners may have died in Woodbury, but their progeny lived elsewhere.

Statistics regarding the Woodbury joiners active in the last twenty years of the eighteenth century parallel those of the earlier period. Locally born and trained craftsmen accounted for just over a third of the total number. Neighboring towns, older communities, and even urban areas provided the other two-thirds. Among the apprentices of Elijah Booth and Bartimeus Fabrique were Eli Hall of Weston, Abner Judson of Newtown, and John Beardslee of Trumbull. The appearance of such urban-trained craftsmen as George Bolt of Norwalk and Nicholas Jebine of New Haven illustrates the continued attractiveness and openness of the joiner's community in Woodbury. Jebine, who rented a house and owned a shop on land leased by Jabez Bacon, the leading merchant in town, provided Bacon with Windsor chairs. In 1807 Bacon's store had an inventory of sixty Windsor chairs, most probably made by Jebine. Jebine and other contemporaries continued to concentrate on woodworking and to depend upon others for foodstuffs. Jebine's payments included potatoes, a steer, and payment of town taxes. Dennis Bradley owned just half an acre, so he depended upon his customers for rye, potatoes, and even the pasturage of his only cow.

The late eighteenth century witnessed a hardening of lines between the various sorts of woodworking in Woodbury. Craftsmen like Jebine, who was explicitly referred to as a cabinetmaker, provided furniture and performed repair work occasionally. They did not work on houses. Instead, crews of house joiners began to take over framing, covering, and finishing dwelling houses. Bartimeus Fabrique was one such master builder. He oversaw his journeymen and apprentices and even contracted individual craftsmen like Charles Prindle when business demanded it. When business was slack, Fabrique let out some of his workforce to other joiners. Independent joiners like Prindle made some furniture such as kitchen chairs, cupboards, and coffins, but tended to concentrate on house joiner's work.

Geographic mobility increased among Woodbury joiners, with almost a quarter of them leaving town. Like their Newtown contemporaries, some moved at the end of their working careers. For example, Isaac Bunce moved to Wakeman, Ohio, when he was sixty-six years old. However, most Woodbury joiners moved in the prime of their careers. Ephraim Munson, Hezekiah Hine, and Dennis Bradley worked in town for a decade or so and then moved along to better opportunities in nearby towns. Other recent arrivals in town or the occasional local apprentice filled the empty places. The short, one-generation shop traditions and great mobility of Woodbury joiners accounted for a rapid and thorough turnover of joiners and shop traditions, which allowed the practicing joiners to select and combine aspects from a multiplicity of furniture traditions.

Many patterns evident during 1780–1800 carried over into the third period, 1800–1820. Woodbury continued to attract urban-trained craftsmen such as Harvey J. Linsley of New Haven and William Peabody of Norwich and Bridgeport. These artisans provided the upper level of the local furniture market. Constantly changing crews of house joiners, composed of craftsmen from the entire region, dominated architectural woodworking. But the third time period revealed a compositional difference in the woodworking trades: neighboring towns contributed fewer young joiners and the local Woodbury boys began to fill the joiners' shops. However, the life cycles of these boys did not resemble those of their Newtown peers. Young native joiners such as brothers Noah Hinman Booth and Ebenezer Booth VI, and Daniel Hurlbut and William Hurlbut probably trained with their fathers but spent their early twenties as handymen carpenters, who performed any sort of necessary work. The Hurlbuts cut and carted wood, performed framing work, bottomed chairs, laid fences, repaired tools, carted dung and hay, and worked in the garden. Some local craftsmen such as the Booths remained restricted to this work, while for others handyman work was simply a temporary situation. The growth of an external market for inexpensive furniture began to offer some hope for Woodbury joiners in the late 1810s. After making a living as handymen, the Hurlbut brothers entered into a partnership in 1816. Later, with the financial backing of Charles Peck, the Hurlbut shop expanded and acquired water-powered machinery by 1824.

Important differences between the mechanized shops in the two communities emphasize fundamental differences in their respective craft structures. In Newtown the Bradleys initiated financial arrangements to expand their operation. They took out mortgages but maintained control of their shop. The Hurlbuts, on the other hand, sought to gain viability as a shop by forming a partnership. When that proved insufficient, they turned to Peck, gaining financial stability in return for loss of control. Peck was recognized as owner of the firm. Lack of precedent and tradition was two-edged: it enabled joiners like the Hurlbuts to search for the best solution to setting up a viable shop, but it left the joiner isolated without the comfort, insurance, or guidance of other furnituremakers in the community. In short, the Woodbury joiner was potentially vulnerable, as the careers of several members of the Booth family reveal.

Ebenezer Booth IV: Continuity and Conservatism

A study of the various woodworking Booths provides an opportunity for a more personal look at the different craft structures in Newtown and Woodbury. Among the children of Ebenezer Booth III (1718–1803) of Newtown were three sons known to have been joiners: Ebenezer IV, born August 16, 1743; Elijah, born October 26, 1745; and David, born November 8, 1754.[12] Circumstantial evidence suggests that Ebenezer IV and perhaps Elijah trained with their uncle, Amos Sanford.[13] Elijah probably trained David. By 1766 Ebenezer IV had completed his training. On November 20 of that year he married Olive Sanford, a relative of his probable master, and on December 4 his father deeded him the family homestead in the Sandy Hook section of Newtown.[14]

On April 9, 1765, Ebenezer III had sold forty-seven acres of his land on Walnut Tree Hill in Newtown to Ebenezer and Sarah Ford of Newtown and had purchased forty-one acres on Good Hill in Roxbury from the Fords.

Apparently he recognized that Ebenezer IV would be firmly established as a joiner in Newtown. To avoid familial competition, he moved the rest of the family to Roxbury to establish his other woodworking sons in a community just beginning to grow. Able to purchase sufficient quantities of land in this more sparsely populated neighboring town, Ebenezer III slowly deeded portions of the family estate to his sons, with the expectation that they would look after him when he grew too old to support himself. Ebenezer III's subsequent relocation documents his concern with the reciprocal responsibilities of the lineal family. In the late 1780s, he left the Roxbury homestead to David and moved to Norfolk, where another son, Amos, lived. In the 1790s, he then returned to Newtown to live with yet another son, Asahel. Ebenezer III died in Newtown in 1803.[15]

Although no account books document Ebenezer IV's furniture production, he apparently fulfilled his father's expectations and established himself as the leading joiner in Newtown. His shop, first assessed for taxes in 1767, maintained a consistently high assessment in relation to other craftsmen's shops. Its value derived from an ideal location: it fronted north on the road from Newtown to Southbury; east on the Sanford gristmill, a site of community gathering, and on the Pootatuck River, an as-yet-untapped source of water power; and west on his cousin's family lands. The Sanford sawmill was just across a street that ran up to the center of Newtown.[16]

As revealed by land records and the estate inventory, Ebenezer's life was circumscribed by traditional family values. Marriage connected him to the Sanford family, who owned much of the land around the Booth homestead. Ebenezer relied on the nearby Sanford sawmill for a ready supply of sawn wood. From 1770 until his death in 1790, Ebenezer consolidated his holdings near the home lot and near the family land at Walnut Tree Hill and Billbury Swamp. Such accumulation and consolidation was not for speculative purposes, but rather to provide for his children. The ability to settle one's children as separate but nearby households was the mark of success in an agricultural community.[17]

Ebenezer IV's inventory revealed the continuation of a mixed agricultural economy in which the household remained the unit and location of production. In addition to a shop located on the home lot and his joiner's tools, Ebenezer owned forty-five acres of arable land and meadow, a quantity of farming tools, two cows, three heifers, two calves, twelve sheep, four swine, one colt, and one mule. The estate also included a loom and tackle, twenty-eight pounds of sheep's wool, and a pair of cards to clean the wool. Ebenezer IV epitomized the Newtown artisan who retained his yeoman-craftsman identity and preserved the strength of the lineal family.[18]

His inventory permits insight into the conservative nature of his shop and its production, much of which was chairs. All of the forms listed in the shop appeared in quantity in the Newtown inventories from the 1770s until the 1820s (see chapter 5). The large supply of already turned and dried chair rounds and posts and the stock of flag to bottom the finished frame demonstrates the local preference for flag-seated turned chairs. The variety of such turned chairs offered by Ebenezer ran from plain chairs (@ 2/) to round-top chairs (@ 3/), horn chairs (@ 4/), and fiddleback chairs (@ 5/6). Similar correlations exist between the storage and table forms in his shop and those listed in the inventories. Case furniture and tables in the shop included a desk with drawers, a chest and drawers, several plain chests, a round fall leaf table, and legs for another round table. Additional evidence of Ebenezer's ties with the local community and its values lies in his extensive stock of local woods—cherry, maple, birch, whitewood, pine, and oak. This selection of woods may reflect his clientele's preference for local woods or his integrated role in the local economy (in the barter economy of a relatively self-sufficient agricultural community, woodworkers often received boards and plank as payment for services or products).[19]

Although based firmly on familial and communal values, Ebenezer IV's career hardly resembles that of an unsophisticated craftsman. His furniture stock, the number of seasoned chair parts, and his ownership of design patterns suggest that Ebenezer, only a part-time craftsman, nevertheless made a variety of forms and organized his work efficiently. The high value given to his sets of planes and saws (70/ and 27/, respectively) implies that he possessed a full range of these tools. Ownership of the perfectly suited tool permitted him to sustain quality production. The stockpile of chair parts and extensive set of patterns also enabled Ebenezer to run a fairly large shop. In 1790 Ebenezer's workforce consisted of his son Joel, one male under sixteen, and two males over sixteen. In spite of the local orientation, the Booth shop was not sealed off from the rest of the world. Publication of a note of administration on his estate in the Danbury *Farmer's Journal* signifies that Ebenezer had commercial contact with people outside the immediate community. Unfortunately, the extent of this contact remains unknown.[20]

The distribution of Ebenezer's estate in 1790 attests to the strength of values that stressed familial continuity. His daughters were established with sufficient dowries of personal estate and land to enable them to marry local men and remain in town. His oldest son, Joel, was left the shop, tools, and a two-thirds share of the home and home lot (the other third went to Olive, Ebenezer's widow). The youngest son, Ebenezer V, received another part of the real estate. In addition to the physical estate that Ebenezer IV distributed to his sons, he passed along a craft identity as a joiner. Joel, born June 17, 1769, must have assumed leadership of the shop when his father had a leg amputated in January 1790. After Ebenezer IV's death that June, Joel inherited the shop and tools and became legal master of the shop. In 1791 Joel took the freeman's oath, which signified one's status as head of a Newtown household.[21]

Although Joel's death in 1794 ended his career just as it was beginning, his inventory supplies valuable information about his work and values. Joel's life reflected an outlook more modern than his father's, but still anchored in local traditional values. Whereas real estate and the dwelling house accounted for more than half of Ebenezer IV's estate (61%), they represented slightly more than a third of Joel's estate (39%). Such a difference cannot be attributed solely to Joel's early death and the resulting inability to accumulate land. He invested more capital in furniture production and personal belongings, such as silver spoons and window curtains. Tools, unfinished furniture, boards, and the shop facility accounted for 24 percent of Joel's total estate, an increase of 11 percent over his father's estate.[22]

Nevertheless, Joel did not abandon the mixed agricultural life of his father. His estate included a wide range of animals—two oxen, one cow, two calves, one mare, one colt, one sow, two goats, three swine, and five sheep. The grasses in storage and grains on the ground included five tons and two stacks of hay, nine bushels of oats, three acres of wheat, and three and a half acres of rye. A detailed tax list from 1790 listed Joel's land by use and quality. He owned ten acres of plowland, four acres of upland meadow and clear pasture, six acres of second-rate meadow, four acres of unmowed bog, and seventeen acres of brush pasture. Such a distribution of lands forced Joel to use his arable acreage in a more intense manner, to keep animals on the unimproved land, and to rely on a craft skill for an increasing part of his livelihood. The debts of Joel's estate, many of them probably accrued by his shop expansion, provide additional evidence of his traditional views. He relied on kin and neighbors for economic assistance. The largest part of the debt was owed to his and his wife's immediate families (44%), and a comparable amount to other inhabitants of the town (43%). People from outside of the community accounted for only 12 percent of the total debt.[23]

The products of Joel's shop provide proof of his solid base in the traditional and less competitive world of kin and neighbors. Spurred on by his own initiative or by some fashionable patrons, Joel made mahogany furniture, including a card table and a desk, and cases for such musical instruments as a spinet, a "violene," and a "voice flute." These cosmopolitan items, however, were only a small part of his total work. The majority of Joel's products were more conservative forms, similar to those of his father. The quantity of chair rounds and slats, the fifteen shillings' worth of flag, and the listing of black chairs and red chairs document the continued popularity of flag-seated turned chairs. Case furniture made in Joel's shop included cases of drawers, desks, chests of drawers, and painted chests. All of these forms appeared frequently in Newtown inventories from the 1770s until the 1820s. Although capable of producing fine furniture in a fashionable manner, Joel's output remained consistent with the community's traditional orientation. Caught between the demands for fashion and the expectations of traditional social relationships, Joel gave more weight to the latter.[24]

Elements of new fashion and old tradition can also be detected in an indenture between Joel Booth and Robert Hazard of Stonington, Connecticut, dated October 10, 1794, for Booth to teach Hazard "the art trad an mistrey of a Sd Cabbennet makeing" in two years. Joel's choice to use the term *cabinetmaker* rather than *joiner* could be considered an affirmation of a more cosmopolitan view. However, the more traditional products of Joel's shop suggest that it may have been only a rhetorical accommodation of more recent styles and techniques. The apprentice's hometown presents equally ambigious evidence: One could conclude that Joel enjoyed a colonywide reputation, but more likely a member of the Hazard family living in Newtown arranged Robert's apprenticeship. Firmer evidence of the conservative organization of Joel's shop was the provision that Hazard was "to be obliged to work out at farming busnes Not to Exceed five Days in Each year." Perhaps Joel had a reputation for concentrating on furniture production while delegating farm responsibilities to journeymen and apprentices. Other rural joiners of the same period followed this practice. Since apprentices were part of the family, masters expected them to contribute to all phases of the household production.[25]

Joel's brother Ebenezer V was only fourteen years old when Joel died in 1794. He was too young to inherit the family shop and tools, but he did become a woodworker. On January 1, 1802, Ebenezer V married Anna Hann of Southford. Three months later he sold his portion of the family lands to his uncle Asahel Booth and his cousin John Sanford and bought land in Southbury. His new home placed him within a mile of his paternal uncle, Elijah Booth. At first Ebenezer V experienced hard times in this new community. He had to mortgage his property several times and, like the Hurlbuts, devoted most of his time to such handyman carpentry work as cart repair, ax helving, and other repairs. Life for Ebenezer V improved by 1825. He built a dam on Eight Mile Brook in Southford and set up a water-powered cabinetmaking and turning shop. According to a local historian, Ebenezer V "made chairs in quantity, which were taken to Derby and sent from there by boat to New York."

An account book kept by Charles Booth (1802–1848), a furnituremaking son of Ebenezer V, reveals that the Booth shop on Eight Mile Brook had strong ties to the external market. The shop provided "Ebenezer Dupinenach" of New York with chair parts that were boxed in Southford and then assembled in New York. Among the parts listed were curled maple posts, bows, and rounds; eagle frets (slats cut out in an eagle profile) and cross frets (X-shaped slats), as well as square frets, oval frets, and crown tops. Besides furniture, the Booth shop produced quantities of hat blocks for Danbury hat manufactories and spindles for nearby spinning manufactories.[26]

Earlier aspects of Ebenezer V's life provide additional evidence of the strong traditional values of the Booths in Newtown. Though not trained directly by his father or brother, Ebenezer V still followed the family calling and became a joiner. He settled in Southbury, presumably because his wife's family and his uncle Elijah lived there. Like his father and brother, he expected family and craft together to provide a means of emotional and economic security, but the different craft structure of Woodbury had a profound effect. Ebenezer V found that he had to adjust his values and rely solely on his own craft skill to survive. Rather than producing entire pieces of furniture and continuing the yeoman-artisan tradition, he turned to the growing industrial market. He provided chair parts for export to the nearest large commercial center and contributed equipment for the area's leading industries. Although able to train his son Charles, Ebenezer V found that the earlier connection between family and occupation had weakened. In fact, he paid his son wages to work in the shop.

Elijah Booth: Competition and Change

Elijah Booth must have moved to Roxbury with his father, Ebenezer III, because in 1768 Elijah's name first appeared on that town's tax list. By 1770 Elijah had established a joiner's shop in Roxbury, for which he was assessed £8. Such a figure suggests a sizable operation. Elijah was not to remain in Roxbury very long, moving to Southbury in 1771. According to the 1771 Southbury tax list, he must have immediately set up shop that year—he was assessed £3 for a faculty (a craft or service shop) in addition to a normal tax. Elijah may have been pushed out of Roxbury by the imminent maturing of his four younger brothers or attracted to the Woodbury area by the open craft structure. On March 2, 1771, Elijah bought a half-acre home lot and house from Edward Hinman, whose sister he married on October 14, 1772.[27]

In several respects Elijah's career as a woodworker in the Woodbury area parallels that of his brother Ebenezer IV in Newtown. According to a May 7, 1777, apprentice agreement between Elijah and Lewis Hurd of Woodbury, Elijah was a shop joiner, a term also applicable to Ebenezer IV. The furniture made by Elijah resembled the conservative forms made in his brother's shop. The "plain desk" Elijah made in 1784 for Shadrach Osborn and the "plain table" and "plain chest" he made in 1787 and 1790, respectively, for Joseph Curtiss suggest that Elijah produced a simple sort of furniture that lacked extensive decorative details, such as elaborate carving or inlay. He concentrated on plain, traditional forms like the chest of drawers, valued at 36/, that he made for Bennet French in 1801. In 1798 Elijah also sold French a bedstead, which was probably made from bedstead timber purchased at David Stiles's sawmill. For Frances Hinman in 1802, Elijah provided a suite of furniture that included "1 Kitchen table £1.8.0; chest two Draws £1.16.0; 7 plain chares £1; and 2 Elbow chairs (inexpensive armchairs) 8/." In February of the next year he provided Frances with a clock case valued at £3. Paint often decorated Elijah's furniture. For David Stiles he made two green chests in 1796, and his accounts with Shadrach Osborn reveal frequent purchases of paints and red lead. An ability to pass along a woodworking legacy further links Elijah and Ebenezer IV. Two of Elijah's sons became woodworkers in Woodbury: Noah Hinman Booth, born January 31, 1783, and Ebenezer Booth VI, born April 7, 1790.[28]

In spite of these similarities, Elijah's career in Woodbury reflects a significant amount of change in structure and values. Unlike his brother, Elijah specialized in woodworking and lacked sufficient land to provide for his own family. Throughout his career he purchased substantial quantities of rye, wheat, meat, potatoes, dairy products, and cider. In contrast to the relative self-sufficiency of Ebenezer IV, such specialization made Elijah more dependent on others in the community. Elijah's widely fluctuating tax assessments indicate a less stable existence than Ebenezer's. Even though he specialized, Elijah did not belong to the upper cadre of furniture producers that developed after the Revolution. For the most fashionable furniture, the townspeople had two choices. They patronized cabinetmakers like Nicholas Jebine or Ephraim Munson, or they purchased imported items from New York through Shadrach Osborn and other local merchants. Shop joiners like Elijah Booth were a second rank of furnituremakers, who provided conservative plain or painted furniture. Yet shop joiners were still distinct from handymen carpenters like Joseph Curtiss, who performed contract work hauling wood, framing barns and sheds, repairing furniture, and bottoming chairs.[29]

After 1790 Elijah's career underwent striking changes. His age or a decreasing demand for traditional furniture may account for the adjustments. He began to devote an increased proportion of time to house joinery and carpentry work. After 1796 Elijah no longer consistently purchased great quantities of sawn cherry and whitewood boards and planks from David Stiles's sawmill. Instead he bought smaller quantities sporadically, as infrequent demand dictated. During the last five years of the eighteenth century, Elijah also bought sash lights (window glass) and great quantities of white lead. These products are more often associated with house joinery than furnituremaking. Elijah's journeymen and apprentices during these years provide additional evidence of his experience in house joinery. Eli Hall, Charles Prindle, Silas Bennett, and Elijah's two sons all became house joiners/carpenters. Only Abner Judson, who returned to Newtown as Rivirius Prindle's journeyman, remained active in furnituremaking.[30] Elijah's traditional role as shop joiner was disrupted in other ways. His attempt to raise livestock for the market after 1800 met with failure because he did not have sufficient land. Frustrated by the lack of opportunity, Elijah took on odd carpentry jobs such as hauling, sawing, and mending during the last twenty years of his life.[31]

Elijah's ideas about his family changed as the nature of his work changed. Whereas Ebenezer IV's life revealed the intertwining of work and family, Elijah's later career reflects a new independence between work and family. The 1790 census listed Elijah as the head of a large household comprising thirteen people, five of whom were not in the immediate family. These five were probably journeymen and apprentices. In 1800, only eight people remained in the entire household; all of them belonged to the immediate family.

Accounts from the late 1790s and early 1800s reveal that Elijah stopped boarding apprentices. Instead he contracted Bartimeus Fabrique's workers or other journeymen for short periods of time. Such a change suggests that less importance was attached to the household as a unit of production. Craftwork, formerly an integral aspect of family life, became separated from it. Such a change in values can be seen even in the relationships between Elijah and his two sons. Although he trained Ebenezer VI and Noah as woodworkers, Elijah provided little additional support after they concluded their training. He did not pass along the family shop or any tools, but rather let his sons fend for themselves. Noah had to purchase his workbench, a gluepot, some tools, and plane stocks from Bartimeus Fabrique in 1809. His purchase of the joiner's most essential possessions reflected a radical new orientation toward a craft skill. No longer did fathers train their sons, establish them in the family shop, and gradually turn the business over to them. A craftsman's skill became more of a marketable commodity for an individual than a means of assuming traditional familial values and preserving the family identity.[32]

Elijah's new attitudes toward land were symptomatic of his new ideas about family and work. Whereas Ebenezer IV accumulated land to provide for his children and passed along his home and shop to his oldest son, Elijah viewed his land speculatively after 1795. He used land as a capital asset to be mortgaged in times of need. Rather than depend on neighbors or relations for economic support as his nephew Joel Booth had, Elijah relied on land. On several occasions he mortgaged his seven-acre wood lot on French's Mountain. He even mortgaged his shop and home in 1803. Although he recovered the property on March 15, 1806, he immediately sold it to his former journeyman Eli Hall. In 1811 he purchased a small lot of eighty-one rods, which included a house but no shop.[33]

Fluctuations in Woodbury's economy or Elijah's own maturing probably account for the changing nature of his work and workforce and his numerous land transactions. Elijah looked after himself instead of relying on kin or neighbors during hard times and old age. His hiring of journeymen by the day lowered his operational costs, and his mortgages provided immediate credit. These solutions distinguish Elijah's individualistic value system from that of his Newtown relatives. He did not consider his home, his shop, or his work as a legacy to be preserved and handed down through the family line. Instead he viewed his work and his land as financial assets. Once Elijah trained his sons, he expected them to become similarly individualistic and entrepreneurial, seizing opportunity unfettered by traditional constraints. He did not provide them with assistance as they established themselves, and they felt no obligation to look after him in his old age. At his death in 1823, Elijah distributed his meager estate to his wife and a spinster daughter with whom he lived in a small house.

The careers of Ebenezer Booth IV and Elijah Booth point to the importance of the social economy in which the joiner worked. Both craftsmen grew up and trained in Newtown. Such apprenticeships must have endowed them with the same skills and concerns as other Newtown yeomen-artisans. Yet Elijah and his nephew Ebenezer V altered their work habits and values when they moved to Woodbury. Elijah trained Abner Judson as a house joiner amid the narrowing craft structure of Woodbury. Judson, however, assumed a different artisanal role when he returned to Newtown. He was able to make furniture, perform house joinery, and combine farming with joiner's work. The lives of joiners who worked in Newtown or Woodbury illuminate striking differences between neighboring rural communities. What caused or contributed to these contrasting craft structures? Why did Woodbury continue to depend on immigrant furnituremakers? Why did immigrant craftsmen start to work in Newtown only in the 1810s? In order to understand the joiners' communities in Newtown and Woodbury, it is essential to explore each town's socioeconomic structure.

F O U R

Socioeconomic Structure in Newtown and Woodbury

In the colonial and early national periods of American history, agriculture was the root of the fundamental values that shaped public behavior and helped participants to comprehend that behavior. To understand an early American community's values and behavior, one must therefore undertake an intensive analysis of that community's agricultural economy. Even slight shifts in farming techniques, size or varieties of crops, or numbers or varieties of animals altered basic agricultural routines and production schedules. Such alterations, in turn, affected all complementary craft and service activities in that town, with resulting adjustments in attitudes toward land and work. These changes and alterations did not occur systematically, but rather in fits and starts that varied from town to town. As one charts the socioeconomic patterns of Newtown and Woodbury and extrapolates the prevalent values in each town, one begins to see how social structure, work activities, and communal values determined career choice, mobility, production rhythms, consumer taste, and technological innovation.[1]

Specific evidence about the patterns of each town are found in inventories, account books, and census schedules. The patterns that emerge reflect two distinct rural experiences during a period characterized by the growth of urban markets, intensified animal husbandry, rural industry, and national financial systems. By necessity, farmers from both towns were *in* the market; by choice, Woodbury farmers were also *of* the market, which their Newtown counterparts were not until the 1810s.

Newtown: A Yeoman Town

Founded in 1711, Newtown was a fairly young community in the last half of the eighteenth century. Its first inhabitants did not migrate as a cohesive unit from the same area. Rather, families from Milford, Stratford, Derby, New Haven, and Guilford purchased shares in the town. Like other towns incorporated at the same time, Newtown received from the Connecticut General Assembly a small grant of sixty-six square miles. Town leaders intended to settle the area slowly, as shown by the first division of land, which provided only twenty-two acres per family. This restraint was short-lived. Five additional divisions followed within the next five years, and by 1723, no common land remained in reserve.

Newtown's quick division of such a small area and its location off the migratory path to the northern or western frontiers made it less attractive to the mobile population of the colony. Nevertheless, Newtown's population did increase, especially between 1756 and 1790 (table 4). The town's growth resulted more from a natural increase in many of the original families than from immigration. Of the 147 people on the tax list of 1739, two-thirds had a surname that appeared on a list of inhabitants from 1717. Furthermore, Newtown's gross rate of persistence remained high until the early nineteenth century (table 5). Newtown's rates of 77 percent in the 1760s, 65 percent in the 1770s, and 62 percent in the 1790s compare favorably to those of stable rural communities such as Hingham, Massachusetts, at the end of the eighteenth century. The exception to these high rates, a surprising low of 50 percent in the 1780s, appears temporary and can be attributed to the dislocations experienced by some of Newtown's Anglicans at the conclusion of the Revolution. Many of those who did not remain in town in the eighteenth century may have been native sons whose move permitted the distribution of viable family farms to one or two other sons. Not until the first two decades of the nineteenth century did Newtown's persistence rate fall to the lower fifties. At that time migrants must have

TABLE 4
Population of Newtown and Woodbury, 1756–1820
(selected years)

	1756	1774	1790	1800	1820
Newtown	1,253	2,229	2,774	2,921	2,879
Woodbury	3,911	5,313	4,400	3,676	3,551

SOURCES: For 1756 and 1774: Evarts Greene and Virginia Harrington, *American Population Before the Federal Census of 1790* (New York: Columbia University Press, 1932), 56, 61. For 1790: U.S. Bureau of the Census, *Heads of Families at the First Census of the United States Taken in the Year 1790—Connecticut* (Washington, D.C.: Government Printing Office, 1908). For 1800: *Return of the Whole Number of Persons Within the Several Districts of the United States* (Washington, D.C.: Wm. Doane & Son, 1802), 23–24. For 1820: *Population Schedules of the Fourth Census of the United States—1820* (National Archives Microfilm Publications, microcopy no. 33), 1:213, 420; 3:38.

TABLE 5
Gross Rates of Persistence for Newtown and Woodbury, 1760–1820
(percentages)

	1760–70	1770–80	1780–90	1790–1800	1800–1810	1810–20
Newtown	77	65	50	62	54	53
Woodbury	73	62	55	53	52	57

SOURCES: Tax lists for Woodbury, Southbury, and Newtown, which are held at the town hall in each of the listed towns. See also note 2.

become more attracted to Newtown or more native sons must have migrated out. Only 46 percent of the taxpayers' surnames on the 1820 list appeared on the 1760 enumeration.[2]

The quick division of Newtown's land and its subsequent transmission through family lines resulted in small differences between great and small estates (see chapter 5). Consequently, life in Newtown was never dominated by only a small number of prominent families. During the third quarter of the eighteenth century, 3.8 percent of Newtown's population served as leaders and only 45.9 percent of its terms of office were filled by men serving at least five years. More than one-half of Newtown's families contributed a town leader. Newtown's deputies to the General Assembly in the years 1760–80 served an average of 4.87 one-year terms each. Furthermore, just over half of the officers were not reelected for the subsequent term. The high deputy turnover rate of 51 percent meant that more townspeople were able to participate in government on the colonial level. Given its dense population, Newtown was surprisingly egalitarian.[3]

The timing and nature of Newtown's settlement put that community at a distinct economic disadvantage in its region during the middle of the eighteenth century. Existing transportation routes converged in older, more socioeconomically stable towns surrounding Newtown and provided those communities with greater economic possibilities. As a result, Newtown inhabitants continued to do business with the shopkeepers and craftsmen of Milford, Stratford, and other coastal towns until the 1760s. Thomas Tousey, a Newtown doctor, patronized Andrew Durand of Milford and Hezekiah Treadwell of Stratford for the furniture in his daughter's dowry in 1740 and hired the services of a Norwalk miller in 1752. Merchants in the older towns of Milford, Stratford, Norwalk, and Danbury organized the limited amount of external trade in agricultural surpluses.[4]

From estates filed at the probate court in the 1760s (tables 6–8), it is clear that Newtown still had a developing economy at that time: crops and oxen

TABLE 6
Grains in Newtown and Woodbury, 1760–1824
(percentage of estates with specified grain)

	1760–64	1770–74	1780–84	1790–94	1800–1804	1810–14	1820–24
NEWTOWN							
Number of estates	15	17	18	17	29	26	48
Wheat (%)	33	53	50	47	17	15	6
Corn (%)	27	35	72	29	41	54	65
Rye (%)	—	29	33	35	59	73	63
Oats (%)	27	29	50	12	31	50	52
Hay (%)	20	29	67	35	41	46	67
Potatoes (%)	—	—	11	24	31	46	5
WOODBURY							
Number of estates	16	13	20	17	20	24	29
Wheat (%)	56	46	55	35	35	25	28
Corn (%)	56	46	35	47	50	67	59
Rye (%)	31	31	40	47	70	71	62
Oats (%)	44	23	25	24	45	50	45
Hay (%)	44	15	25	29	50	42	52
Potatoes (%)	—	15	10	12	25	38	45

SOURCES: Estate inventories for Woodbury, Danbury, and Newtown probate court districts (Connecticut State Library, Hartford).
NOTE: Dashes indicate that data were unavailable.

TABLE 7
Animal Ownership in Newtown and Woodbury, 1760–1824
(percentage of estates with specified animal; mean number per estate in parentheses)

	1760–64	1770–74	1780–84	1790–94	1800–1804	1810–14	1820–24
NEWTOWN							
Number of estates	15	17	18	17	29	26	48
Oxen (%)	20 (2.3)	65 (3.1)	56 (6.5)	65 (4.4)	59 (3.4)	81 (4.3)	83 (2.8)
Cows (%)	73 (3.8)	76 (6.2)	94 (5.8)	100 (5.1)	79 (6.0)	88 (8.4)	44 (4.8)
Horses (%)	73 (1.9)	76 (1.9)	67 (2.9)	82 (1.9)	83 (2.2)	85 (2.0)	60 (1.5)
Pigs (%)	53 (5.9)	76 (9.0)	67 (10.3)	88 (9.5)	72 (7.1)	73 (6.5)	71 (4.1)
Sheep (%)	47 (8.7)	59 (11.8)	94 (12.5)	71 (20.3)	48 (13.2)	81 (17.6)	56 (13.2)
WOODBURY							
Number of estates	16	13	20	17	20	24	29
Oxen (%)	50 (4.5)	54 (4.9)	60 (4.1)	47 (5.0)	80 (3.6)	71 (3.7)	52 (5.7)
Cows (%)	75 (9.7)	100 (5.2)	95 (6.5)	88 (6.7)	100 (6.6)	92 (7.6)	90 (8.5)
Horses (%)	94 (2.3)	69 (3.0)	100 (2.0)	71 (3.3)	95 (2.4)	83 (2.0)	55 (1.9)
Pigs (%)	56 (10.6)	92 (8.2)	65 (8.7)	65 (7.7)	80 (8.1)	88 (8.8)	69 (10.3)
Sheep (%)	69 (25.6)	69 (31.4)	75 (14.7)	53 (21.9)	75 (13.5)	58 (29.4)	72 (21.9)

SOURCES: See table 6.

TABLE 8
Packed Meat and Dairy Products in Newtown and Woodbury, 1760–1824
(percentage of estates with specified items; mean value in parentheses)

	1760–64	1770–74	1780–84	1790–94	1800–1804	1810–14	1820–24
NEWTOWN							
Number of estates	15	17	18	17	29	26	48
Meat (pork, beef, lard) (%)	13 (£10.18.6)	18 (£13.14.5)	28 (£6.11.4)	41 (£3.17.1)	52 (£7.7.10)	77 (£7.15.0)	52 (£3.12.0)
Dairy (cheese, butter) (%)	7 (£0.10.0)	12 (£5.17.10)	22 (£2.11.6)	29 (£1.2.8)	38 (£1.14.3)	35 (£0.17.0)	33 (£1.8.0)
WOODBURY							
Number of estates	16	13	20	17	20	24	29
Meat (pork, beef, lard) (%)	44 (£2.18.3)	38 (£3.7.5)	15 (£10.10.1)	44 (£6.9.9)	50 (£12.18.4)	71 (£7.1.0)	52 (£6.10.0)
Dairy (cheese, butter) (%)	13 (£3.16.2)	8 (£1.4.0)	15 (£1.15.5)	18 (£1.15.0)	40 (£1.15.10)	33 (£4.11.0)	48 (£2.7.0)

SOURCES: See table 6.

teams appear in few inventories, and most inhabitants seemed to rely on cattle raising while local economic services developed. But these farmers were not really raising cattle for market. Rather, established settlers exchanged surplus food and cattle for goods brought by new arrivals. The high value of packed local meat seen in table 8 is not indicative of the town's economy, but rather reflects the unequal weight of the considerable amount of packed meat belonging to Donald Grant, the town's Scottish-born storekeeper.

In the last three decades of the eighteenth century, Newtown exhibited a relatively self-contained barter economy. Danbury assumed great economic and political power in northern Fairfield County and precluded any possibility that Newtown would become an important gathering center. Danbury's preeminence in the region was manifest in various ways: it was the seat of the probate court, target of a British attack in 1779, and home of a newspaper in the 1790s. Newtown's insignificant commercial role in Fairfield County is evident in its commercial index, a figure derived by dividing the town's tax by its total area to compute property values. Newtown's index of 0.563 was the second lowest in its region; only New Fairfield, laid out in 1740, possessed a smaller index.[5]

Newtown's social structure further discouraged the development of a market economy. The absence of dominant wealthy leaders in Newtown meant that no local figures would naturally take the initiative to coordinate and organize production. In addition, many of Newtown's inhabitants may not have been interested in the external market. They continued to emphasize permanence in their hometown, even as the town became more densely populated. The smaller size of subdivided lands did not encourage farmers to turn to the market for relief. Instead the yeomen-artisans depended on their kin and neighbors. The ensuing network of obligations drew the community together. Custom and communal sanctions continued to guide Newtown families in the distribution and allocation of resources. This conservatism is explicit in a late eighteenth-century apprenticeship agreement in which Zachariah Clark was to instruct his nephew in the "Art of Farming and Common Business of Husbandry." The use of artisanal language, such as *art* and *common business*, and the articulation of social obligations in other sections of the agreement document the continued strength of the traditional social economy.[6]

The inventories from the 1770s reflect Newtown's prewar mixed agricultural economy. Grains, in particular, appear frequently in this group of inventories and signal the end of Newtown's unsettled frontier period. Wheat, the traditional English grain, remained the preferred crop over rye or corn. The slight increase in corn and additional references to hay occurred in conjunction with the increased number of cows and the increase in both the number of oxen and frequency of their mention. The greater number of oxen also had a causal relationship with the increase in grain crops because teams of oxen were necessary to plow the fields. Although a noticeable increase in the frequency and number of pigs accompanied the increases in other animals, the average livestock holdings in Newtown still remained lower than those in towns that concentrated on animal husbandry.[7]

The balance of grain and animals in Newtown inventories implies a concern for domestic needs. Account book references provide additional proof of this emphasis. The ledger of Thomas Stilson, a native yeoman-joiner whose family remained in Newtown during the entire period of this study, shows that Newtown families exchanged agricultural produce, farm labor, specialized services, and craft goods according to the rhythms of the mixed agricultural economy. Early in his career Stilson made furniture, performed house joinery, and wove cloth in the various slack periods between winter threshing, spring plowing and planting, and fall harvesting. At those times, he worked on his own farm with the assistance of customers indebted to him or on other farms to speed the work. These intricate mutual obligations, not always based on skill or efficiency but rather on expediency or the task itself, ensured stable social relationships.[8]

Newtown's experiences during the Revolutionary War differed significantly from those of Woodbury and Danbury, both of which experienced short-term dislocations but then parlayed the mobilization effort into commercial prosperity after the war. In fact, no agricultural dislocation was evident in Newtown estates during 1780–84. Continuity, indeed growth in crops and animals, implies that Newtown did not contribute much of its labor and produce to the war cause. Such lack of involvement can be attributed to an economic structure not well enough organized on the local level to collect surpluses for market, a dominant conservative cultural outlook, and pro-British sympathies. The roots of this conservatism were threefold: the persistence of so many families; the strength of the conservative Anglican faith, in which more than half of the town's population worshipped; and the dominating influence of the Anglican minister, John Beach. In a small inland community, Beach commanded great respect and deference as the link to a learned society. In the years of the Revolution, Beach's role as a cultural leader even increased: he was unchallenged by a commercial elite, kept the church open to comfort his congregation during a period of great uncertainty, and continued to offer prayers for King George III. As a result of Beach and the town's kinship network, the town petitioned the English king and Parliament rather than the Continental Congress in March 1775. Not until 1783 did Newtown's Loyalists pledge allegiance to the new United States of America.[9]

After the war, Newtown inhabitants continued a mixed agricultural economy based on an interrelationship among crops, animals, and craftwork, in spite of the inevitable encroachment of market pressures. In the inventories from the 1790s and early 1800s, the frequency of wheat, the most marketable grain, declined dramatically. Corn, a less labor intensive crop that yielded more per acre, and rye, a more dependable grain less susceptible to blasts and other natural disasters, replaced wheat as the favored grain (see table 6). Animal ownership in Newtown inventories from this period also manifests an emphasis on prudence and frugality. Estates listed sizable numbers of pigs and sheep, the most independent and low maintenance sorts of animals, while horses, oxen, and cows, which required more attention and care, appeared less often and in smaller numbers (see table 7). Newtown farmers did not concentrate on meat and dairy products as did many Connecticut farmers at the end of the eighteenth century.

Very few Newtown estates listed a specialized shelter for their livestock (table 9). Instead Newtown farmers continued to use barns, multipurpose buildings that were perfectly suited for mixed agricultural production. Packed meat appeared in a number of local inventories, but the low average value of the meat suggests that it was merely held aside for familial consumption. The frequency and value of packed dairy products provides similar evidence of domestic priorities.[10]

Continuation of a balanced mixed agricultural economy, frugal management of limited resources, and preference for local exchange is evident in other patterns revealed by the Newtown inventories (table 10). Cider mills and barrels of cider appeared in an increasing number of estates. Locally produced cider and cider brandy rather than imported rum remained the favored drinks in Newtown. Newtown inventories also demonstrated an increased capacity to produce and process wool and linen cloth. Many households listed flax, sheep, a great wheel to spin wool, a Dutch wheel to spin flax, and a loom. In addition to this agricultural processing equipment, Newtown inventories from this period contained great quantities of other artisanal tools (table 11).[11]

The life of Samuel Beers, a native hatmaker-farmer, provides detailed insight into the town's mixed agriculture and some of the changes it experienced during the late eighteenth century. On his seventy-seven acres of

TABLE 9
Cowhouses and Horsehouses in Newtown and Woodbury, 1760–1824
(percentage of estates with either specified item)

	1760–64	1770–74	1780–84	1790–94	1800–1804	1810–14	1820–24
NEWTOWN							
Number of estates	15	17	18	17	29	26	48
Cowhouses/ horsehouses (%)	7	0	6	0	3	7	13
WOODBURY							
Number of estates	16	13	20	17	20	24	29
Cowhouses/ horsehouses (%)	6	14	25	18	20	42	21

SOURCES: See table 6.

TABLE 10
Cider and Clothmaking in Newtown and Woodbury, 1760–1824
(percentage of estates with specified item)

	1760–64	1770–74	1780–84	1790–94	1800–1804	1810–14	1820–24
NEWTOWN							
Number of estates	15	17	18	17	29	26	48
Cider (%)	20	29	44	35	52	65	42
Cider mills (%)	13	0	17	18	28	23	23
Clothmaking items[a] (%)	7	6	17	41	24	31	21
WOODBURY							
Number of estates	16	13	20	17	20	24	29
Cider (%)	31	23	30	12	45	46	59
Cider mills (%)	0	0	0	12	30	13	7
Clothmaking items[a] (%)	19	0	15	29	35	8	17

SOURCES: See table 6.
[a]Sheep, flax, a great wool wheel, a Dutch flax wheel, and a loom.

TABLE 11
Ownership of Artisanal Equipment in Newtown and Woodbury, 1760–1824
(mean value)

	1760–64	1770–74	1780–84	1790–94	1800–04	1810–14	1820–24
Newtown	£3.05	£1.0	£2.45	£5.35	£2.5	£7.3	£10.3
Woodbury	£2.65	£3.15	£1.0	£1.1	£3.3	£1.95	£3.65

SOURCES: See table 6.

land, Beers grew corn, rye, buckwheat, oats, potatoes, and hay to provide for his family, feed his animals, and have a small surplus to use as needed. The animals included oxen, steers, cows, a horse, sheep, and pigs. The oxen helped to prepare the tillage and to haul wagons of produce or hats; the pigs, cows, and steers provided meat and dairy products for familial consumption and limited export as well as skins for Beers's hatmaking shop. Sheep served a similar multipurpose role: mutton became part of the family diet, and the wool was used for cloth and hats.

Local demand and an intricate web of local obligations, services, and products characterized the bulk of Beers's craftwork. His account books shed light on how he balanced these various economic roles. Agricultural rhythms restricted hatmaking to the winter months of December and January, a few weeks in the late spring after plowing, and a few weeks in the fall after harvesting. Most of his customers purchased small quantities of hats and lived in Newtown or in such neighboring towns as New Stratford, Huntington, Redding, and Southbury. For credit these customers supplied Beers with carded wool, craft goods, specialized services, or agricultural labor or produce. Beers drew on these obligations to supply labor for major tasks like plowing and harvesting. Sons and daughters were another important source of labor for both agricultural work and preparation of hatmaking materials.

The large size of Beers's shop, valued at £60, occasionally allowed him to enter the external market in the 1790s. Large hatmaking establishments such as James Hurlbut & Company of Norwalk and Peleg Wood and Selah Conkling of Long Island shipped various sorts of skins to Beers. By providing the raw materials, these large firms assumed the greatest expense of hatmaking. Beers did not have to incur debts to increase his production. Freed from the expense and time of procuring and processing skins, Beers used his standard tools in a more intense manner to make greater quantities of hats. He then hired local lads such as Ely Dikeman and Abraham Wheeler to cart casks of these hats to Bridgeport, Danbury, or Norwalk.[12]

A detailed tax list from 1798 documents Newtown's mixed agricultural economy (table 12). Woodlands and unimproved land accounted for 33 percent of the town's land, which indicates that woodlands remained an important resource. A breakdown of Newtown's improved land shows that tillage represented 25 percent; hayland, only 25 percent; and pasture, 51 percent. Newtown farmers did not set aside more land for hay because they preferred to let their animals forage on pastureland. This method allowed farmers to raise crops and perform craftwork with the time saved. Although ownership of chaises, riding chairs, watches, and clocks implies that some Newtown inhabitants had access to the fashion and trade of the larger world and the means to purchase some of its material products, the market's lure did not overwhelm the community. Money tied up in interest, evidence of commercial expansion, totaled only $1,248.

The strength of a culture that venerated the past and emphasized frugal and efficient use of resources can also be inferred from the breakdown of house types in Newtown. Just over four-fifths of Newtown's dwellings were depreciated at three-fourths, indicative of smaller size or older age. Most surviving eighteenth-century houses in Newtown feature traditional single-pile floor plans (a room on either side of a central chimney), with a kitchen in a lean-to or ell along the back.

TABLE 12
1798 Tax List for Woodbury and Newtown

	Woodbury	Newtown
Polls 18–21 years of age	80	53
Polls 21–70 years of age	512	495
ANIMALS		
4-year-old oxen, bulls	789	648
3-year-old cows, steers, heifers, bulls	1,677	1,370
2-year-old cows, steers, heifers, bulls	891	607
stallions	10	2
3-year-old horses	848	663
2-year-old horses	133	84
1-year-old horses	105	46
TOWN'S LAND *(in acres)*		
Plowland	4,869	4,304
Upland mowing pasture and clear pasture	6,213	1,503
Mowed boggy meadow	789	1,348
Unmowed boggy meadow	41	156
Other meadow	986	1,314
Bush pasture	9,651	8,843
1st-rate quality unenclosed[a]	1,242	2,708
2d-rate quality unenclosed	4,626	2,204
3d-rate quality unenclosed	3,560	3,689
CONSUMER GOODS		
Chaises	10	2
Riding chairs	2	4
Gold watches	3	2
Silver or other watches	52	26
Steel- or brass-wheeled clocks	10	16
Wooden-wheeled clocks	10	2
MONEY ON INTEREST	$5,793.35	$1,248.00
DWELLING VALUE		
1st-rate quality[b]	6	8
2d-rate quality	104	20
3d-rate quality	469	163
4th-rate quality	507	802
FACULTIES *(mean/median value in parentheses)*		
Professionals and human services		
Attorney	5 ($172.00/$167.00)	1 ($167.00/$167.00)
Physician	5 ($37.20/$34.00)	4 ($44.50/$42.00)
Merchant	7 ($98.86/$100.00)	4 ($104.75/$95.00)
Tavern keeper	10 ($51.00/$50.00)	11 ($59.91/$50.00)
Mixed agricultural economy craftsmen		
Blacksmith	14 ($19.07/$17.00)	14 ($25.57/$17.00)
Goldsmith (silversmith)	—	3 ($17.00/$17.00)
Joiner	7 ($24.43/$17.00)	14 ($19.36/$17.00)
Carpenter	1 ($17.00/$17.00)	3 ($19.67/$17.00)
Cooper	5 ($17.00/$17.00)	5 ($20.60/$17.00)
Wheelwright	1 ($17.00/$17.00)	2 ($17.00/$17.00)
Shoemaker	13 ($25.77/$17.00)	22 ($21.22/$17.00)

(continued)

TABLE 12
Continued

	Woodbury		Newtown	
Tailor	5	($17.00/$17.00)	5	($22.20/$17.00)
Clothier	2	($30.00/$30.00)	7	($17.00/$17.00)
Weaver	—		1	($17.00/$17.00)
Hatter	2	($18.50/$18.50)	4	($25.25/$17.00)
Saddler	3	($17.00/$17.00)	3	($17.00/$17.00)
Mason	1	($25.00/$25.00)	3	($17.00/$17.00)
Combmaker	—		1	($17.00/$17.00)
Mills				
Sawmill owner	7	($24.29/$20.00)	13	($21.62/$20.00)
Gristmill owner	7	($57.14/$60.00)	9	($19.44/$15.00)

SOURCES: Tax lists for 1798 for Woodbury, Southbury, and Newtown (Connecticut Historical Society, Hartford).
NOTE: Dashes indicate that data were unavailable.
aSoil or grass quality of land that was not under plow.
bIn the tax lists, these categories were specified as fireplaces @ $2.50, fireplaces ¼ depreciated @ $1.88, fireplaces ½ depreciated @ $1.25, fireplaces ¾ depreciated @ $0.63.

Even more revealing from the 1798 tax list is the composition of the artisanal community within Newtown. One hundred and twenty-four heads of households (25% of all males older than twenty-one) had faculties assessed in Newtown. Professionals or providers of human services (attorney, physician, merchant, tavern keeper) operated 16 percent of these faculties, and artisans who worked with the products of mixed agriculture (joiner, carpenter, cooper, wheelwright, shoemaker, saddler, hatter, combmaker, weaver, tailor, clothier) owned 67 percent. Shoemakers, clothiers, and joiners were in particular abundance in Newtown. These trades offered the easiest means of making a living on a small farm. The needed raw materials—leather, wool, flax, and wood—had always been a part of mixed agriculture. Work could be done at home with the help of the household at one's discretion. Furthermore, the plentiful supply of farmer-artisans meant that the demand for a particular product never became so great that it forced the craftsman to relinquish his agricultural responsibilities. Craftsmen like Samuel Beers only entered the external market if time permitted and familial and local demands had already been met.

In the early nineteenth century, a turnpike was constructed from Bridgeport to New Milford, with Newtown at the halfway point. At first the town resisted the "great inconvenience and expense" of the proposed turnpike and pointed out the advantages of a free public road. Within a year the town reconsidered and accepted the road, which opened in 1809. Even though the road linked Newtown with Bridgeport and intensified Newtown's exposure to the market, inhabitants responded in terms of existing socioeconomic norms. Rather than embracing commercial agriculture or catering to the changing demands of the external market, they merely intensified their existing activities. Crop patterns evident in inventories from the 1810s and 1820s indicate that wheat continued to fall from favor as rye and corn dominated the references to grain. Newtown farmers sought to maximize crop yields by fertilizing the plowland with lime, plaster of paris, and manure. Each of the three fertilizers were listed in several Newtown inventories in this period and reflect the Newtowner's continued emphasis on grains and an awareness of agricultural advances.[13]

The opening of the Bridgeport–New Milford Turnpike provided a new market for meat and grain. Initially, Newtown farmers explored the possibilities of the Bridgeport trade. Frequencies of animals and numbers of cows and oxen in the inventories jumped in the 1810s. The number of estates with packed meat also rose. Some inventories even listed meat and grain sold in Bridgeport. Yet Newtown farmers did not follow the pervasive western Connecticut shift toward dairy exports during the first two decades of the nineteenth century. The quantities that each household had available for market remained small. Newtown production remained decentralized, with each farmer continuing the custom of selling grain and meat in "dribbles . . . as he may want to raise a few Dollars for immediate necessity."[14] In economic as well as political matters, the individual yeoman seemed to possess the power to participate on his own terms.

The account books of three Newtown artisans active in the first two decades of the nineteenth century shed additional light on developing changes in the Newtown craft structure. Philo Beardslee, a native farmer-weaver, followed the more traditional route. Listed as a weaver in the 1798 tax lists, Beardslee made coverlids (coverlets), blankets, carpets, bed ticking, and fabrics such as Irish stitch and diaper. In the winter months he also performed such coopering tasks as making barrels, tubs, pails, kegs, and firkins. He even occasionally bottomed chairs and made brooms.[15]

John Hubbell was a Newtown-born farmer-craftsman who followed a slightly different course. Hubbell supplied the local community with tools for woodworking and farming, shoes for animals, chains, locks, nails, and other iron or steel goods. Additional evidence of his integral role in the Newtown economy was his having trained and set up another local lad, Josiah Curtiss, and teamed with carpenters such as Samuel Northrup and David Parmelee to make wagons. Hubbell retained his local focus and interaction with other craftsmen even though his shop gave him the capacity and technology to expand his clientele and to concentrate on his own work. His shop included five benches, three anvils and one horn, and a trip hammer. In 1821 Hubbell began to ship quantities of his axes to New Haven.[16]

The career of a third Newtown artisan, Eden Burchard, reveals a slightly different pattern. Born in Danbury, Burchard came to Newtown in 1799 to work as a partner with Isaac Wheeler in the saddling business. He used skins available from local sources to make saddles, bridles, and harnesses, essential products in the mixed agricultural economy. The majority of Burchard's customers lived in Newtown, but he also sold leather goods in Danbury. In the sales of his products, Burchard resembled the hatter Samuel Beers. Hatmakers, saddlers, and shoemakers in Newtown all occasionally performed outwork for establishments in Danbury or other commercial towns. But Burchard's move to Newtown distinguished him from his contemporaries and signaled the beginning of a new trend in the Newtown craft community. In the 1810s, more craftsmen like the joiners Arcillus Hamlin and the Bradleys were attracted to Newtown, probably because of the artisanal heritage of the town and the existing water-power sites.[17]

Woodbury: A Gentry Town

A particular sort of land distribution determined a different social structure in Woodbury. Woodbury was settled in 1673 by a cohesive group of Stratford families. Like most Connecticut towns incorporated before 1680, it received a large grant from the General Assembly. Only a small fraction of the original 150-square-mile patent was initially laid out for the original settlers. The remainder was parceled out piecemeal over the next century by a series of proprietary divisions. In this process, areas of common land within the town boundaries were divided up among the town's proprietors, whose members included descendents of the original settlers or recent arrivals who possessed the means to purchase a proprietary share. Membership in this group became more closed after 1730 as the price of a share increased.[18]

Since divisions continued throughout the eighteenth century, the proprietary system played a significant role in Woodbury. Proprietors determined why and when new lands were needed and thereby shaped the town's economic life. If proprietors wished to increase their capacity for crops or livestock or if they wished to provide their children with sufficient land to begin new farms, they had the power to do so. This enabled descendents of proprietors to own substantial acreage and remain in their hometown. As a result, proprietary families achieved the continuity and stability that determined local prominence and became a gentry class.

From 1730 until 1770, Woodbury's population grew dramatically. It reached a peak of 5,313 in 1774 (see table 4). Although some of this growth was natural, some can also be attributed to an influx of migrants or transients. Because of its location at the edge of Connecticut's northwestern frontier, which is the present Litchfield County, Woodbury served as the staging area for that developing region after 1730. Migration into Woodbury was particularly noticeable in the years between 1737 and 1743, the same years in which the northwestern lands were divided into towns, auctioned off, and first settled. Newly arrived families accounted for 25 percent of all Woodbury families in 1738. Some of these families may have stopped in Woodbury for only a short time on their way to Cornwall or Salisbury, but many remained. A gross persistence rate of 73 percent for 1760–70 attests to Woodbury's ability to accommodate native children and recent arrivals (see table 5).[19]

In the fifty years after 1770, the proprietary system affected the townspeople unequally. It helped proprietors such as the Hinmans, Minors, Strongs, and Pearces achieve local prominence. They acquired land to increase their own production or to settle descendents on large estates in town. Many proprietors began to view land as a commercial commodity as population and demand for land increased in the last half of the eighteenth century. These entrepreneurs were willing to sell or rent portions of their estates to recent arrivals in town. For example, the proprietors Zadok Hurd Jr. and Edward Hinman sold small parcels of land to Ebenezer Bull and Elijah Booth in 1758 and 1771, respectively. Simeon Judson rented a house and half an acre in the late 1770s; Amos Hicock rented out a portion of his inherited estate; and John Edwards and Matthew Morris were among many newcomers who leased entire farms including dwelling house, barn, farm tools, and animals.[20]

Children of nonproprietors and more recent arrivals such as John Dulivan, William Wilmot, Joseph Ferry, and Samuel Moody found access to economic resources more difficult. Some could afford to purchase or rent only a home having less than twenty-five acres, while others had to work small farms that had been subdivided from their parents' estates. To achieve some sort of livelihood, these family heads relied on part-time craftwork or raised grain and pastured animals on someone else's land. In the early nineteenth century, young men such as Jesse Green, Simeon

Munn, and William Guyre made a living by hiring themselves out as farm laborers, receiving payment in cash and provisions. Each of these three men worked for a six-month period, April to October, on Matthew Minor's farm in 1801–3, 1803, and 1807, respectively.[21]

The increased demand on a fixed supply of land contributed to the high cost of land and prohibited many townspeople from buying land in town for their children. Consequently, these families remained in town for a generation and were then replaced by another generation of migrants. The decline in the gross rate of persistence after 1770 points out that population turnover intensified after that time. Only slightly more than half of the taxpayers remained in Woodbury long enough to be listed ten years later. In the eighteenth century, a persistence rate in the low fifties was more characterisitic of urban centers. Another indication of mobility was that only 36 percent of taxpayers' surnames on the 1820 tax list also appeared on the 1760 list.[22]

A statistical analysis of leadership patterns in Woodbury during the third quarter of the eighteenth century reveals a more stratified social structure than in Newtown. Only 1.4 percent of the town's population served in the major town offices, and 56.1 percent of the leadership terms were filled by men serving at least five years. Closer examination of these leaders reveals that less than one-fifth of Woodbury's families contributed to the leadership pool. This suggests not only the prestige of a few prominent families but also the lack of an extended kin network. Such oligarchal patterns were more common in Connecticut's urban or commercial centers, where a local gentry class held political, economic, and cultural power. Officeholding patterns of Woodbury's deputies to the General Assembly reveal a similar deference to a small elite. In the twenty years from 1760 to 1780, Woodbury's deputies served an average of 11.43 one-year terms each, a figure that surpassed those of all other Connecticut towns. Futhermore, the town consistently returned the previous deputies to office. The low turnover rate of Woodbury's deputies (19%) was comparable to the rates of New Haven and New London. It is thus accurate to label Woodbury a gentry town, a term further clarified by examination of its economy.[23]

Time of settlement and the social structure had a profound affect on Woodbury's economy. The town's early establishment and role as seat of the probate court influenced transportation networks in southern Litchfield County. People grew accustomed to traveling to Woodbury to settle estates and record wills, and they found it just as easy to take along their few surplus products to exchange for needed goods. Woodbury became the gathering point for agricultural surpluses from its northern backcountry, and a class of men arose in town to assume control of the trade. This modest trade formed an important part of the town's economy. Aware of its importance to the region, Woodbury even petitioned the General Assembly in 1748 to form a separate county out of southern Litchfield County, with Woodbury as the shire town.[24]

After 1760, Woodbury entered increasingly into the agricultural export market based in New York. This marketing network, established to procure provisions during the Seven Years' War, continued in peacetime as New York's population grew and its merchants shipped grain and meat to southern Europe and the West Indies. Woodbury's stratified social structure was well suited to this trade and provided leaders to organize and direct marketing. Truman Hinman, a wealthy proprietor, gathered farmers' surplus cattle and drove them overland to New York as early as 1765. Individual Woodbury farmers continued to produce mainly for familial and kin consumption, but merchants such as Hinman and Jabez Bacon collected substantial quantities of wheat, beef, and pork for the New York market. Bacon was perhaps the best-known Woodbury merchant. He attracted New Haven merchants to buy from him and even controlled the New York pork market. In return these merchants offered imported and fancy goods such as textiles, English tools, ceramics, and rum to the people of Woodbury. The town's leading economic role in northwest Connecticut can best be seen in its commercial index. Woodbury's index of 0.618 was Litchfield County's highest in 1774, with Litchfield a distant second at 0.476.[25]

Evidence gathered from probate inventories of the 1760s and 1770s reveals the existence of agricultural surpluses. The varieties of grains mentioned included wheat, corn, and rye (see table 6). The equal number of corn and wheat references and the slightly fewer references to rye suggest that the Woodbury farmer could have used rye and corn for home consumption and exported the wheat. Similarly the large herds of cows, pigs, and sheep, larger than those of Massachusetts towns from the same period, encouraged the trading of surpluses (see table 7). Scholars' calculations indicate that three cows, eight pigs, and ten sheep fulfilled domestic needs for a family of nine in the mid eighteenth century. Woodbury had a particular abundance of cows and sheep. The latter were important: they provided wool for yarn, could be driven to market, and provided mutton for local consumption, thereby allowing the export of pork, a meat more easily preserved for shipping. Apparently some Woodbury farmers must have recognized the demand for beef and pork and the relative ease of animal husbandry. They began to view the external market as a means of maximizing productivity and gaining extra income from their small farms. About 40 percent of the inventories listed packed meat valued at an average of £3, the approximate value of one barrel of pork (see table 8).[26]

The orchestration of local surpluses by leading Woodbury merchants assumed greater significance during the Revolution. The Continental army continually demanded packed beef and pork and wool, products that formed the base of the community's economic structure. To supply these needs, merchants Truman Hinman and Shadrach Osborn served as commissaries and sutlers. They drew on the already existing informal commercial patterns and used Woodbury as a collection and storage center. A contemporary description noted that all the streets around the Woodbury meetinghouse were "piled high on either side for a hundred yards or more with barrels and hogsheads of pork, beef, lard, and flour, besides the great quantities of bales of blankets, tents, and clothing."[27]

The war effort gave the people of Woodbury experience in a more intense market economy and legitimized the local merchant's role. Farmers now depended on local merchants to market their produce, and their first exposure to trade may have whetted their appetite for more. The war also exposed Woodbury inhabitants to a variety of values that would affect subsequent choices. Woodbury's role as the major recruiting center for the region contributed to the drop in persistence rates and the presence of a greater number of men from surrounding towns. The approximately five hundred Woodbury men who entered military service between 1775 and 1783 gained additional exposure to the external world. When they returned to Woodbury, they may have been more receptive to change.[28]

Grain and animal statistics from the years 1780–84 (see tables 6–8) reflect the economic dislocation of war. Woodbury soon returned to its prewar economic health. In fact, account books and inventories from 1785 to 1820 document increased economic activity with external markets. Extensive marketing of English exports in America in the late 1780s and increased American shipping during the Napoleonic wars of the 1790s and early 1800s fueled the growth of urban ports. This commercial prosperity affected both the ports and their hinterlands, which became better linked by newly built or improved transportation routes.[29]

In 1783 a new road between Derby and Woodbury, along the east bank of the Housatonic, provided an easy overland route for Woodbury exports. Shadrach Osborn and Nathan Preston used this turnpike to cart their collected surpluses to such Derby ship owners as Joseph Hull, William Clark,

S. Clark, L. Stone, C. Gillet, Hitchcock & Company, Gorham, and Morris. These Derby contacts then sailed for New York or the West Indies. The road to Derby also provided Woodbury with easier access to New Haven, the fastest-growing city in the state. Among Osborn's customers in New Haven were Shipman & Denison, Bradley & Huggins, Forbes & Henry, William Beecher, E. Austin, and T. Beecher. The greatest number of transactions involved pork, especially from November through February. Osborn would purchase four or five hogs each from fifteen to twenty farmers; commission local coopers to build barrels and hogsheads; hire part-time butchers Adam Wagner or William Pardee to cut, salt, and pack the meat; and then contract teamsters Lewis Stiles or Abraham Lines to carry a wagonful of pork barrels to Derby or New Haven.[30]

A petition to the General Assembly drafted by the Southbury town meeting in 1795 explicitly stated the area's dependence on commerce. This address sought to prevent the erection of a bridge across the Housatonic River near Stratford because such a structure would "greatly impede the Navigation of Said River, from the Mouth to Derby Landing: from which place the greatest part of the Produce from this Town, and most of the Towns in the South part of Litchfield County, is Shipped for the New York and foreign Markets."[31]

Stratification and mobility played important roles in Woodbury's increased involvement in the external market. Proprietary families could divide up additional lands to increase their pasturage and hayland. Nonproprietors, who usually lacked the emotional and economic reinforcement of extended kinship, confronted the problem of earning a livelihood on small holdings as individual units. For them, animal husbandry and the market provided a means to maximize the productivity of limited labor or limited land.

The 1798 tax list provides insight into Woodbury's livestock-based economy (see table 12). Only 29 percent of the town's land was woodland or unimproved land. The high percentage of improved land implies that local farmers allotted as much land as possible to tillage, pasturage, and meadow for their commercial farming. A breakdown of the improved land reveals that tillage accounted for 22 percent; hayland, for 36 percent; and pasture, for 43 percent. The high proportion of hayland and the balance between hayland and grazing land approximates the land allocation in Concord and Brookfield, Massachusetts, where farmers emphasized animal husbandry rather than mixed agriculture. But whereas an average Brookfield farmer owned two or three cows and a single horse, his Woodbury counterpart owned about six cattle (oxen, bulls, cows, steers, and heifers) and two horses. Such large herds ensured an annual surplus for the external market.

The influence of the market can also be seen in several taxable consumer categories. Ownership by Woodbury residents of twelve chaises or riding chairs, fifty-five watches, and twenty clocks demonstrates awareness of current fashion and cultural change. More than half of Woodbury's homes were valued at one-fourth or one-half depreciation, indicative of large-scale or fairly recent construction. In contrast to the smaller, single-pile houses common in Newtown, a significant number of large double-pile houses with gambrel roofs, elaborate doors, extensive interior paneling, and other expensive features still survive in Woodbury. More substantive evidence of commercial involvement is the nearly six thousand dollars of money on interest, a sum five times greater than Newtown's.[32]

The assessments for faculties further distinguish Woodbury's economy from Newtown's. In 1798 only ninety-five heads of households (18% of all males older than twenty-one) were assessed for a shop. Of the total number of shops, 28 percent of shops were devoted to professionals or providers of human services and 39 percent to artisans who worked with the products of mixed agriculture. In Woodbury, there were a greater number of lawyers, but craftwork was not widespread. Limited participation in craftwork in Woodbury can also be seen in the low proportion of estates with cider mills and clothmaking equipment and the low mean value of artisanal equipment in Woodbury estates (see tables 10–11). Craftwork and processing were limited to a few inhabitants. Estates of the 1810s and 1820s offer particularly strong evidence regarding the concentration of artisanal activity in Woodbury and imply the town's absorption with animal husbandry.

In the early nineteenth century, the new Oxford Turnpike offered a second access route to Derby and New Haven. The matriculation of Woodbury youths at Yale College and the work of Woodbury factors in New Haven further enhanced Woodbury's ties to that city. As a result, imported items entered Woodbury more easily and less expensively. Not only did the local storekeeper offer the farmer an increased selection of goods but the farmers began consciously organizing their production around the market. Beginning about 1800, account books include a significantly greater number of references to butter and cheese. At the same time, merchants like Shadrach Osborn were purchasing greater quantities of firkins, butter pails, and other dairy containers from local coopers. Osborn filled these wooden vessels with cheese and butter gathered from local farmers and had them carted to New Haven.

During the first decade of the nineteenth century, Osborn continued to send pork and grain to Derby, but demonstrated greater involvement in the dairy trade with New Haven. In 1811, a contemporary observer explained this shift to dairy production in relation to the Woodbury farmers' market orientation: "The habits of the Farmers have ever been in favor of raising Pork for Market. But it is doubtful whether they can raise it and fatten it as easily as they do where Corn is raised with less expense of ploughing and manual labor. Some are convinced of their bad economy in this respect, and are turning their attention to Dairies." A particularly noticeable symbol of Woodbury's increased involvement in the market was the popularity of horse teams in Woodbury. Even though oxen permitted better plowing in the region's hard soil and would eventually provide beef, Woodbury farmers preferred a combination of oxen and horses for their teams because "horses for their speed are thought preferable to carry produce to market."[33]

Woodbury's increased involvement in commercial animal husbandry after the Revolution can also be traced in inventories (see tables 6–8). Local farmers grew less wheat because of its susceptibility to disease and because of the plentiful supply of wheat exported by the Middle Colonies. What little wheat was grown in Woodbury was probably exported, as the increased corn and rye crops served local needs. A decreased emphasis on grains is evident in the decline of fertilizer use. Woodbury estates listed lime in the 1770s and 1780s, but fertilizer was listed only once in the 1810s and 1820s. Grains had become less important to the town's economy except as feed for animals. References to hay, potatoes, and corn—the favored foodstuffs for cattle and pigs—increased at the beginning of the nineteenth century. More frequent references to these fodder crops paralleled the increased frequency and size of cattle and pig holdings.[34]

Livestock ownership further demonstrates the influence of the external market on Woodbury farmers. Although Woodbury estates had always listed large numbers of animals, significant changes became evident at the turn of the century. Inventories included fewer oxen and horses, a pattern attributable to the decreased emphasis on grain agriculture and the use of teams mainly for transportation. A corresponding interest in animal husbandry can be seen in the increased numbers of cattle and pigs in the same inventories. Some of these animals provided meat for export, but Woodbury farmers began to use their cattle more for the production of cheese and butter. In fact, the inventories imply that the Woodbury farmers even began to place greater value and importance on their cattle. Instead of using multipurpose barns for grain storage and animal shelter, a greater number of Woodbury estates referred to a cowhouse or horsehouse in addition to a barn (see table 9). Such a specialized structure manifests an increased emphasis on cattle.

Continued interest in the meat market, which became more widespread in the nineteenth century, and the shift toward dairying after 1800 can be seen in table 8. Estates filed after 1810 reveal a resurgence in sheep raising, a shift that also can be attributed to the influence of the external market on the decisions of Woodbury farmers. The Oxford Turnpike provided a direct, newly improved road from Southbury to Humphreysville, Connecticut's first extensive woolen manufactory. The three carding machines, two spinning jennies and one spinning billy, twelve looms, eighteen stocking frames, three fulling mills, and other equipment demanded great quantities of raw wool and prompted Woodbury farmers to increase the size of their sheep herds.[35]

In comparison to Newtown's decentralized mixed agricultural economy, Woodbury became increasingly stratified and dependent on animal husbandry toward the end of the eighteenth century. By the early nineteenth century many of the town's inhabitants relied exclusively on sales of packed meat or dairy products. The prominence of the proprietor/shopkeeper class, the farmers' market orientation, the amount of money borrowed to participate in the market, and centralization of artisanal work combined to support such a dependence on animals. Newtown farmers and yeoman-artisans, on the other hand, continued to choose when and how to participate in the larger external market and were not dependent on that market.

FIVE

Consumer Behavior in Newtown and Woodbury

The striking differences in social structure that characterized Newtown and Woodbury in the colonial and early national periods affected not only production but also consumption and the relationship between production and consumption of locally made goods. Probate inventories, itemized lists of decedents' real and personal estate, offer the best "picture" of domestic environments in the late eighteenth century and remain one of the best means of exploring household consumption during this time period. From the listing and valuation of a person's property one can discern the relative allocation of resources and chart the use of new descriptive language or the introduction of a type of domestic object. It also is sometimes possible to reassemble objects into room groupings.[1]

To discern broad patterns of consumer behavior over time and between towns, all Newtown and Woodbury probate inventories filed between 1760 and 1825 were surveyed. A more intense, systematic analysis was done of seven five-year groups (1760–64, 1770–74, 1780–84, 1790–94, 1800–1804, 1810–14, and 1820–24). From these estates, data on real estate, personal estate, and consumer goods were collected and collated to chart specific trends.[2] Under the consumer goods heading, specific attention was given to furniture, which was further divided into three categories: seating forms, storage forms, and tables. The focus on furniture within the broader context of household assemblage permits an understanding of the joiner's products within their theater of use, the domestic environment. Furniture was a single but very prominent genre of household assemblage. The integrated use of quantitative analyses (numbers, frequencies, and values) and qualitative analyses (types and descriptors) permits a thorough investigation of consumption and ownership of household goods in Newtown and Woodbury. Examination of types, numbers, and relative values of furniture forms among different economic classes over time provides evidence about changing attitudes and changing furniture traditions. Explained in relation to the towns' socioeconomic and craft structures and general furnishing trends, these patterns permit a richer understanding of furniture's context in the two towns.[3]

General Patterns of Consumption

During the sixty-five-year period under study, each town displayed a different pattern of consumption (chart 1). In Newtown the mean value of consumer goods grew fairly constantly until a noticeable drop in the early 1820s. Only the years 1780–84 demonstrated a counter trend. However, a downturn at this point is not unexpected because of the Revolutionary conflict from 1779 to 1781. Although the war had little effect on the town's agricultural economy, it may have temporarily slowed local production of household goods and limited the flow of goods into Newtown. The decrease was small in any case, and the growth evident in subsequent inventories indicates that the effects of the war were short-lived.

Steady growth in the consumer assets of Newtown estates most likely is the result of the town's high rates of persistence. As families remained in town, they gradually added items to their inherited estates. In addition,

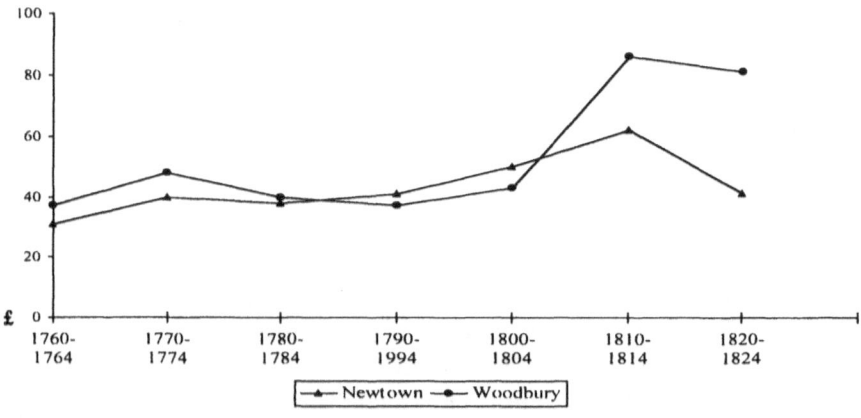

Chart 1. Consumer goods in Newtown and Woodbury, 1760–1824 (*mean values*). *Sources:* Estate inventories for Woodbury, Danbury, and Newtown probate court districts (microfilm of the original record books is held by the Connecticut State Library, Hartford).

persistence may have preserved strong communal values that permitted only gradual changes in standards of material living. Not until the 1820s did the value of consumer goods drop. This decline coincided with an increased population turnover that had begun earlier in the nineteenth century and was just starting to affect probated estates. Increased mobility contributed to a decrease in consumer goods in two ways: fewer native families would be distributing goods to succeeding generations in town, and more transients or people with fewer possessions would be entering the community.

Greater fluctuations in the mean value of consumer assets can be found in the Woodbury inventories. After increasing between 1760 and 1770, the mean value dropped and stagnated during the next thirty years. During the last two periods of the study (1810–14 and 1820–24), it rose dramatically. The dislocations of war and the gradual accumulation of material goods do not fully explain the prolonged downs and sudden ups of the mean value. Indeed such patterns preclude the possibility of natural accumulation. More valid explanations link these patterns to the town's socioeconomic structure. The decline noted in the inventories from 1770 through 1804 occurred during a period when Woodbury's persistence rates dropped. As in Newtown in the 1820s, population turnover limited substantial estate building. The increase in the last two periods can be ascribed to the inhabitants' close connections to the commercial world. During that time, Woodbury farmers began to orient their production and consumption to the external market.

Further refinement of these temporal breakpoints and an understanding of the quantitative differences between the two towns can be achieved through the breakdown of consumer catagories. The mean and median values of household goods echo the respective patterns of each town's general consumer trends (chart 2). Mean values of household goods in Newtown gradually increased until the 1820s. In addition, the mean values remained fairly close to the median values. Such proximity can be attributed to Newtown's relatively egalitarian social structure. Few inhabitants of the yeoman town accumulated unusually large collections of household goods. The mean and median figures provide additional circumstantial evidence that Newtown inhabitants shared common attitudes regarding standards of material living.

The Woodbury estates of the early 1770s revealed an increased mean value of household goods and a considerable difference between the mean and median values. The higher figure reflected the valuable household possessions of Timothy Hinman, a proprietor and shopkeeper in Southbury. As high mobility continued for the rest of the century, the mean value

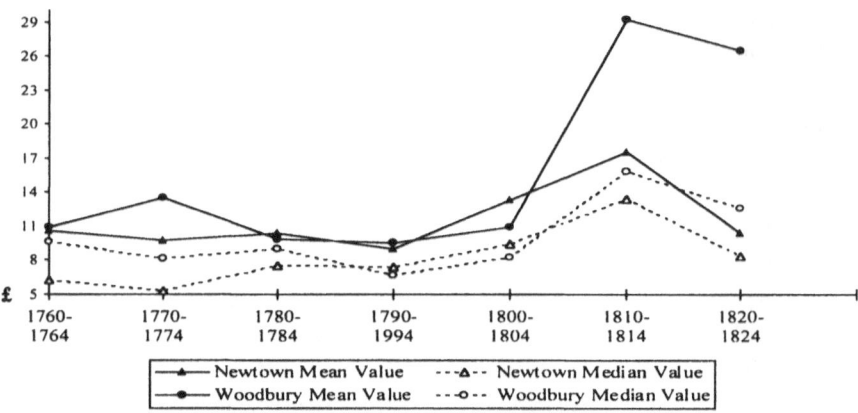

Chart 2. Household goods in Newtown and Woodbury, 1760–1824 (*mean/median values*). *Sources:* See chart 1.

of household goods remained low. Significant changes occurred in the estates included in the last two periods. Availability and desirability of imported goods contributed to a greater average investment in household goods. Increased allocation did not occur evenly. Some estates listed especially expensive household goods and thus contributed to a greater difference between mean and median values. Such patterns attest to some sort of consumer stratification in the gentry town of Woodbury. Consumer spending on the whole was greater in Woodbury than in Newtown, and several different levels of material comfort existed in Woodbury.

The raw frequencies of such specific household goods as tea dishes and silver provide additional insight because these goods usually were imported.[4] These items confirm the patterns of consistency in Newtown and fluctuations in Woodbury (table 13). Newtown inhabitants increasingly listed such imported wares, but only gradually. Woodbury estates reveal a decline in frequency of tea dishes and silver during the Revolution, with a subsequent period of growth that began in the 1790s and accelerated in 1810. Throughout these years more inventories in Woodbury listed the specified goods than in Newtown. Woodbury's fluctuations demonstrate that its people lacked common standards of consumption and were subject to the vagaries of the marketplace. Economic dislocations during the Revolution restricted Woodbury consumption, but expansion of commercial re-

TABLE 13
Raw Frequencies of Selected Household Goods, 1760–1824
(percentage of estates with specified item)

	1760–64	1770–74	1780–84	1790–94	1800–1804	1810–14	1820–24
NEWTOWN							
Number of estates	15	17	18	17	29	26	48
Tea dishes (%)	20	24	28	39	48	65	60
Silver (%)	27	29	33	35	41	54	58
WOODBURY							
Number of estates	16	13	20	17	20	24	29
Tea dishes (%)	37	15	20	65	70	83	69
Silver (%)	37	38	30	47	35	75	72

SOURCES: Estate inventories for Woodbury, Danbury, and Newtown probate court districts (Connecticut State Library, Hartford).

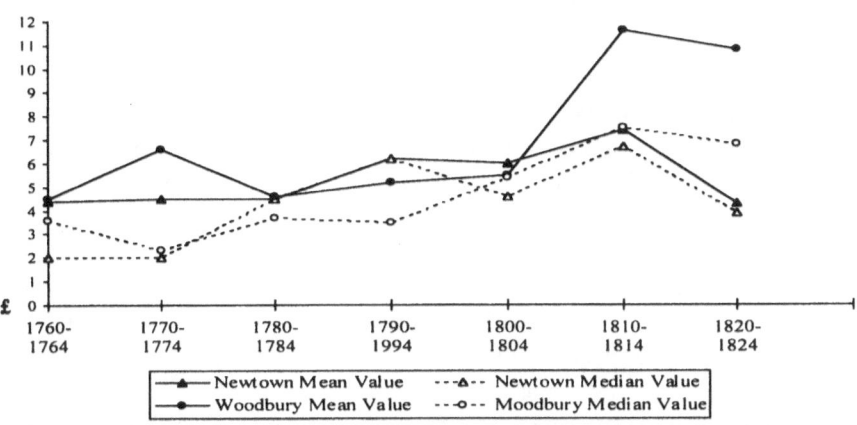

Chart 3. Furniture, 1760–1824 (*mean/median values*). *Sources:* See chart 1.

lations with the external markets, especially around the turn of the century, profoundly affected Woodbury households.

Furniture listed in Newtown and Woodbury estates provides specific evidence of the communities' different consumer patterns. The mean and median values of furniture, which were 9 to 15 percent of consumer assets, parallel general consumer patterns and values of household goods (chart 3). In Newtown gradual growth and small differences between mean and median values substantiate the durability of commonly accepted standards for furniture consumption. Only in the 1820s did furniture values decline as more immigrants settled in town. Nevertheless, the difference between mean and median values remained small. Consumer stratification connected to market capitalism did not affect Newtown inhabitants.

In Woodbury the greatest increases in overall value of furniture occurred during those years when the difference between mean and median values was largest (1770–74, 1810–14, and 1820–24). During the years of declining or stagnant values (1780–84, 1790–94, and 1800–1804), the mean and median values became closer. Such shifts point out that some consumer stratification had occurred by the 1770s but great mobility contributed to a decline in values for the next three decades. In the last two periods of this study, market capitalism took hold, and the wealthier segment of Woodbury's population allocated great sums for furniture.

Newtown Furniture Forms: The Persistence of Tradition

Chairs

The numbers and patterns discussed above take on deeper meaning if we consider the qualitative similarities and differences that were inextricably interwoven with the quantitative ones. In seating furniture, most Newtown inhabitants expressed a preference for traditional, flag-seated turned chairs (table 14). Inventories from the last forty years of the eighteenth century specify turned chairs such as slat-back chairs (similar to that shown in fig. 7, with two to five horizontal slats tenoned into the rear posts to form a back support), crown chairs (high-back chairs with reeded banisters and scrolled, sawn-out crests that often were pierced with a heart-shaped hole), York chairs (like fig. 8, with round-shouldered, yoke-shaped crest rails), and white chairs (an unpainted, simple slat-back chair). The same chair types represented the range of turned chairs in contemporary western coastal Connecticut, from Guilford to Norwalk.[5]

Painted turned chairs with flag seats were technically and socially suitable in the mixed agricultural economy of Newtown, where all households frugally managed their limited resources. Turned construction allowed the yeoman-craftsman to make efficient use of his time and tools. According to the rhythms of turned chair production, the joiner turned large quantities of rounds and posts at his discretion when breaks in agricultural production permitted. Then, as chairs were demanded, he drew on his stock of parts,

TABLE 14
Chairs, 1760–1824
(percentage of estates with specified form)

	1760–64	1770–74	1780–84	1790–94	1800–1804	1810–14	1820–24
NEWTOWN							
Number of estates	15	17	18	17	29	26	48
Turned flag-seated (<5/) (%)	67	94	100	88	97	100	97
Joiner's or crookedback (>5/) (%)	—	—	—	—	3	8	4
Windsor (%)	—	—	—	12	14	27	27
Fancy (%)	—	—	—	—	—	4	17
Mahogany or cushion bottom (%)	—	—	—	—	—	—	—
WOODBURY							
Number of estates	16	13	20	17	20	24	29
Turned flag-seated (<5/) (%)	75	85	90	88	95	96	83
Joiner's or crookedback (>5/) (%)	—	8	5	12	15	28	13
Windsor (%)	—	—	5	6	30	54	52
Fancy (%)	—	—	—	—	—	—	10
Mahogany or cushion bottom (%)	—	—	—	—	—	17	—

SOURCES: See table 13.
NOTE: Dashes indicate that data were unavailable.

some of which may have been shaped several years earlier. As a result, the actual assembling of chairs for customers took little time. Other townspeople's ability to paint and bottom chairs further freed the joiner to maintain a farm. These services and the large number of part-time joiners provided additional obligations and ties within the interdependent community. In short, turned chair production in Newtown was a social act rather than a labor-intensive one.

New chair types that appeared in the late eighteenth and early nineteenth centuries demonstrated the continued dominance of conservative values, with small concessions toward new taste. The most popular chairs from 1790 until the 1820s were fiddlebacks and Windsors. Both were painted turned chairs. Fiddleback chairs, first listed in the 1774 inventory of Ebenezer Ford, became the most frequently specified seating form in the Newtown estates from 1790 through 1824. These chairs retained the structure, proportions, and flag seat of the older York chairs, but featured a different crest rail (see figs. 9–14). The sweeping crest rail of the fiddleback ended in upward and backward flaring ears. Such movement represented more recent fashion than the rounded shoulders of the York chair's crest. Fiddleback chairs afforded the maker or the owner the opportunity to express an awareness of fashion without introducing a radically new design.[6]

Windsor chairs, which achieved moderate popularity in inventories after their first appearance in 1791, provide another example of Newtown's selective acceptance of new fashion. Plank-seated Windsors (see figs. 38–39) represented the latest fashion in chair forms throughout the new nation. Yet they gained ready acceptance in conservative Newtown because their separate elements were already familiar to maker and owner. Windsors were made largely from turned parts, which had been shaped in quantity during slack times. Sawmill owners often supplied quantities of plank seats. The craftsman assembled, glued, and then painted these parts. The standard rhythms of joiners' production in Newtown, varied contributions of parts and services by other members of the community, and customer preference for painted turned chairs permitted the easy accommodation of the new Windsor chair. Another new seating form, the fancy chair, appeared in the last ten years of the survey. It had a painted turned frame with a plank or a flag seat. Consequently, local furniture traditions and clientele readily accepted fancy chairs. In Newtown, the Windsor chair, and later the fancy chair, served as the more expensive chair form. The chairs complemented rather than replaced the earlier turned forms.[7]

Flag-seated cherry chairs first appear in the 1777 inventory of the Reverend David Judson, but are found only sporadically afterward. Sometimes referred to as crookedback or hollowback chairs, they had proportions and seats like the fiddlebacks and older turned chairs (see fig. 15) but had more concessions to fashion. The front remained essentially an early eighteenth-century chair with decoratively turned front posts, turned front round, and carved feet. But the frame was not turned; the joiner sawed out all the vertical posts, the rear ones with an ogee profile.

Even less popular were framed chairs or joiner's chairs, which differed from crookedback chairs in seat construction and decoration (see fig. 37). Joiner's chairs featured straight, sawn-out legs, no turned elements or decoration, and framed seats consisting of four rectangular rails with tenons cut on each end. These tenons fit into rectangular mortises cut into the vertical posts and were pinned in place. Into this joined frame was set a cushion bottom—a mortise-and-tenoned frame, which supported an upholstered seat consisting of webbing, sackcloth, stuffing, and a leather or textile cover. Because of the greater time and effort expended in cutting mortises and tenons and the cost of upholstery materials (most webbing, sackcloth, and fabric was imported), joined chairs tended to be twice as expensive as crookedback chairs, ten to twelve shillings versus four to six shillings apiece. Only one inventory in all of the Newtown inventories surveyed listed chairs with values high enough to suggest a completely joined chair. The Reverend David Judson owned six leather-seated crookedback chairs appraised at ten shillings apiece.[8]

Several other types of chairs were specified in the Newtown inventories filed after 1790. Kitchen chairs and dining chairs, especially the former, were listed, but their appearance in the inventories represented semantic rather than formal or stylistic changes. The similarity in value with the older white and crookedback chairs, respectively, and the sudden disappearance of the older terms just as kitchen and dining chairs began to be listed strongly suggest a simple terminological change. Inventories of the second decade contained the first references to rocking chairs, but the consistently low value attached to them suggest that such chairs were merely old armchairs with rockers added rather than a new form designed specifically as a rocker.[9]

Storage Forms

Inventory references to storage forms also illustrate the traditional nature of material culture in Newtown. Plain chests and their slightly larger relatives, chests with one, two, or three drawers, appeared frequently in inventories throughout the survey period. More than 90 percent of all Newtown inventories listed a plain chest, even in the nineteenth century. A consideration of the plain chests' values reveals that mere inheritance does not fully explain this pattern—there were as many chests that received high valuations, indicative of recent manufacture, as received low evaluations, indicative of older age. Later or more complex furniture did not replace these chests or chests with drawers. Rather they coexisted, just as the various types of turned chairs did (table 15).

The more complex and expensive storage forms—cases of drawers, dressing tables, and desks—appeared quite often in inventories after 1770. Apparently these forms continued to serve their intended function and

TABLE 15
Storage Forms, 1760–1824
(percentage of estates with specified form)

	1760–64	1770–74	1780–84	1790–94	1800–1804	1810–14	1820–24
NEWTOWN							
Number of estates	15	17	18	17	29	26	48
Plain chest (%)	67	82	100	82	97	100	94
Chest with drawer(s) (%)	53	76	72	76	79	62	67
Other drawered case furniture (%)	27	35	50	65	41	69	56
WOODBURY							
Number of estates	16	13	20	17	20	24	29
Plain chest (%)	75	77	90	82	95	75	83
Chest with drawer(s) (%)	44	56	50	71	60	63	55
Other drawered case furniture (%)	31	25	35	59	55	67	72

SOURCES: See table 13.

satisfy their owners' stylistic demands because few Newtown estates included the more fashionable replacements: the bureau, the toilet table or washstand, and the desk-and-bookcase and later the secretary. Continued recruitment of native sons and the long working careers of Newtown joiners in a culturally stable community also contributed to the limited constellation of forms.

Susannah Shepard's inventory of 1800 included a bureau, but this particular piece of furniture was not the fashionable, neoclassical storage form usually denoted by the term *bureau*. Rather, her "old bureau" was appraised at eighteen shillings, a value more consistent at that time with a chest with two drawers. A true bureau, a chest of drawers in the neoclassical style, would have been worth two or three pounds. The Shepard bureau, like the references to kitchen tables and chairs, represents the application of new terminology to older forms, not the introduction of a form. Bureaus priced commensurate with the new form were listed in only two Newtown inventories before 1820, and only two desk-and-bookcases and one toilet table were designated in all Newtown estates prior to 1825.[10]

The traditional practice of painting the most-used seating and storage forms persisted into the early nineteenth century in Newtown. Paint permitted the restitution of old furniture or, since paint often was used to cover cheap wood, the purchase of greater quantities of furniture. Painted furniture also contributed to household decoration. Nathan Washbon coordinated the colors of his painted chairs and chests; other people gradually accumulated differently colored sets of furniture. Black and red remained the most common colors.

Even in the later years of this study, the larger estates with more expensive furniture listed substantial quantities of painted furniture. For example, Ezra Booth furnished his house with six red fiddleback chairs, six black chairs, four black crown chairs, a red chest, a cherry case of drawers, and cherry fiddleback chairs. Green, or Windsor, chairs and blue chairs and chests began to appear in the first decade of the nineteenth century, when coloring agents other than lampblack, red lead, and Spanish brown became more readily available (see table 17). Painting was also a service performed by many townspeople. Painting and painted furniture were particularly important to Newtown's economy and consumption habits.[11]

Tables

Descriptions of table forms in the Newtown inventories reveal a preference for traditional forms. Newtown tables continued to be multifunctional, characterized by size (large or small), by shape (round, square, or oval), or by a physical trait (fall leaf, colored, or drawered) rather than by specific function (table 16). Specific sociofunctional terms had not evolved because Newtown inhabitants had not deemed the particular social activities associated with table use to be important. The exception to this pattern was the term *kitchen table*, which became common in the nineteenth century.

Differentiation of kitchen tables from other tables could be interpreted as a reflection of old values or as an acceptance of modern ones. On the one hand, the kitchen and its artifacts served as the symbolic heart of the house and its inhabitants. The large fireplace provided heat and light, and the food preparation and consumption that transpired there fostered and ritualized family behavior. Denoting a table used in that room as a kitchen table may therefore be seen as a formalization of traditional family relations. On the other hand, the emergence of a distinctive kitchen table could be interpreted as a symptom of the differentiation of life processes that characterize more modern attitudes. Full acceptance of these modern values would be

TABLE 16
Tables, 1760–1824
(percentage of estates with specified form)

	1760–64	1770–74	1780–84	1790–94	1800–1804	1810–14	1820–24
NEWTOWN							
Number of estates	15	17	18	17	29	26	48
Round (%)	20	41	56	53	24	38	25
Square (%)	13	24	33	29	34	38	4
Oval (%)	—	—	11	—	—	4	2
Fall leaf (%)	—	—	—	24	21	19	8
Kitchen (%)	—	6	—	—	24	27	54
Dining (%)	—	—	—	6	3	4	19
Breakfast (%)	—	—	—	—	3	—	4
Tea (%)	—	6	—	—	—	8	25
Card (%)	—	—	—	—	—	4	—
Toilet (%)	—	—	—	—	—	4	—
WOODBURY							
Number of estates	16	13	20	17	20	24	29
Round (%)	19	23	40	35	30	29	7
Square (%)	13	23	25	12	15	13	10
Oval (%)	—	—	—	—	—	4	—
Fall leaf (%)	—	—	—	6	20	33	3
Kitchen (%)	—	—	—	12	25	42	69
Dining (%)	—	—	—	—	—	25	48
Breakfast (%)	—	—	—	6	10	29	34
Tea (%)	6	8	—	—	—	33	31
Card (%)	—	—	—	—	—	13	3
Toilet (%)	—	—	—	—	—	17	10

SOURCES: See table 13.
NOTE: Dashes indicate that data were unavailable.

reflected in ownership of separate dining tables, dining chairs, kitchen tables, and kitchen chairs in one estate. Among the Newtown inhabitants whose estates were recorded before 1825, only David Baldwin possessed such a suite of furniture. Other indications of cultural separation—card tables, breakfast tables, and tea tables—were equally rare. On the basis of this evidence, the practice of referring to certain tables as kitchen tables was Newtown's way of accepting semantic elements of newer ideology while reaffirming older values.[12]

Wood Choices

Mahogany, an imported wood often used in joiner's chairs, gained little favor in Newtown for chairs. None of the inventories referred to mahogany seating furniture. In fact, even the locally available cherry achieved infrequent mention. When cherry was specified, it was in conjunction with fiddleback chairs or chairs with values equivalent to fiddlebacks (approximately four shillings apiece). In Newtown, painted maple or yellow poplar, typical stock for turned chairs, remained the favored materials (table 17).

Newtown estates were more likely to identify the particular wood used for tables and storage furniture than for chairs. Local cherry remained the most frequently mentioned wood. Cherry round and square tables, fall leaf tables, cases of drawers, desks, chests of drawers, and dressing tables appeared in Newtown inventories. Imported mahogany forms were found

TABLE 17
Woods and Colors of Seating Furniture, 1760–1824
(percentage of estates with specified form)

	1760–64	1770–74	1780–84	1790–94	1800–1804	1810–14	1820–24
NEWTOWN							
Number of estates	15	17	18	17	29	26	48
Woods (%)							
Mahogany	—	—	—	—	—	—	—
Cherry	—	—	—	—	—	12	—
Colors (%)							
Black	13	29	50	18	24	15	6
Red	—	12	33	29	31	19	8
Green	—	—	—	—	3	—	4
Yellow	—	—	—	—	—	—	2
Blue	—	—	—	—	—	8	—
WOODBURY							
Number of estates	16	13	20	17	20	24	29
Woods (%)							
Mahogany	—	—	—	—	—	13	—
Cherry	—	6	—	6	—	13	7
Colors (%)							
Black	31	38	15	47	40	13	7
Red	—	6	5	12	35	13	7
Green	—	—	5	—	10	42	14
Yellow	—	—	—	—	—	4	3
Blue	—	—	—	6	—	—	3

SOURCES: See table 13.
NOTE: Dashes indicate that data were unavailable.

TABLE 18
Mahogany and Cherry Tables and Case Furniture, 1760–1824
(percentage of estates with specified form)

	1760–64	1770–74	1780–84	1790–94	1800–1804	1810–14	1820–24
NEWTOWN							
Number of estates	15	17	18	17	29	26	48
Tables (%)							
Mahogany	—	—	—	—	—	8	2
Cherry	—	8	6	18	17	27	13
Case furniture (%)							
Mahogany	—	—	—	—	—	4	—
Cherry	—	—	—	—	10	23	—
WOODBURY							
Number of estates	16	13	20	17	20	24	29
Tables (%)							
Mahogany	—	—	—	—	—	8	7
Cherry	6	8	15	29	40	46	21
Case furniture (%)							
Mahogany	—	—	—	—	—	4	10
Cherry	—	8	10	18	—	17	14

SOURCES: See table 13.
NOTE: Dashes indicate that data were unavailable.

only a few times toward the end of the survey period (table 18). Other woods specified in Newtown inventories included maple, butternut, and whitewood (yellow poplar) for tables and pine and whitewood for case furniture. Much of the pine and whitewood furniture was painted.

Patterns of Furniture Ownership

These patterns of furniture ownership in Newtown should not be attributed mistakenly to lack of awareness or to limited means. Conservative attitudes and satisfaction with existing forms are not uniformly the result of cultural ignorance or material poverty. Neither joiners nor patrons were unconcerned with cultural currents outside Newtown. The contract for a new town house in 1766 explicitly expressed awareness of the larger world: It specified the building of good seats "in form as in the State House at Hartford." The single reference to inlaid furniture, the few pieces of mahogany furniture in Joel Booth's shop, and the extremely small number of references to mahogany furniture, card tables, and desk-and-bookcases indicate that few Newtowners chose to partake of the new, even though they had been been exposed to more fashionable items. The mean and median values of furniture imply that such traditional preferences were widely held. A surprisingly large number of inhabitants of various estates owned expensive furniture or household goods such as looking glasses, clocks, cases of drawers, and desks, but not new-fashioned furniture (table 19). If Newtown could be considered a cultural backwater in regard to furniture, this conservatism was selective and self-imposed. Its roots lay in the town's persistence rate and recruitment of local joiners.[13]

How pervasive was Newtown's conservatism? To understand the extent of the town's preference for traditional furniture, let us examine the raw frequencies of seating, storage, and table forms in relation to four value categories (table 20).[14] Various furniture forms were evenly distributed among estates with consumer assets totaling less than £10. The possessions of William Seger, appraised in 1800, were typical of this group. At his death, Seger owned five old chairs, a chest, a square table, and a stand, as well as bedding, clothing, and household goods.[15]

Earlier estates with consumer assets valued between £10 and £25 contained furniture with an average value only slightly more than one pound. Compared to William Seger, men belonging to this class had more items of a certain form. David Dunning, a farmer who died in 1783, owned more

TABLE 19
Raw Frequencies of Selected Artifacts, 1760–1824
(percentage of estates with specified artifact)

	1760–64	1770–74	1780–84	1790–94	1800–1804	1810–14	1820–24
NEWTOWN							
Number of estates	15	17	18	17	29	26	48
Cases of drawers (%)	27	29	44	47	31	50	29
Desks (%)	7	12	11	18	17	23	19
Clocks (%)	7	24	6	12	24	50	42
Looking glasses (%)	40	53	78	82	79	81	81
WOODBURY							
Number of estates	16	13	20	17	20	24	29
Cases of drawers (%)	25	31	40	53	50	58	52
Desks (%)	6	15	10	12	10	50	48
Clocks (%)	—	15	20	18	15	54	62
Looking glasses (%)	44	62	85	65	90	83	79

SOURCES: See table 13.
NOTE: Dash indicates that data were unavailable.

TABLE 20
Distribution of Furniture by Four Value Categories
(mean number of form; mean percentage of total furniture value in parenthesis)

	1760–64	1770–74	1780–84	1790–94	1800–1804	1810–14	1820–24
NEWTOWN							
<£9.9							
Number of estates	2	1	1	—	1	—	1
Mean furniture value	£0.12.0	£0.8.6	£1.2.0	—	£0.9.7	—	£1.6.10
Seating forms	4.5 (55%)	5 (29%)	10 (25%)	—	5 (28%)	—	6 (22%)
Storage forms	0.5 (14%)	2 (24%)	2 (41%)	—	1 (25%)	—	3 (62%)
Tables	1 (30%)	1 (47%)	2 (34%)	—	2 (47%)	—	2 (16%)
£10–24.9							
Number of estates	4	7	4	4	8	4	14
Mean furniture value	£1.7.9	£1.1.11	£1.11.9	£3.3.10	£2.7.11	£1.2.10	£2.0.10
Seating forms	4.5 (17%)	4.7 (24%)	3.5 (25%)	10.5 (39%)	7.8 (35%)	7.5 (43%)	10 (35%)
Storage forms	2.5 (63%)	1.3 (43%)	3.5 (55%)	2.5 (43%)	3.3 (47%)	2.3 (48%)	2.7 (40%)
Tables	1 (20%)	2 (33%)	2.8 (20%)	2.8 (18%)	2 (17%)	1.5 (9%)	3.1 (25%)
£25–49.9							
Number of estates	3	4	8	8	8	8	18
Mean furniture value	£3.5.7	£3.1.0	£4.14.11	£5.0.2	£5.4.5	£4.6.10	£4.5.1
Seating forms	12 (34%)	10.7 (33%)	11.5 (24%)	17.5 (32%)	14 (41%)	15 (31%)	17 (43%)
Storage forms	3 (43%)	3 (39%)	3.3 (61%)	5.3 (55%)	3.5 (45%)	4 (51%)	4.3 (35%)
Tables	3 (22%)	2.2 (28%)	3 (15%)	4.3 (30%)	2.8 (13%)	2.8 (18%)	4.2 (22%)
>£50							
Number of estates	2	5	5	5	12	14	14
Mean furniture value	£13.17.3	£11.4.7	£6.18.0	£10.10.2	£9.1.10	£10.19.9	£7.6.7
Seating forms	34 (35%)	20 (22%)	15.5 (27%)	18.8 (29%)	20.3 (33%)	21 (29%)	22.3 (33%)
Storage forms	8.5 (46%)	5.8 (54%)	5.5 (56%)	5.6 (55%)	6 (47%)	6.5 (44%)	6 (39%)
Tables	4.5 (16%)	5.6 (24%)	4.5 (18%)	3.8 (16%)	4.8 (22%)	5.4 (28%)	5.2 (28%)

(continued)

TABLE 20
Continued

	1760–64	1770–74	1780–84	1790–94	1800–1804	1810–14	1820–24
WOODBURY							
<£9.9							
Number of estates	1	1	—	2	—	—	1
Mean furniture value	£0.7.0	£0.7.0	—	£0.7.6	—	—	£0.2.0
Seating forms	—	—	—	4 (54%)	—	—	—
Storage forms	—	1 (100%)	—	1 (13%)	—	—	1 (100%)
Tables	1 (100%)	—	—	1 (33%)	—	—	—
£10–24.9							
Number of estates	2	4	7	2	4	3	4
Mean furniture value	£0.8.7	£0.15.2	£1.10.9	£2.6.2	£2.4.5	£1.13.10	£1.9.8
Seating forms	4 (59%)	3.7 (46%)	6 (30%)	7 (25%)	7.5 (24%)	6 (25%)	6.5 (23%)
Storage forms	1 (40%)	1.5 (38%)	3 (45%)	3.8 (58%)	2.5 (46%)	2.7 (55%)	2.5 (65%)
Tables	—	0.7 (16%)	2 (25%)	1.6 (17%)	2 (29%)	2.3 (19%)	1 (12%)
£25–49.9							
Number of estates	6	7	4	5	9	7	10
Mean furniture value	£4.13.8	£3.6.3	£3.18.6	£5.7.6	£4.6.3	£3.10.6	£4.9.3
Seating forms	9 (27%)	10 (27%)	7 (15%)	15 (25%)	11 (35%)	15 (45%)	15.7 (30%)
Storage forms	4 (55%)	3.4 (48%)	2.5 (64%)	4.8 (56%)	4 (43%)	3 (18%)	4.3 (44%)
Tables	3 (17%)	2.4 (25%)	2 (21%)	3.4 (20%)	3 (23%)	4 (36%)	3.9 (26%)
>£50							
Number of estates	4	1	9	4	7	14	14
Mean furniture value	£7.4.9	£59.15.4	£6.6.3	£11.8.10	£8.18.4	£17.15.2	£18.16.8
Seating forms	12 (25%)	60 (19%)	16 (25%)	23 (26%)	18 (29%)	26 (29%)	29.6 (32%)
Storage forms	6 (50%)	20 (68%)	4.5 (46%)	7.5 (54%)	4.6 (48%)	7 (45%)	7.2 (39%)
Tables	3 (25%)	12 (14%)	4 (29%)	5.5 (21%)	4.9 (23%)	7.4 (27%)	6.8 (29%)

SOURCES: See table 13.
NOTES: Dashes indicate that data were unavailable.

storage and table forms. His possessions included an armchair, three old chairs, a chest with drawers, an old pine chest of drawers, two old chests, an oval table, and two old tables. Beginning in the 1790s, furniture values in this economic group doubled. A greater number of chairs and storage forms account for this increase. John Crofut's estate of 1822 listed seven kitchen chairs, an old case of drawers, a chest with drawers, three plain chests, two tables, and two stands. The descriptions and values of Crofut's furniture reveal a mixture of new traditional forms and old inherited furniture. Numbers and values of furniture holdings had grown, but the types of furniture remained the same. They included painted turned chairs, chests and chests with drawers, and multifunctional tables. Some estates specified cherry tables in the nineteenth century, but real changes can be noted only in the inventories from the 1820s. At that time, Windsors and fancy chairs began to complement older, turned chairs in this class of inventories. There were just a few references to tea tables and bureaus.[16]

A third group of estates, with consumer assets valued between £25 and £50, contained greater quantities of furniture than the previous group. Painted chairs, simple storage forms, and inexpensive tables could be found in all the estates from these two middling classes. What distinguished the estates valued between £25 and £50 was the number of each form and the increased likelihood of owning a more expensive case of drawers or a new form, like a Windsor or fancy chair. Jonathan Northrop, whose estate was filed in 1783, owned six black turned chairs, six white turned chairs, a chest with drawers, two plain chests, a trunk, a round table, a square table, and a stand. For this segment of the population, chairs accounted for about one-third of total furniture value, storage forms slightly more than one-half, and tables one-sixth. The inventory of George Northrop, appraised thirty-eight years after Jonathan Northrop's, included more chairs and similar storage forms and tables. His household consisted of ten Windsor chairs, eleven kitchen chairs, two chests with drawers, two plain chests, a round table, a kitchen table, and a chest.[17]

Many of the same forms appeared in the estates of the fourth and final group. The same painted chairs are found in these inventories, but each household owned three different sets of different colors or styles of turned chairs. Members of this class owned a case of drawers and dressing table in addition to chests and chests with drawers and owned, along with various smaller tables, a large fall leaf table. The Reverend John Beach furnished his house with four Windsors, four black chairs, six white chairs, three chests with drawers, several plain linen chests, three tables of various shapes, and two stands. A desk provided sufficient storage space for his extensive library. Lemuel Nichols, who operated a water-powered clothier's shop, owned furniture similar to that of Ebenezer Booth IV or Ebenezer Ford, who died twenty and forty years earlier, respectively. Nichols's furniture included fiddleback and kitchen chairs, a case of drawers, a desk for his business accounts, a chest with drawers, four plain chests, a kitchen table, a round table, a square table, and three stands. The only new item in his household was a set of fancy chairs, which were very similar to the older types.[18]

Several observations can be made from analysis of the four value categories. Newtown inventories of all sizes manifest an even distribution of forms and values. Differences between groups and over time tended to be in number, not in kind, and relatively gradual through all levels. In fact, the composition of each value group further documents the slow accumulation of consumer goods and furniture in Newtown. During the first two periods, the greatest number of people had consumer goods appraised between £10 and £25. The third group became the largest for the next two decades, but then was superceded by the wealthiest class in the early nineteenth century. Only in the 1820s did this pattern change. At that time the upper three groups each accounted for about a third of the inventoried population.

In Newtown the persistence of traditional forms illustrates the inherently conservative consumer and producer values of a yeoman town. Those who remained in town passed artifacts down through generations, and these material precedents continued to influence new production. At the same time, local training of joiners in a restricted number of traditions reinforced the standards of appropriateness. Semantic changes and selective adaptation of new forms characterized Newtown's furniture consumption between 1760 and 1820.

Woodbury Furniture Forms: New Fashion and New Lifestyles

Certain patterns of furniture ownership in Newtown can also be found in Woodbury. The Woodbury inventories of the 1760s included chests, chests with drawers, round tables, and square tables, many of them painted. Colored turned chairs predominated in these estates. References to slat-back, crown, York, and the generic black, red, and white chairs were common. Even some of the wealthier estates from the end of the survey period contained such traditional forms. At his death in 1810, David Mitchel of

Southbury owned a set of old chairs, a set of red chairs, a large black chair, and two red chairs, in addition to a set of cherry chairs, a set of birch chairs, a desk-and-bookcase, and a chest of drawers. Truman Hurlbut often painted chairs and bedsteads for the Woodbury merchant Nathaniel Bacon.[19]

Chairs

In spite of such general similarities, attention to specific forms reveals a widening split in consumer behavior between Newtown and Woodbury. Taste in chairs provides one clear way of recognizing the difference. Crookedback chairs and joiner's chairs (both also referred to as dining chairs in the early nineteenth century) gained greater acceptance in Woodbury than in Newtown. Beginning in the 1770s, Woodbury estates began to list crookedback chairs with flag seats and joiner's chairs with cushion bottoms. Several estates listed joiner's chairs or cherry chairs with values double those of cherry chairs with flag bottoms. An 1813 inventory listed the highest valued variation of this seating form: "10 mahogany hair bottom chairs $30."[20]

The popularity achieved by crookedback and joiner's chairs came at the expense of their turned cousin, the fiddleback chair. In Woodbury, fiddlebacks first appeared in an 1800 inventory, but never became a very common chair type.[21] However, Woodbury did not totally reject turned chairs. The most frequently specified chair in estates recorded from 1810 until 1825 was the Windsor, or green, chair. Its desirability in Woodbury may have been due less to the familiarity of its turned construction and painted decoration than to its symbolic connections with the world beyond Woodbury's boundaries. Nicholas Jebine, the New Haven–trained cabinetmaker, was a prominent Windsor chairmaker in Woodbury. The Windsor, and later the fancy chair, did not coexist with the other chair types in Woodbury. They replaced some of the more expensive chairs and, eventually, even the cheaper turned ones. By 1820 traditional, inexpensive turned chairs had lost their former pervasiveness (see table 14).[22]

Upholstered seating furniture further distinguished Woodbury estates from those of Newtown. Several inventories listed chairs with cushion bottoms. Gary Bacon's 1821 estate included a sofa and an easy chair, appraised at the high values of $60 and $18, respectively. Contemporary values for other chairs help put these figures into proper perspective. Joiner's chairs averaged $2 per chair; flag-seated chairs, $1.16; fancy chairs, $1.26; Windsor chairs, $0.67; and kitchen chairs, $0.22.[23]

Patterns of chair ownership in Woodbury demonstrate higher value, greater competition among styles, and shorter swings in popularity. A division existed between traditional, less expensive chairs and more expensive types. The latter—crookedbacks, joiner's chairs, and fancy chairs—replaced one another in succession as the most expensive chair form. Windsors began to encroach on the less expensive furniture. Older turned chairs became less common in the inventories from the end of the study period. These patterns are quite different from those of Newtown. In that conservative town, both inexpensive and expensive chair types were relatively timeless. They did not continually succeed one another, but grew only gradually in number.

Storage Forms

New fashions in case furniture after 1770 and especially after 1800 also document different consumer behavior in Woodbury. In contrast to Newtown's continued preference for such traditional forms as chests and chests with drawers, Woodbury inventories listed a smaller percentage of traditional forms. After 1790, Woodbury estates included a greater proportion of more sophisticated case furniture (see table 15).

Such patterns are uncovered further in the analysis of specific storage forms. Many of those specified forms provide evidence of new styles and changing social attitudes and relationships within Woodbury. The neoclassical taste of federal America was very apparent in Woodbury estates. Whereas only two Newtown inventories before 1820 listed bureaus, Woodbury examples from the same period contained nine bureaus, including three mahogany and two cherry examples.[24] The sideboard, a second type of neoclassical furniture, was absent from Newtown inventories. In Woodbury, sideboards appeared in the estates of the community's leaders—the Reverend Elijah Wood, merchant Gary Bacon, and proprietor Curtis Hinman owned them. Aesthetically, technologically, and functionally, the sideboard was the quintessential manifestation of the American Federal style. In both outline and volume, it embodied the taut, geometric symmetry and light, angular appearance of the neoclassical style. Various decorative practices of the period further emphasized the new style. Veneer created geometric panels of contrasting color or figure, and carving and inlay provided neoclassical details and motifs.[25]

To achieve the desired geometric structure and classical decoration, the joiner drew on the latest technology and organizational practices. During this time, veneer became easier and cheaper to make because of sawing improvements and organizational developments in urban cabinetmaking centers. Such centers supported craftsmen who specialized in veneer or in the making of stringing and pictorial inlays. This decorative inlay was then marketed throughout the surrounding region. Widespread use of veneer permitted fabrication of carcasses with curved members made from laminated boards of a secondary wood such as pine. Standard-sized carcasses could be customized with different veneers or inlay. Bacon's mahogany sideboard was appraised at $60, a value commensurate with a mahogany-veneered sideboard with some inlay or carved decoration. Hinman's sideboard, with a lower value of $20, more likely was a plainer version. Even so, the value of Hinman's sideboard was double that of a case of drawers. Like joiner's chairs, sideboards demonstrate that the Woodbury consumer was willing to invest more money for fashion.[26]

The sideboard was a fashionable storage area for bottles, silver, and china, and a display surface for various dining accoutrements. It implies the formalization of dining behavior, the symbolic importance of holding the key to lock the silver drawer or bottle compartment, and even the existence of a household servant to mediate between sideboard and dining table. In conjunction with the dining table, dining chairs, and extensive sets of fine ceramics, it signaled a different attitude toward dining than existed in Newtown. In that town, multifunctional chests with drawers and tables served similar storage and display functions. Dining in Woodbury started to become more of a social than familial activity. Certain Woodbury inhabitants attached great importance to formal dining, as is clear from their purchases of a constellation of specific objects. It was a way to tie bonds with like-minded people and to distinguish themselves from other groups.[27]

In addition to desks, Woodbury estates featured other furniture designed specifically for books and business papers. Simple forms such as book cupboards and bookcases appeared irregularly throughout the survey period. The more expensive desk-and-bookcase, a form that first appeared in the 1770 inventory of Timothy Hinman, reflected the emergence of new reading patterns, which also spurred a group of Woodbury residents to establish their own social library in 1772.[28]

Earlier in the eighteenth century, New Englanders tended to own a small number of religious or devotional texts. Read over and over and passed among family and friends, these books taught a religiously structured reality. This traditional world of print, based on strong relationships between oral and printed culture and between different classes, resulted in a collective mentality shared by most New Englanders in the late seven-

TABLE 21
Book Ownership, 1760–1824
(percentage of estates with books; value of books)

	1760–64	1770–74	1780–84	1790–94	1800–1804	1810–14	1820–24
NEWTOWN							
Number of estates	15	17	18	17	29	26	48
Books							
% Estates	53	82	100	65	79	85	85
Mean value	£1.8.0	£0.10.0	£0.12.0	£0.18.0	£0.10.0	£1.6.0	£0.14.0
Median value	£0.12.0	£0.4.0	£0.10.0	£0.12.0	£0.6.0	£0.16.0	£0.10.0
WOODBURY							
Number of estates	16	13	20	17	20	24	29
Books							
% Estates	75	85	65	65	85	67	76
Mean value	£1.6.0	£1.6.0	£1.6.0	£1.14.0	£0.16.0	£1.16.0	£6.6.0
Median value	£1.6.0	£0.4.0	£0.18.0	£1.0.0	£0.10.0	£1.4.0	£1.4.0

SOURCES: See table 13.

teenth century. Certain ideological and economic changes in the eighteenth century began to fracture this unity. Enlightenment thought and the lessons of the Great Awakening attached greater weight to an individual's self-determination, while the postrevolutionary republican emphasis on virtuous citizenship provided additional justification for self-education. Consequently, the more cosmopolitan and rational merchants, ministers, and magistrates began to withdraw from the world of popular culture.[29]

Alongside this increasing emphasis on self-improvement were changes in the marketplace of print. Increased imports, greater production by the growing local presses, and more active marketing along the trade networks established after the Revolution brought greater quantities of historical, legal, and romantic literature to more people. The larger number of books available in Woodbury is reflected by the value of books listed in that town's estates (table 21) and by contemporary sources. In 1788, Shadrach Osborn sold Chauncey Hide "the Scots Rouge, Mol Flanders & another Romance." Gary Bacon assembled an extensive collection of adventures. Curtis Hinman's library featured $180 worth of books, most of which were legal studies. Replacing an intensive reading style with an extensive one necessitated a special piece of furniture to hold the increased number of books.[30]

The plentiful storage space of a desk-and-bookcase also facilitated storage and organization of the voluminous business papers accumulated by an active merchant. For example, the surviving receipts and ledgers of just one Southbury merchant, Shadrach Osborn, are plentiful enough to occupy several feet of shelf space. As merchants drew up more bills of credit, corresponded more extensively with agents and middlemen, and sought to preserve the gentlemanly nature of commerce, the desk-and-bookcase assumed functional and symbolic significance.[31]

Whether used to hold an increasing library or to organize a home office, the desk-and-bookcase symbolized its owner's involvement in a cosmopolitan and commercial culture that was distinct from the traditional popular one. Five desk-and-bookcases were listed in the twenty-four inventories from 1810 through 1814. Estates from the last study period included three desk-and-bookcases and two secretaries, a newer style of desk-and-bookcase. In contrast, the Newtown inventories listed several desks and many small portable writing desks, but only two desk-and-bookcases.[32]

Tables

The increased number of tables for specific uses further documents Woodbury's cultural change after 1800. Inventories from the nineteenth century listed card tables, tea tables, breakfast tables, and washstands (see table 16). Card tables first appeared in a 1797 Woodbury inventory. They permitted that frivolous and fashionable pastime to be carried on at home rather than at the tavern. Often listed in pairs along with other expensive furniture, this gaming furniture denoted the genteel orientation of its owners, who preferred to enjoy their leisurely activities at home and thereby aspired after the fashionable ideal of domestic sociability. The socialization and gambling that was part of card playing may also have served to endow the community's fashionable members with a cohesive group identity, distinct from the rest of the town folk.[33]

Similarly, the tea table, first listed in 1753 and especially numerous in the estates of the 1810s, signified the increased importance of the domestic environment as a place for leisurely socialization. Tea drinking at home, like card playing at home, was an individualized form of entertainment. It differed significantly from the more traditional social entertainment that accompanied town meetings, religious services, and harvesting.[34]

The distinction among breakfast, kitchen, and dining tables represents a third example of the tendency to structure and formalize social interaction and entertainment in the home. Division of the preparatory and eating activity into such specific units implies more elaborate meals or the importance of meals and drinking as social events. Six of the twenty-four inventories from the early teens and seven of the twenty-nine from the early twenties specified ownership of kitchen, dining, and breakfast tables. The increased number of these specialized tables in Woodbury inventories foreshadows the importance of cultivated domesticity later in the nineteenth century, when the home became a controllable social environment that provided refuge from the competitive, vexatious, and unpredictable world of business.[35]

Another group of table forms reveals increased attention to appearance and hygiene. Toilet tables and washstands, usually equipped with a basin and ewer, first appeared in an 1807 inventory and sporadically thereafter. Jabez Bacon, Samuel Tomlinson, Joel Hinman, Reverend Elijah Wood, and other cosmopolitans interested in self-image purchased furniture specifically designed to hold the accoutrements necessary to keep clean and polished. In contrast, a Newtown inventory of 1801 listed a toilet table, but only one more reference followed in the next twenty-four years. Apparently the inhabitants of Newtown did not accept the new importance attached to personal appearance with the same enthusiasm that spurred Bacon and others to buy special furniture. Instead, Newtown inventories continued to list the older multifunctional form, the dressing table.[36]

Patterns of Furniture Ownership

Examination of furniture owned in the four economic classes permits additional insight into the effect of mobility and market orientation on Woodbury consumers (see table 20). Estates in the lowest value category lacked an even spread of resources and often contained just a single piece of furniture. Most had mainly clothing and personal possessions. Job Martin, who died in 1774, owned a single chest; 89 percent of his consumer assets were clothing.[37]

Furniture ownership in Woodbury estates with consumer assets valued between £10 and £25 remained relatively penurious, especially before 1780. Furniture in comparable Newtown estates was consistently appraised at higher values. These Newtown estates often had more drawered storage forms and a few more chairs. After 1780, total furniture values for this group in both towns converged, but composition of the values remained different. Newtown inventories were characterized by greater numbers of forms per estate, while their Woodbury counterparts derived similar values from small quantities of newer or more expensive furniture. Instead of a set of nine turned chairs, a chest with one or two drawers, a couple of plain chests, and two small tables, Woodbury estates filed after 1780 included more cherry furniture and stylish forms in smaller numbers. The 1800 inventory of Justus Hinman included six Windsors, a cherry table, a cherry stand, and a breakfast table.[38]

Woodbury estates from the third class reveal a similar pattern. They approximated the total furniture values of Newtown estates, but compositional analysis reveals that Woodbury households contained smaller numbers of the traditional inexpensive forms and more examples of the expensive forms. Simeon Judson owned furniture with the same total value as Jonathan Northrop of Newtown. Judson owned fewer chairs and plain storage forms, but a case of drawers accounted for about half the total value of his furniture. In the nineteenth century, cherry tea tables, breakfast tables, Windsor chairs, bureaus, and very expensive cases of drawers and tables appeared in this group of Woodbury inventories. Joel Down's household featured an expensive bureau, three chests of drawers, two painted chests, six painted chairs, eleven other chairs, an expensive tea table, a stand, a small table, and a kitchen table.[39]

In the fourth and final value group, estates from both towns between 1780 and 1804 showed consistent value proportions among the three formal categories. The total values for furniture holdings were very similar. Common perceptions of an appropriate assemblage of furniture linked these more established inhabitants. After 1804 this segment of Woodbury's population altered its furniture taste. Some of the smaller Woodbury estates from this group listed crookedback chairs, breakfast tables, bureaus, and dining tables.

More significant shifts occurred in the great number of large estates. The merchant Truman Hinman owned furniture valued at £35.16.0. His furnishings combined a touch of the traditional with a great deal of newer fashion. His seating furniture included hair-bottomed mahogany joiner's chairs, eight cherry joiner's chairs, seventeen Windsor chairs, and twelve kitchen chairs. A desk-and-bookcase housed his business papers, and he filled a mahogany bureau, two cherry cases of drawers, and several trunks with his vast wardrobe. Hinman owned a large number of mahogany, cherry, and function-specific tables to use with an expensive array of eating and dining equipment. Among these were a mahogany breakfast table, a mahogany candlestand, a cherry dining table, cherry breakfast table and stands, a toilet table, and two card tables. Curtis Hinman, who operated a Woodbury clothier's manufactory, owned completely different furniture than his Newtown counterpart, Lemuel Nichols. Hinman's furniture included a sideboard, mahogany and cherry breakfast tables, a bureau, a desk-and-bookcase, a desk, several trunks, a number of Windsor chairs, and some older chairs, chests, and tables.[40]

Before 1770 the material culture of Woodbury was relatively similar to neighboring Newtown. After that date, the inventories of middling and wealthy Woodbury inhabitants began to contain more expensive chairs, different styles of chairs, and more complex storage forms in addition to traditional painted furniture. The town's mobility affected both producer and consumer. Joiners who were trained in a number of different traditions provided a wide variety of formal and decorative options. The stratified social structure produced a gentry class eager to distinguish itself with new fashion and a middle class, many members of which were not born in Woodbury, less influenced by precedence. Beginning around 1800 another shift in Woodbury inventories can be noted. A broader segment of the population purchased great quantities of consumer goods and owned more expensive and fashionable furniture. Ties with the external market became widespread and secure. At the same time, the proliferation of specialized furniture types and the development of a suitable language to describe them reflected acceptance of different customs and habits. In short the consumption patterns of the neighboring towns document two different responses to cultural change. Close examination of the surviving artifacts provides material evidence of the kind and degree of difference.

SIX

Workmanship of Habit: The Furniture of Newtown

While manuscript sources such as probate inventories and account books permit the study of patterns of distribution, usage, and patronage, actual artifacts also provide essential evidence about the context of furniture production and usage. Rigorous analysis of surviving furniture from Newtown and Woodbury proves invaluable for a number of reasons. The artifacts provide a different type of evidence, which corroborates or even elaborates upon the data presented in the previous chapter. Attention to technical and decorative details often reveals qualitative differences concealed by general inventory terms like *black chair* or *cherry table*. Artifactual analysis and comparison also help to investigate craftsmen's behavior. Structural and decorative features of a surviving piece of furniture provide essential information about the training, habits, and values of its maker. Rather than judging each surviving object merely on its aesthetics or historical associations, one needs to analyze a body of furniture in a collective, comparative manner. Examination of a significant object pool, with items linked by common place of origin, reveals the workings of past minds and serves as a graphic index of cultural continuity and change.

Furniture production in Newtown and Woodbury was related in several respects. The shared topographical features provided each town with the same raw materials for furniture. Particularly common in contemporary sources and surviving artifacts are cherry (*Prunus serotina*), yellow poplar (*Liriodendron tulipifera*), which was referred to as whitewood in the period, and red oak (*Quercus rubra*). For the better case furniture and tables, joiners of both communities used cherry and occasionally sugar maple (*Acer sacchrum*) for the exterior wood. A combination of yellow poplar, red oak, white pine (*Pinus strobus*), or even post oak (*Quercus stellata*) was favored for the less visible interior structure. As late as the early nineteenth century, red oak remained a popular choice for drawer linings. Cherry was used for the more expensive chairs, but maple, yellow poplar, and ash (*Fraxinus americana*) were used for the less expensive turned chairs and for Windsor chairs. Joiners throughout the region turned legs and front rounds or stretchers from maple; sawed out and modeled crest rails, banisters, and shoe rails from yellow poplar; and rent and shaved side rounds and slats out of ash. Painted yellow poplar and white pine storage forms and tables served utilitarian needs. Imported walnut (*Juglans nigra*) and mahogany (*Swietenia mahogani*), which were less common than the locally available woods, were used only in the most fashionable furniture and enjoyed greater popularity in Woodbury than in Newtown.

Although the species of trees in Newtown and Woodbury were similar, the quality of the wood often differed. In Newtown, surviving examples indicate that joiners used good grades of yellow poplar, red oak, and white pine for drawer linings, interior structural elements, and backboards of case furniture. An even grain and a lack of defects characterize the look of these woods. Similarly the cherry or maple used as the primary, or exterior, wood is rarely marred by the contrast between heartwood and sapwood; color and grain are uniform. In contrast, much of the white pine and oak found in Woodbury furniture is knotty and rough, and the cherry exterior wood often contains both heartwood and sapwood.

This evidence indicates that Newtown joiners had access to and valued the best-quality primary and secondary woods. Several explanations could account for this supply: sawmills carefully sawed around the log, constantly rotating it, and thereby removed the greatest number of better-grade boards and kept the knotty defects in the central portion; Newtown inhabitants maintained carefully harvested wood lots as part of the mixed agricultural economy; or the community internalized an allocation system in which the best lumber used in furnituremaking was designated for the local joiners, while lesser quality lumber was earmarked for other purposes such as framing or fuel. The lower grades of woods in Woodbury furniture could be attributed to greater use of "through and through sawing," a more efficient way of ripping boards from logs that produces lumber of varying quality; and careless harvesting practices, in which farmers cleared wood lots to allow more pasturage for animal husbandry. There was also no systematic local allocation of wood; instead, the Woodbury joiner found himself restricted to local woods of widely varying quality and to lumber purchased from surrounding areas that still maintained good stands of the necessary cabinetmaking woods.[1]

Coastal Connecticut cabinetmaking traditions also linked the furniture made in Newtown and Woodbury, for craftsmen such as Timothy Jordan and Samuel Curtiss of Stratford and Alexander Bryan and David Miles of Milford moved to Newtown and Woodbury in the mid eighteenth century. They introduced elements of the coastal traditions into the two inland towns' styles of construction and decoration. As a result it can be hard initially to distinguish between furniture made in the different communities of the Housatonic Valley. The confusion resulting from this shared heritage can be seen most clearly in the common turned vocabulary (both the shape and placement of turned elements such as balusters or rings) of the posts and front rounds, or stretchers, of fiddleback and crookedback chairs and the widespread use of scrolled knees and carved fans on case furniture. In Stratford, Newtown, and Woodbury, joiners occasionally executed a similar decorative scroll on the outside edges of crooked legs and often carved a distinctive fan, characterized by concave, spoon-handled ribs, on the lower central drawer of a case of drawers or dressing table. The movement of joiners between Newtown and Woodbury also contributed to similarities in the towns' furniture. Members of the Fabrique and Booth families worked in both towns, and Abner Judson was born in Newtown, trained in Woodbury, and returned to Newtown to work. As a result of this mobility, joiners in one town were aware of design, techniques, and workmanship in the other.[2]

In spite of these similarities, subtle constructional and decorative differences help to distinguish Newtown furniture from Woodbury furniture. These differences became more noticeable toward the end of the eighteenth century. After 1760 Newtown continued to selectively blend the coastal furniture traditions of its earlier joiners. The compatibility of the original coastal traditions, limited immigration of new craftsmen, and training of local youths resulted in a relative homogenization of furniture production. Stability in the craft structure restricted sustained challenges to the available shops. Differences between Newtown shops became very subtle by the end of the eighteenth century as a distinctive Newtown style of traditional forms and restrained decoration evolved. However, one should not view this as totally derivative or static material culture. Even though Newtown joiners drew on existing technical and stylistic ideas, they reordered and combined these parts in a variety of new ways. Occasionally they adapted new features to their conservative forms or added elaborate decoration. Analysis of Newtown's turned chair production, comparison of similar case furniture made in three shops (which researchers have not yet been able to identify), and examination of several other examples of locally made furniture help us to understand Newtown's traditional culture.

Chairs

The chairs in figures 7 through 14 illustrate some of the most popular chair types produced in Newtown between 1770 and 1810. Consumers of the eighteenth century, like those of the present, chose from various products on the basis of cost and stylishness. Ebenezer Booth IV (1743–1790) was one Newtown joiner who offered a variety of chairs to meet the townspeople's differing demands. His inventory included, in order of increasing cost, "plain," "round top," "horn," and "fiddleback" chairs. Although it has been impossible to determine what a horn chair looked like, the other three chair types specified in Booth's estate can be identified.[3]

The illustrated plain chair (see fig. 7) embodies simple design and decoration and ease of manufacture. The bowed profile of the back slats and the ball-and-reel finial at the top of each rear post are the only decorative details on this very chaste chair. Its method of construction contributes to its modest appearance: slats sawn from yellow poplar boards, visible elements of the frame easily produced on a lathe, rounds and seat lists shaped with a drawknife and inserted into holes drilled in the four posts, and flag seat quickly woven over the lists. The ease of construction and lack of time-consuming decorative work made this chair available at the lowest price.[4]

The term for the common chair underwent several changes during the period of this study. The modifying term for this type of chair changed from surface description to formal trait to functional delimitation. From 1760 until about 1790 these chairs were referred to as white chairs, indicating an unfinished or unpainted surface. The 1777 inventory of Ebenezer Johnson, which listed "8 white plain chairs 10/," foreshadowed a terminological shift that was completed by the century's end. In 1790 these common chairs, valued between one and two shillings each, began to be called plain chairs or kitchen chairs. The latter term became predominant in the early nineteenth century.[5]

With the terminological change, the chair experienced a stylistic evolution during the late eighteenth and early nineteenth centuries. The earlier examples featured thin posts, each embellished with a baluster, or vase-shaped decorative turning, on the rear posts and crisply executed ball-and-reel finials. The nineteenth-century version had shorter, heavier plain posts and finials with softer turnings. Although the chair in figure 7 has undecorated posts, its sharply turned finials and the height and relative thinness of its posts suggests a date of manufacture in the late eighteenth century. This stylistic transformation of plain/kitchen chairs in Newtown paralleled a similar process in Milford and may have begun there because of the Milford origin of several Newtown families, particularly the joiners Alexander Bryan and James Briscoe Jr. Many of the techniques and styles introduced by Bryan and Briscoe became part of the Newtown joiners' stock of ideas.[6]

The "round top" or "round back" chair, first listed in the 1776 inventory of Moses Platt, was a moderately priced chair that never gained the same popularity as the plain/kitchen chair or the later fiddleback chair.[7] The round-top chair (see fig. 8) was the rural joiner's response to expensive joined chairs in the early Georgian style (1720–40), what collectors of antiques commonly call the Queen Anne. Georgian chairs were distinguished by yoke-shaped crest rails, short and broad backs, baluster-shaped banisters, sawn-out rear legs with ogee, or S-shaped, profiles, sawn-out crooked front legs with claw or round feet, joined seat frames, and carved decoration. To make this new type of chair, the craftsman sawed the parts from expensive woods such as walnut or mahogany; shaped the parts with a drawknife, rasp, and scraper; and joined them with mortises and tenons. Turning, if used at all, was confined to shaping the round feet and making rounds, which were not common on chairs of this type.

Newtown joiners became aware of the new Georgian style through their own and their clients' exposure to it, possibly during a trip to Danbury, Fairfield, New Haven, or some other larger town. The appearance of the urban chair, however, conflicted with the traditional concept of a chair in Newtown. Therefore the Newtown joiner sought to reproduce the feeling of this fashion within the locally accepted idiom, which demonstrated a preference for chairs with turned frames and flag seats. He was technically capable of producing a version of the early Georgian joined chair, but instead assessed the new type in light of his accustomed practice of turning parts. He employed a combination of turned and joined construction, updating the highly visible upper-back area with a smoothly modeled yoke-shaped crest rail, baluster-shaped banister, and rounded rear posts. These posts resembled the rounded stiles on some early Georgian chairs rather than posts on turned chairs. To balance this new fashion with the old style, he preserved the stretcher system, turned decoration, turned vertical posts, flag seat, and verticality of the older chair types. Extensive use of turned construction also permitted fast and easy manufacture. The round-top chair was a fairly inexpensive seating form that conformed to traditional expectations but also incorporated elements of newer taste.[8]

The round-top chair in figure 8 provides evidence of Newtown joiners' origins and attests to the persistence of certain cultural ideas in the inwardly focused community. The turned intermediate spindles, running from the rear post to the front leg just under the arms, and the simple decoration of the rear posts (a long column surmounting a flattened ball) can be seen on contemporary chairs from Milford and Stratford. Joiners trained in these communities, such as Alexander Bryan and Benjamin Latten, could have introduced these features, or Newtown families with relatives still in Milford or Stratford may have desired furniture similar to that of their cousins. Other details link this round-top chair with earlier turned chairs from Norwalk, Fairfield, and New York. The rounded profile and molded upper surface of the arms' handgrips and the barrel-shaped turned elements on the front posts (where the intermediate spindles tenon into the front post) suggest the influence of a Norwalk-area chairmaking tradition. Several crown chairs with histories of ownership in Norwalk families exhibit the prototypes of such features. The baluster turnings on the front round and the ring turnings of the front posts resemble those on a slat-back chair attributed to Ozias Buddington of Fairfield. Aspects of the front round also reflect the influence of York chairs made in New York. The rounds of those urban chairs featured bulging baluster termini at each end and a tripartite central element that consisted of a thin central ring flanked on either side by a well-articulated reel. The Newtown craftsman drew individual elements from these four different traditions and combined them in his own way.[9]

Beginning in the 1780s, round-top chairs appeared infrequently in Newtown inventories, and fiddleback chairs (see figs. 9–14) became the most common chair form. Fiddleback and round-top chairs shared the same turned structural system derived from several coastal chairmaking traditions, but differed in their crest rails. The fiddleback had only a vestige of the yoke shape at its center between sweeping sides with squared-off ears curving up and back. The sweeping shape of the crest rail originated in English furniture in the style of William Kent during the 1740s and was adapted to American furniture in the 1750s. The fiddleback was thus a slightly more fashionable turned chair in the 1780s, and its popularity coincided with a time of gradually increasing furniture value in Newtown (see chart 3).[10]

Close examination of fiddlebacks with histories of ownership by Newtown families and comparison with related chairs without definite provenance reveal the existence of at least four groups of chairs, each of which probably represents a different shop tradition. Within each group, the joiner had several options for particular features such as the rear posts or the termini at the top of the rear posts. Comparison of the feet, front rounds, front posts, splat profile, rear post, and termini of the rear post indicates that the front stretcher and the handling of the baluster shape on the front and rear posts are the most important distinctions between shops.[11]

One shop produced a simplified fiddleback with minimal turned decoration (see fig. 9). The use of two front rounds rather than one, simple ring turnings on the front posts, and a "turnerly" seat construction, in which the front posts continue up through the seating plane, link the chair type to the plain/kitchen chair tradition. The type is distinguished from plain/kitchen chairs by a fiddleback crest rail, baluster-shaped banister, or splat, very simplified baluster turnings on the front rounds, and turned rear posts with two baluster-shaped elements of different lengths, the lower one of which features crisp, well-defined rings at the base and the top. The joiner did not, however, turn any sort of decorative termini at the top of the rear posts, as found on figures 10 through 12. The seat construction and the abridgment of the turned decoration on the rear posts allowed the craftsman to make this type of chair more quickly than the other fiddlebacks discussed below. Its simplicity demonstrates why certain fiddlebacks had a slightly lower value than most others in inventories or account books.[12]

A fiddleback (see fig. 10) originally owned by a member of the Blackman family incorporates several features that made it more "joinerly" and more expensive. To endow the seat with the appearance of a joined seat, the craftsman shaped the front seat list to include a square block at each end. He then tenoned the front posts into the undersides of the blocks and the side seat lists into the rear edges of the blocks. This practice resulted in a single-plane seat, which was not disrupted by protruding front posts. The substitution of a single, more decoratively turned front round for two simple front rounds was another way in which the joiner distinguished this type of fiddleback from plain chairs and added decoration. The turnings of the rear post feature thinner baluster shapes and softer rings than those on figure 9, but both types resemble the posts on crown and painted chairs from Milford. While the front rounds of figure 9 resemble those on Milford chairs, the turnings of the front round in figure 10—long, baluster-shaped termini with ring transitions to the coffin-shaped balusters, which flank a central element consisting of a thick, reeded disk between reels—echo those found on examples from Norwalk and suggest a second shop tradition.[13]

A joiner in a third shop produced very similar fiddlebacks distinguished by a different front round, in which the central element was a single reel, and a different handling of turning gouges. He favored robust transitions between turned elements, turning a flaring reel at the top of the attenuated rear post baluster to provide a lively flow into the baluster terminus or turning crisp tapered rings at the bases of the balusters. The chair in figure 11 descended in the Stiles family of Southbury, but its overall form, crest rail, splat, and turnings closely follow Newtown conventions and relate to a number of other local examples. A craftsman working in a fourth shop favored conical-shaped termini rather than baluster-shaped stops on the front rounds and baluster-and-cone turnings rather than double-baluster turnings at the top of the front legs; a chair that passed down in the Beers family illustrates the turning vocabulary of this Newtown shop (see fig. 12). The lack of a ring under the baluster on the front post, the consistent use of a ring on the back post just above the seat plane, and a distinctive terminus at the top of the rear post, consisting of a small reel with a large baluster above it, are also distinguishing features of chairs produced in this shop.

Several fiddleback chairs combine features of two shops. One chair (see fig. 13), originally owned by Solomon Glover (1750–1842), combines baluster-shaped termini on the front round (seen on figs. 10 and 11) and baluster-and-cone turnings on the front post (seen on fig. 12). The rear posts illustrate the second type of back post found on Newtown fiddlebacks: a long column mounted on a thick, flattened ball. The same back post can be found on Stratford examples from the last two decades of the eighteenth century; however, the Newtown joiner eliminated the termini at the top of the back post and used the typical Newtown crest rail rather than a Stratford crest.[14] The survival of sufficient numbers of fiddleback chairs to identify specific shop traditions and the existence of several examples that combine elements from different shops suggest that Newtown joiners either drew easily from each other's repertoire to offer slight variations of a commonly understood form or freely exchanged surplus parts, made in efficient batches according to the rhythms of yeomen-craftsmen, as other neighboring craftsmen needed them. The common understanding of fiddleback chairs drawn from coastal turning traditions and preserved by the artisanal continuity of Newtown and the shared sense of economic role within the mixed agricultural economy combined to defuse a competitive spirit and contribute to a mutuality of interests.

Great fiddlebacks are more difficult to assign to specific shop traditions, but they still provide invaluable information about furnituremaking in Newtown. A great fiddleback with rockers (see fig. 14) documents that joiners who made fiddlebacks in the nineteenth century continued to draw from the same repertoire of parts. The maker preserved the traditional fiddleback form, particularly the crest, turned structure, and front round, but endowed it with a newer feeling by lightening the decoration and thinning the structural members (the front round is noticeably thinner in comparison to the front rounds on earlier fiddlebacks). Such alterations reflect the influence of the neoclassical style. Rather than use a new type of arm, the maker searched through his repertoire for an old form compatible with the neoclassical feeling and chose arms just like those on figure 8.[15]

The constant, unaltered characteristics of the illustrated Newtown fiddlebacks—painted turned frame, flag seat, and specific type of crest rail and front round—constituted the essential definition of the Newtown fiddleback chair. Within these parameters there was room for considerable diversity. Newtown joiners continued to draw from a familiar collection of older coastal and New York chairmaking traditions to vary the turnings and arms. The structural consistency, persistence of older details, and accommodation of only the general feel of the neoclassical style document the relatively unchallenged homogenization of several Newtown joiners' shops.

Even the more fashionable crookedback chair, which appeared very infrequently in Newtown inventories, reflects the existence of a selective conservatism that drew upon coastal material culture. A Newtown crookedback chair (see fig. 15) is linked to the fiddleback tradition through its front round, which is identical to that on the fiddleback in figure 12. The crest rail, banister, and rear stiles on this example are plain interpretations of a Stratford crookedback made in the middle of the eighteenth century. Unlike his Stratford counterpart, the Newtown joiner did not run a decorative molding along the lower edge of the shoe rail, and he employed a more traditional substructure. The use of double, decoratively turned side rounds rather than single sawn-out stretchers and uncarved feet suggest the influence of Newtown's preference for turned structure and plain decoration. Even on one of the most fashionable chair types in Newtown, qualities of traditional form, uniform structure, and plain decoration predominate.[16]

Newtown seating furniture manifests the influence of the workmanship of habit. The relationships among the illustrated chairs document turning's consistency over two or three generations. The chairs also draw attention to the interdependence of technology and demand. In some respects the means of production for turned chairs perpetuated the dominance of those

Fig. 7. Plain chair, Newtown, 1770–1800. Maple, yellow poplar; overall height (OH): 38¾", seat height (SH): 15", seat width (SW): 17", seat depth (SD): 12". Plain chairs with two or three slats were the most common inexpensive chair form throughout the Housatonic Valley region. Simple turned construction and limited decoration made them extremely affordable utilitarian chairs. In the early nineteenth century they were often referred to as kitchen chairs, suggesting that they were used in domestic workspace rather than social space. Collection of Newtown Historical Society; photograph courtesy of Mattatuck Museum.

Fig. 8. Great round-top chair, Newtown, 1760–1790. Maple, yellow poplar, and ash; OH:44", SH:16½", SW:23", SD:15¼". The round-top chair was a turnerly adaptation of the fashionable joiner's chairs made in the early Georgian style. Round-top chairs never gained great popularity in Newtown, having been superseded by the fiddleback form in the 1770s, but some of their features can be seen on later fiddlebacks. For example, the turned front round of this example closely resembles that on figure 13; the arms, those on figure 14. Collection of Newtown Historical Society; photograph courtesy of Mattatuck Museum.

Facing page:
Fig. 9. *Top left:* Fiddleback chair, Newtown, 1780–1800. Maple, yellow poplar, and ash; OH:40⅜" (bottom 1¼" of front feet added), SH:17", SW:19", SD:13½". The seat and substructure identify this fiddleback as a simple, inexpensive version, only slightly more stylish than a plain chair. Privately owned.

Fig. 10. *Top right:* Fiddleback chair, Newtown, 1770–1790. Maple, yellow poplar, and ash; OH:40½", SH:17", SW:20⅜", SD:13". In contrast to figure 9, this chair manifests a greater concern with fashion within the parameters of the turned chair tradition. Blocks at the end of the front lists give the flag seat the appearance of an upholstered cushion seat in a joiner's chair (in this example, tapestry fabric is nailed over the flag seat), while the turned decoration at the top and bottom of the front posts provide the visual interest of a joiner's chair's rounded knee and pad foot. Collection of Newtown Historical Society.

Fig. 11. *Bottom left:* Fiddleback chair, Newtown, 1780–1800. Maple, yellow poplar, and ash; OH:38⅜", SH:15⅞", SW:20", SD:13⅞". The maker of this chair was an exuberant turner, whose flair with the turning gouge is quite recognizable. The seat's deterioration (the jute webbing is a later addition) permits a closer look at how the front list was shaped integrally between the two blocks at its ends. Privately owned.

Fig. 12. *Bottom right:* Fiddleback chair, Newtown, 1770–1790. Maple, yellow poplar, and ash; OH:40½", SH:16⅛"; SW:19⅞"; SD:13¼". The joiner who made this and similar chairs employed conical-shaped termini at the ends of the front post and front round. Privately owned; photograph courtesy of Chipstone Foundation.

Fig. 13. Fiddleback chair, Newtown, 1780–1800. Maple, yellow poplar, and ash; OH:40½", SH:15½", SW:17¼", SD:13". This particular fiddleback is unusual for its combination of conical-shaped termini on the front posts and baluster-shaped termini on the front round. The blend suggests that craftsmen might have borrowed ideas from each other or exchanged products as particular needs arose. Privately owned.

Fig. 14. Great fiddleback rocking chair, Newtown, 1800–1820. Maple, yellow poplar, and ash; OH:39⅝", SH:13½", SW:22¼", SD:16". The rocking chair form, not common until the early nineteenth century, and the thinness of the front round on this example suggest that Newtown joiners adapted the fiddleback to new forms and lighter elements in the early nineteenth century. Privately owned; photograph courtesy of Mattatuck Museum.

Fig. 15. Crookedback chair, Newtown, 1790–1810. Maple, yellow poplar, and ash; measurements unavailable. The uncarved feet, double side rounds, and lack of incised or molded decoration on the shoe rail, rear stiles, or crest rail of this rare Newtown form document the conservative style of craftsmen there. The use of different woods means that the black paint on the chair is original. The plain decoration and painted surface of the Newtown example contrast with the more joinerly appearance and resin-finished cherry of the Woodbury examples in figures 34–36. Privately owned.

Fig. 16. Desk, Newtown, 1760–1780. Cherry and yellow poplar; height (H): 35¼", width (W): 36", depth (D): 19". The integral construction—the skirt, sides, and back are tenoned into the upper sections of the legs—makes this form unusual. Throughout New England at the time, most desks resembled chest of drawers with four full-width drawers surmounted by a desk interior with slant-front writing surface. Privately owned; photograph courtesy of Chipstone Foundation.

Fig. 17. Dressing table, Newtown, 1760–1780. Cherry, yellow poplar, and red oak; H:32½"; W:30½", D:20⅝". Dressing tables (or lowboys, as they are commonly called today) were a common form in Newtown during the last half of the eighteenth century. Newtown dressing tables are noticeably taller and wider than Boston and Massachusetts examples. Privately owned.

Fig. 18. Case of drawers, Newtown, 1770–1790. Cherry, yellow poplar, and red oak; measurements unavailable. This plain, flat-top case of drawers is an example of the most common form of large storage furniture in Newtown and was usually placed in a chamber or bedroom. A flat-top case of drawers cost less than the more complexly constructed crown case of drawers, but the handling of the scroll and the quality of the interior joinery suggest that the maker of this and several related examples was an accomplished craftsman who responded to local needs and expectations. Privately owned.

Fig. 19. Dressing table, Newtown, 1770–1790. Cherry and yellow poplar; H:30½", W:30", D:18". In making this plain dressing table, the joiner even eliminated the scroll on the knee that he had included on the case of drawers in figure 18. A number of other plain Newtown versions have been located. Privately owned; photograph courtesy of Mattatuck Museum.

Fig. 20. Crown case of drawers, Newtown, 1769. Cherry, yellow poplar, and red oak; H:84½", W:40", D:19". Made for the daughter of a successful shopkeeper in town, this unusual case of drawers chronicles the decorative repertoire of the same Newtown shop that made figure 18. The carving of the ball-and-claw feet and "snakeskin" carving of the knees suggest a connection to high-style work in New York City, but the piercing and carving in the pilasters and the chain-like carving on the tympanum of the upper section are rarely seen on such forms. Collection of Connecticut Historical Society, Hartford.

Fig. 21. Dressing table, Newtown, 1770–1790. Cherry, yellow poplar, red oak, birch, and red pine; H:31", W:31 3/8", D:19". Made in the same shop as the plain version in figure 19, this elaborately carved dressing table provides additional evidence of the maker's decorative capabilities. Courtesy of Historic Deerfield, Inc.; photography by Helga Photo Studio.

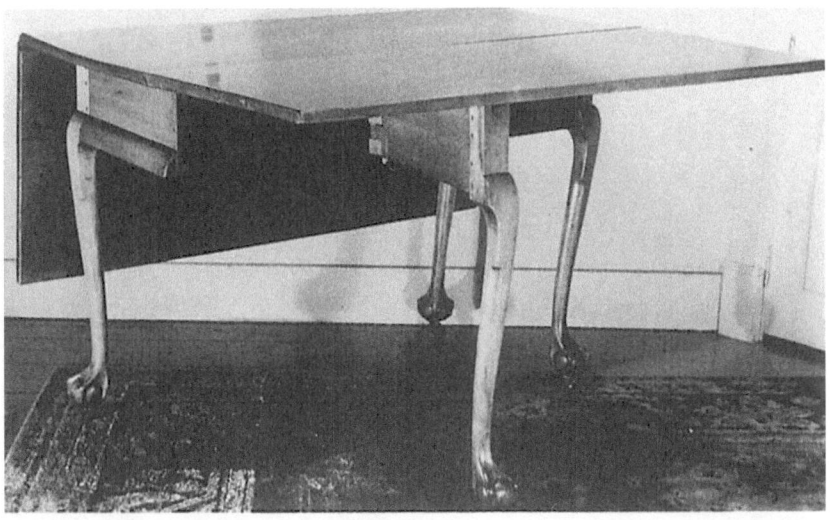

Fig. 22. Fall leaf table, Newtown, 1770–1790. Cherry and yellow poplar; measurements unavailable. The crooked legs and carved ball-and-claw feet suggest that this table was made in the same shop as figures 18–21. Such a table was used primarily for dining, but with its leaves down could be moved about the house for general use. Privately owned.

Fig. 23. Dressing table, Newtown, 1790–1810. Cherry, red oak, and white pine; H:31¾", W:32¼", D:18¼". Although distinctive constructional practices distinguish this dressing table from those in figures 19 and 21, it nevertheless retains the large size and general appearance of other Newtown examples. Yale University Art Gallery, Mabel Brady Garvan Collection.

Fig. 24. Case of drawers, Newtown, 1790–1810. Cherry and yellow poplar; H:90½″, W:41½″, D:20¼″. Even though the composition and construction of this case of drawers links it firmly to a Newtown shop, several of its decorative elements—contrasting fans, fluted pilasters in the upper section, and treatment of the plinth—resemble Woodbury features. Privately owned.

Fig. 25. Table with one drawer, Newtown, 1780–1810. Cherry and yellow poplar; H:27", W:35¼", D:24". Turned frame tables remained popular in Newtown into the early nineteenth century, but they were sometimes made more formal by the use of cherry and the addition of a drawer or two. Privately owned.

Facing page:
Fig. 26. Desk, Newtown, 1790–1810. Cherry and white pine; H:40½", W:36", D:18½". This simple desk typifies the timeless furniture produced and purchased in Newtown in the last quarter of the eighteenth century. Neither the shape of the bracket feet nor that of the brackets for the pigeonholes in the desk interior can be assigned a narrow date range of popularity or fashion. Privately owned.

Fig. 27. Desk, Newtown, 1790–1810. Cherry, yellow poplar, white pine; H:42½", W:39⅜", D:17¾". Although the maker of this desk had many recent techniques at his command, he used them to build a plain, traditional form. Privately owned; photograph courtesy of Mattatuck Museum.

forms. Stockpiling seasoned rounds and lists and the turning of quantities of posts meant that many structural details were prepared far ahead of demand and were thus relatively free from the immediate caprice of fashion. Although such production rhythms limited experimentation and fostered slow change over time, certain consumer preferences must have continued to call for and legitimize these traditional techniques. In short, workmanship of habit was causally linked with consumption by habit. As old forms remained in demand, old methods continued to be applicable.

Case Furniture and Tables

Newtown case furniture and tables, identifiable through histories of ownership and constructional details, encompassed a relatively limited number of forms. What was preferred in the 1750s remained fashionable in Newtown into the early nineteenth century. Plain chests, chests with drawers, cases of drawers, and dressing tables appeared frequently in inventories throughout the entire period of this study. Desks appeared in inventories after 1772. Most people in Newtown were satisfied with the limited number of forms and did not acquire new ones as early as did their Woodbury counterparts. The work of three related Newtown shops and several other pieces of Newtown furniture demonstrate this preference.

The products of a Newtown joiner working in the 1760s demonstrate the proficiency of the town's furnituremakers and the conservative base of their few learned traditions. The desk in figure 16 was owned by the same Beers family that owned the fiddleback in figure 12. The desk on crooked legs had limited popularity in preindustrial New England. Unlike desks with four drawers underneath the writing surface, few desks on long crooked legs have survived and most have origins in southwestern Connecticut. However, the Newtown desk manifests an entirely different structural conception than that of a contemporary example made in Fairfield. The latter is a desk on a crooked leg frame, in which the upper section was dovetailed together and set on top of a base formed by tenoning the back, sides, front rail, and skirt into the legs. Its two-part construction resembles that of a case of drawers and would have required more time to construct than the Newtown example, which was built as an integral unit, more like a dressing table. The Newtown maker tenoned the back, sides, and front rail and skirt into the extended leg posts. The desk had closer links to the joined tables and case furniture with turned legs made in the early eighteenth century than to the dovetailed carcasses of the later eighteenth century. However, these qualities do not reflect the maker's backwardness or incompetence, but may be attributed to a conscious, innovative approach to a new need based on familiar composition or to the influence of Anglo-Dutch work in the Long Island basin. The form itself, the flow of the legs, and the slight scrolls at the edge of the knees indicate an accomplished joiner aware of fashion. Yet he limited decoration to the knees, the sawn-out profiles on the skirt, and the brackets above the pigeonholes.[17]

Identical legs (except without the knee scroll) and drawer construction link the dressing table in figure 17 to the same Newtown shop. The outline of the legs and shaping of the knees and feet suggest use of the same template to cut out the legs and a consistent approach to shaping the leg blank, using a lathe to define the underside of the foot and a spoke shave, files, and gouges to shape the ankle and knees. To fit together the parts of the drawers, the joiner laid out the pins and tails in a consistent fashion and then dovetailed the yellow poplar sides to the cherry drawer front and the yellow poplar back to the sides (see fig. 5). Decorative and constructional features link the dressing table to Stratford examples from the mid eighteenth century and further demonstrate the coastal towns's influence on Newtown furniture. The plastic feeling of the undulating ribs of the small carved fan can be found on case furniture from Stratford. Like some Stratford craftsmen, the Newtown joiner nailed side drawer supports to a piece of scrap yellow poplar that had been nailed to the inside of the sideboards.[18]

Furniture made in a second Newtown shop also manifests technical proficiency and understated ornament. Typical is a flat-topped case of drawers (see fig. 18) that belonged to the Walter Johnson (1802–1889) family of Newtown's Huntingtown district.[19] The joiner limited decorative work to round feet, beading on the edge of the knees, and a simple carved fan on the lower central drawer front. He devoted considerable time and energy instead to the finish and fit of the different parts of the chest, even those interior parts that would not be visible. The dovetailed corners lack the long, deep kerf marks (usually seen on the inside front corner of a drawer) of rushed production, and the interior structural members were planed to even dimensions and smooth surfaces. The joiner even ran a smoothing plane on both sides of the backboards. Various constructional features, none of them indicative by themselves, can be found on a number of similarly chaste but well-constructed flat-topped cases of drawers (some with histories of ownership in the Newtown area) and together represent the signature of this Newtown shop.[20]

Dressing tables, whose values were generally between one-quarter and two-fifths the cost of a case of drawers, were often listed just before or just after cases of drawers in inventories. This pattern suggests that they were used in the same room or that they shared similar designs. Constructional and decorative features link the dressing table in figure 19, which descended in the Curtiss family of Newtown, with the Johnson case of drawers. It has the same drawer construction, drawer support systems, dished front skirt, and tenoning techniques. However, two minor visible differences distinguish it: the fan on the dressing table contains four additional ribs for a total of fifteen and its knees lack beaded scrolls. The joiner laid out the design of a slightly larger fan in order to alter the decoration slightly, but the odd number of ribs points out the consistency in his workmanship of habit. He eliminated the beaded knees either on his own accord or at his customer's specification, given that he possessed the techniques, tools, and stock leg patterns to produce the beaded effect. Distinctive features of this Newtown type of dressing table include its large size, particularly its height and width, and the lack of a rail above the top drawer.

Diagnostic constructional features observed in figures 18 and 19 can be found in two other pieces of furniture, one of which has an early Newtown history of ownership. The case of drawers in figure 20 was made for Hannah Grant of Newtown on the occasion of her marriage in 1769. A similar form was referred to in 1801 as a "crown case of drawers" because of its broken pediment.[21] The aesthetic similarities with furniture from many regions, competent workmanship, and amount of decorative detailing have caused great confusion about the origin of this case of drawers. Similarly carved rosettes are found on furniture from Norwich and Glastonbury, the finial design resembles examples on Woodbury and Stratford cases of drawers, and the carving on the knees suggests the influence of New York furniture.[22] The good workmanship evident in the interior of figure 20 has always been attributed to an urban origin. Furthermore, the ornamental exuberance seems greatly out of place in Newtown.

Analysis of proportions, construction, and workmanship in this piece of furniture document its origin. It was made in the same way as figure 18 and is therefore the product of the same Newtown shop. Biographical facts about Hannah Grant help to explain how such an elaborately decorated case of drawers came to be made in Newtown. Hannah was the daughter of Donald Grant, a successful Newtown storekeeper born in Scotland, and she married Stephen Mitchell of Wethersfield, a thriving community at the time. Her lack of Newtown roots, her father's status as one of the only shopkeepers in Newtown, and her Wethersfield connections may have influenced her demands for the unusual quality and quantity of decoration on this piece of furniture. Many flat-topped Newtown cases of drawers with simple fan carving in the lower section have survived, but few of the more complex crown-topped ones have been identified. The Hannah Grant example was the exception rather than the rule in Newtown, but does document the upper limits of the craftsman's skills.[23]

A dressing table with no documented history of ownership (see fig. 21) shares many decorative and structural features with the Grant case of drawers. The sharply articulated knuckles, softened fingers, and distinctly sloped ankles of the feet; the carved floral motif on the knees; and the fan's design link the dressing table to the case of drawers. The consistent workmanship of this shop is also evident in the drawer construction, double-thickness skirt, placement of pegs in tenoning, and drawer supports. Like the Curtiss dressing table, this example lacks a rail between the full-width drawer and the top of the table.

The scrolled knees, crooked legs, and claw feet in figures 20 and 21 can also be seen on several fall leaf tables found in the Newtown area (see fig. 22). The method of fastening the top to the frame of these cherry tables denotes the maker's sophisticated understanding of the properties of wood. On the underside of the top board, he cut two wedge-shaped dados, or grooves, which then slid over the end boards of the frame. The upper edges of the end boards had been cut as dovetail keys that corresponded to the dado. This housed dovetail groove permitted movement across the grain in the top board and thereby prevented the splitting that is caused by directly screwing or pinning a top to the frame.[24]

A third, related Newtown shop produced conservative case furniture that can be distinguished from figures 18–21 through subtle differences. At first glance the dressing table in figure 23, which descended in the Johnson family of Newtown, seems to be the work of the joiner who made the preceding five pieces of furniture. Its appearance closely resembles that of figures 18 and 19: its scale is larger than Massachusetts dressing tables; there is no upper rail; its similarly conceived and carved fan contains an odd number of ribs; and the knees feature beaded scrolls. Certain aspects of its carcass and drawer construction seem similar as well. Even the method of attaching the top to the frame resembles that on the table in figure 22. The joiner nailed a piece of scrap oak near the upper edge of the side between the legs, cut a dovetail key along its protruding upper edge, and cut a wedge-shaped dado on the underside of the top. He then slid the top on from the front side.[25]

However, closer examination of figure 23 reveals differences in both appearance and construction: the feet lack the same articulation along their backs; the drops on the lower edge of the skirt resemble inverted nozzles rather than acorns; the front corners of the drawer dovetails lack a half pin at the bottom; the skirt is only a single cherry board; and the joiner used a rabbeting plane instead of a panel plane along the edges of the drawer bottoms. Such changes indicate a different shop tradition, not just the drift in technique from master to apprentice within a single shop. The shop tradition also may be a slightly later one, since rabbeted drawer bottoms tend to appear around the turn of the century, but such small differences between two shops over time also provide strong evidence of the strength of local forms and traditions. That a joiner with a different set of tools and construction practices made dressing tables so close in appearance to those of another, possibly slightly earlier, shop underscores the coherence of Newtown's furniture trade and the closely intertwined performance of its different shops.[26]

Identical drawer construction, leg shapes, and drops can be seen on the case of drawers in figure 24. The profiles and construction of the moldings in particular point out the distinction between this third shop and the second one: the midmolding on the lower section of figure 24 has a long cove that pinches the width of the upper section, and the cornice molding has only a projecting quarter-round along its upper edge rather than a cyma recta and astragal detail found on the Johnson and Grant cases of drawers. The joiner who made figure 24 used a different series of molding planes. He favored a more pronounced series of fascia moldings and an extra ovolo molding along the top of cornices and substituted a flat cove for a cyma recta on the upper part of the midmolding attached to the lower section. The joiner who made figures 18 and 20 ran a cavetto, astragal, large cove, and fascia molding on one piece of cherry and nailed it to the upper edge of the carcass. He then decorated a smaller piece of cherry with a cyma recta and astragal molding and nailed this second cherry piece to the upper edge of the first. The maker of figure 24 used a two-piece cornice molding in which the molding was cut on a single thin cherry board. The joiner nailed this cherry molding to a piece of secondary wood, triangular in cross section, which had been attached to the carcass. This sort of construction can also be found on Woodbury furniture in figures 42 and 46–50. A third point of distinction in figure 24 is the full-depth dustboard below the third drawer from the top; figures 17 and 19 lacked this structural feature. Similar dustboards were found in the upper sections of two other flat-topped cases of drawers made in the same shop as figure 24.[27]

The decorative detail seen on the exterior of figure 24 also suggests Woodbury furniture's influence at the turn of the century. The mismatched shells of the upper and lower sections, four-channel fluting in the upper section, and flame-twist finials are features found on case furniture from the neighboring town, as will be shown in the next chapter. However, the joiner applied this Woodbury aesthetic to a distinctively Newtown carcass, for its interior construction firmly links it to a body of documented Newtown case furniture. Even the proportional system suggests a Newtown origin: Newtown crown cases featured broad bases and tall upper sections, while Woodbury cases were thinner with shorter upper sections. The proportions of the Newtown cases more closely resemble New York and Long Island examples, and the Woodbury cases more closely follow Boston and Massachusetts types.

The artifactual evidence of the three Newtown shops thus shows that an Anglo-Dutch furniture tradition derived from coastal Connecticut and Long Island formed the basis of the Newtown furniture trade and that the Woodbury tradition, derived from a different synthesis, began to have a more pronounced influence on Newtown ornament at the turn of the century. Certainly the mobility of joiners like Abner Judson and David Fabrique account for such accommodations of Woodbury decoration.[28]

Several other pieces of furniture possess strong histories of ownership in Newtown but have less certain connections to the three shops already discussed. Nevertheless they can be attributed to the Newtown area and provide additional insight into Newtown's furniture production and consumption. Tables with turned legs, such as the example in figure 25, were the logical table forms made by joiners working according to the craft rhythms of Newtown's mixed agriculture: legs could be turned in quantity when the lathe was set up; stretchers, sides, and top could be roughed out at the sawmill and required little finishing; and decoration consisted largely of turned elements and sawn profiles. The most common table form in Newtown probate inventories—the turned frame table—represents a timeless design, which remained popular throughout the period of this study. Owned by a descendent of the Johnson family, this particular table was an expensive version of a conservative table form. The joiner used cherry throughout, rather than maple for the legs and yellow poplar for the frame and top, and spent time cutting, assembling, and fitting a drawer. Yet many of the Newtown turned tables featured drawers, an extra detail consistent with the fastidious interior finish of other case furniture in the community.[29]

Two desks with local histories of ownership provide additional evidence of the local aesthetic. A cherry desk (see fig. 26) purchased from a family that lived in the Sandy Hook section of Newtown features the distinctive Newtown drawer construction found on figures 16 through 21 and the wide quarter-round and shallow fillet edge molding on the drawer fronts (see fig. 5) so typical of Newtown drawers. Even though the joiner possessed sufficient skill to fasten the bracket feet with half-blind dovetails, he did not use his skills fully in making this very simple desk with understated bracket feet, simple cove molding along the base, and plain interior, in which the main decorative feature is two different arch profiles above the pigeonholes. It is one of the simplest forms of desks, without any sort of carved or time-consuming decoration.

A second desk (see fig. 27), originally owned by a branch of the Beers family from the Palestine district of town, retains many aspects of older furniture types, but several structural features indicate that it can be dated to the early nineteenth century. Features such as the cusped return of the bracket foot and the serpentine curve of the pigeonhole brackets recall the fashionable elements of furniture from the third quarter of the eighteenth century. The edges of the drawer fronts reveal the use of old techniques to produce new stylish features. In the late eighteenth and early nineteenth century, some furnituremakers ceased to use molding planes along the edges of their drawer fronts, instead applying a protruding strip around the edge of each drawer to produce a cock-bead molding. On the desk in figure 27, the joiner chose not to use the old quarter-round-and-fillet molding, but he did use a molding plane to achieve a fashionable result. Along the drawer blades and the inner edges of the carcass sides, he used a molding plane to produce the appearance of cock-bead molding. Early nineteenth-century structural and decorative practices include the use of cut rather than wrought nails and an integral base molding. The combination of old forms, old motifs or approaches updated, and new conventions parallels the same sort of blend seen in figure 14 and attests to the continued strength of tradition in the Newtown joiner's trade.[30]

Compatibility and Continuity

The artifactual evidence of figures 7 through 27 confirms the conclusions drawn from the craftsmen's biographies and the analysis of probate inventories. Most of the joiners active in Newtown at the beginning of this period of study had been trained in one of several coastal Connecticut traditions. As

Robert Trent's *Hearts and Crowns* implies,[31] the furniture traditions of the various coastal communities that contributed craftsmen to Newtown were relatively compatible. When earlier craftsmen began to train local youths, they found it easy to merge these traditions. Joiners active in the last quarter of the eighteenth century assimilated one another's regulating habits and tools through local recruitment and the handing down of shops, sets of tools, and customers. Consequently, similar techniques and workmanship predominated in most Newtown shops.

Homogeneity of the shops contributed to a recognizable Newtown style. Sturdy, long-lasting turned chairs, with fashionable elements confined to the most visible areas—the backs and crest rails—characterize Newtown seating forms; traditional cases of drawers, dressing tables, desks, and chests with flat, taut facades, broken only by a single carved fan or a scrolled knee, its case furniture; and turned frame tables, its tables. Yet economical conservatism implies not a static state but rather an emphasis on slow evolution rooted in precedence. The trained, fully competent Newtown joiners viewed new fashion through a lens shaped by their training and cultural climate. They borrowed a few new details, reordered existing motifs, or used older techniques in new ways to introduce limited decorative innovation into old forms. The result was slight variation within appropriate and acceptable norms determined by past products. Although the forms were traditional and the decoration plain, Newtown furniture was not a watered-down interpretation or misunderstood copy of urban styles.[32]

In addition to documenting the roots of the local homogeneous traditions and the existence of a dominant local style, surviving Newtown furniture provides insight into the values of the community's joiners. Workmanship reveals that the joiners shared the traditional attitudes of the inwardly focused town. Many pieces of Newtown case furniture demonstrate a greater concern for time-consuming, quality workmanship and the properties of wood than do examples from more competitive urban areas of New England such as Boston. Whereas the latter tend to be elaborately decorated but shoddily built with an unspoken concern for ease and cheapness of carcass and drawer construction, the former tend to be sturdily built with techniques that accounted for the movement of wood across the grain. Newtown joiners took time to saw and pare tight-fitting dovetails. The carcass construction shown in figure 16, the drawer support systems and double skirts in figures 18–21, and the rabbeted drawer bottoms and dovetailed top of figure 23 provide evidence of the overengineered quality of Newtown case furniture. The joiners even finished off structural members that would not be visible in normal use and used secondary woods in a consistent fashion. They were not apt to utilize any scrap wood indiscriminately. If one drawer of a case piece had red oak sides, a yellow poplar back, and a yellow poplar bottom, then so did the other drawers.[33]

Customer demand and craft structure explain this labor-intensive approach to furniture construction and indifference to ostentatious decoration. As the patterns of consumption indicate, high rates of persistence in the eighteenth century meant that many Newtown families passed along furniture to the succeeding generations. Continuity and cultural cohesion ensured that these traditional forms would remain acceptable and appropriate. Newtowners put a premium on construction rather than ephemeral decoration. They wanted furniture that would last, yet not be outdated. The preference for traditional products rather than ever-changing popular ones allowed the local joiners to turn legs or rounds, saw out crooked legs or crest rails, and dress structural timbers in quantity when it was convenient. Craftsmen could then use these parts at any time. Predictable demand enabled the joiners to perfect the workmanship of habit necessary for these few forms.

The lack of external market challenges also influenced the production of traditional furniture in Newtown. The dominance of native craftsmen and their role as yeomen-joiners resulted in a lack of competition. Different conventions introduced by craftsmen trained outside the community did not challenge the dominant local traditions. Since yeoman-joiners derived much of their livelihood from their farm and could be assured of requests for some supplemental craftwork from their kin and neighbors, they did not have to rely entirely on craftwork or compete with one another.

The joiners' embedded and secure roles within Newtown society and economy made them very aware of their responsibility to their customers. They did not organize their work to distinguish themselves, increase production, or maximize profits. Instead they made furniture to provide needed material goods for their relatives and neighbors and to complement their agricultural work. As in all aspects of life in Newtown, continuity and stability guided the joiners' values and actions.

SEVEN

Workmanship of Competition: The Furniture of Woodbury

A survey of identifiable furniture from Woodbury and the study of several shops' products reveal a different pattern of material culture in Woodbury than in Newtown. Several early Woodbury joiners synthesized the same coastal traditions as their Newtown peers, but they also incorporated parts of other traditions. The presence in Woodbury of several joiners trained in the Farmington and New Haven areas contributed to this more extensive structural and decorative repertoire. Continued mobility and increased involvement in the external market around the time of the Revolution combined to expand this repertoire further. Newly arrived mature joiners from several geographically and culturally diverse regions introduced new techniques, forms, and decoration. The changing composition of the Woodbury population eased the acceptance of these new stylistic options. Since many townspeople lacked a common value system achieved through longevity or continuity in Woodbury, they were less likely to be guided by precedent and more willing to purchase different types of furniture. Greater involvement with the market provided Woodbury craftsmen with additional knowledge of technical and decorative options and Woodbury inhabitants with additional knowledge of fashion systems. The emergence of a proprietary gentry class eager to use material trappings to affirm status also created a receptive environment for the extensive use of new or elaborated forms and ornament. The qualitative differences in Woodbury furniture production after 1770 become striking through analysis of surviving examples.

Chairs and Case Furniture, 1750–1770

Painted, turned, flag-seated chairs represented the bulk of common seating forms in eighteenth-century Woodbury. Only in the nineteenth century did Windsor chairs, first found in the households of the wealthier inhabitants in the 1790s, begin to compete with these traditional black or red chairs as the favored sturdy, inexpensive turned chair. A great black chair (see fig. 28), which descended in the Minor family of Woodbury, is a good example of a mid eighteenth century turned chair rooted firmly in the banister-back chair tradition of the early eighteenth century rather than the more fashionable round-top form of the 1750s or fiddleback forms of the 1770s. However, the Woodbury chair does not resemble the Boston version of such a turned chair, which is characterized by tall, thin proportions, turned banisters between the rear posts, and complexly sawn out and carved crests. Instead the broader proportions, scooped crest rail, reeded banisters, and downward-sloping arms link the Minor chair to a broader Anglo-Dutch tradition characteristic of the New York and Long Island region. The turned vocabulary of the rear posts and configuration of the reeded back with scooped crest rail demonstrates the persistence of Milford joiners' traditions farther up the Housatonic River and thus confirms the demographic pattern of such joiners as David Miles.[1]

A New York rather than Boston orientation is also found in the second type of turned chair popular in Woodbury during the 1760s—the round-top, or York, chair. Throughout the greater New York cultural region, the York chair was a local turnerly interpretation of the early Georgian joined chair. The great round-top chair in figure 29, originally owned by the Reverend Noah Benedict of Woodbury (1737–1813), shows that the town leaders in the third quarter of the century still found a turned chair to be satisfactory, with some concession to new fashion, even for more prestigious armed great chairs. The distinguishing features of a Woodbury round-top chair—the high arch of the crest rail, wide expanse of the banister, horizontal sweeping movement of the flat arms, and large central disk between the flanking bulbous balusters on the front round—resemble the same features on examples from Stratford and further document the coastal foundations of Woodbury furnituremaking.[2]

Several Woodbury cases of drawers from the third quarter of the eighteenth century (see figs. 30–32) document additional traditions that influenced furnituremaking in Woodbury and demonstrate how these various strains were blended to form a coherent Woodbury look before the Revolution. The case of drawers, referred to as a high case of drawers in a 1768 inventory, was the most popular large storage form in Woodbury during most of the last half of the eighteenth century. Analysis of such a complex form sheds valuable light on the nature of furniture production and consumption at that time.[3]

Two Woodbury cases of drawers of this period (see figs. 30–31), linked primarily by structural and stylistic features, illustrate how one joiner's shop drew upon the conventions of several different regions to offer options within a consistent approach to design.[4] Like Newtown case furniture, these Woodbury cases of drawers share many structural and decorative features with examples made in the Stratford area. For example, the upper carved fan and the squarish knees in figures 30 and 31 resemble corresponding aspects of furniture made by Brewster Dayton (worked 1755–97) and other Stratford joiners; and the vertical orientation of the backboards and inclusion of a horizontal tie bar behind the upper tier of drawers can be found on a case of drawers made in 1784 by Eli Lewis (1738–1818) of Stratford. The square pediment on figure 31 may have been suggested by the cornice molding on a scroll-pedimented chest-on-chest made by a joiner who trained in England and then worked in Stratford during the second quarter of the eighteenth century.[5]

However, the Woodbury joiner did not depend as heavily on Stratford aesthetic or structural traditions as his Newtown counterparts. Instead his work attests to the vitality of traditions other than those of Milford and Stratford. For example, the heavy three-drawer arrangement along the upper tier of drawers in figure 30 can be seen on earlier New Haven cases of drawers and differs from the favored Stratford convention of a large central drawer flanked by a smaller drawer on each side (as seen in fig. 24). The use of two fans and of fans with concave ribs can also be found on case furniture from the greater Hartford area. The Hartford and New Haven traditions may have provided the Woodbury joiner with certain construction conventions, such as the lack of a concealed joint where the drawer blade fits into the carcass sides in the upper section, the simple single-piece midmolding, and nailed drawer supports. Newtown craftsmen, like Dayton and his Stratford contemporaries, glued vertical cherry strips along the front edges of the sides to conceal the joints of the drawer blades, glued drawer supports into grooves run in the sides, used more complex midmoldings, and limited carved fans to the lower central drawer. In comparison to his Newtown and Stratford counterparts, the Woodbury joiner was more willing to reduce time in the construction stages in order to devote additional time to decoration. By nailing in drawer supports and not concealing drawer blades, the craftsman could carve an extra fan on a case of drawers without increasing the price.[6]

Eastern Connecticut traditions may have influenced the Woodbury shop. An architectonic handling of the cornice molding and an elaborately decorated pediment, often found on case furniture from New London County, are seen on the case of drawers (see fig. 32) made in Woodbury in 1755 by Silas Butler, who trained in eastern Connecticut and worked briefly in Woodbury from 1755 to about 1760. Other aspects of the Butler example that may have influenced Woodbury aesthetics include wide midmolding around the top edge of the lower section, use of double fans (one in the upper section and one in the lower), deeply modeled concave ribs of the fan, and upwardly angled framing ribs in the fans. Similar shells can be seen on the bottom cases of figures 30 and 31 and are different than the coastal shells seen on the top sections.[7]

Although the Woodbury craftsman picked from many traditions to introduce variations into his designs, he limited these changes to a restricted area of the form or to a small decorative detail. Within the constant formal parameters of a case of drawers, the Woodbury joiner achieved visual diversity by altering the cornice and uppermost tier of drawers, the most visible part of the object. On one example (see fig. 30), he repeated the same configuration that he used on the lowermost tier, resulting in a line of three very substantial drawers that stretched full-width across the top. In the other example (see fig. 31), the same craftsman experimented and produced a more successful, vertically oriented case of drawers by emphasizing the large central drawer of the upper section with its own pediment and by flanking this drawer with single short drawers and a stepped cornice. Through all these changes, the joiner preserved the same basic proportioning system for the overall form, for the lower and upper section, and even for the full-width drawer fronts.[8]

Chairs and Tables, 1770–1800

In about 1770, production of furniture in Woodbury began to change more dramatically. Joiners started to make chairs that more closely resembled joiner's chairs than turned ones, function-specific tables, and more varied and elaborate case furniture. The chairs in figures 33 through 37 represent the full line of chairs produced during the last quarter of the eighteenth century by a single Woodbury shop, whose master worked comfortably in both the turned and the joined furniture traditions. The Woodbury fiddleback (see fig. 33) bears a general resemblance to its Newtown counterpart. Certain features, however, establish it as a Woodbury fiddleback: the lack of termini on the back posts, a convex-bowed central portion of the crest rail, and a front round with heavier, more pronounced baluster-and-ring turnings. Yet fiddlebacks like figure 33 never achieved widespread ownership in Woodbury, according to inventory references. Instead the estates indicate that the more expensive, more fashion-laden crookedback chair began to encroach upon the dominance of chairs with completely turned frames.[9]

The same Woodbury shop provided its patrons with two different versions of the crookedback chair (see figs. 34–35) that were differentiated by style rather than by cost. Figure 34 is a crookedback with a mixture of old and new fashion. Vestiges of the older turned chair tradition include the flag seat, the turned decoration on the front stiles, and the decoratively turned rounds. However, the frame was noticeably different from the fiddleback in figure 33. Sawn-out, or hewn, front and rear stiles replaced the turned posts, and carved claw feet replaced turned ball feet. Even the woods of the crookedback frame were different. The joiner used cherry rather than painted maple and ash for the crest rail, stiles, and rounds of the crookedback. For the banister and shoe rail, he continued to use yellow poplar, whose grain closely approximates cherry.

A second crookedback chair (see fig. 35) shows the evidence of even less work on the lathe. Rectangular side and rear stretchers that were tenoned and pegged into the rear legs and into the block elements of the front legs impart the look of a joiner's chair to this crookedback. Yet this chair was not necessarily a more expensive model than that shown in figure 34, which had expensive features such as a cherry frame, hewn stiles, carved feet, and decoratively turned side and rear rounds. The work evident in these features made the chair comparable in price to figure 35. The chair in that figure represents the craftsman's desire to make, or a client's to own, a more stylish chair.

Woodbury crookedback chairs such as figure 35, in which turned construction accounts only for the flag seat, the front round, and some ornamentation on the front legs, offer a sharp contrast to Newtown fiddlebacks. Whereas the Newtown craftsman who made a fiddleback emphasized the older turned chair tradition while incorporating just a bit of the new fashion, the Woodbury craftsman who made a crookedback chair emphasized the newer fashion while preserving only a vestige of the older turned tradition. Apparently, Woodbury joiners favored sawn-out frames over turned frames, a preference that may reflect both clients' demands and the technological orientation of the joiners. The limiting of turned work to the low-end chairs as well as the widespread use of sawn-and-dressed members suggest a different artisanal value system in Woodbury. Unlike their counterparts in Newtown, the Woodbury joiners did not fit craftwork in among other tasks and thus were not dependent on turning as the appropriate technology for efficiency. Woodbury craftsmen relied solely on their trade and often had to give greater weight to fashion than to traditional rhythms. Thus they sawed up stock throughout the year and offered more crookedback chairs than fiddlebacks.

The most stylish flag-seated crookedback chair made in this shop was a great chair (see fig. 36).[10] In this case the joiner totally eliminated the decorative turning on the front legs and round. To replace the visual vitality of turned decoration, the artisan employed other decorative techniques more consistent with joined construction. He incorporated a hewn front stretcher and front legs, sawed out parts of the banister to produce a pierced pattern identical to one favored in Boston, ran decorative quarter-round moldings along the outer edges of the front legs and along the upper edge of the stretchers, and shaped the upper part of the arm supports with a drawknife instead of a lathe in order to give them an octagonal cross section rather than a circular one. Yet the conceptualization of the chair form remained rooted in the turned chair tradition. The flag seat, arrangement of the stretchers, and set-back arms mounted on uprights mortised into the upper edge of the side stretchers and notched into the seat list link this chair with turned great chairs of the late eighteenth century. The Woodbury joiner thought turnerly, but executed joinerly.

Stylishness reached a climax with a fifth chair made in the same shop (see fig. 37). This seating form, referred to in the inventories as a joiner's chair or a cherry chair, contained neither turned elements nor turned arrangement of parts. Every part was hewn cherry, joined by mortises and tenons, and pegged. In this example, originally owned by the Hinman family of Southbury, the joiner not only hewed the stretchers but also used a medial stretcher running between the two side stretchers rather than a front stretcher running between the two front posts. This H-shaped bracing system was common on Boston joiner's chairs made in the last quarter of the eighteenth century and thus more appropriate for a joiner's chair than the front stretchers or rounds of turned chairs. In addition to running a molding along the edges of the front stiles and sawing out a pierced Gothic pattern in the banister, the joiner carved an incised line along the upper edge of the crest rail and along the outer edge of the rear stiles and continued the quarter-round molding along the upper outside edges of the seat rails. Most important, he made a cushion bottom to fit into rabbets cut into the inside upper edges of the seat rails.[11]

Joiner's chairs first appeared in the 1770 inventory of Timothy Hinman, but other seating forms listed only as cherry chairs were probably joiner's chairs rather than crookedback chairs, even though both types were made from cherry. This distinction is based on valuation. Crookedback chairs tended to be valued between four and six shillings each, whereas joiner's chairs commanded twice that amount. Such a variation in price can be attributed to the different sorts of seat construction. It was easier, less time consuming, and therefore less expensive to construct a flag seat than to hew seat rails, cut tenons on the rails and mortises in the stiles, glue and peg the joints, and then construct a joined seat frame and upholster it. Imported upholstery materials such as webbing, sackcloth, and worsted cover fabrics also increased the price of a joiner's chair. Such distinctions in the values of cherry chairs remain applicable as the term *cherry chair* gave way to *dining chair* in the early nineteenth century. Dining chairs appraised between four and six shillings apiece were more likely flag-seated crookedback chairs, and chairs appraised at double that value were more likely cherry joiner's chairs with cushion bottoms.[12]

The exclusive use of cherry and a completely joined frame make the joiner's chair in figure 37 one of the most cosmopolitan seating forms in Woodbury, but it still retained close visual ties with the slightly less expensive and less stylish crookedback chairs and with even the less common fiddleback of the same shop. Use of a single crest rail pattern facilitated the joiner's work. He did not need to lay out each crest rail freehand, and he could entrust the tracing of the pattern and the cutting out of the part to an apprentice or less-skilled member of his shop. As a result, his work became efficient without losing quality or consistency. Patterns for hewn legs and for three different sorts of banisters—a solid banister, a pierced interlaced scroll, and a pierced Gothic pattern—also link the more stylish products of this particular shop. Just as these patterns assisted in the production process, so they played a major role in the purchasing process. Affluent Woodbury patrons were better able to purchase matching sets of seating furniture to furnish the various social spaces of their homes. The familiar legs and crest rail of the joiner's chair also made that form less imposing or made the crookedback seem more fashionable, depending upon the customer's perspective.

Another chair form rare in Newtown but made and owned in Woodbury was the Windsor chair. The first reference to a Windsor chair in Woodbury inventories occurred in the 1784 estate of Thomas Tousey, who owned "2 green Windsor chairs 16/." Windsors appeared frequently in inventories after 1795 and became the predominant middle-value, inexpensive chair in all estates after 1805. They were appraised at approximately four shillings apiece, the price of a fiddleback. Although most Windsors were painted green, others were painted black, white, or yellow. The continued use of the generic term *black chair* precluded any conclusions that there were black-painted Windsors in Woodbury, but black was a popular color for Windsors in all other parts of New England. White Windsors, which first appeared in 1807, were colored rather than unpainted chairs. References to specific types of Windsors remained infrequent and identified only "green fan chairs," beginning in 1804, and "armed chairs green," as early as 1803.[13]

The bow-back Windsor (see fig. 38), stamped on the underside of the seat with the initials "I.M." for Josiah Minor (1789–1820), was probably made by Nicholas Jebine of Woodbury (worked 1794–1819), a New Haven–trained cabinetmaker, who settled in Woodbury by 1794.[14] The Minor example displays a combination of several different regional Windsor chairmaking characteristics. Its swelled spindles are usually associated with Windsors made in eastern Connecticut or by craftsmen trained there. But the Minor bow-back has many other attributes atypical of eastern Connecticut work, including the incised line that delimits the spindle area of the seat, tenoning of the legs through the seat, shape of the turnings, and decorative molding along the face of the bow. The tapered column, crisp urn, and large-bellied baluster of each leg resemble New York examples, and the triple-bead molding on the bow is seen most frequently on Windsors from the Connecticut River Valley.[15] The blending of features from eastern Connecticut, New York, and the Connecticut River Valley reflects Jebine's training in New Haven. Because that growing commercial center had ties to all three regions, Jebine would have been exposed to craftsmen or furniture from those areas or to craftsmen who had been trained in those traditions.

The armed high-back Windsor (see fig. 39), formerly owned in the Munson family of Southbury, has a base similar to the one used for the bow-back, but substituted a new back-support system. This was a popular Windsor type for the Woodbury region: the Masonic Lodge in Waterbury, Harmony

Lodge 42, purchased similar chairs in the late 1790s, and the Reverend Joseph Bellamy of Bethlehem, the renowned New Divinity leader, owned a writing-arm version. Patronage by these members of the region's leadership attests to the high status of the Windsor chair and the prestige of this particular Woodbury shop.[16]

The Woodbury furniture illustrated in figures 40 and 41 are some of the various function-specific cherry tables that inventories first listed in the 1790s. Earlier estates tended to list multifunctional tables, whose price indicates that most featured turned frames and were made of maple, yellow poplar, and white pine that had been painted. By the end of the century, increasing numbers of Woodbury inventories listed specialized forms made from woods with decorative grains, especially stands, tea tables, and fall leaf tables of cherry. Stands with a turned central pedestal supported by three legs dovetailed into it became the favored surface for candlesticks and other artificial-lighting devices, while tea tables with large tilting tops were designed to display the silver and ceramic equipage for tea drinking and other genteel pursuits. A single Woodbury shop made a number of such forms, including the large stand and tea table in figure 40. On the tea table the turned vocabulary of the pedestal and use of the box (the "birdcage" mechanism that revolved on the central shaft and held the pintels on the underside of the top, thereby allowing the top to rotate and tilt up) reveal the influence of New York tea tables and suggest that the maker or his clients were familiar with the fashionable tables of that city and their uses in polite society. The change to the elaborated, specialized forms seen in figure 40 and a specific language to describe them shows the significant new attention Woodbury's leaders devoted to the increasing number of domestic comforts and social rituals.[17]

Cherry fall leaf tables (or tables with hinged leafs) were first listed in the 1793 inventory of Sherman Hinman and appeared frequently and regularly in the inventories of the next fifteen years. References to fall leaf tables became less common in the teens, when the term *dining table* gained favor. All dining tables were not necessarily fall leaf tables, but the newer functional term apparently subsumed the older descriptive one.[18] The cherry fall leaf table in figure 41, whose straight or Marlborough legs reflect stylish features that became fashionable in urban centers in the 1770s, exemplifies the most common type that has survived and, with the tables in figure 40, illustrates the ability of Woodbury joiners to keep up with current fashion and client demand for such forms. The legs' simplicity is somewhat deceiving and needs to be understood in terms of fashion rather than technique.

Although such legs were relatively easy to make in comparison to the crooked legs seen on the Newtown table in figure 22, the latter actually represent an older style. The Newtown joiner relied on the template he used for case furniture legs to make the more traditional elaborate crooked leg for fall leaf tables, but his Woodbury counterpart followed the latest trends of the 1770s to make a simple leg that he then embellished with fluting, a decorative feature popular in late eighteenth-century Woodbury (see figs. 46, 51–52). Such legs linked his products more with the current work of shops in New York City or Newport, Rhode Island, than with the past work of local shops.[19]

Two Cosmopolitan Shops

Woodbury case furniture built before 1780 was characterized by the retention of old-fashioned forms, with a limited amount of decorative variety derived from the traditions in which the town's joiners were trained. After the Revolution, the emergence of a fashion-conscious gentry class of proprietors and the continued influx of mature joiners, especially from urban areas such as New Haven, greatly altered the furnituremaking trade in Woodbury. Although a few earlier structural and decorative conventions persisted, locally made furniture became increasingly diverse in form and decoration. The work of two identifiable Woodbury shops from that period documents the proliferation of different forms and the competitive mixing and matching of decoration. The great variety of forms suggests that these joiners were trained in a cosmopolitan or similar environment where they gained experience in or exposure to a number of different traditions. The masters of these shops derived decorative details from many different regions and from one another, but each continued to use this decoration on forms distinctive to his shop.

For the Hurlbut family of Woodbury, one Woodbury shop made a case of drawers (see fig. 42). At first glance, this conservative form resembles the Newtown examples in figures 18 and 24, especially the latter. The shape of the legs, the scrolled knees, lower fan, two-piece midmolding, vertical strips along the front edges of the upper sides to cover the joints for the drawer blades, and use of a wedge-shaped piece of tulip inside the single-piece cherry cornice molding recall similar features on figure 24. These similarities may be attributed to the training of several Newtown joiners in Woodbury during the late eighteenth century. Craftsmen such as Abner

Judson and Timothy Jordan may have retained certain constructional conventions when they returned to Newtown but altered their decoration in accordance with their Newtown clientele.

However, several important aesthetic and technical features distinguish the Woodbury case of drawers in figure 42 from its Newtown relatives, including layout of the fan, edge moldings on the drawer fronts, drawer construction, and orientation of the backboards.[20] Most revealingly, the Woodbury example displays a different standard of workmanship. Unlike the well-finished surfaces and tight joints of Newtown case furniture, figure 42 demonstrates a greater concern for cost-efficient production. The joiner did not completely finish the backboards with a smoothing plane. The long, deep kerf marks on the inside corner of the drawer fronts indicate that the joiner cut out his dovetails in the fastest way possible. By cutting with his dovetail saw more, he used his chisel less to shape and trim the pins. An emphasis on sawing rather than paring saved time but did not produce as clean or as tight a joint. Additional evidence of technical shortcuts can be seen on the central drawer supports. Rather than dovetail them to the back of the drawer blade or skirt, the joiner simply bevel-tenoned them. Other time-saving conventions include nailing drawer supports to the sides and use of an unfinished upper rail in the lower section. The joiner left the rear edge and underside of this slab-cut board in an unsmoothed state. Similar features appear on all the furniture made in this shop. On many of the shop's products, one can even find bark left on the inside edges of rough slab-cut boards used for rails or drawer blades.

A desk owned in the Stiles family of Southbury (see fig. 43) is another conservative form made in the same shop. Identical drawer construction, drawer side and back dimensions, and drawer front moldings link this desk to the case of drawers in figure 42.[21] Features of this desk found on other work of the shop also include the distinctive carved feet, bulbous rounded knees with a delicate scroll on the knee, and a framed base structure (rather than carved feet tenoned into the bottom board or bracket feet and corner blocks attached to the corners of the bottom boards). For this desk, the joiner tenoned thin skirt boards into the legs, sat the carcass on top of this frame, and fastened it with nails driven from the underside of the frame. He then pinned the base molding to the upper edge of the protruding frame. In designing this desk, the craftsman focused his decorative effort on the desk interior, running a coved molding along the front of the upper tier of drawers and a reeded facade along the document drawers flanking the central drawer. The great number of examples from Woodbury with this type of interior suggests that the craftsmen must have planed long boards with this cove molding, cutting them up as needed, and used a special scratch plane to produce the reeding.[22]

A chest of drawers (see fig. 44) made in the same Woodbury shop demonstrates an indebtedness to local ornamental features and more distant regional constructional traditions. The squarish central toe and two flanking thinner toes are identical to the carved feet of the desk in figure 43, both echoing the carved feet executed in Stratford by Brewster Dayton and his English-trained master. Such carved feet, often called Spanish feet by antique collectors, are frequently viewed as old-fashioned, *retardataire* features on a piece of furniture made after the Revolution. However, as in Stratford, the use of such a foot was not a restricted act based on limited knowledge of fashion or technique, but rather the deliberate choice of a decorative foot associated with the English Georgian style and produced with less-intricate carving than a ball-and-claw foot. While the layout and carving of the latter could be very labor intensive, the joiner making a carved foot like that on figure 44 relied on a template to derive the basic shape of the leg and foot, then used a spokeshave or drawknife, file, and veining gouge to articulate an animated foot in less than half the time it took to make a ball-and-claw foot.[23] The rope-twist turnings of the quarter-columns in the front corners of figure 44 were another common form of decoration found on case furniture made in western Connecticut. The design and workmanship of the rope-twist columns on this Woodbury chest of drawers bear close resemblance to those on a slightly earlier chest-on-chest from the Glastonbury area and on later examples from Kent and Canaan.[24]

In figure 44, these locally popular decorative details were grafted onto a form whose construction linked it to more distant regions, particularly Hartford and New London Counties. The method of securing the top to the carcass resembles that used in furniture from those two areas. A joiner fastened the sides to the top with half-blind dovetails and then pinned a mitred cornice molding along the front and sides to conceal this joint. The competent workmanship and delicacy of the molding suggest that the craftsman was trained in a sophisticated shop, where he had many opportunities to observe and perfect these techniques. The execution of the refined rope-twist quarter-columns reflects the joiner's familiarity with making and fitting quarter-columns and provides additional evidence that he received skilled training, perhaps in an urban area, before moving to Woodbury. The competent resolution of this complex technical problem

Fig. 28. Great black chair, Woodbury, 1750–1770. Maple, yellow poplar, ash; measurements unavailable. In the third quarter of the eighteenth century, painted turned chairs remained the most popular seating furniture in Woodbury. This great chair closely resembles Milford prototypes and is firmly rooted in the Anglo-Dutch tradition of the Long Island Basin. Privately owned.

Fig. 29. Great round-top chair, Woodbury, 1750–1770. Maple, yellow poplar, ash; OH:42¼", SH:15⅞", SW:22½", SD:15". In the middle of the eighteenth century, a great round-top chair was a fashionable seating form in Woodbury in spite of its turned frame. The Reverend Noah Benedict, one of the town's more prominent citizens, owned this example. Courtesy of the First Congregational Church, Woodbury.

Fig. 30. Case of drawers, Woodbury, 1760–1780. Cherry, red oak, white pine, and yellow poplar; H:80", W:39⅝", D:19⅝". Although its general proportions, squarish knees, and blocky legs link this case of drawers to examples made in Stratford and neighboring coastal communities on Long Island Sound, its mismatched carved fans and construction features reveal ties to the Connecticut River Valley. Collection of New Haven Colony Historical Society.

Fig. 31. Case of drawers, Woodbury, 1760–1780. Cherry, yellow poplar, and white pine; H:80½″, W:40″, D:19⅜″. The square pediment, perhaps derived from the cornice molding treatment seen in figure 32 or that on a Stratford example, reveals the joiner's ingenuity in developing a more architectonic vertical thrust to the case of drawers. This example was originally owned in the Sherman family. Privately owned; photograph courtesy of Mattatuck Museum.

Fig. 32. Case of drawers, signed by Silas Butler, Woodbury, 1755. Cherry and white pine; H:86", W:40", D:20". One of only two signed examples of furniture made in Woodbury, this case of drawers illustrates the leg shape, skirt profile, fan carving, and midmoldings of the Connecticut River Valley and eastern Connecticut. Butler was from Lebanon, in the eastern part of Connecticut. Wadsworth Atheneum, Hartford, the Evelyn Bonan Starrs Trust Fund and the gift of Henry and Walter Keney and the American Decorative Arts Purchase Fund; photograph by Joseph Szaszfai.

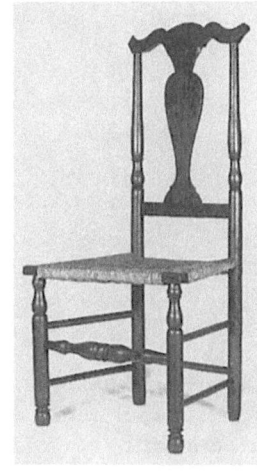

Fig. 33. Fiddleback chair, Woodbury, 1770–1790. Maple, yellow poplar, ash; OH:42⅛", SH:17", SW:20½", SD:14". Although over several decades Newtown joiners made many fiddlebacks, their Woodbury counterparts made very few. The heavier turnings of the front round, softness of the turned elements, lack of termini at the top of the back posts, and convex-bowed central portion of the crest rail distinguish this Woodbury example from Newtown examples such as figures 10–12. Collection of New Haven Colony Historical Society.

Fig. 34. Crookedback chair, Woodbury, 1780–1800. Cherry, yellow poplar, ash; OH:40¼", SH:17", SW:20¼", SD:13½" (feet have been cut down). This Woodbury chair seems to resemble the Newtown example in figure 15 (both even have two side rounds), but the use of cherry for the frame and rounds, more pronounced ogee profile of the back posts, more extensive shaping of the back sides of the rear posts, decorative molding on the lower edge of the shoe rail, and more up-to-date triple-bowed crest rail make the Woodbury chair a more stylish example. Privately owned; photograph courtesy of Mattatuck Museum.

Fig. 35. Crookedback chair, Woodbury, 1780–1800. Cherry, yellow poplar, ash; OH:41½", SH:17⅞", SW:20⅛", SD:13¼". The hewn, or sawn-out, stretchers on this example identify it as a more joinerly crookedback than that in figure 34. Privately owned; photograph courtesy of Mattatuck Museum.

Fig. 36. Great crookedback chair, Woodbury, 1780–1800. Cherry, yellow poplar, ash; OH:39", SW:23", SD:19". The basic form of this great chair is a turned great chair, but the straight legs with molded edges, sawn-out stretchers, pierced banister, and triple-bowed crest rail make this a very fashionable Woodbury crookedback. Privately owned.

Fig. 37. Joiner's chair, Woodbury, 1780–1800. Cherry and yellow poplar; OH:38", SH:16¾", SW:19⅞", SD:15⅝". This chair belongs to one of several sets of Woodbury joiner's chairs that have survived. The degree of finish evident in the molding along the edges of the crest rail and back posts and in the molding along the edge of the front legs and seat rails, the number of mortise and tenon joints, the intricate piercing of the banister, and the cost of upholstery materials make this chair the most expensive model offered by the shop that made the chairs in figures 33–37. Privately owned; photograph courtesy of Mattatuck Museum.

Fig. 38. Bow-back Windsor chair, attributed to Nicholas Jebine, Woodbury, 1795–1810. Maple, yellow poplar, and ash; OH:35½″, SH:15″, SW:15⅜″, SD:17¼″. The turned vocabulary of the legs and rounds of this Windsor and of the one in figure 39 resemble that found on New Haven examples. Nicholas Jebine, who made chairs for the Minor family, was trained in New Haven. Privately owned; photograph courtesy of Mattatuck Museum.

Fig. 39. Armed high-back Windsor chair, Woodbury, 1790–1810. Maple, white pine, and red oak; OH:36¼″, SH:16⅜″, SW:16¼″, SD:16 9/16″. This Woodbury Windsor descended in the Munson family. Yale University Art Gallery, Mabel Brady Garvan Collection.

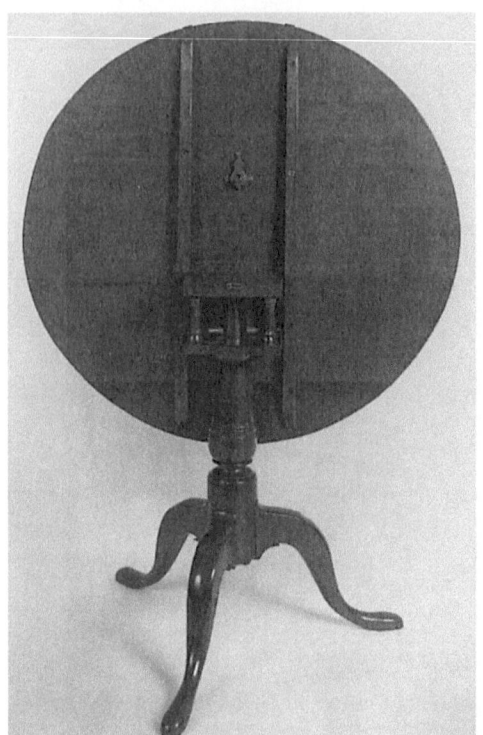 

Fig. 40. Tea table (*left*), Woodbury, 1790–1810. Cherry; H:27″, D(top):33″. Battens are replacements. Stand (*right*), Woodbury, 1780–1800. Cherry and yellow poplar; H:27″, D(top):21⅞″. Several other stands and tea tables that descended in Woodbury families have similar legs, pillars, and, on the tea tables only, columnar spindles in the box that supports the tilting table surface. Such features suggest that the maker was familiar with New York City examples and may have received some training there or in a shop with New York ties. Privately owned; photographs courtesy of Chipstone Foundation (tea table) and of Mattatuck Museum (stand).

Fig. 41. Fall leaf table, Woodbury, 1780–1800. Cherry, red oak, and yellow poplar; H:28″, L:53¾″, W(closed):18½″, W(one leaf up):36″, W(both leaves up):53½″. Many Woodbury fall leaf tables survive; all of them feature straight fluted legs, the latest fashion for New York and Newport tables of the period. Privately owned; photograph courtesy of Mattatuck Museum.

Fig. 42. Case of drawers, Woodbury, 1770–1800. Cherry and yellow poplar; H:79¼″, W:39½″, D:19¾″. Cases of drawers with long crooked legs, a dressing table configuration of drawers in the lower section (a small full-width drawer above a line of three small drawers), and a fairly short upper section were common throughout southwestern Connecticut. This particular case of drawers from the Hurlbut family is the only surviving example of such a form made in the Woodbury shop the works of which are illustrated in figures 42–50. Privately owned.

Fig. 43. Desk, Woodbury, 1770–1800. Cherry, yellow poplar, and red oak; H:41¾", W:37⅞", D:22⅞". This desk's writing interior was a stock design for the Woodbury shop that produced it. Of the various feet offered by the shop, the carved foot shown here was the most popular for chests of drawers and desks. Either Woodbury patrons preferred such feet for substantial forms or the joiners favored them, because these feet, in comparison to ball-and-claw feet, provided the most decorative effect for the least amount of work. Photograph courtesy of Mattatuck Museum.

Fig. 44. Chest of drawers, Woodbury, 1770–1800. Cherry, red oak, yellow poplar, and white pine; H:33¼", W:34⅜", D:20½". The carved feet and scrolled bulbous knees link the chest of drawers to the desk in figure 43 and to many other pieces of Woodbury case furniture. The intricate handling of the rope-twist quarter-columns and use of a cornice molding to conceal a blind-dovetailed joint suggest the sophisticated training of the shop's master. Such workmanship further reinforces the notion that the carved feet were used intentionally by the maker. Privately owned; photograph courtesy of Mattatuck Museum.

Fig. 45. Bureau, Woodbury, 1790–1800. Cherry and yellow poplar; H:37", W:44", D:18¾". The Woodbury shop that produced the chest of drawers in figure 44 revealed its flexibility and ability to follow fashion changes by making this plain bureau. Privately owned.

Fig. 46. Crown case of drawers, Woodbury, 1770–1800. Cherry, red oak, yellow poplar, and white pine; H:90″, W:44″, D:22¾″. The crown top, fluted pilasters, carved fans, and carved ball-and-claw feet made this case of drawers an expensive piece of furniture in the late eighteenth century. Its basic form and many of its decorative features have close ties with work from the Norwich-Colchester region of eastern Connecticut. Ball-and-claw feet were the most common feet on large case furniture; only a few examples with simple pad feet have survived. Collection of Colonial Williamsburg Foundation.

Fig. 47. Case of drawers, Woodbury, 1770–1800. Cherry, yellow poplar, red oak, and white pine; H:82″, W:42⅞″, D:21¼″. Even the flat-top versions of the preferred Woodbury case of drawers form—characterized by mid-length crooked legs and two deep drawers in the lower section—featured elaborate ornament and must have served as powerful social props. Consistent use of ball-and-claw feet is also unusual and indicates the availability of good carvers, the shop's ability to set up efficient production of the feet, and consistent demand for the period's most complicated foot design. Photograph courtesy of Mattatuck Museum.

Fig. 48. Desk-and-bookcase, Woodbury, 1770–1800. Cherry, yellow poplar, and red oak; measurements unavailable. The distinctive Woodbury desk interior, bulbous knees, and carved feet are readily apparent. The fall front on the desk features an inlaid mariner's compass, and the panels set into the door frames in the upper section are fielded, or chamfered, along their edges. Both of these decorative conventions had been fashionable in the second quarter of the century. Privately owned.

Fig. 49. Desk-and-bookcase, Woodbury, 1778. Cherry, yellow poplar, white pine, and red oak; H:83⅝", W:39¼", D:22". Many of the same features on figure 48 are found here, especially the shape of the dividers in the upper section and the desk interior, but the joiner has updated certain other aspects. He substituted flush panels for fielded panels, used inlay to compose neoclassical motifs rather than traditional motifs like the compass, and offered bracket feet rather than carved feet. Privately owned; photograph courtesy of Mattatuck Museum.

Fig. 50. Chest-on-chest, Woodbury, 1780–1800. Cherry, yellow poplar, and red oak; H:82½″, W:40¾″, D:19¾″. As in figure 49, the joiner substituted inlaid decoration for modeled, or carved, decoration, chevron inlay instead of carved rope-twist moldings just under the cornice molding, interlaced stringing instead of fluted pilasters along the front edges of the carcass, and stringing and cock beading along the edges of drawer fronts instead of thumbnail moldings. Privately owned.

Fig. 51. Crown case of drawers, Woodbury, 1780–1800. Cherry and yellow poplar; H:91", W:43⅞", D:20". Wooden pulls are replacements. Although this case of drawers seems decoratively linked to the work of the shop that made figures 42–50, its composition displays a very different tradition, one based more in Philadelphia than in Boston or Newport. Constructional differences also distinguish this example from the previous group. Privately owned.

Fig. 52. Desk-and-bookcase, Woodbury, 1780–1800. Cherry, yellow poplar, and white pine; H:84″, W:38″, D:20¾″. A Pennsylvania basis of this Woodbury shop's traditions is clear in this form of a desk-and-bookcase and contrasts with the examples in figures 48 and 49. Privately owned.

resulted from specific skills learned and refined during apprenticeship. It is unlikely that it represents a mature craftsman's experimentation with new features.[25] The Woodbury joiner's use of a framed base to support a chest of drawers also links figure 44 to case furniture traditions in New London and Hartford Counties. To relieve the monotony of the skirt, the joiner added a special decorative touch along the front by sawing out a central drop, a motif also seen on chests of drawers from Norwich, Connecticut, and on cases of drawers from Salem, Massachusetts.[26]

At the end of the century this Woodbury shop offered a second type of chest of drawers, one more likely to be referred to as a bureau (see fig. 45). The thin, outward-flaring bracket feet, simple cove base molding, applied cock-bead drawer edging, neoclassical brasses, and slightly overhanging plain-edged top all link this example to the bureaus characteristic of the Federal style. The joiner secured the top in a different manner than in the previous example: he blind-dovetailed three thin, horizontal members to the sides and then ran screws through these boards to secure the top. Nevertheless he relied on other familiar structural conventions: the carcass sits on a three-piece frame whose edges are run with cove molding, the dimensions of the drawer stock are consistent with other work from the shop, and the joiner chalked half circles on the inside surfaces of the drawer backs.[27]

From surviving evidence we have determined that the case of drawers in figure 42 was not the most common large storage form produced in this particular shop; rather, the most common form was a case of drawers with ball-and-claw feet, mid-length crooked legs, and two deep drawers in the lower section. Many examples have survived and manifest a variety of options: crown top or flat top; fluted pilasters, quarter-columns, or plain edges on the upper section; various skirt profiles on the lower section; and a wide assortment of carved decoration. The most exuberant example of this type (probably also called a case of drawers since Woodbury inventories before 1825 did not distinguish between cases of drawers and chests-on-chests) was owned by a member of the Stiles family (see fig. 46).[28] Several characteristics link this piece of furniture with pieces shown in figures 42–44: the bulbous knees with scrolls, which are slightly longer versions of those in figures 43 and 44; the fastening of drawer supports and drawer blades; layout and execution of the carved fan; the cornice molding construction; and the deep, unfinished upper rail in the lower section.[29]

On this particular case of drawers (fig. 46), the joiner used decorative ornamentation from a variety of regional traditions. The stop-fluted pilasters, the uppermost drawer's resemblance to a fielded panel, and the full-depth cornice molding on the inside of its crown echo characteristics of Rhode Island and New London County furniture. Stop-fluted pilasters with carved half-shell termination and a distinctively carved drawer-front fan link this case of drawers even more specifically with furniture from the Colchester-Norwich area of New London County. Structural evidence provides additional documentation of a connection with that part of eastern Connecticut. Several chests of drawers from the Colchester-Norwich area have the same medium-length crooked legs and tall, carved claw feet with very rounded balls. A case of drawers with these feet and a deep drawer in its lower section has been attributed to the same area.[30] Such structural and stylistic evidence suggests that the master of this particular Woodbury shop trained in the Norwich-Colchester area or in an area that sent mature joiners to both Norwich-Colchester and Woodbury.[31] A flat-top version of the same form (see fig. 47) illustrates some of the other decorative options offered by this shop: a different skirt profile, unadorned lower section, elimination of carved fans, addition of fluted quarter-columns on the front corners of the upper section, and use of rope-twist quarter-round molding at the base of the cornice.[32]

Widespread use of such varied decoration distinguishes these two cases of drawers and others made in the same shop from the Newtown case of drawers in figure 18. The Newtown joiner could draw on many of the same decorative traditions as his Woodbury counterparts but very rarely was encouraged to do so by his customers. Newtown inhabitants preferred to have a very limited amount of decoration and the same conservative forms. The environment in Woodbury encouraged joiners to alter their decoration continually and to offer multiple variations of the same basic forms. The cases of drawers made in this one shop document the competitive atmosphere.

The effect of competitive performance can also be seen in two different types of desk-and-bookcases offered by the same Woodbury shop for aspiring genteel customers. The carved feet, scrolled bulbous knees, mortise-and-tenoned base frame, desk interior, and four-channel fluted pilasters surmounted by carved rosettes identify figure 48 as an example of this shop's desk-and-bookcase form.[33] While the carved feet and fielded panels in the upper section bestow this example with a somewhat conservative look more typical of the first half of the century, in figure 49 (which has traditionally been identified as a dowry present for Sarah Curtiss, who married Joel Hinman in 1778) the bracket feet and reliance on inlaid neoclassical decoration seem to indicate a different hand at work in a later style.

However, the desk interior and the shape of the vertical compartment dividers in the upper section match the corresponding features in figure 48, and the base construction relates to that on the bureau in figure 45. The drawer construction, drawer support systems, and drawer edge moldings provide corroborative structural proof of its shop of origin. The base and splayed bracket feet—the third type of foot made in this Woodbury shop—constitute the most up-to-date structural elements of this desk-and-bookcase.[34]

In figure 49, the inlaid decoration on the upper section and on the exterior of the fall-front writing surface represented the latest decorative fashion. The string inlay seen on the pilasters was used commonly throughout America to provide accents or to create contrasting geometric shapes. The Woodbury joiner also strung together two-tone ovals to form a large oval on each door of the upper section and a swag on the fall front. Such pattern inlay was most commonly used in Providence furniture after the Revolution. The string inlay and berry pictorial inlay at each corner of the fall front reveals more distant connections. Although it is usually associated with the Chester County, Pennsylvania, region, it is hard to pinpoint exactly the direct influences on the Woodbury joiner because string and pictorial inlays more often were shared by several furniture production centers than were indigenous to certain regions. The inlaid decoration on figure 49 provides little help in the positive identification of the maker's origins, but it does manifest the sophistication of his decoration, his ties with inlay producers, and the customer's progressive taste.[35]

The same shop also made the chest-on-chest in figure 50, whose base construction and foot profile duplicate those same features on figure 49. Originally owned by Newton and Ruth Pearce Tuttle of Southbury, who were married in 1786, this chest-on-chest demonstrates several new conventions and provides additional evidence of the joiner's competence and creativity. The type of chevron inlay that runs horizontally between the cornice molding and upper drawer often can be found on furniture made in Hartford, Providence, or the Connecticut River Valley in the late eighteenth century; yet the Woodbury joiner used it in a different way. Instead of using it to outline doors or drawers or to create geometric patterns on bookcase doors, the Woodbury craftsman used a single line of the chevron inlay, as he had used the quarter-round rope-twist molding on figure 47, to provide some horizontality to the piece and to balance the vertical mass. Such distinctions suggest that the Woodbury joiner did not train in the same tradition; rather, he must have purchased his string and pattern inlays from the same sources as his Hartford, Providence, and Connecticut River Valley counterparts.

A second distinguishing feature of this chest-on-chest is the decoration of the drawer front edges. Rather than use a molding plane to run a quarter-round-and-fillet molding along the edge, the joiner applied a cock-bead molding around the edges of the drawer fronts, as he had on the bureau in figure 45. This technique was favored in urban shops during the late eighteenth and early nineteenth centuries. In short, figure 50 documents the Woodbury joiner's ability to produce another large storage form in a fashionable style with fashionable decoration.[36]

Compilation of all the artifactual evidence in figures 42–50 suggests that the master of that shop was trained in a sophisticated shop that had extremely strong ties with the Norwich-Colchester furnituremaking traditions and slightly weaker connections with the Hartford area traditions. When this craftsman moved to Woodbury, he took advantage of the open craft structure. He satisfied requests for plain or familiarly decorated furniture (figs. 42–43); grafted elements of the local decorative vocabulary onto his own forms (figs. 44, 48); and introduced totally distinctive forms with distinctive ornament (figs. 45–47, 49–50). His products also demonstrate a diverse assortment of options in regard to legs, feet, carved ornament, or inlaid decoration. Variations were not limited to a few forms, a restricted area of each form, or small decorative detail. Some of the fashionable decorative elements were soon embraced by Woodbury inhabitants eager to increase their ties with the world of fashion. Motifs like carved plinths, fluting, and quarter-columns then became part of the local style as competing craftsmen sought to appeal to Woodbury's developing sense of fashion.

A second cosmopolitan joiner in Woodbury used some of the same decorative motifs but executed them in his own manner on his own forms. A case of drawers (see fig. 51) made for Anna Curtiss Sherman of Southbury (1771–1847) shares several features with figure 49: full-depth cornice molding on the inside of the crown, scroll base for the central finial, stop-fluted pilasters on the upper section, and central profile of the skirt. In spite of these decorative parallels, figure 51 was made in a different shop. Differences in drawer dovetailing, molding profiles and construction, securing of drawer supports, orientation of backboards, and layout of decoration suggest the work of another joiner.[37] Compositionally, the case of drawers in figure 50 also reveals a different hand at work. In proportions it more closely resembles examples from the Philadelphia area, whereas the joiner who made figure 42 used proportions more typical of Boston-influenced New England examples. Philadelphia cases of drawers are characterized by deep skirts, wide and heavy lower sections, and vertically oriented upper sections. New England examples, on the other hand, tend to have long legs, lighter lower sections, and shorter upper sections. Within the basic Philadelphia form, the Woodbury craftsman used a drawer arrangement and knee shape more typical of New England.[38]

The use of similar ornamentation on different forms and the increased specialization within the woodworking trades in Woodbury raise the possibility that a specialized carver worked for several different shops in Woodbury. However, inconsistencies between carved features on figures 46 and 51 discredit such a hypothesis. Although some of the decoration looks similar, there are noticeable differences in the execution of this ornament, especially in the fans and the feet.[39] The small claw feet on figure 46 feature very full and round balls and thin, well-articulated claws. Such a combination endows the feet with a feeling of height. In contrast, the larger, flatter balls and more broadly articulated talons on the feet of figure 51 are more similar to Philadelphia work. If a specialized carver worked in both of these shops, one would expect to see some consistency in all aspects of the carved elements rather than in just a few general ones. Consistent layout and execution is of critical importance to the carving of fans and claw feet.[40] A more credible explanation for similar decoration on furniture from two different Woodbury shops is the joiners' willingness to borrow motifs from competing shops and to graft them onto their own forms.

The competent workmanship of the craftsman who made figure 51 can also be found on a desk-and-bookcase (see fig. 52), originally owned by Nathaniel Smith of Woodbury (1762–1822). The case of drawers and the desk-and-bookcase feature similar drawer construction; large, somewhat flattened balls in the ball-and-claw feet; distinctly fluted talons; and stop-fluted pilasters. The possibility that the maker trained in a Philadelphia tradition is suggested by the specific form of desk-and-bookcase, which substitutes doored shelves for drawers below the writing surface, as well as by the reeded decoration of the prospect and its flanking columns. These features are usually associated with examples from the Philadelphia area and suggest that the Woodbury craftsman hailed from Philadelphia or trained with a master from that area.[41] Benjamin Burnham of Colchester and Eliphalet Chapin of East Windsor are the best-known Philadelphia-trained furnituremakers who worked in Connecticut, but there likely were others. Ephraim Munson, who lived with his family in Pennsylvania for eight years, was one Woodbury joiner who may have been familiar with Philadelphia furniture.[42]

The desk-and-bookcase in figure 52 was a very fashionable and decorative form, but structurally it was easier to produce than the desk-and-bookcases in figures 48 and 49. The substitution of doored shelves for a series of drawers saved significant time and energy. Similarly the deletion of a sliding candle tray below the bookcase reduced the amount of time needed to make the object. A set of four drawers required a great deal of sawing and dovetailing, and the joiner had to be sure that the drawers and the trays fit and slid properly in the carcass. The second Woodbury shop also simplified the structure of the desk-and-bookcase by eliminating any sort of a framed base. Instead the craftsman merely tenoned the claw feet through the bottom board and fastened the upper posts of the feet to the sides with screws. These conventions demonstrate that economic considerations guided some of the structural choices of Woodbury joiners. The availability of many technical and decorative options and the demand for reasonably priced, fashionable furniture reinforced each other.

Diversity and Competition

Like their Newtown counterparts, the illustrated examples of Woodbury furniture shed invaluable light upon the joiner's world. Most obviously the variety of forms and decoration reflect the origins of the community's craftsmen. Woodbury joiners hailed from more varied and more geographically diverse regions than their Newtown contemporaries. Furthermore, these artisans arrived in Woodbury as fully trained, mature craftsmen. Whereas compatible traditions and subsequent local recruitment nurtured a selectively conservative furniture tradition in Newtown, more diverse traditions and constant in-migration fostered a more progressive tradition in Woodbury. The new arrivals brought new techniques and tools to Woodbury and therefore prevented the establishment of a single appropriate solution or method for each act of furniture construction. For example, joiners affixed feet to large case furniture in a variety of ways: they could tenon the front skirt, sideboards, and backboards into the legs (see figs. 46–47); build a frame on which the carcass sat (see figs. 43–44); build up a series of corner blocks behind bracket feet (see figs. 45, 49–50); or tenon the tops of the feet through the bottom boards and secure the upper tenons to the carcass sides (see fig. 52). Different tools also permitted technical variety. The master of the shop that made the furniture illustrated in figures 42–50 introduced a small skew rabbet plane and the knowledge of when and how to use it. In Woodbury, the joiners constantly had choices.[43]

The availability of a far greater range of techniques and decoration pressured existing conventions in Woodbury and contributed to a very dynamic regional style. The changing composition of the craftsmen's customers and stronger ties to the external market in the last quarter of the century added to this dynamism. A continued influx of people with slightly different tastes and expectations greatly influenced the joiners, who could not anticipate what forms or decorative motifs would be popular. As a result they constantly had to be prepared to alter their techniques to meet their clients' demands and to distinguish their own shops from those of their competition. Imported household goods and greater awareness of fashion's short swings of popularity also forced the local joiner to be more competitive. Precedence and consumption by habit played a smaller role in Woodbury than in Newtown. Instead, nascent self-conscious gentility and a concern with social distinction led to competitive consumption, in which the Woodbury furnituremakers were forced to participate because of their economic reliance on their craft and the highly visible role of the objects they created in sustaining domestic refinement. Woodbury crookedback and joiner's chairs seemed to follow Boston fashion; the stands, tea tables, and fall leaf tables seemed more closely linked to New York fashion; and the case furniture of one shop resembled work from New London County, while that of another featured ties to Pennsylvania. The Woodbury craftsmen's need and ability to select forms and decoration from a variety of local and distant sources bespeaks a state of cultural flux in Woodbury.[44]

Competition among the joiners affected not only their design and decoration but also their workmanship. Furniture made in Woodbury at the end of the eighteenth century manifests a concern for quick, easy construction and extensive, time-consuming decoration. Such values were the opposite of those in Newtown. Woodbury joiners did not spend the extra time to dress completely the interior structural timbers. Backboards, drawer bottoms, drawer blades, and even the inside surfaces of stretchers in crookedback or joiner's chairs were often left rough or with evidence of saw marks. The craftsmen also relied on dovetail saws rather than chisels to cut dovetails. Many of the resulting joints have subsequently lost their tightness. In other joints, the joiners replaced dovetails with lap joints, which were more easily made. Central drawer supports were simply bevel-tenoned and nailed to the front skirt. Inconsistent use of available wood, often of inferior grade, characterizes much of Woodbury furniture made in the last quarter of the eighteenth century. The joiner used yellow poplar, red oak, or white pine in no apparent pattern. The evidence reveals that the Woodbury craftsmen favored the easiest and least time-consuming method, in which they relied more on saws and nails than planes and chisels.

Woodbury joiners devoted a greater proportion of time to visible and ornamental features. Each shop offered a great variety of forms, legs, banisters, and other parts. Much of the furniture featured widespread use of expensive decoration like fluted pilasters, fluted or rope-twist quarter-columns, carving in several locations, and inlay. This concentration on the most stylistically sensitive areas resulted from the unpredictable demands of customers who became increasingly fashion-conscious and consumption-oriented at the end of the eighteenth century. Unlike their Newtown peers, the Woodbury joiners competed with one another for customers and sought to maximize profits. They therefore organized their shops to make the most ostentatious or fashionable furniture for the least price.

CONCLUSION

The Response to Market Capitalism

Account books, inventories, census materials, and surviving furniture from Newtown and Woodbury point out that it is impossible to depict a single, typical rural economy in New England during the early national period. The social economy of each community blended older structures and values with newer ones derived from the rapidly changing world around it. These changes included a network of banks, corporations, federal tariffs, and state aid which provided new business opportunities; erosion of community social order and deference in the face of heightened social stratification and factional politics; and implementation of a national system of communication, finance, and rule over the existing local and regional systems.[1] The two towns of this study present very different responses to the economic opportunities of the period and reveal the dynamic possibilities of the term *social economy*. The contrasts provide surprising and invaluable evidence about the origins and paces of consumerism and industrialization and emphasize the need to examine consumption and production together.

Newtown remained an inwardly focused community during the last several decades of the eighteenth century. A stable cultural core and common values of permanence gave Newtown furnituremakers a valuable role, embedded in both the economic structure and the value system of their community. Part-time craftwork, which was spread among many inhabitants, fit in well with the rhythms of mixed agriculture, prevented the glut of artisans that might have accompanied full-time activity, and provided products and services that further bound the inhabitants together in a community characterized by economic and social balance.

From 1760 until 1810, native traditionalists dominated the Newtown furnituremaking trade. Born and trained in town, these joiners internalized the older furniture traditions and the communal values and thus continued to produce traditional, well-constructed furniture that featured little decoration. Locally invested joiners, who determined the number and types of furniture, may have played a major role in determining the relative correlation of mean and median values of furniture ownership in Newtown inventories after 1780 (see chart 3). The nature and result of their production both checked and was checked by their fit in the town's network of reciprocal relationships. The balance of local production and local demand resulted in little incentive for structural changes, such as water power, specialized production, wider markets, or even drastically different forms. In short, consumption of furniture as well as of many other locally produced household goods was directly linked to the mixed agricultural economy's web of goods and service exchanges.

After 1800, the inhabitants of Newtown faced increasing opportunities to participate in the external market as nearby towns such as Danbury and Bridgeport became centers of production and trade. Danbury developed as a major center of the hatmaking trade and also supported extensive shoe and saddlery trades; Bridgeport began to eclipse Stratford as a major port town with several small industries. The Newtown community, however, responded to the external market in a manner different from that of its Woodbury neighbors. Rather than forsake its balanced agricultural economy to orient production for external demands, the community drew on existing structures and habits to test the external market. Farmers started to send meat and dairy products to Bridgeport, but interest in commercial agriculture proved short-lived in Newtown. By the 1820s involvement in the agricultural market had waned—numbers and frequencies of cows, horses, and sheep declined, the average number of oxen and pigs per estate also dropped, and the quantity of packed meat and dairy products returned to their 1790s level.

Traditional agricultural practices, which emphasized the town's economy, can be found in the continuation of the common sheep flock as late as the 1830s. Communal cooperation and concern with efficiency were important reasons for this continued custom, but they were not the only reasons. Farmers valued sheep manure as a fertilizer and therefore viewed the flock as a mobile, communal fertilizing service that made calls at everyone's farm. In this manner, old forms flourished in new ways.[2]

Rather than concentrate on meat and dairy products, the many yeomen-artisans of Newtown intensified their traditional artisanal skills to participate in the external market. The town's strong craft roots were combined with its numerous water-powered sites and improved access to the urban and coastal markets to shape its economy in the 1810s. The first few water-powered industries included Lemuel Nichols's clothier's shop, A. & G. Bradley's furniture manufactory, and John Hubbell's blacksmith shop, which featured a trip hammer. These establishments show how Newtown built on the past to adapt to changing economic patterns. In each case, the craftsmen applied water power and new equipment to their shops without changing their product, the size of their workforce, or their personal involvement. The Bradleys produced plank-seated kitchen and Windsor chairs, seating forms closely linked to the turned chairs produced easily by Newtown joiners and favored by Newtown inhabitants during the last quarter of the eighteenth century.

Even the capital used to expand shops had local roots. When Newtown joiners began to mortgage their property in the first decade of the nineteenth century, they turned to relatives, fellow craftsmen, or neighbors. For example, brothers-in-law Rivirius Prindle and Abner Judson often worked together and mortgaged their properties to various relatives and neighbors from 1802 through 1806, and Charles Glover mortgaged his property, including his wheelwright shop, to fellow woodworker Clement Fairchild in 1828. The shift to water power and reliance on local credit were locally based structural changes that reveal a greater intensification of the craft as the craftsmen responded to increasing demand for similar furniture among a wide regional audience.[3]

In the 1810s, Newtown also attracted entrepreneurial craftsmen who established shops in town to supply high-end goods. These new joiners did not succumb to the external market, but rather took it on full tilt. Arcillus Hamlin, born in Sharon, Connecticut, established a partnership with William Chappell of Danbury, and then settled in Newtown by 1816. He offered mahogany, cherry, and veneered furniture in the latest neoclassical styles. In 1829, William G. Smith, a new arrival, advertised that he manufactured and sold "an elegant assortment of furniture, not inferior to any in this country." His stock included "Sofas, Secretaries, Book Cases, Lockers, Bureaus, Pillar and Claw Tables, Mahogany and Cherry Tea Tables . . . together with Venetian Window Blinds made to order as cheap as can be bought in New York."[4]

The intensification of craftwork can be seen in the rising mean value of artisanal equipment in Newtown inventories, which grew noticeably from £2.5 to £10.3 in the first quarter of the nineteenth century (see table 11). The importance of artisanal work can also be seen in the population schedules of the 1820 census, the first census to gather statistics on general occupational categories. In Newtown, 1 percent of the males older than eighteen were engaged in commerce; 31 percent, in manufacturing; and 68 percent, in agriculture.[5] Only in the 1840s did Newtown's water-powered industry undergo additional changes, which included new products like fire hoses and buttons; new organizational structures like absentee ownership and incorporation; and new forms of work dependent on larger, wage-earning workforces.[6]

Woodbury's economy flourished in the last quarter of the eighteenth century. The proprietary system and early settlement had provided the town with a mobile population and service functions more typical of urban, commercial, or distribution centers. Such features had a very strong effect on the supply of and demand for furniture. They provided a constant replenishment of craftsmen and techniques from a variety of regions. Many craftsmen arrived in Woodbury eager to establish themselves and found it necessary to focus on craftwork as a full-time activity. The resulting environment was a competitive one. Mobility also brought to Woodbury people with diverse attitudes who needed to establish new households. The turnover of craftsmen and customers prevented the dominance of any shop traditions, welcomed alternative practices, and supported new syntheses of traditions. In addition, a social structure in which several proprietors and shopkeepers began to direct the town's involvement in the external market also provided the aspiring joiners with an eager, fashion-conscious clientele. This local elite sought to solidify their social position by the ownership, use, and display of household goods. Through distribution systems that were growing increasingly efficient, they purchased quantities of British goods, while at the same time commissioning local joiners to build large, expensive furniture with distinctive types of elaboration or decoration, seating upholstered with imported materials, and function-specific furniture, which was used in conjunction with imported ceramics, glassware, and textiles to cultivate gentility and sociability.[7]

Routinized ties between Woodbury and the external market in Derby, New Haven, and New York contributed to a flourishing, dynamic furniture tradition in the last quarter of the eighteenth century. But the demand-driven consumerism also contained the seeds for the demise of the local furnituremaker. Shopkeepers such as Jabez Bacon and Shadrach Osborn imported textiles, pewter, looking glasses, ceramics, glassware, and many household items from New York dry goods merchants and retailers and greatly increased the "material literacy" of their neighbors. Farmers relying on the local shopkeepers began to enjoy multiple choices in various categories of goods, acquired a more discerning eye for quality and variety, and developed a more elaborate descriptive vocabulary for furnishings. In Woodbury, shopkeepers and local elite engaged in commercial husbandry became the catalysts for increased consumerism and the accumulation of household possessions. Initially they commissioned "imported" local joiners to make their furniture, but they soon found their commercial contacts able to supply various types of fashionable furniture from the external marketplace at good prices.[8]

The emphasis on commercial husbandry and the encroachment of nonlocal custom or batch craft production can be seen in the community's craft structure. The intensive processing work involved in large-scale meat and dairy production conflicted with the customary seasons of craftwork and forced yeomen-craftsmen to choose either husbandry or craftwork. Cooperage, wagonmaking, hauling, and services ancillary to commercial animal husbandry provided jobs for those without sufficient land to raise cows or pigs. For other woodworkers, the lines of demarcation between tasks became firmer. House joinery, in which work had to take place on location, experienced significant growth during this period of rebuilding and developed its own organization based on loosely affiliated regional teams of woodworkers. A large number of handyman carpenters were needed to maintain the structures and equipment of animal husbandry. As a result many local youths found it easier to enter this lower end of the woodworking spectrum. Furniture production in the first two decades of the nineteenth century was limited to a few shops, which had to compete with the high-end fashionable furniture and low-end painted work offered by urban cabinetmakers and furniture warehouses.[9]

Increased marketing of manufactured goods threatened the monopolies of local crafts not directly connected to commercial animal husbandry. The probate inventories show that the mean value of artisanal equipment in Woodbury remained fairly constant at around £3 during the first quarter of the century (see table 11). Size of operation allowed large house joinery and clothier shops to survive, but many other craftsmen experienced a degradation of tasks and were forced to do lower-end work. Joiners who sought to maintain or increase their shop often found themselves mortgaging their properties to people from outside the community or seeking a partnership with someone not in the trade. William H. Peabody mortgaged his shop and property to the New York merchant Robert Bowne, from whom Shadrach Osborn often purchased goods, and to the Plymouth merchant Victory

Tomlinson; Daniel and William Hurlbut formed a partnership and shared a shop with the wheelwright William Deforrest, but still found it necessary to take on Charles Peck as a partner. Joiners often were restricted to performing handyman work, producing simple furniture, or making parts for furniture to be assembled and decorated in the city.[10]

Population schedules from the 1820 census further document the emphasis on commercial agriculture in Woodbury. Two percent of the males older than eighteen were engaged in commerce; 22 percent, in manufacturing; and 76 percent, in agriculture. In comparison to Newtown, Woodbury had a few more commercial enterprises and many more people involved in animal husbandry. Nathaniel Perry, who gathered the census information for the Woodbury area, stated that "there was no manufacturing establishment of any considerable importance within my division except one for making Hats owned by Hamilton & Brush & situated in the town of Woodbury." Employing about fifteen men, the establishment had an annual market value of $25,000, about ten times greater than that of the larger Connecticut furniture firms such as James English of New Haven, Samuel Hawley of Ridgefield, or Amos D. Allen of Windham. Instead, as Perry's notes indicate, there was widespread production of butter and cheese; craftwork included several shops making shoes and boots, several blacksmiths, four wagonmakers, two coopers, two tanners, and a nailmaker, bridlemaker, saddler, harness maker, and tinware producer.[11]

Differing experiences in Newtown and Woodbury cannot be attributed to a "transportation revolution" or a "technological revolution." Comparison of two period maps of Connecticut, a 1777 map by Bernard Romans (see fig. 1) and an 1811 federal map (fig. 53), reveal many of the same roads crisscrossing the towns, connecting them to Bridgeport, Derby, New Haven, and to each other. The basic routes were well established by the time of the Revolution; what differed was how each community used these roads. As early as 1783 Woodbury's economic leaders enjoyed improved routes to Derby that facilitated market access, while the Bridgeport Turnpike did not connect Newtown to Bridgeport and New Milford until 1809. In spite of this late link to a port, craftsmen such as Joel Booth had already intensified their work in the early 1790s. Like other furnituremakers in the area, Booth did not rely on new technology, but simply made more efficient use of his neighbors and fellow craftsmen. The scale of shops and the types of tools remained relatively uniform into the 1820s. Neither turnpikes nor technology were the primary agents of change.[12]

What is more striking is that the towns reflect different sorts of consum-

196 *Making Furniture in Preindustrial America*

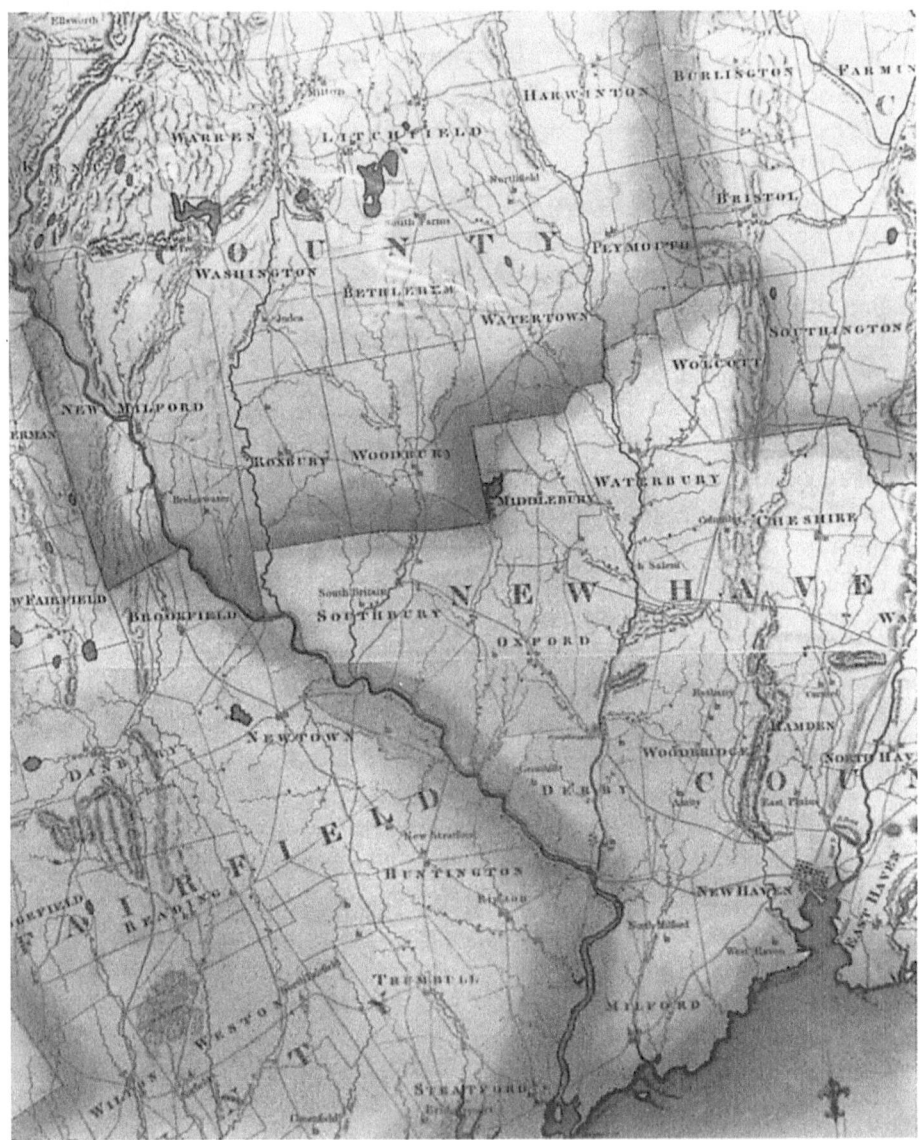

Fig. 53. Detail of map of Connecticut, 1811. RG 77; US 20 in the National Archives, Washington, D.C.

erism. Beginning in the 1760s, Woodbury became increasingly involved in the North Atlantic commercial world. Local shopkeepers fostered involvement in the external market by gathering agricultural surpluses and helping determine farmers' choices and by selling English imports or New York products shipped by that port's merchants. Shopkeepers held a powerful position in Woodbury but possessed less power outside the community. The market for foodstuffs—affected by the quantity and cost of goods from other production centers, cost of shipping, natural disasters, and so on—determined their potential profits, and the New York suppliers determined the types of goods for sale in Woodbury. The Woodbury merchant and proprietary farmer thus held a rather tenuous economic position, but one firmly linked to the world of fashion. They therefore used the power of household goods to maintain their perceived social status.[13]

Newtown, on the other hand, had a few shopkeepers such as Donald Grant or Elijah Nichols, but consumption was much less stratified. Newtowners did not depend on the external economic network to the same extent and thus did not have to rely on their furniture and household possessions as symbols of social status. Instead, furniture in Newtown seemed to serve as familial or communal reification. In the early nineteenth century, intensification of decentralized production for a primarily local market was an integral part of the consumerism in town. Different social economies produced different responses to the changes of the early national period.

The examples of Woodbury and Newtown, when linked to other scholarship on material culture and social history, refine our knowledge of the pace and nature of rural capitalism in Connecticut. Gentry towns like Woodbury, as well as others such as Windsor or Colchester, tended to develop an economy based on commercial agriculture and a stratified social structure with a fashion-conscious elite. Related by marriage or business dealings, these elite patrons necessitated that joiners develop certain specialties and freely combine different traditions to offer individualized variations. In each community the highly competitive custom furniture market was dominated by one or two shops that drew ideas from a wide variety of shop traditions. In Windsor, Timothy Loomis III catered to a growing number of storekeepers and market-oriented farmers. He specialized in elaborate architectural paneling and case furniture. The production of turned chairs in the Spencer family shops of Hartford and joined chairs in the Chapin shop of East Windsor allowed Loomis to develop a niche. For the elite of New London County, the shop of Benjamin Burnham and Samuel Loomis in

Colchester provided a great variety of elaborate case furniture, while Jabez Huntington concentrated on joiner's chairs.[14]

Beginning in the 1810s, changes in agricultural practices and increasing competition from regions such as Pennsylvania and western New York began to drive many Connecticut farmers from their farms. The demise of New England agriculture at this time undermined the precarious position of the shopkeepers and proprietors who had risen to prominence in the last quarter of the eighteenth century. As the patronage of these local gentries waned, urban merchants and manufacturers gained the upper hand and local craftsmen found themselves with limited opportunities. Shipments of furniture from urban centers encroached on the high end of the market, and local craftsmen found themselves limited to only some of the local work. In fact many of these gentry towns prospered for a brief moment after the Revolution and then began to stagnate in the 1810s.[15]

In Woodbury only a few furnituremakers such as Charles Booth, who began to make parts to be assembled and sold in New York chairmakers' shops, were able to adapt. Yet these craftsmen, working for a broad New York–based market, lost control of their craft. In Woodbury most manufacturing in the 1820s was geared toward supplying parts for large-scale manufacturing elsewhere: Burton Canfield expanded an old mill site in South Britain to create a three-story structure that produced carpet yarns for weavers in New Haven; Harvey Bronson owned a ropeworks that made clock cords for the great clockmakers of Waterbury and Bristol; and Charles Booth also made hatblocks for hatmakers and reels and spools for spinning operations. A few small shops remained along the Eight Mile Brook in South Britain, but most Woodbury firms supplied parts for an emerging mass production section of manufacturers. Such bulk production was characterized by a fixed product with a uniform look achieved through routinized production and widespread marketing. The evidence from Woodbury and other gentry towns delivers a surprising insight: a hierarchical community structure with entrepreneurial leaders and an early bent toward capitalist production was not necessarily the most fertile ground for industrial capitalism.[16]

In yeoman towns like Newtown, the lack of fashion competition and a decentralized shop system resulted in a broad-based furnituremaking tradition that retained its vitality through the commercial expansion of the 1810s and 1820s. Joiners were accustomed to being an integral part of their town's economy and therefore took part in its transformation. Throughout the hill towns of the Connecticut River Valley and Worcester County, Massachusetts, artisans in yeoman towns parlayed their knowledge and skills.[17] Craftsmen in these communities participated in industrial capitalism in a number of ways: as developers of batch production shops, as owners of small shops catering to local custom or specialty markets, as machinists who made equipment for new manufactories, or as outworkers. Newtown craftsmen retained flexible technologies and progressive skills that allowed them to adapt and change their products while maintaining the importance of quality. As economic historians have only recently argued, the rise of mass production and new technology was closely intertwined with the vitality of the small shop staffed by broadly skilled artisans.[18]

Furnituremaking, like other Connecticut crafts of the late colonial and early national period, was not simply an economic task, a means to supplement an income or increase self-sufficiency. Rather it was an essential part of the region's mixed agricultural economy from the earliest settlements. Making chests, chairs, and tables was one facet of the agricultural cycle and fit in neatly with the responsibilities of animal and grain husbandry. Ultimately, furnituremaking—like animal husbandry, dairy production, grain cultivation, or special crops such as onions—was just one option in the formerly multifaceted New England economy that was developed more intensely during the early national period. The increased consumer activity of the period played an important role in this intensification, but its impact was uneven. In Woodbury, increased reliance on commercial agriculture and interest in imports led first to a dynamic centralization of furnituremaking and then to its demise as firms from outside the community encroached on the local market. In Newtown, a social economy based on broad artisanal activity responded favorably to increased interest in household goods and the expansion of markets. Thus, in terms of local realities, Americans encountered the market revolution unevenly and adjusted to it in fits and starts.

APPENDIX A

Biographies of Newtown Joiners, 1760–1820

Information for the capsule biographies in appendixes A and B comes principally from the following sources, with additional sources cited at the end of each entry:

BC   Barbour Collection of Connecticut Births, Marriages, and Deaths
CCR   Connecticut church records
CR   Connecticut census records
DPR   Danbury probate court records
HC   Hale Collection of Connecticut Headstone Inscriptions and Newspaper Death Notices
NLR   Newtown land records
NPR   Newtown probate court records
NTL   Newtown tax lists
SLR   Southbury land records
STL   Southbury tax lists
WLR   Woodbury land records
WPR   Woodbury probate court records
WTL   Woodbury tax lists

Thomas Allin (?–1778)   Allin, who first appeared on the Newtown tax list in 1775, owned tools more suited for a housewright, but the inclusion of jointers and cherry boards and planks imply that he also made furniture. At his death he owed Ebenezer Booth IV £4.12.0.

SOURCES: DPR; NTL.

John Beardslee (1772–1820)   Beardslee, son of Jonathan and Huldah Beardslee, was born and died in Newtown. His inventory reflects a combination of farming and joiner's work. He owned a full set of farming tools and agricultural processing equipment, which included a loom. On his twenty-acre farm he grew corn, rye, and potatoes and kept three cows, twelve sheep, and two pigs. Listed as a joiner on the 1798 assessment list, Beardslee owned a joiner's shop and half a sawmill. The variety of his tools and products indicates that he performed the work of a joiner, wheelwright, and cooper. His estate included cherry and butternut boards, jointing planes, a lathe and turning chisels, many augers, broad chisels, cart and wagon spokes, cart hubs, heading, staves, and window sashes. On several occasions, Beardslee provided coffins as payment of his town taxes.

SOURCES: NPR; NTL; HC; CCR; CR; Newtown Town Book, 1802–12 (Newtown Town Hall).

Ezekiel Bennett (worked 1790–1801)   Bennett, born and trained in nearby Weston, moved to Newtown in 1795 and was listed as a joiner in the 1796 assessment list. In 1801 he sold his eight-and-a-half-acre home lot and dwelling house back to William H. Fairchild. Fairchild then sold it to Isaac Scudder, another Newtown joiner.

SOURCES: NTL; NLR; CR.

Ebenezer Booth IV (1743–1790)   See chapter 3.

Joel Booth (1769–1794)   See chapter 3.

John Boyer (?–1801)   Possibly from Maryland, Boyer had settled in Newtown by 1785, when he was taxed £20.2.6 and assessed £5 for a faculty. His wife was Mehitable Briscoe, daughter of James Briscoe. On the 1796 tax list, Boyer was listed as a house joiner. For the next two years the assessments listed him only as a joiner. However, his inventory indicates that he was more of a shop joiner, whose two-bench shop made chairs in quantity. Appraised by Alanson Northrop, the inventory included:

Cherry plank 9/   Pine Ditto 4/   Bass Ditto 4/   Whightwood bord £1.16.0   Cherry Bords £1.12.0   Remnants of bords and Timber 18/   Chare Bows 3/   Ditto Rounds 4/6   1 Brass wimble & bits £1.0.6   1 Ditto Iron 2/6   1 Carpenders Saw 15/   2 hand Saws £1   1 fine saw 10/   1 Ditto 5/   1 Ditto 4/6   1 Ditto 4/   2 Drawing Knives 3/6   1 Iron Square 1/6   1 froe 1/6   1 Broadax 8/   1 Small Ditto 3/   3 hammers 3/6   2 broad Carpenders Chizels 9^d 1 Narrow Do 10^d 3 pr Compersis 1/   2 pr nipers & 9 gimblets 2/3   4 Duck Bill Chizels 2/   4 Broad Do 1/10   4 inch Ditto 1/4   6 narrow Ditto

1/8   2 Compas Saws 1/9   4 gogus 2/   7 fiels 2/   1 rasp 1/3   1 Taper Auger 1/6   3 Jointers 12/   1 Jack Plaine 5/   1 tooth Plain 2/6   1 Dubble Iron tooth plain 3/   1 Single Iron Ditto 2/   1 round Ditto 1/   1 Short Jinter 2/   1 wood Square 1/   3 Duble plaines 3/   2 Irons for plaines 1/   1 Box of gouges 1/6   2 Jack plaines No Irons 5/   1 Small Do 2/   1 round Plaine and Iron 1/9   6 Augers 12/6   4 turning Chizels 4/   7 Ditto gouges 3/6   1 Turning Lathe & C. £2.2.0   1 Glue Pot 1/6   1 Box of paints 6/   Brushes Cups Boles & C. 2/   2 Plows 9/   1 paniel plain 4/6   1 Iron Skillet 1/6   5 rounds 11/6   3 hollows 6/6   3 Noesings 10/   2 astickels 4/10   1 pare of Match planes 5/9   3 Small Ogees 8/   3 Back Ogees 11/9   3 rabet plaines 4/9   1 pare Table match Do 6/6   6 Beads 10/   1 quarter round 2/   1 Sash plaine 2/   1 Dubble Ditto 6/   1 Duftaile Do 2/   one Do 1/   3 Molding Plaines no Irons 4/   1 grinding Stone & C. 4/   1 rule 6^d 1 ax 1/3   Shop with two benches £7

The shop and tools were distributed to his son John.

SOURCES: DPR; NTL; NLR; Rev. Charles Boyer, *American Boyers* (Allentown, Penn.: H. Ray Haas, 1940).

Abijah Bradley (1790–1881)   Bradley's father, Abijah Bradley Sr., bought land on the Halfway River that had a gristmill, sawmill, and two houses in 1801. The property was deeded to his son George Bradley by 1816, when the property was mortgaged. Abijah Jr. moved to Newtown to join his brother in 1818. Together they formed A. & G. Bradley & Co., manufacturers of furniture. In 1821 they bought sixty-six acres of woodland with the help of a mortgage by Philo Bassett of Derby. Throughout the 1820s the Bradleys also bought adjacent lands to ensure water rights. Their shop produced Windsor chairs, bedsteads, kitchen chairs, and coffins.

SOURCES: NLR; NTL; Account Book of Caleb Baldwin of Newtown, 1800–1846 (Yale University Library, New Haven).

Eliphalet B. Bradley (1777–1849)   Eliphalet Bradley, who does not appear to be related to Abijah or George Bradley, was baptized at the Fairfield/Greenfield church and had moved to Newtown by 1797. He was assessed for a faculty beginning in 1804, although the only reference to his woodworking career involves a coffin he made for the town in 1811.

SOURCES: NTL; CCR; BC; Newtown Town Book, 1802–12.

George Bradley (1796–1875)   Brother of Abijah (see entry for Abijah Bradley above).

Nathaniel Brisco (worked 1820)   A Nathaniel Brisco made and carved a coffin for the town in 1820. The Newtown tax lists from the first two decades of the nineteenth century show a Nathaniel Brisco and a Nathaniel Brisco Jr.; it has proved impossible to distinguish which was the coffin maker.

SOURCES: NTL; CR.

James Briscoe Jr. (?–1765)   Briscoe, referred to as a carpenter in the account book of Thomas Tousey, was first assessed a town tax in 1740. From 1749 to 1753 his work for Tousey included making a plow, working on a mill wheel, working on a door and a frame, making window casements, procuring timber, and making a "Candlestick Stand" valued at 8/. The lack of real estate in Briscoe's inventory suggests that he had already deeded the homestead that he inherited from his father in 1753. Although never assessed for his own shop, Briscoe did make chests, tables, and chairs in addition to performing carpentry work. The contents of his shop well document his furniture production.

1 Joyners bentch 6/   broad ax 8/   1 small ax 3/   1 Large Joynter 4/   1 small Do 2/   1 fore plain 1/3   Smothe Do 1/3   1 upright Ditto 1/3   one Round facd Plain 10^d one Tooth Ditto 1/3   1 pannel Do 1/6   1 Scue Rabbit Do 9^d one plow 3/   1 Cornish 1/6   1 Bedmold 1/6   a Topmolding plain 2/   1 Back OG 3/   one pair of Round Table plains 4/   1 ¾ OG 1/6   1 bede 1/6   1 halving Plain 1/6   1 Short Rabbiting Do 10^d 1 Small nosing Do 1/6   1 ¼ Round 1/   1 2 inch Do 2/   one 1 inch Do 1/6   one ½ inch Do 1/6   one Sash Halving Do 1/6   1 Sash beed Stock 1/3   one Small Hollow Stock 8^d one Spring Stock 1/6   2 Joyners Rules 2/6   one Steal Plate Saw 11/   one Iron Do 4/   1 fine Do 10/   1 Lock Do 1/   one Slitting Ditto 6/   one Intch augre 1/6   one ½ Intch Do 1/3   1 Large File 1/   two Small Dos 3^d 1 Rasp 1/3   1 broad Chissel 1/   1 Intch & ¼ firmer Do 8^d 1 Intch Do 7^d one ¾ Do 6^d 1 ½ Intch Do 5^d 1 ½ Intch Do 4^d 1 ¼ Do 4^d Small Do 3^d 1 table Chissel 6^d 1 winscoot Do 6^d small Do 4^d 1 ¼ Gouge 6^d one hammer 1/6   1 pr of pinchers 8^d 3 Turning Chizels 1/6   1 Turning Gouge 6^d two Lathe Straps 10^d 1 Lathe 1/6   1 Large brest Wimble & bit 1/6   1 Long bitt Do 1/3   1 Do 8^d 1 ½ Inch bit 6^d 1 Large Gimblet 4^d Spike Do 6^d 4 Small Dos 6^d 1 hold fast 2/   two Gages 6^d two Squares 8^d 1 Sail whetstone 4^d 1 Plain Iron 4^d 48 wood Scrues 2/   14 brass buttons 2/6   Sundry things in a baskit 1/3   17 brass Handles 5/8   1 Led glue pott 1/   100 brads 5^d Some 4^d Nails 3^d 1 Jugg & oyl 1/   1 pr Table Hinges 2/8   1 Jugg & varnish 1/6   two sets of Drawer Locks 6/   2 lb of Glue 3/4   2 ¾ lb of Chalk 4^d 1 ½ lb of Spanish Brown 3^d 1 lb Red oaker 3^d 1 pint of Lam black 4^d two set of Table Legs 2/   some birch sawed Timber 10/   60 foot of birch board 2/   10 foot of birch plank 8^d 320 foot of Cherry boards 48/   a Stack of

Shaggy whitewood boards 1/ 68 foot Cherry boards 12/6 35 foot of birch boards 1/2 a Quantity of flags 5/

SOURCES: DPR; NTL; NLR; Account Book of Thomas Tousey of Newtown, 1716–1761 (Newtown Historical Society); J. J. St. Mark, "Newtown Joyners: Alexander Bryan and James Briscoe, Jr.," *Antiques and the Arts Weekly* (Oct. 6, 1978): 1, 64–69.

Joseph Bristol (1713–1791)   Born in New Haven, Bristol moved to Newtown, where he married Jemima Foot. His estate listed a shop, half a sawmill, and some old woodworking tools.

SOURCES: DPR; Warren Bristol, *Bristol Genealogy* (Bristol Family Association, Inc., 1967).

Alexander Bryan (1709–1760)   Born in Milford and probably trained there, Bryan had settled in Newtown by 1739, when his name appeared on the earliest surviving tax list. Several bits of evidence suggest that Bryan was the leading joiner in town during the middle of the eighteenth century. The tax list of 1743 recorded an assessment of £20 "for making Chairs, Tables, & c." Such a description of a faculty was rare and points to the importance or size of that shop. Additional evidence of Bryan's reputation can be found in the account book of Thomas Tousey, who commissioned the following furniture for his daughter Mehetable in April 1750: "2 doz & 1 Chairs, Chest or Case of Draws, Round Table & Dressing table all from Andrew Durand att Milford" and "2 Tables, a Stand & Chest wth Draws from Bryans In Newtown." This patronage pattern reveals how Newtown still relied on the coastal towns for their cultural leadership but was beginning to develop its own culture. In 1747 Bryan had turned a set of rounds and made a stand, a chest with two drawers, and two tables for Tousey, who supplied the boards for the last three items.

Although not descriptively detailed, Bryan's inventory reveals his continued activity and scope of work in his later years. New chairs and tables prove that he was still making those forms, the escutcheons imply that he still made chests with drawers, and the presence of shingles and casements demonstrate that he also performed house joinery tasks. Bryan left his tools and shop to his son Ezra, who may have continued the family craft. Ezra appraised James Briscoe Jr.'s estate and was taxed for a faculty until 1769, when he sold a homestead, dwelling house, and joiner's shop to Samuel Peck, a member of his wife's family. By 1786, Ezra was living in Dutchess County, New York. Alexander Bryan's inventory included great quantities of land and farming apparatuses, which represented 76 percent of the total value of the estate.

SOURCES: DPR; BC; NTL; NLR; Account Book of Thomas Tousey of Newtown, 1716–1761; and St. Mark, "Newtown Joyners."

Samuel Burrill (1737–1767)   Burrill inherited his father's homestead in 1760. He provided window frames for Joseph Prindle when Prindle was building a house for John Tousey. Prindle also appraised Burrill's estate, listing sash planes and chisels and 108 squares of sashes in addition to other woodworking tools.

SOURCES: DPR; NLR; CCR; Account Book of Thomas Tousey of Newtown, 1716–1761.

David Fabrique (1745–1798)   A first cousin of Ebenezer and Elijah Booth, Fabrique was born in Newtown, then lived and worked in Derby. He returned to Newtown in 1780 but soon moved to Southbury in 1785. In 1791, Fabrique returned to Newtown, probably to work on the Anglican church (the drawings for this church are in the Fabrique family papers at Yale University). He also worked on the Southbury Meeting House (1778) and the Oxford Meeting House (1793–95). Listed as a carpenter in the 1796 and 1797 tax assessments, Fabrique was more of a house joiner and often worked with his brother, Bartimeus, of Woodbury (see appendix B). The tools in his estate confirm his specialization: many augers and chisels, several axes and hatchets, an adze, and a few planes.

SOURCES: DPR; NTL; STL; WTL; NLR; SLR; William Warren, "The Oxford Meeting House," *Connecticut Antiquarian* 33, no. 1 (1981): 4–8; Warren, "The First Two Southbury Meeting Houses," *Connecticut Antiquarian* 33, no. 2 (1981): 22–32; Fabrique Family Papers (Yale University Library, New Haven).

Clement Fairchild (1764–1849)   Clement Fairchild, son of Ebenezer and brother of Edward, was born in Newtown. He was listed as a shoemaker in the assessments of 1796–98, but he may also have done some woodworking. He made a coffin for Betty Brown in 1820.

SOURCES: BC; CCR; NTL.

Edward Fairchild (1752–1784)   Edward Fairchild, brother of Clement, was a Newtown-born Tory who was killed racing horses with British officers on Long Island. His inventory consisted largely of joiner's tools, including a lathe, a set of planes, and "shakey cherry board," but his estate amounted to only £2.1.6. Such a low valuation may be explained by his Loyalist stance; perhaps the remainder of his estate had been confiscated.

SOURCES: DPR; F. C. Sanford, *Genealogy of the Fairchild Family and Allied Families of Newtown and Vicinity* (Hartford: Connecticut State Library, 1948).

Joseph Ferris (1746–1833)   A native of Newtown, Ferris was a Tory whose estate reverted to his father, Peter, when he fled to Long Island in 1776. He joined the British army, but broke his leg in 1777. He never regained full health, but he did return to Newtown in December of 1783. Even though some of his movables had been sold prior to appraisal of his estate, the confiscated inventory still included a "Joyners Bench 36/ Layth 24/."

SOURCES: DPR; NLR; BC; Peter Coldham, *American Loyalist Claims* (Washington, D.C.: National Genealogical Society, 1980).

Daniel Foot (1752–1819)   Daniel Foot was born in Newtown, as was his brother, Edward. Daniel was listed as a house joiner in 1796 and a joiner in 1798.

SOURCES: NTL; CCR; HC; Nathaniel Goodwin, *The Foote Family* (Hartford: Case, Tiffany, 1849).

Edward Foot (1748–1835)   Like his brother, Daniel, Edward Foot was listed as a house joiner in 1796.

SOURCES: NTL; BC; CCR; HC.

George Foot (1754–?)   George Foot, first cousin to Daniel and Edward, was a house joiner in 1796, a carpenter in 1797, and a joiner in 1798.

SOURCES: NTL; BC; CR.

Joseph Foot (1748–1801)   Joseph Foot was born in Stratford, but he had moved to Newtown by 1771. He was assessed as a house joiner in 1796. His inventory listed forty-three dozen chair rounds of various kinds.

SOURCES: DPR; NTL; BC.

Charles Glover (1798–1884)   Glover was a Newtown-born wagonmaker who moved to Roxbury sometime between 1840 and 1850. A 1828 mortgage of his shop reveals that he made posts for kitchen chairs and bedsteads, in addition to wagons and carts.

SOURCES: NLR; HC; CR.

Samuel Griffin (1698–1773)   Griffin was born in Stratford, but he was working as a carpenter in Newtown in 1748.

SOURCES: DPR; Account Book of Thomas Tousey of Newtown, 1716–1761.

Arcillus Hamlin (1782–1827)   Hamlin was born in Sharon, Connecticut, but he had moved to Newtown by 1816, when he married Jerusha Botsford on February 13. He apparently formed some sort of a partnership with William Chappell, a Danbury cabinetmaker. An 1816 account with the Glover and Beers shop of Newtown referred to a balance from the Chappell and Hamlin account. Hamlin's inventory, appraised by Abner Judson, offers a valuable glimpse into furniture production in the 1820s and how much it differed from the more traditional manner.

1 Double Iron Jointer .42   1 Do No 5 .50   1 do No 6 .42   1 Jack plane .34   1 Smooth plane .25   1 do No 7 .20   1 Circular Saw .20   1 Gard Rabbet .25   1 Plough No 11 & 8 Irons 1.25   1 Gage Rabbet .50   2 Double Irons .34   1 Bead Plane .12   1 Brace for Chairs .75   1 do Cabinet 2.25   1 handsaw No 1 .25   1 No 2 .25   1 Brass Back Saw .75   1 do .58   1 Whip Saw .34   1 Sash do .10   1 do small .17   1 Gage .25   Screwbox & Tap .20   1 Small Saw .10   1 Iron back .12   3 Carving tools .30   1 holdfast .40   1 adds .75   Fro .25   3 Gages .25   1 Set augers 1.67   5 turning Chissels .50   1 set turning Gouges .34   1 Shave .12   Oil Stone .34   3 Stock shaves .25   1 Cramp .25   2 Match plains .50   1 Shaving knif .25   1 Large Square .42   1 Small do .12   2 wood rules .06   1 Set wax tools .12   Bevel .03   7 duckbil Chissels .42   4 screw drivers .17   8 Files .37   5 Carving Gouges .25   7 small Chissels .25   1 Gril .10   Brad Awls .06   1 Taper bit .06   2 Compass .12   1 pr pinchers .12   1 Screwdriver .38   2 Wrenches & Screws .30   2 rivet hammers .20   1 hinge punch .06   1 Set old Chissels .17   1 Box small instruments .08   8 hand screws .64   1 Box small tools .25   1 Screw .08   1 Small brass square .07   1 Chalk line .08   1 Large wood square .10   1 Iron vice 3.34   1 Box old iron .25   1 Saw Clamp .10   3 work benches 3.   1 Stock Shave .06   3 Bottles .04   1 old Grind stone 1.25   1 pit Saw 1.   1 Hatchet .34   old linds .25   4 unfinished trunks 1.   Glue pot & Kettle .37   1 Bench .08   Stove & pipe 3.34   1 unfinished Bureau 4.50   1 Lathe & apperatus 2.   paint Stone & pots 1.75   1 Whip saw .25   1 unfinished stand .50   Screws & c. .50   1 unfinished Chest .50   3 set window blinds 4.   1 Chest .75   1 dining table frame .75   1 Large trunk unfinished .50   2 unfinishd table frames .25   1 Lot Mahogany 1.25   1 Kitchen table 2   1 Red frame .12   1 Lot white wood boards 1.   part

of a bedstead .50   1 ax .50   2 Cherry plank .25   Bedstead timber
1.25   Cherry plank .17   500 Feet whitewood Boards 4.17   1 Shop 17.

SOURCES: NPR; BC; Account Book of Glover & Beers of Newtown, 1814–19 (Newtown Historical Society); H. Franklin Andrews, *The Hamlin Family* (Exira, Ia.: H. Franklin Andrews, 1902).

Ichabod Johnson (1719–1772)   In the 1750s Johnson hewed timber, rent clapboards, and fitted mantletrees for Thomas Tousey. He owned a sawmill on the Pootatuck River.

SOURCES: CCR; BC; NLR; Account Book of Thomas Tousey of Newtown, 1716–1761.

Philo M. Jordan (1788–1822)   Philo Jordan, son of Timothy, owned sash tools, an extensive set of planes, a fine backsaw, several axes, several augers, and squares of differing sizes.

SOURCES: DPR; NTL; NLR; BC.

Timothy Jordan (1766–1829)   Timothy Jordan was born in Stratford, worked in Woodbury from 1788 until 1790, then moved to Newtown in 1791. Referred to as a carpenter in the 1796–98 assessments, he was taxed for a faculty beginning in 1794. From 1804 until 1818, his shop was assessed at a high rate. Jordan seems to have been in semi-retirement at his death, but still owned a carpenter's adze, several augers, some wide chisels, a few molding tools and planes, and a large iron square. Additional indications that he worked mainly as a house joiner were his oak boards, chalk line, and chalk.

SOURCES: DPR; BC; WTL; NTL.

Abner Judson (1777–1848)   Born in Newtown, Judson trained with Elijah Booth in Southbury and returned to work in Newtown, where he gained Freeman status in 1801. Judson may have worked as a journeyman for Rivirius Prindle, and later may have had some working relationship with Arcillus Hamlin, whose estate he appraised. Judson lived and worked in the Sandy Hook area of Newtown, frequently mortgaging or selling his properties in the first two decades of the nineteenth century. By his death in 1848, he must have reduced his woodworking activity, because his inventory included only "12 New chairs 6.   1 Stove in shop .50   3 Unfinished chairs .50   1 Stand Frame .25   1 Paint Stone .25   1 Work Bench 1.   1 Grind Stone .25   Chest of Tools 7."

SOURCES: DPR; NPR; BC; NLR; Account Book of Shadrach Osborn and Nathan Preston of Southbury, 1790–1796 (Winterthur Museum).

David Judson (1783–1822)   The estate of David Judson, who was a first cousin of Abner, included a lathe, a few planes and chisels, some other woodworking tools, and a quantity of chestnut shingles. The inventory also refers to a house and shop. Isaac Scudder was an appraiser of Judson's estate.

SOURCES: NPR; BC.

Benjamin Latten (1736–1802)   The Latten family originated in Stratford. Benjamin Latten's father first bought land in Newtown in 1755, but Benjamin did not appear on the tax lists until 1765 and did not gain possession of the family home until 1769. In the following year, he also bought his father's shop. Most of Benjamin's tools were old and of little value, but at his death he did still own fifteen molding planes and a wide assortment of other tools in addition to fifty-two acres of land and a variety of animals. The bulk of his estate, including tools, was given to his son Nathan.

SOURCES: DPR; NTL; NLR; Samuel Orcutt, *A History of the Old Town of Stratford and the City of Bridgeport* (New Haven: Tuttle, Morehouse & Taylor, 1886).

Ebenezer Mallery (1762–1816)   Mallery was born in Newtown and married Eunice Judson there. He was listed as a shop joiner in 1796 and a joiner in the following two years. In 1797 his shop was assessed a faculty tax of $20, the same amount as John Boyer's. In 1807 Mallery and his wife moved to New York state. He died in Catherine, New York.

SOURCES: NTL; Special Genealogical Files (Connecticut State Library, Hartford).

Alanson Northrup (1765–1812)   Related to the Prindle family through his mother, Northrup married Lydia Hull of Newtown in 1792 and took the Freeman's oath in 1800, but had his life cut short when he was thrown from a horse and killed in 1812. A family genealogy refers to him as a carpenter and builder, but the extent of his skills cannot be determined by his inventory, which merely listed "Saw & Joiner Tools $10.25" and a shop. Nevertheless his work as an appraiser of John Boyer's estate may imply an ability to make furniture or indicate a business connection with furnituremakers. The 1796 assessment list referred to him as a shop joiner. The lists of the following two years included him in the joiner category, not in the carpenter category. Northrup remained a yeoman-craftsman as demonstrated by the major portion of his estate (92%) consisting of land, buildings, and animals. His tools and shop were distributed to his son Oliver.

SOURCES: DPR; A. Judd Northrup, *The Northrup-Northrop Genealogy* (New York: Grafton Press, 1908).

David Northrup (1771–1801)   David Northrup's relationship to Alanson is not clear. His probate included house joiner's tools, window sashes, and window frames.

SOURCES: NPR; NTL.

Nathaniel Norton (worked 1771–1793)   Norton covered a barn and made a coffin for Samuel Beers in 1789. A Nathaniel Norton appears in the tax lists, but no specific genealogical facts can be found.

SOURCES: NTL; Account Book of Samuel Beers of Newtown, 1776–1810 (privately owned).

Amos Parmelee (1771–1858)   Listed as carpenter in 1796, Parmelee's shop was assessed from 1796 through 1820. His relationship to David Parmelee and Nathaniel Parmelee is unclear.

SOURCES: NTL.

David Parmelee (worked 1796–1819)   Listed as a carpenter in 1796, David Parmelee worked with John Hubbell to make a wagon in 1819.

SOURCES: NTL; Account Book of John Hubbell of Newtown, 1805–1823 (Old Sturbridge Village, Sturbridge, Mass.).

Nathaniel Parmelee (1761–1834)   A cousin of the Parmelee woodworkers in Guilford, Connecticut, Nathaniel seemed to specialize in making turned chairs. He made six chairs, valued at £1.4.0, for Samuel Beers in 1795, and made eight chairs of various values and bottomed and colored other chairs for Andrew Leavenworth of Monroe in 1805. The few tools listed in his inventory and among the personal property sold at vendue after his death included "1 turning Lathe & bench .22   1 shaving horse .26" and several turning tools. Although he was born in Newtown, Parmelee did not take the Freeman's oath until 1804, when he was forty-three. Such a delay may have been determined by his father's continued authority or by Nathaniel's relegation to journeyman status.

SOURCES: NPR; NTL; Mrs. E. Warren Mason, *Parmelee Family: Nine Generations* (Hartford: Connecticut State Library, 1952); Account Book of Samuel Beers of Newtown, 1782–1805 (privately owned); Account Book of Andrew Leavenworth of Monroe, 1791–1816 (Yale University Library, New Haven).

Daniel Peck (1776–1846)   Daniel Peck appears on the 1798 assessment list as a joiner. He worked in Newtown his entire life.

SOURCES: NTL; BC.

Joseph Peck Jr. (1778–1833)   Joseph Peck Jr. apprenticed with Lazarus Prindle and worked in his own shop as a joiner in 1797. His tools consisted primarily of house joiner's equipment: augers, floor planes, chalk line, and so on.

SOURCES: NPR; NTL; HC; Apprenticeship agreement between Lazarus Prindle and Joseph Peck Jr., June 5, 1793 (privately owned).

Samuel Peck (1775–1817)   A family genealogy refers to Samuel Peck as a joiner by trade. He married Nancy Mallery and had his own joiner's shop in 1798. Peck's inventory reveals that he continued agricultural activity. His single-bench shop included a good selection of planes.

15 Rabits and plowes for Joiners 2.13   1 Corner plain .12   1 Smooth Plain .17   1 four plain .20   2 Jointers .51   8 olde augers .25   3 Small Do .50   1 Do Skrew .34   1 large Do .42   1 Frow .34   1 Skrew .25   lot of old Iron .34   8 small bits & augers .25   8 Small gouges & Plows .50   2 files & one rasp .20   2 large gouges .25   5 Chizils .60   2 Nale hammers .12   2 old plains .25   2 Squares .08   3 Small Saws 1.50   1 Shaving knife .73   1 pr Compass .75   1 Iron Square .40   1 broad ax .42   1 hatchet .36   pare Smoothing Irons .85   Small grindstone .12   Shaving hors .17   1 Chisel .12   1 Gouge .08   1 hand Saw 1.06   1 worke bench .37.

SOURCES: DPR; NTL; Ira Peck, *A Genealogical History of the Descendants of Joseph Peck* (Boston: Alfred Mudge & Son, 1868).

Daniel Perry (1768–1823)   Listed as a house joiner in 1796, Perry's inventory included sashes, window frames, and joiner's tools. Perry worked with Rivirius Prindle and held notes against Cyrus and Lewis Prindle.

SOURCES: NPR; NTL; HC; Account Book of Caleb Baldwin of Newtown, 1800–1846.

Nathan Platt (1761–?)   Platt was a millwright-carpenter in the 1790s.
SOURCES: NTL; BC.

Cyrus Prindle (1760–?)   Cyrus Prindle was the son of Joseph, brother of Lazarus, and father of Lewis. Among his documented products and services are chests, coffins, bedsteads, doors, and sashes, and putting up mantlepieces, helving axes, and bottoming chairs.
SOURCES: NTL; Account Book of Caleb Baldwin of Newtown, 1800–1846; Newtown Town Book, 1802–12; Account Book of Anonymous Dyer/Fuller of Newtown, 1802–1808 (privately owned); Account Book of Ziba Blakeslee of Newtown, 1789–1822 (Winterthur Museum Library).

Joseph Prindle (1730–1795)   Joseph Prindle was the father of Cyrus and Lazarus and uncle of Rivirius. He supplied Samuel Beers with a painted chest of drawers and bottomed some chairs in 1776. Fifteen years later, he supplied Beers with a chair, some sashes, and two window frames. He also did the joinery work on John Tousey's house in 1755.
SOURCES: Account Book of Samuel Beers of Newtown, 1776–1810; Account Book of Thomas Tousey of Newtown, 1716–1761.

Lazarus Prindle (1763–1845)   Lazarus Prindle, son of Joseph, was a shop joiner from whom Samuel Beers purchased three chairs, one chest, and sashes between 1781 and 1783. He moved to Salisbury, Connecticut in 1796 and died in Hartford, New York.
SOURCES: NTL; Account Book of Samuel Beers of Newtown, 1776–1810.

Lewis Prindle (1782–1850)   Cyrus Prindle's son, Lewis, operated his own joiner's shop in the middle of town beginning in 1804. His tasks ranged from repair work and ax helving to gun stocking and furniture production.
SOURCES: NTL; NLR; HC; Account Book of Caleb Baldwin of Newtown, 1800–1846; Account Book of Samuel Beers of Newtown, 1794–1815 (privately owned); Account Book of Philo Beardslee of Newtown, 1804–1833 (Litchfield Historical Society).

Rivirius Prindle (1768–1811)   Joseph Prindle's nephew Rivirius seems to have been the leading furnituremaker in the family. In 1801, he and Abner Judson appraised a second inventory, solely of furniture, for the estate of Henry Glover. Since Glover's regular inventory, appraised by

Jotham Sherman and Jared Botsford, included a normal amount of household furniture, it seems likely that Prindle and Judson listed and appraised furniture in their shop that had been ordered by Glover. The list offers valuable information about what was produced at that time and what constituted a stylish suite of furniture: "1 Crown Case £9   1 Fall Leaf Table £2.5.0   1 Tea Table £1.13.0   1 Candle Stand 6/   1 Kitching Table £1   1 Chest with one Drawer £1.4.0   1 Plane Chest 10/   9 Dining Chares £3.12.0   6 Elbow Do £3   6 Kitchen Chares £1.10.0   1 Toilett Table 6/." In the first decade of the nineteenth century, Prindle provided Caleb Baldwin with a cupboard, a fire screen, and a pine table, and also bottomed four chairs and performed hours of joinery for him.

SOURCES: DPR; NTL; BC; Account Book of Caleb Baldwin of Newtown, 1800–1846.

Amos Sanford (1733–1779)   Sanford was born in Newtown and may have been Ebenezer Booth IV's master. He made a case of drawers for Thomas Tousey. In 1765, Sanford moved to Sharon, Connecticut, where he died in 1779. His inventory included cherry and whitewood boards, a lathe and turning tools, a full range of joiner's planes, and six "new fashion york chairs."

SOURCES: Sharon Probate District; NTL; BC; Account Book of Thomas Tousey of Newtown, 1716–1761.

Stephen Sanford (1771–1855)   Sanford was born in nearby Redding, but he moved to Newtown in 1793. After working as a shop joiner until 1804, he sold his three-acre home lot, home, shop, and horse shed, and moved to Roxbury. Sanford's shop had a particularly high assessment from 1798 until 1804.

SOURCES: NTL; NLR.

Isaac Scudder (1776–1845)   Scudder was a native woodworker whose speciality was house joinery. He built the town's second meetinghouse in 1808 and constructed several bridges for the town's highways.

SOURCES: NPR; NLR; Newtown Town Book, 1802–12; Jane Eliza Johnson, ed., *Newtown's History and Historian, Ezra Levan Johnson* (Newtown: Jane E. Johnson, 1917).

Elijah Sherman (1762–1844)   Sherman operated a sawmill and house joiner's shop. He still owned many of his joiner's tools at his death.

SOURCES: NPR; NTL; BC; HC.

Elnathan Skidmore (?–1801)   Elnathan Skidmore was Nehemiah's son and continued the family's carpenter shop.
SOURCES: DPR; NTL.

John Skidmore (1767–1820)   John Skidmore, son of Thomas, was referred to as a house joiner.
SOURCES: NTL; *Thomas Skidmore of Westerleigh, Gloustershire, and Fairfield, Connecticut* (privately printed by Warren Skidmore, 1980).

Nehemiah Skidmore (1718–1781)   Nehemiah Skidmore was a carpenter and house joiner like his father, Thomas. He had part ownership of a sawmill and an old shop, in which there were twenty squares of glass, augers, a frow, and other rougher carpentry tools.
SOURCES: DPR; NTL; BC.

Zardis Skidmore (1772–?)   Zardis Skidmore, Elnathan's son, was also a carpenter. His Newtown shop was assessed from 1797 until 1813, when he moved to Patterson, New York.
SOURCES: NTL; *Thomas Skidmore of Westerleigh, Gloustershire, and Fairfield, Connecticut.*

Israel Stilson (1742–1827)   Stilson apprenticed to Peter Fairchild, a Redding house joiner who built Thomas Tousey's house. He never had a shop appraised, but he did make window frames for Samuel Beers in 1792.
SOURCES: NTL; Account Book of Thomas Tousey of Newtown, 1716–1761; Account Book of Samuel Beers of Newtown, 1776–1810.

James Stilson (1771–?)   Listed as a shop joiner in 1796 and 1797, Stilson's last appearance on the Newtown tax lists was in 1805. Charles Prindle of Woodbury did some work for Stilson in 1802.
SOURCES: NTL; BC; Account Book of Charles Prindle of Woodbury, 1801–1806 (Connecticut Historical Society, Hartford).

Thomas Stilson (?–1815)   In addition to weaving, general farm work, hewing wood, and framing outbuildings, Stilson made some furniture. In 1776 and 1777 he provided Eunis Johnson with "1 Chest of draws £1.7.0   3 white chears 8/   3 white chears 7/6," and in 1778 he made a table with a drawer and an oval table for James Whitney.
SOURCES: BC; Account Book of Thomas Stilson of Newtown, 1772–1803 (Newtown Historical Society).

Andrew Wheeler (1772–1828)   Wheeler was referred to as a house joiner. His inventory included one joiner's bench, a set of joiner's tools appraised at $10.43, and some hewed timber.

SOURCES: NTL; NPR; Newtown Town Book, 1802–12.

APPENDIX B

Biographies of Woodbury Joiners, 1760–1820

William Adee (?–1765)   Adee of New Haven bought 2,400 square feet of land near David Minor in 1750 and married Sarah Hotchkiss in 1751. At his death he owned a fairly extensive quantity of tools, especially of the turning variety. His estate listed seventy dozen chair rounds. He may have concentrated on making chairs, even though he made a coffin for Ephraim Minor in 1762. His agricultural possessions included only a mare for transport and a cow for basic family needs. Adee distributed portions of his shop and tools among five children. His artisanal equipment included:

an ax 3/   a Small Broad ax 4/   a draw Shave 2/   a Large Hansaw 15/   a fine Hansaw 4/6   Dito 1/6   a Compas Saw 2/   one Joynter 2/3   a panel plain 2/   a Groving Plow 5/   a haveing plain 1/6   a qirter Round 1/   a Beed 6^d a fore plain 1/   a Smoothing plain 1/   a pair of Sash plains 4/   an Back oge 2/   a fore oge 1/9   a Rabit plain 1/3   a Small oge 1/6   Dito 1/9   2 wooden Squares 1/6   a Broad turning Chisel 2/   a turning Gouge 2/   a narrow turning Chisel 1/3   a Small Gough 1/3   a Scribing Gough 1/   a winscot Duks Bill 1/   a Sash Duks Bill 9^d a Small narrow Chisel 4^d a Sash Gouge 4^d a Heading Chisel 6^d a former 6^d a Bench hook 6^d a pair of Compases 4^d a Gunters Rule 1/9   a fro 3/   a Breast wimble 2/   a 3 qirter auger 1/6   a nail Hamer 1/   a Small Rasp 1/   a taper Bit 10^d an old pair of pinchers 1/   a pair of nipers 9^d 2 nail Gimblets 1/   a hone 1/6   4 pound of old iron 8^d a turning Lathe 5/   70 dosen of turned Chair Rounds at 3^d pr Dusen 17/6   a Shop with all the Loos Bords in it £5.10.0.

SOURCES: WPR; WLR; WTL; BC; loose bill in the Minor Family Papers (privately owned).

Seth Bacon (1768–1805)   Bacon was a carpenter who hailed from Farmington, Connecticut.

SOURCES: WTL; BC.

Josiah Baldwin (1728–1761)   A native of Woodbury, Baldwin owned a lathe and a variety of carpenter's or house joiner's tools. His estate was appraised by two other carpenters, Eldad Spencer and Zimri Moody.

SOURCES: WPR; CCR.

David Beardslee (1769–1846)   Beardslee was a joiner in his hometown of Southbury from 1793 until 1800. His shop was assessed the rate of $40 in 1798, when he was listed as a joiner and a carpenter. Beardslee's last appearance on the Southbury tax list was in 1799. He died in Catherine, New York.

SOURCES: STL; BC; *Beardsley Genealogy* (MS, Connecticut State Library, Hartford).

Silas Bennett (1767–1853)   Born and trained in nearby Huntington, Bennett moved to Southbury in 1793. He was listed as a joiner on tax assessments and purchased hardware and tools from Joel Pierce, a Southbury shopkeeper.

SOURCES: STL; BC; CR; Account Book of Joel Pierce of South Britain, 1795–1807 (Yale University Library, New Haven).

George Bolt (worked 1793–1820)   Little exact genealogical information exists for Bolt. The Bolt family came from Norwalk, where a John Bolt was a joiner. George first arrived in Woodbury in 1793 and married Dorcas Johnson of Southbury the next year. A nineteenth-century historian described Bolt as "one of the best builders of his time and most skillful as a joiner." Most surviving references to Bolt involve house joinery and coffin building.

SOURCES: WTL; STL; BC; DPR; J. L. Rockey, ed., *History of New Haven County, Connecticut* (New York: W. W. Preston, 1892); Account Book of Shadrach Osborn of Southbury, 1796–1806 (Winterthur Museum); Account Book of Shadrach Osborn of Southbury, 1801–1803 (Litchfield Historical Society); Account Book of Daniel Hinman of Southbury, 1807–1815 (Connecticut Historical Society, Hartford).

Ebenezer Booth V (1779–1836)   See chapter 3.

Ebenezer Booth VI (1790–1864)   See chapter 3.

Elijah Booth (1745–1823)   See chapter 3.

Noah Hinman Booth (1784–1867)   See chapter 3.

Dennis Bradley (1773–1862)   Bradley was born in Woodbury and began his career there, but by 1810 he had moved to Watertown. He had settled in Litchfield by 1820 and died there. In 1802, Bradley provided Matthew Minor of Woodbury with "two Brecfast tabels £2   one kitching tabel of pine 18/   two Bread trays 6/   one Poor Chest made of Bass wood" in return for rye, cider, potatoes, care of a cow, and payment of taxes.

SOURCES: BC; CR; WLR; Account Book of Matthew Minor of Woodbury, 1801–1810 (privately owned).

Ebenezer Bull (1732–1760)   Originally from Farmington, Bull purchased a one-acre home lot and five acres of land in Woodbury in 1758, at which time he was taxed for a faculty. Although he died a single man in January 1760, his inventory describes a fairly active, established shop. The lathe and turning tools enabled him to make chairs, the presence of brasses and cherry boards indicate that he also made case furniture, and the large number of sash squares reveal his additional activity in house joinery.

One Small Hatchet 1/   one Joynter 3/   one Ditto 4/   Corniss 6/   Groveing Plow 5/   halfing Plow 3/6   Great Round 3/   Pannel Plain 4/   Billection 3/   asticle 1/3   Smll Hollow 1/6   Rabit Plain 1/4   Sprung Rabit 1/4   Sash Plain 1/8   fore Plain 6^d Smoothing Plain 1/   one Smoothing Plain 2/   one Smll Round 2/   two Smaller Ditto 2/8   Small Ojee 1/3   Quarter Round 1/4   Inch Ojee 1/6   Smll Quarter Round 1/3   Smll Philister 1/3   half Inch Philister 1/4   Compass Plain 6^d Quarter Round 1/4   Broad Turning Chizel 1/6   one Narrow Turning Chizel 1/3   Large Turning Gouge 1/6   Smaller Ditto 1/3   Smaller Ditto 1/   Large Hand Saw 12/   Tennon Saw 10/   Smaller Ditto 12/   Compass Saw 2/   one Pareing Chizel 2/   Inch furmer 1/   Scribing Gouge 1/   Smaller Gouge 9^d two smll Ditto 6^d Mortising Chizel 6^d Winscott Ducks Bill 9^d Sash Chizel 9^d two smll Furmers 1/   two smll Ditto 9^d Sash Gouge 3^d Plain Iron 9^d Six smll files 3/   one half Round file 6^d two rasps 1/4   two pair Compasses 1/   one Gunters Rule 1/8   one Pare smll Pinchers 1/6   Small Brads 8/6   two nail Gymblets 6^d 3 Wooden Squares 3/   four Gages 1/   Shaveing Knife 2/   half Inch Auger 2/   one hold fast 1/6   three hammers 2/   Brest Wimble and two bitts 1/   Spike Gymblet 6^d two Whet Stones 6^d Chalk Line and Roal 6^d Glue and Glue Pott 2/   Three Dusson Brasses £1.2.0   Turners Lathe 5/   Grindstone 10/   three Hundred and Seventy Six Sash Squares £4   40 feet Maple Board 1/6   Slit Work 5/   Pine Boards 431 feet £1.5.10   946 feet

Whitewood Board £2.16.10   200 feet of oak Board 6/   23 feet Cherry Board 2/10   16 feet Whitewood Board 10^d Nails 1/2   Glue 1/   Eighteen pound & half 4^d nails 16/6.

SOURCES: WPR; BC; WLR; WTL.

Isaac Bunce (1770–1846)   Bunce was a joiner, according to tax lists. A native of Woodbury, he moved to Ohio in 1832 at the end of his woodworking career.

SOURCES: WTL; BC; Alice Howard, *Genealogy of the Bunce Family* (MS, Connecticut State Library, Hartford).

Silas Butler (1733–1779)   Butler was baptized in Edgartown, Massachusetts, on November 11, 1733, but his family most likely lived in Lebanon, Connecticut, at the time. A Silas Butler appears on the Woodbury tax lists for the first time in 1755. A case of drawers, signed by Silas Butler and dated March 25, 1755, is in the collection of the Wadsworth Atheneum, Hartford. On March 15, 1758, Butler married Jerusha Spencer, daughter of the joiner Eldad Spencer (see entry below). Sometime around 1760, Butler moved to western Massachusetts. A 1763 deed from Stockbridge mentions "Silas Butler, Joiner, of New Framingham." Later he lived in Sheffield, where he died. His inventory, taken March 2, 1779, included "1 grindstone 1/   a Slay Partly made 5/   joiners tools 42/6."

SOURCES: WTL; Berkshire County Probate District, Docket 960; Frederick Chesson, "The Great Highboy Hunt" (MS, Aug. 1992, in author's possession).

Naboth Candee (1734–1786)   Candee was born in New Haven, but had moved to Oxford by 1760, when he married Esther Trowbridge. He lived on the border of Southbury and Oxford on three acres of land. His tools, which he distributed equally among his six brothers and sisters, indicate that he concentrated on house joinery.

SOURCES: WPR; BC; CCR; WLR.

Philemon Cherevoy (1749–1801)   This joiner was born of French parents in Acadia. When the family was expelled in 1755, Cherevoy's parents fled south to Haiti, but he was sent to Woodbury with a brother and a sister. Treated as an orphan, Cherevoy was apprenticed to a joiner, perhaps Bartimeus Fabrique, a son of another French immigrant. Cherevoy often worked with Fabrique.

SOURCES: WTL; *Boston Evening Transcript;* Account Book of Shadrach Osborn of Southbury, 1777–1784 (Connecticut Historical Society, Hartford); Account Book of Nathaniel Bacon of Woodbury, 1798–1849 (Connecticut Historical Society, Hartford).

Amos Crammer (worked 1777–1800)   Crammer provided Nathaniel Bacon with two bedsteads worth twelve shillings each, a small chair valued at four shillings, and 135 feet of oak studs. Biographical information on Crammer was not available, but the Crammer family is from New London County.
SOURCE: Account Book of Nathaniel Bacon of Woodbury, 1798–1849.

Samuel Curtiss (1736–1813)   Born, trained, and married in Stratford, Curtiss moved to Southbury in 1759. He had a faculty assessed in the 1760s and 1770s. His inventory listed 114 acres of land, a sizeable number of livestock, packed pork, a chaise, and a set of house joiner's tools. Apparently Curtiss foresook his woodworking career and concentrated on animal husbandry.
SOURCES: WPR; BC; STL.

William DeForrest (1786–1857)   This wheelwright was born in Stratford, but moved to Woodbury in 1808. He made wheels, hubs, and spokes. With Daniel and William Hurlbut, he owned a sawmill and shop.
SOURCES: WTL; WLR; BC; Account Book of Matthew Minor of Woodbury, 1802–1826 (privately owned).

Bartimeus Fabrique (1751–1829)   Fabrique was born in Newtown, but moved to Woodbury sometime around 1775, when a deed to his father's land referred to "Bartimeus late of Newtown and now resident in Woodbury." The 1796 tax assessment listed Fabrique as a carpenter, but the lists for the following two years referred to him as a joiner. His account book for the period 1791–1810 and several plans and elevations are deposited in the Yale University Manuscript Collection. The drawings are of the Newtown Anglican Church, Roxbury Meeting House, the Ebenezer Smith house and the Gad Bristol house in Woodbury, and the Buell house in Litchfield. Bartimeus and his brother David of Newtown often worked together (see appendix A). They collaborated on the Oxford Meeting House and the Sherman Hinman house, although the division of their responsibilities is unclear. Bartimeus seems to have been the most prominent house joiner in the area during the last two decades of the eighteenth century. He had many apprentices and journeymen working for him, including Charles Prindle, Philemon Cherevoy, Herman Hinman, Silas Lewis, Noah Tuttle, Simeon Clinton, John Beardslee, Eli Hall, and Curtis Mallery.

SOURCES: NLR; SLR; WLR; STL; Fabrique Family Papers (Yale University Library, New Haven); Account Book of Charles Prindle of Woodbury, 1801–1806 (Connecticut Historical Society, Hartford); William Warren, "The Oxford Meeting House," *Connecticut Antiquarian* 33, no. 1 (1981): 4–8; Warren, "The First Two Southbury Meeting Houses," *Connecticut Antiquarian* 33, no. 2 (1981): 22–32.

John Whitehead Gould (1754–1781)   Born in Branford, Gould never married, but apparently he carried on an active business. His shop included an unfinished case of drawers, a lathe, a good selection of tools, and several gunstocks. Other than a single mare worth £8, Gould's personal estate amounted to very little. His status as a single man with only commercial connections with the Woodbury community was clearly demonstrated by the need for his sister to file suit against two court-appointed administrators of his estate, Ebenezer Tallman and Benjamin Rusco.

SOURCES: WPR; BC.

Eli Hall (1776–1859)   Referred to as a mechanic in his death notice, Hall was born in Weston but came to Southbury to train with Elijah Booth. Upon completion of his apprenticeship, Hall engaged himself in house joinery and performed contract work for Bartimeus Fabrique. In 1806 Hall married Irena Hinman and bought Elijah Booth's home, home lot, and shop. Jervis Summers worked with Hall in 1807 (and with Noah Booth in 1808). Like Fabrique, Elijah Booth, Ebenezer Booth V, and Samuel Munn, Hall depended on Shadrach Osborn for tools, brass hardware, glass, and even nails. Hall's activities after 1806 included making coffins and making and repairing farm equipment. No references document his ability to make furniture other than coffins or chests.

SOURCES: BC; SLR; STL; Account Book of Shadrach Osborn of Southbury, 1801–1803; Account Book of Shadrach Osborn of Southbury, 1777–1784; Account Book of Daniel Hinman of Southbury, 1807–1815; Account Book of Shadrach Osborn and Nathan Preston of Southbury, 1790–1796 (Winterthur Museum); Account Book of Bartimeus Fabrique, 1791–1810 (Yale University Library, NewHaven); Account Book of Shadrach Osborn of Southbury, 1783–1792 (Yale University Library); Account Book of Shadrach Osborn of

Southbury, 1805–1806 (Connecticut Historical Society, Hartford); Account Book of David Stiles of Southbury, 1789–1815 (privately owned); Account Book of Shadrach Osborn of Southbury, 1796–1806 (Winterthur Museum); Account Book of Ephraim Stiles of Southbury, 1785–1817 (Connecticut Historical Society); Account Book of Shadrach Osborn of Southbury, 1806–1807 (Winterthur Museum); Account Book of Shadrach Osborn of Southbury, 1807–1808 (Winterthur Museum); Account Book of Erastus and Benjamin Osborn of Southbury, 1808–1810 (Winterthur Museum); Account Book of Erastus and Benjamin Osborn of Southbury, 1808–1812 (Winterthur Museum).

Billious Hill (1735–?)   Born and married in Goshen, Hill moved to Woodbury in 1765. He made a "Cherry Chest with Draws" worth £5 for Thomas Bull in 1773. The upper section of a desk-and-bookcase sold at Christie's in 1992 was signed "Billious Hill" in chalk on the backboards. Hill left Woodbury in 1778 and moved to Lenox, Massachusetts. In his army enlistment papers in 1781, he was referred to as a carpenter.

SOURCES: WTL; WLR; BC; Account Book of Samuel and Thomas Bull of Woodbury, 1719–1790 (Connecticut State Library, Hartford); Christie's Sale #7492 (June 17, 1992), lot 178; *Massachusetts Soldiers and Sailors of the Revolutionary War* (Boston: Wright & Potter Printing, 1900), 7:869–70.

Hezekiah Hine (1757–1830)   Hine was born in Southbury but was working in Derby early in 1790. Later that year he moved to Southbury, where he was listed as a joiner in the 1790s. He was paid £14.12.3 for his work on the Southbury school house in 1797. In 1801 he sold his house, home lot, and shop to the blacksmith Veron Dyke and moved to Oxford.

SOURCES: BC; CR; SLR; STL; Account Book of Shadrach Osborn of Southbury, 1796–1806; *Descendants of Thomas Hine of Milford, Connecticut* (St. Paul, Minn.: privately printed, 1898).

Herman Hinman (1782–1841)   Hinman was a native lad who worked as part of Bartimeus Fabrique's crew and with Charles Prindle. Little is known about him and his relationship with the other Hinmans in town.

SOURCES: CCR; Account Book of Bartimeus Fabrique of Southbury, 1791–1810; Account Book of Charles Prindle of Woodbury.

John Hurd (1717–1766)   Hurd was a native carpenter whose tools consisted of adzes, augers, drawknives, and saws.

SOURCES: WPR; BC.

Solomon Hurd (1768–1814)   Hurd, who lived in Woodbury his entire life, was assessed as a joiner in Woodbury in 1796.

SOURCES: WTL; CCR.

Daniel Hurlbut (1786–1828)   Like his father, Truman, and brother, William, Daniel Hurlbut performed a great deal of general carpentry and handyman work for Nathaniel Bacon. Such limited woodworking opportunities were common in the early nineteenth century. Unlike other young woodworkers, Hurlbut was able to improve his situation. He formed a partnership with his brother in 1816 and bought a mill site to undertake furniture production. His estate listed his share (with William and Charles Peck) of partly finished "cabinet stuff" and a share in the new shop. Charles Peck had become a financial backer of the Hurlbuts early in the 1820s. Daniel and William Hurlbut also held a farm jointly.

SOURCES: WPR; WTL; WLR; HC; Account Book of Nathaniel Bacon of Woodbury, 1798–1849.

Truman Hurlbut (1750–1819)   Truman Hurlbut was born in Roxbury, but he moved to Woodbury as a young man. He owned a home and shop near Jesse Minor in Woodbury. He bottomed chairs for Matthew Minor and performed various handyman jobs for Nathaniel Bacon, including painting and fixing chairs and bedsteads.

SOURCES: WTL; WLR; Account Book of Matthew Minor of Woodbury, 1801–1810; Account Book of Nathaniel Bacon of Woodbury; Thomas Hurlbut, *The Hurlbut Genealogy* (Albany, N.Y.: Joel Munsell's Sons, 1888).

William Hurlbut (1784–1835)   William Hurlbut's estate included a joiner's bench, a full selection of bench and molding planes, chisels, and a paint stone and paintbrushes. He had only six and a half acres of land, one horse, two cows, and two pigs. The wheelwright William DeForrest, who shared the Hurlbut's sawmill and machinery, was one of the appraisers of the estate.

SOURCES: WPR; WTL; WLR; HC; Account Book of Nathaniel Bacon of Woodbury.

Nicholas Jebine (worked 1794–1819)   Jebine trained in New Haven, where he married Mary Munson in January 1790. Their sons were baptised at the First Congregational Church on September 22, 1794, but the family must have moved to Woodbury shortly thereafter because Jebine was assessed on the 1795 tax list. Jebine lived in a house, formerly owned by Benjamin Price, that stood just east of the meetinghouse. He built a joiner's shop just south of the dwelling house.

Of great enough skill and reputation to be referred to as "Cabbinet Maker in Woodbury" in an account book, Jebine made a wide variety of furniture. For Jabez Bacon he made a suite of furniture in 1798 that included "1 Bureau £5.5.0   1 High Post Button Bedstead £1   2 Low Post Common Bedsteads £2.2.0   12 Windsor Chairs £4.16.0   1 Kitchen Table £1.4.0   1 Breakfast Table £2.2.0   2 Tea Tables £6   2 Candle Stands £1.1.0   1 Dining Table £3." Windsor chairs may have been a particular specialty of Jebine's; Matthew Minor purchased sets of Windsors on three different occasions. Jabez Bacon may have sold some of Jebine's Windsor chairs in his shop because his inventory included sixty Windsors in addition to his household furniture. In 1798, Jebine also made picture frames for Daniel Bacon. In return for his specialized skills, Jebine received foodstuffs and even had his patrons pay his town taxes.

SOURCES: CCR; WTL; WLR; Account Book of Nathaniel Bacon of Woodbury; Account Book of Matthew Minor of Woodbury, 1800–1820; Account Book of Bennet French of Southbury, 1793–1804 (privately owned); Account Book of Daniel Bacon of Woodbury, 1799–1800 (Connecticut Historical Society, Hartford).

Thomas Kimberly (1760–1802)   A native Southbury artisan, Kimberly owned only eight acres of poor soil, one cow, and one horse at his death. For his livelihood, Kimberly relied more on his joiner's skills. He owned a vast array of tools that included:

50 feet of pine boards 3/   small grindstone 1/   3 small whetstones 3^d 1 Chalk line & spool 6^d 2 junk oil bottles 6^d 1 Broad ax 1/8   1 Carpenters Hatchet 7/6   1 Narrow ax 4/   1 Post ax 1/6   1 Carpenders Adze 6/   1 Hammer 1/   1 Hand Saw 3/6   1 Do 3/   2 Fine Saws 6/   Wooden Vice 1/6   Broken iron Square 6^d Joiners rule 1/   1 Coopers Fro 1/6   1 Led Glue Pot 1/   1 Breast piece & bits 5/   2 Bits 1/   1 Joiners plow & M plains 2/6   Joiners Tools No. 1 9^d Do. No. 2 9^d Do. No. 3 9^d Do. No. 4 6^d Do. No. 5 6^d Do. No. 6 8^d Do. No. 7 7^d Do. No. 8 9^d Do. No. 9 7^d Do. No. 10 2^d Smoothing plains No. 1 9^d Do. No. 2 6^d Do. No. 3 6^d Do. No. 4 3^d 2 Jointers 1/   2 Fore plains 4^d 2 Round plains 4^d 3 Mortice chisels 1/6   6 Very Small Do. 1/3   3 Turning Do. 1/   1 Gouge & Chisel 8^d 1 Broad Chisel 3^d 4 Turning Gouges 4/4   2 pr of Compases 1/   1 pr of Nippers 2^d 3 Files & one rasp 1/   1 Large Gimblet 4^d 1 Compass Saw 4^d 1 paint box & sieve 1/   1 Saw set 2^d 1 Inch Chisel 8^d 1 Inch and ½ Do. 6^d 1 Inch ½ Auger 1/   ½ Inch Do. 6^d Inch Do. 6^d 3 Quarter Do. 6^d 1 Large Gimblet

4ᵈ   1 Small Do. 3ᵈ   1 Wooden Square 6ᵈ   Lathe with the irons and work bench 4/6   Old Chest with tools and patterns and Nos. of Wheels Mopsticks turning sticks & C & C 1/.

Of particular note is the old chest with patterns and the turning sticks. A turning stick, probably what is now called a strike pole, turning verge, or pattern stick, had sharp spikes driven through it. When the joiner held it against a post in his lathe, it made a series of scored rings that acted as reference points for turned decoration or for drilling holes. The turning stick thus allowed uniform posts or chair rounds that were interchangeable.

SOURCES: WPR; STL; BC.

Simeon King (1748–1776)   This native Woodbury joiner followed the craft in its more traditional nature. He worked in his hometown, made furniture and architectural elements, and oversaw a small farm. He owned joiner's tools appraised at £3.2.4. In his shop were a set of black chairs (£1.10.0), 6 white chairs (11/), 1 "case of draws part done" (£1.16.0), 28 window frames (£4.18.0), and sash and sash stuff (£1.13.8). His shop and tools were sold by his widow to the joiner Richard Smith and cooper Abraham Lines.

SOURCES: WPR; WTL; BC; WLR.

Amos Leavenworth (1753–1793)   Born and married in Roxbury, Leavenworth had settled in Woodbury by 1775. He contracted to build a house and kitchen for Nathaniel Smith for £20, £16 of which would consist of horses. Leavenworth also did some house joinery and tool repair for Dr. Samuel Orton in 1791.

SOURCES: WTL; BC; CCR; Contract between Amos Leavenworth and Nathaniel Smith (privately owned); Account Book of Dr. Samuel Orton of Woodbury, 1788–1798 (Woodbury Town Hall).

Harvey J. Linsley (1797–1853)   Born in Branford and trained in New Haven, Linsley moved to Woodbury in 1820. He owned one acre of land with a house and shop. An 1822 bill reveals that Linsley made Matthew Minor "1 kitchen table $2.34   1 cherry candlestand $1.75   1 bureau $16.   1 cherry breakfast table $5.50."

SOURCES: WTL; WLR: HC; November 20, 1822, bill for Matthew Minor (privately owned).

David Miles (1731–1771)   Miles was born in Milford, but he moved to Woodbury in 1769 when he bought eighty and one-half acres, including a gristmill and a sawmill, from James Burgiss. Miles combined joinery, sawing, milling, farming, and shopkeeping. In the distribution of his estate, he bequeathed his tools to his daughters and gave part ownership of the sawmill to his widow and each of his children.

SOURCES: WPR; WLR; WTL; BC.

Timothy Minor (1702–1760)   Minor was a native farmer-carpenter.

SOURCES: WPR; BC.

Zimri Moody (1736–1796)   A joiner, Moody was born in Farmington and later moved to Woodbury in 1760.

SOURCES: BC; WTL; Account Book of Shadrach Osborn and Nathan Preston of Southbury, 1790–1796; Account Book of Anonymous Shopkeeper of Woodbury, 1770 (Connecticut Historical Society, Hartford).

Daniel Munn (1719–1796)   Munn was a wheelwright whose faculty was assessed from 1761 until 1778.

SOURCES: WTL; HC; Account Book of Samuel and Thomas Bull of Woodbury, 1719–1790.

Samuel Munn (1753–1813)   At his death, this Southbury native still owned a number of axes, augers, and chisels; an adze; a chalk line and roller; a few saws and planes; and other carpentry and house joinery tools. These tools were distributed between his two daughters. His two sons received land, stock, farming tools, and shoemaking tools. Munn bought hardware from Shadrach Osborn.

SOURCES: WPR; BC; CCR; STL; Account Book of Shadrach Osborn of Southbury, 1801–1803.

Ephraim Munson (1763–1834)   Although Munson was born in Wallingford, his father moved the family to Farmington in 1766 and then to the Wyoming Valley in Pennsylvania in 1771. In 1779 the Munsons moved back to New Haven for a year and then settled in Plymouth, Connecticut. Since the family was in New Haven when Ephraim was sixteen years old, he may have trained there. By 1785 he lived in Bethlehem and owned a home and a shop southeast of the town center. He sold this eight-and-a-half-acre lot in 1796 and bought thirty-nine and a half acres in the northeast corner of Woodbury. This location situated Munson near a sawmill, the highway, and good woodland. In 1811 he sold the land, with its shop and dwelling house, and moved back to Bethlehem, where he bought a farm on Carmel Hill. Apparently he retired as a joiner at this time, although his inventory shows that he kept many of his tools, the price of which imply that they were well aged.

SOURCES: WPR; WLR; WTL; Bethlehem land records (Bethlehem Town Hall); Myron Munson, *The Munson Record* (New Haven: Tuttle, Morehouse & Taylor, 1896).

Barnum Osborn (1764–1852)   Barnum Osborn and his brother, Josiah, were native house joiners in Southbury. Together they framed a shop for Shadrach Osborn and Nathan Preston in 1796. Barnum alone framed a shop for an anonymous South Britain shopkeeper.

SOURCES: STL; HC; Account Book of Shadrach Osborn and Nathan Preston of Southbury, 1790–1796; Account Book of Anonymous Shopkeeper of South Britain, 1788–1789 (Connecticut Historical Society, Hartford).

Josiah Osborn (1755–183?)   Most of Josiah Osborn's work consisted of framing and building tools and board fences. For a South Britain shopkeeper he also made doors, benches, and a chest. Neither Josiah nor his brother, Barnum, was ever assessed for a faculty, nor were they listed as joiners or carpenters on the tax lists.

SOURCES: STL; CR; Account Book of Shadrach Osborn and Nathan Osborn of Southbury, 1790–1796; Account Book of Anonymous Shopkeeper of South Britain, 1787–1789; Account Book of Shadrach Osborn of Southbury, 1777–1784; Account Book of Shadrach Osborn of Southbury, 1801–1803; Account Book of Shadrach Osborn of Southbury, 1806–1807.

William H. Peabody (1769–1841)   Peabody was born and trained in Norwich. In 1797 he moved to a part of Stratford that eventually became Bridgeport. A nineteenth-century history of that city referred to Peabody as Bridgeport's first cabinetmaker. In May 1804, Peabody sold his half-acre home lot, dwelling house, and shop, and purchased eight acres with a house, barn, and outbuildings in Woodbury. In order to purchase the Woodbury estate, Peabody mortgaged it to Robert Bowne, a New York merchant. Several times in the next decade Peabody mortgaged this lot, which lay just west of the meetinghouse. Finally, in 1816, Peabody sold his Woodbury land and returned to Bridgeport.

Matthew Minor's account book recorded that Peabody made a bureau, breakfast table, square stand, and birch kitchen table in 1805. For Minor, Peabody also performed various other jobs such as making a coffin, putting on shovel handles, and mending wooden tools. In return Peabody received foodstuffs, bedstead timber, bass boards, oak boards, maple boards, and plowing service. These transactions, typical among the Woodbury joiners, imply that Peabody concentrated on his woodworking and relied on his customers for food, for whatever labor was needed on his own meagre holdings, and even for wood.

SOURCES: WLR; HC; Account Book of Matthew Minor of Woodbury, 1801–1810; Account Book of Nathaniel Bacon of Woodbury, 1798–1849; Stratford Land Records (Stratford Town Hall); Samuel Orcutt, *A History of the Old Town of Stratford and the City of Bridgeport, Connecticut* (New Haven: Tuttle, Morehouse & Taylor, 1886).

Joseph Prentice (1714–1760)   Like other early Woodbury woodworkers, Prentice combined craftwork and farming. His "carpenders tools" made him more suited to carpentry and house joinery than to furniture production.

SOURCES: WPR; BC.

Arthur Prindle (?–1798)   Prindle lived in Woodbury in 1794, when he became a guardian to his nephew Charles Prindle. Four years later he died. Nevertheless, his inventory reveals a great deal. It consisted largely of house joinery tools: clapboard saw, sash tenon saw, chalk lines, twist augers, broadaxes and hatchets, adzes, carpenter's chisels, panel and molding planes, and compasses. The lack of real estate in his inventory, his low tax rate, and the paucity of household products imply that Prindle was a tramping house joiner. His inventory was appraised by Bartimeus Fabrique and Philemon Cherevoy, two other house joiners. This connection suggests that Prindle may have worked for Fabrique, a relative by marriage.

SOURCES: WPR; WTL.

Charles Prindle (1777–1858)   Charles Prindle was the son of Isaac and Elizabeth Prindle of Huntington. His mother was Bartimeus and David Fabrique's sister. When Isaac died in 1794, Charles became the ward of his uncle Arthur Prindle and probably apprenticed with either of his uncles, Arthur or Bartimeus. Primarily a house joiner who worked on his own and with Elijah Booth and Bartimeus Fabrique of Southbury and James Stilson of Newtown, Prindle did make some furniture. He made four kitchen chairs for Reuben Mitchell in 1803 and a cupboard for Luman Ovit in 1805. In 1806 he also painted a chest and a bedstead for Mitchell. His diary provides valuable information on the mobility and operations of house joiners during this time. He moved to Bethlehem in the 1810s and then to Roxbury in the 1830s.

SOURCES: BC; WLR; Account Book of Charles Prindle of Woodbury, 1801–1806; Account Book of Bartimeus Fabrique of Southbury, 1791–1810.

David Roots (1763–1796)   This native Woodbury joiner led a poor life in town. For Jabez Warner of Washington, Roots made a chest and did some interior joinery in 1786. In 1789, he made six black chairs for Israel Minor, who also had Roots do odd carpentry work.

SOURCES: WPR; CCR; Account Book of Jabez Warner of Washington, 1754–1847 (Connecticut Historical Society, Hartford); Account Book of Israel Minor of Roxbury, 1762–1800 (privately owned).

Cyrus Sherman (1792–1872)   Sherman was a native Woodbury lad who engaged in house joinery for Matthew Minor in the late 1810s and early 1820s. In return he received pork, hay, and potatoes.

SOURCES: HC; BC; Account Book of Matthew Minor of Woodbury, 1802–1826.

Richard Smith (1774–1826)   Smith's inventory revealed a one-bench shop with lathe, gluepot, eighteen planes, and several saws and edge tools. Together with Abraham Lines, a cooper, Smith owned Simeon King's old house, barn, shop, and home lot at Bullit Hill in Southbury. Smith's estate indicated that he was a man of many interests—it included a tavern sign and post, a set of surveying tools, and an extensive library.

SOURCES: WPR; WLR; WTL; BC.

Eldad Spencer (1710–1768)   This Hartford-born joiner owned a large selection of planes in addition to a lathe, chisels, and pine boards. He also owned a farm, animals, and a barn. Spencer divided up his tools and personal estate between his widow and son.

SOURCES: WPR; BC.

Nathan A. Stoddard (1768–1848)   Stoddard contracted with Nathaniel Smith in 1798 to build a woodhouse, chairhouse, and cowhouse. He was listed as a joiner on the tax list of 1798. Stoddard only appeared on the town tax lists from 1791 through 1802. Census records confirm that he left Woodbury sometime between 1800 and 1810.

SOURCES: WTL; CR; Contract between Nathaniel Smith and Nathan A. Stoddard; *Anthony Stoddard and His Descendants: A Genealogy* (New York: J. B. Bradstreet & Son, 1865).

Jervis Summers (1791–1833)   Left fatherless at the age of eleven, Summers became the ward of Abraham Lines, a cooper who lived in the Bullit Hill area of Southbury. Summers probably apprenticed with Eli Hall, for he was performing odd jobs for Hall in 1807. In 1816 Summers bought two acres with a dwelling house, barn, and cooper's shop in the southerly part of Southbury. The tools listed in his estate were probably typical of the Woodbury joiners in the second tier of Woodbury furnituremakers:

1 sett joinerz bench plains 3.50   1 do 2.   1 broad ax 1.50   1 do hatchet .20   1 carpenterz adze 1.   1 Joinerz plow & 4 irons 3.   1 Sash tool gouge & gauges 1.50   1 match plain & bead 1.   6 hollow & round plains 1.50   1 ovelow & bead .34   1 OG & bead .25   1 Ozen .34   1 ½ Bead .20   1 Rabbit plain .25   1 do small .20   1 philister .25   1 Brace & 25 bittz 4.   1 Iron square 1.50   1 do do .50   1 hand saw .50   1 Joint saw .25   1 sash saw .25   1 trying square .50   1 drawing knife .17   1 broad chisel .75   1 two inch do .25   1 inch do .17   1 ½ inch do .12   1 two inch auger .50   1 inch & one half do .25   1 inch & one fourth do .40   1 inch do do .17   1 three fourth inch do .12   1 half inch do .10   1 small trying square .34   1 1 ½ inch firmer .20   2 1 inch do .17   1 ½ inch do .06   1 ½ inch do do .04   1 duck bill chisel .12   1 small gouge .08   1 do chisel .02   18 files & rasps .34   2 Screw drivers .04   1 nail hammer .20   1 rule .34   1 oil stone .25   3 chalk lines & rolls .25   1 pair compasses .10   1 cupboard lock .08   3 turnerz chisels & gouges .34   1 paint stone 1.   2 paint ballz .10   1 grind stone & crank 1.   2 paint potz & 5 paint brushez .25   1 small drawing knife .12   1 tap borer & riveting hammer .17   1 set boltz & screwz .12   1 small paper prussian blue .37   1 lot different kindz paint .75   7 sticks bedstead timbers .08   1 lot cherry boards .50   5 pine boards .75   1 lot butternut boardz .34   1 tool chest part finished .25   1 lot of whitewood & chesnut boards 3.   1 small lot of flaggs .25.

SOURCES: WPR; SLR; BC; *History of New Haven County, Connecticut* (New York: W. W. Preston, 1892).

Notes

Abbreviations

The following source abbreviations appear in the notes, along with those used in the appendixes (see appendix A).

BHS	Bethlehem Historical Society
CHS	Connecticut Historical Society, Hartford
CSL	Connecticut State Library, Hartford
FHS	Fairfield Historical Society
FPR	Fairfield probate court records
LHS	Litchfield Historical Society
MHS	Milford Historical Society
NHHS	New Haven Colony Historical Society
NHS	Newtown Historical Society
OSV	Old Sturbridge Village, Sturbridge, Massachusetts
STHS	Stratford Historical Society
STPR	Stratford probate court records
YUL	Yale University Library, New Haven
WML	Winterthur Museum Library, Delaware

Introduction

1. Samuel Goodrich, *Peter Parley's Own Story* (New York: Sheldon & Co., 1866), 33, 31.

2. Ibid., 18, 320–45. Goodrich's phrase "articles of use" is noteworthy in its resemblance to the Marxist concept *use value*. For a historiographical review that characterizes the intense nonmarket exchanges of rural New England households, see Allan Kulikoff, "The Transition to Capitalism in Rural America," *William and Mary Quarterly* 46, no. 1 (1989), esp. 122–26.

3. For example, see Toby Ditz, *Property and Kinship: Inheritance in Early Connecticut, 1750–1820* (Princeton, N.J.: Princeton University Press, 1986); Susan Geib, "'Changing Works': Agriculture and Society in Brookfield, Massachusetts, 1785–

1820" (Ph.D. diss., Boston University, 1981); Christopher Jedrey, *The World of John Cleaveland: Family and Community in Eighteenth-Century New England* (New York: W. W. Norton, 1979); and Bettye Pruit, "Self-Sufficiency and the Agricultural Economy of Eighteenth-Century Massachusetts," *William and Mary Quarterly* 41, no. 3 (1984): 333–64.

4. Christopher Clark, *The Roots of Rural Capitalism: Western Massachusetts, 1780–1860* (Ithaca, N.Y.: Cornell University Press, 1990). See also Steven Hahn and Jonathan Prude, eds., *The Countryside in the Age of Capitalist Transformation* (Chapel Hill: University of North Carolina Press, 1985); Myron Stachiw and Nora Pat Small, "Tradition and Transformation: Rural Society and Architectural Change in Nineteenth-Century Central Massachusetts," in Thomas Carter and Bernard Herman, eds., *Perspectives in Vernacular Architecture III* (Columbia: University of Missouri Press, 1989), 135–48; and Kulikoff, "Transition to Capitalism," 120–44.

5. John Schlotterbeck first used the term *social economy* to analyze the diverse local economy in Virginia during the second quarter of the nineteenth century. "The 'Social Economy' of an Upper South Community: Orange and Greene Counties, Virginia, 1815–1860," in Orville Burton and Robert McMath Jr., eds., *Class, Conflict, and Consensus: Antebellum Southern Community Studies* (Westport, Conn.: Greenwood Press, 1982), 3–28. I refine this term drawing important insights from sociologists and folklorists who study craftsmen. Using *social economy* to describe particular relationships in a period of involution seems far more flexible and accurate than the European-based terms *moral economy* or *proto-industrialism*. E. P. Thompson, "The Moral Economy of the English Crowd in the Eighteenth Century," *Past & Present* 50 (Feb. 1971), 76–136; Thompson, "Patrician Society, Plebian Culture," *Journal of Social History* 7, no. 4 (1974): 382–405; Franklin Mendels, "Proto-industrialization: The First Phase of the Industrialization Process," *Journal of Economic History* 32 (1972): 241–61; and Hans Medick, "The Proto-Industrial Family Economy: The Structural Function of Household and Family During the Transition from Peasant Society to Industrial Capitalism," *Social History* 3 (Oct. 1976): 291–315. For a discussion of why the term *proto-industrialization* is not appropriate for the early national period in America, see James Henretta, "The War for Independence and American Economic Development," in Ronald Hoffman et al., eds., *The Economy of Early America: The Revolutionary Period* (Charlottesville: University Press of Virginia, 1988), 45–87.

6. Michel Foucault, *The Order of Things: An Archaeology of the Human Sciences* (New York: Random House, 1973). For an example of a contemporary skilled craftsman who works within a similar network, which cannot be defined by economic transactions alone, see Douglas Harper, *Working Knowledge: Skill and Community in a Small Shop* (Chicago: University of Chicago Press, 1987).

7. For example, see Clark, *Rural Capitalism;* and Gregory Nobles, "The Rise of Merchants in Rural Market Towns: A Case Study of Eighteenth-Century Northampton, Massachusetts," *Journal of Social History* 24, no. 1 (1990): 5–23.

8. Rolla M. Tryon, *Household Manufactures in the United States, 1684–1860* (Chicago: University of Chicago Press, 1917). In "Organization and Extent of Textile Manufacture in Eighteenth-Century Rural Pennsylvania: A Case Study of Chester County" (Ph.D. diss., University of California, San Diego, 1988), Adrienne Hood

demonstrates the weaknesses of Tryon's thesis. Eighteenth-century Pennsylvania communities were not totally self-sufficient. Owing to limits such as the small number of looms, local production never met the community's needs. Indeed a great variety of imported materials were purchased, ranging from inexpensive necessities to costly luxuries. Throughout the century, local economic pressures and opportunities determined how much cloth was made and how much was imported by each household. The importation of cloth freed up potentially productive time for other livelihoods and therefore played an important part in each family's decisions.

9. Carl Bridenbaugh, *The Colonial Craftsman* (New York: New York University Press, 1950). For a recent appraisal of Bridenbaugh's work, see Ian Quimby, ed., *The Craftsman in Early America* (New York: W. W. Norton, 1984), esp. 3–16.

10. For a fuller discussion, see Edward S. Cooke Jr., "Craftsmen: Product, Process, and Context," in Kenneth L. Ames and Gerald W. R. Ward, eds., *Decorative Arts and Household Furnishings Used in America, 1650–1920: An Annotated Bibliography* (Winterthur, Del.: Henry Francis du Pont Winterthur Museum, 1989), 333–36.

11. Auction catalogues, for example, often attribute much surviving work to the general New England region but provide very specific attributions for urban examples. On the need to look at rural furniture on its own terms, see Robert F. Trent, *Hearts and Crowns* (New Haven: New Haven Colony Historical Society, 1979).

12. Good examples of the limited classical approach include Charles Hummel, *With Hammer in Hand* (Charlottesville: University Press of Virginia, 1968); and Philip Zea, "Rural Craftsmen and Design," in Brock Jobe and Myrna Kaye, *New England Furniture: The Colonial Era* (Boston: Houghton Mifflin, 1984), 47–72.

13. Edward S. Cooke Jr., "The Study of American Furniture from the Perspective of the Maker," in Gerald W. R. Ward, ed., *Perspectives on American Furniture* (New York: W. W. Norton, 1988), 113–26.

14. On the place of wood in the New England pysche, see William Cronon, *Changes in the Land: Colonists and the Ecology of New England* (New York: Hill and Wang, 1983); and Edward S. Cooke Jr., "Bridging Artifice and Nature: Wood in American Material Culture," in Jeff Hardwick, ed., *Wood: Timber, Transformation, and Design* (New Haven, Conn., and Washington, D.C.: Yale-Smithsonian Seminar on Material Culture, forthcoming).

15. Brooke Hindle, ed., *America's Wooden Age: Aspects of its Early Technology* (New York: Sleepy Hollow Restoration, 1975); Robert St. George, "Fathers, Sons, and Identity: Woodworking Artisans in Southeastern New England, 1620–1700," in Ian Quimby, ed., *The Craftsman in Early America* (New York: W. W. Norton, 1984), 89–125.

16. Grant McCracken, *Culture and Consumption: New Approaches to the Symbolic Character of Consumer Goods and Activities* (Bloomington: Indiana University Press, 1988), esp. 58–89, 118–29; and Mary Douglas, *The World of Goods: Towards An Anthropology of Consumption* (New York: W. W. Norton, 1979), esp. 4–5, 59–65.

17. Mihaly Csikszentmihalyi and Eugene Rochberg-Halton, *The Meaning of Things: Domestic Symbols and the Self* (New York: Cambridge University Press, 1981), 58–64.

18. For the traditional view of craftwork as a form of supplemental income, discrete and separable from "real" agricultural work, or as a new strategy, see Jack-

son Turner Main, *Society and Economy in Colonial Connecticut* (Princeton, N.J.: Princeton University Press, 1985), 241–56; and Kenneth Lockridge, "Land, Population and the Evolution of New England Society, 1630–1790; and an Afterthought," in Stanley Katz, ed., *Colonial America: Essays in Politics and Social Development* (Boston: Little, Brown, 1971), 466–91. A regional study of woodworkers in the seventeenth century provides a good example of how craft skills operated within an earlier cultural system. St. George, "Fathers, Sons, and Identity."

19. Among the increasing literature on consumption, the most pertinent studies include Neil McKendrick, John Brewer, and J. H. Plumb, *The Birth of Consumer Society: The Commercialization of Eighteenth-Century England* (Bloomington: Indiana University Press, 1982); Carole Shammas, *The Preindustrial Consumer in England and America* (Oxford: Clarendon Press, 1990); Cary Carson, Ronald Hoffman, and Peter Albert, eds., *Of Consuming Interests: The Style of Life in the Eighteenth Century* (Charlottesville: University Press of Virginia, 1994); and Ann Smart Martin, "Makers, Buyers, and Users: Consumerism as a Material Culture Framework," *Winterthur Portfolio* 28, nos. 2/3 (1993): 141–57.

One

1. Robert St. George has shown that the number of southeastern Massachusetts woodworkers who combined several related trades increased toward the end of the seventeenth century. "Fathers, Sons, and Identity: Woodworking Artisans in Southeastern New England, 1620–1700," in Ian Quimby, ed., *The Craftsman in Early America* (New York: W. W. Norton, 1984), 120–24. Other pertinent discussions on the New England woodworker in the late seventeenth and early eighteenth centuries include Robert Trent, "New England Joinery and Turning Before 1700," in *New England Begins: The Seventeenth Century* (Boston: Museum of Fine Arts, 1982), 3:501–50; Abbott Cummings, *The Framed Houses of Massachusetts Bay, 1625–1725* (Cambridge: Harvard University Press, 1979), 42–44; and Patricia Kane, *Furniture of the New Haven Colony: The Seventeenth-Century Style* (New Haven: New Haven Colony Historical Society, 1973), 6–7, 78–93.

2. The concept of a spectrum of woodworkers based on specific tasks is derived from Jeannette Lasansky, *To Draw, Upset and Weld: The Work of the Pennsylvania Rural Blacksmith, 1742–1935* (Lewisburg, Penn.: Oral Traditions Project of the Union County Historical Society, 1980), esp. 16–17. The differences in ranges of tools can be identified in R. A. Salaman, *Dictionary of Tools Used in the Woodworking and Allied Trades, c. 1700–1970* (London: George Allen & Unwin, 1975).

3. Account Book of Daniel Bishop of Bethlehem, 1801–1818 (BHS); Account Book of Joseph and Simeon Curtiss of Southbury, 1783–1827 (YUL). The career of Jedidiah Williamson, who lived in Stony Brook, Long Island, suggests that such a pattern was not indigenous to western Connecticut. Edward Fix, "A Long Island Carpenter at Work: A Quantitative Inquiry into the Account Book of Jedediah Williamson," parts 1 and 2, *Chronicle of the Early American Industries Association* 32, no. 4 (1979): 61–63; 33, no. 1 (1980): 4–8.

4. On the growth of the Connecticut meat and pork trade, see Richard Bushman, *From Puritan to Yankee* (New York: W. W. Norton, 1970), 108–16; Glen Weaver,

Jonathan Trumbull, Connecticut's Merchant Magistrate (1710–1785) (Hartford: Connecticut Historical Society, 1956); and chapter four. The best overall work on coopering is Kenneth Kilby, *The Cooper and His Trade* (London: Baker, 1971).

5. WPR 7:142–43.

6. Account Book of Shadrach Osborn and Truman Hinman of Southbury, 1775–1781 (CHS).

7. Percy Bidwell, "Rural Economy in New England at the Beginning of the Nineteenth Century," *Connecticut Academy of Arts and Sciences Transactions* 20 (1916): 302–4, 337–38; and Howard Russell, *A Long, Deep Furrow* (Hanover, N.H.: University Press of New England, 1976), 234–36, 249, 271–72. The increasing use of dairy products as a medium of exchange and the seasonal production rhythms of coopers are clearly revealed in the account books of Shadrach Osborn. Account Book of Shadrach Osborn of Southbury, 1786–1788 (WML); Account Book of Shadrach Osborn and Nathan Preston of Southbury, 1790–1796 (WML); Account Book of Shadrach Osborn of Southbury, 1796–1806 (WML); and Account Book of Shadrach Osborn of Southbury, 1801–1803 (LHS).

8. DPR 5:69–70, 7:544–46.

9. WPR 9:134, 10:104; DPR 7:138. Salaman's discussion in *Dictionary of Tools* of the wheelwright's tools and tasks also demonstrates wheelwrights' differences with other woodworkers. The effect of transportation improvements on the wagonmakers and wheelwrights of eastern Long Island is noted by Charles Hummel in *With Hammer in Hand* (Charlottesville: University Press of Virginia, 1968), 238.

10. The effect of the Revolution on spinning and weaving is examined by James Walsh in *Connecticut Industry and the Revolution* (Chester, Conn.: Pequot Press, 1978), 13–27. Carolyn Cooper and Patrick Malone discuss the importance of the textile market for woodworkers in "The Mechanical Woodworker in Early 19th-Century New England as a Spin-off from Textile Industrialization" (paper presented at Old Sturbridge Village, Mass., March 1990). Local owners of spinning and weaving manufactories included John Curtiss and Samuel Beers of Newtown and Curtis Hinman of Woodbury. NPR 1:31–33, 37–40, 72; Woodbury Probate District, Docket 2021 (CSL).

11. WPR 11:214; New Milford Probate District, Docket 2530.

12. NLR 32:553.

13. The 1796 Assessment for Newtown distinguishes between house and shop joiners, but the 1797 list lumps the two groups together as joiners. In eighteenth-century western Connecticut, the term *shop joiner* denoted a craftsman who spent the bulk of his time producing, finishing, or repairing furniture. 1796 and 1797 Assessments for Newtown (CHS); Benno Forman, "The Crown and York Chairs of Coastal Connecticut and the Work of the Durands of Milford," *Antiques* 105, no. 5 (1974): 1147–54; and 1777 apprenticeship agreement between Elijah Booth and Daniel Hurd (facsimile printed in the *Newtown Bee*, Oct. 27, 1967, sec. A, p. 1).

Throughout this study, bedsteads have been considered separately from furniture. Several different types of woodworkers produced bedsteads. Individual parts of bedsteads were also sold by sawmill owners, a custom that allowed anyone to assemble a bedstead. In inventories, bedsteads were listed with beds and bedding rather than with household furniture.

14. Account Book of Charles Prindle, 1801–1806 (CHS); and Account Book of Nehemiah Pray of Huntington and Brookfield, 1810–1820 (NHS). The main difference between Prindle and Pray and earlier ambidextrous craftsmen such as Joseph Brown Jr. and James Briscoe Jr. is the proportion of work devoted to different tasks. Whereas earlier craftsmen divided their time almost equally among several tasks, Prindle and Pray spent most of their time on house joinery.

15. The different spheres of the house joiner and shop joiner is best shown by an account book reference in which Elijah Booth, a shop joiner, received forty window sashes and journeyman's work on a cupboard from Bartimeus Fabrique, a house joiner. Account Book of Bartimeus Fabrique of Southbury, 1785–1820 (YUL), 13.

16. Joseph Moxon, *Mechanick exercises; or, The doctrine of handy-works* (1703; New York: Praeger, 1970), 118.

17. Account Book of Charles Prindle of Woodbury, 1801–1806 (CHS); William Warren, "The Oxford Meeting House," *Connecticut Antiquarian* 33, no. 1 (1981): 4–8; Warren, "The First Two Southbury Meeting Houses," *Connecticut Antiquarian* 33, no. 2 (1981): 22–32; and Account Book of Nehemiah Pray of Huntington and Brookfield, 1810–1820 (NHS). E. J. Hobsbawm discusses formalized tramping and its roots in "The Tramping Artisan," in *Labouring Men: Studies in the History of Labor* (New York: Basic Books, 1964), 34–63.

18. On the etymological roots of the term *joiner* and its popularity in New England, see Benno Forman, "Urban Aspects of Massachusetts Furniture in the Late Seventeenth Century," in John Morse, ed., *Country Cabinetwork and Simple City Furniture* (Charlottesville: University Press of Virginia, 1970), 5, 15–20. In the Newtown-Woodbury area, the first reference to cabinetmaker was a 1794 apprenticeship agreement between Joel Booth of Newtown and Robert Hazard. A 1797 entry in Bennet French's account book lists Nicholas Jebine as a "Cabbinet Maker in Woodbury." *Newtown Bee*, Feb. 12, 1904, p. 3; and Account Book of Bennet French of Southbury, 1793–1804 (privately owned), 22. Dean Failey found continued use of *joiner* and the first use of *cabinetmaker* in the 1790s on Long Island. *Long Island Is My Nation* (Setauket, N.Y.: Society for the Preservation of Long Island Antiquities, 1976), 191.

19. Good introductory studies of woodworking techniques and tools include Moxon, *Mechanick exercises*; Hummel, *With Hammer in Hand*; Salaman, *Dictionary of Tools*; Henry Mercer, *Ancient Carpenter's Tools* (Doylestown, Penn.: Bucks County Historical Society, 1951); Robert St. George, *The Wrought Covenant* (Brockton, Mass.: Brockton Art Center, 1979); and W. L. Goodman, "Tools and Equipment of the Early Settlers in the New World," *The Chronicle of the Early American Industries Association* 29, no. 3 (1976): 40–51. Analysis of specific furniture and inventories from rural western Connecticut has refined further these studies' findings.

20. For a wide drawer, joiners in western Connecticut used a single board with grain parallel to the front, or two boards with a shiplap joint between them, and secured it only along the back edge. Since the bottom board or boards floated within grooves along the interior surface of the other three sides, they could easily expand and contract with climatic changes. For smaller drawers, the joiner would orient the grain of the bottom board so that it ran perpendicular to the front and then secure it with a single nail along the back, thus allowing necessary movement. This tech-

nique of bottoming drawers differed significantly from the dominant Boston tradition.

21. WPR 7:18; see also FPR 10:544-48.

22. On the different types of inlay, see Benjamin Hewitt, "Regional Characteristics of American Federal-Period Card Tables," in *The Work of Many Hands: Card Tables in Federal America, 1790-1820* (New Haven: Yale University Art Gallery, 1982), esp. 73-84.

23. DPR 1:298; Account Book of Charles Prindle of Woodbury, 1801-1806 (CHS). Other references to oil, varnish, and paints in joiners' inventories can be found in the FPR 14:160-63, 16:109, 19:477-81. The best discussions of eighteenth-century finishes are Robert Mussey, "Transparent Furniture Finishes in New England, 1700-1825," *Old-Time New England* 72 (1987): 287-311; and Dean Fales Jr., *American Painted Furniture, 1660-1880* (New York: E. P. Dutton, 1979). The preference for unstained cherry and maple is in contrast with furniture made in eastern Connecticut, eastern Massachusetts, and New Hampshire, where joiners used a dark stain on curly maple or cherry to make the wood look like mahogany.

24. *Farmer's Journal* (March 26, 1792), 4; Account Book of Samuel and Thomas Bull of Woodbury, 1719-1790 (CSL), 132; and Account Book of George Northrop of Newtown, 1792-1827 (CSL), 47.

25. FPR 12:434-38.

26. Account Book of Samuel Beers of Newtown, 1794-1815 (privately owned), 34; Account Book of Samuel Beers of Newtown, 1776-1810 (privately owned), 40; Danbury Probate District, Docket 866 (CSL); Account Book of Ziba Blakeslee of Newtown, 1789-1822 (WML), 57; Account Book of Matthew Minor of Woodbury, 1800-1820 (privately owned), 38; Account Book of Nathaniel Bacon of Woodbury, 1798-1849 (CHS), 73; Receipt of Matthew Minor, Nov. 22, 1822 (privately owned); Account Book of Caleb Baldwin of Newtown, 1800-1846 (YUL), 79, 139; Account Book of an Anonymous Dyer/Fuller of Newtown, 1802-1808 (privately owned); and Account Book of Philo Beardslee of Newtown, 1804-1833 (LHS), 143.

27. STPR 3:267.

28. Charles Hummel, "The Business of Woodworking: 1700 to 1840," in Paul Kebabian and William Lipke, eds., *Tools and Technologies: America's Wooden Age* (Burlington, Vt.: Robert Hull Fleming Museum, 1979), 52-53; Frank White, "The Involuntary Legacy of Samuel Wing, Cabinetmaker/Chairmaker," *Old Sturbridge Visitor* 22, no. 3 (1982): 8-9; and Fairfield Probate Court Records, 12:452-54, 14:160, 16:109, 19:477-81. As John Light demonstrates, investigation of old shop sites might prove important to the understanding of a craftsman's world. "The Archeological Investigation of Blacksmith Shops," *Journal of the Society for Industrial Archeology* 10, no. 1 (1984):55-68.

29. *1820 Census of Manufactures—Connecticut Schedules* (National Archives Microfilm Publications, microcopy no. 279), 146.

30. The only known account book of a joiner working in northern Fairfield County or southern Litchfield County does not reveal seasonal rhythms. Account Book of Elisha Hawley of Ridgefield, 1786-1800 (CHS). For examples of estates with unfinished furniture, see the inventories of Ebenezer Bulkley and Daniel Dimon of Fairfield, Andrew Sherwood and Hezekiah Treadwell of Stratford, Joel

Booth and Alexander Bryan of Newtown, and Simeon King of Woodbury. Fairfield Probate District, Dockets 1162 and 1963; FPR 13:177, 16:109; Danbury Probate District, Docket 866; DPR 1:222–23; and Woodbury Probate District, Docket 2612. Exceptions to this seasonal rule were the larger shops run by Daniel Hoyt of Fairfield, Brewster Dayton of Stratford, and Ebenezer Booth of Newtown. FPR 19:312–14; STPR 3:267; and Danbury Probate District, Docket 861.

31. On the seasonal rhythms of John Dunlap, see Ann Dibble, "Major John Dunlap: The Craftsman and His Community," *Old-Time New England* 68, nos. 3/4 (1978): 50–58.

32. FPR 19:477–81; Danbury Probate District, Dockets 861 and 866; Woodbury Probate District, Docket 2608; and WPR 7:18. Patterns used by the woodworkers of the Dominy family are illustrated in Hummel, *With Hammer in Hand*, 96–100. Patterns belonging to Samuel Wing, a chairmaker from Barnstable, Massachusetts, are owned by Old Sturbridge Village. White, "Involuntary Legacy of Samuel Wing."

33. WPR 7:18; Woodbury Probate District, Docket 26; Danbury Probate District, Dockets 861 and 1854; FPR 14:160–63, 19:477–81; and STPR 3:267. For a dendrological and technological discussion of this technique, see John Alexander Jr., *Make a Chair from a Tree: An Introduction to Working Green Wood* (Newtown: Taunton Press, 1978), esp. 53–101. Benno Forman points out the historical implications of this technology in "Delaware Valley 'Crookt Foot' and Slat-Back Chairs," *Winterthur Portfolio* 15, no. 1 (1980): 45–46. Forman refers to this technology, and the use of patterns, as an urban-based phenomenon caused by the collaboration of several different craftsmen. The evidence from rural Connecticut suggests otherwise. The inventories of Ezekiel Hawley, Brewster Dayton, and Joel Booth, which also listed stockpiles of slats, are another indication of efficiency in the larger shops. FPR 19:477–81; STPR 3:267; and Danbury Probate District, Docket 866.

34. Trent, "New England Joinery," 506–7; and Benno Forman, "Mill Sawing in 17th-Century Massachusetts," *Old-Time New England* 60, no. 2 (1970): 110–30. The restrictions and perils of early water-powered machinery and the eventual role of the market in overcoming such shortcomings is well documented by Anthony Wallace in *Rockdale* (New York: W. W. Norton, 1980), esp. 124–34.

35. NLR 28:612–13, 29:80, 30:58, 499, 31:443–44, 33:24–25; Stratford Probate District, Docket 821; and WLR 37:265. Beginning in 1827, Charles Booth of Southbury used water power to turn chair posts and to saw and plane other chair parts for shipment to New York. Account Book of Charles Booth of Southbury, 1827–1834 (YUL). In 1774, the southern towns of Stratford, Newtown, Redding, and Danbury had moderate population density, with about 32 to 47 people per square mile; the northern towns of Derby, Woodbury, New Milford, and Litchfield had a sparser population, about 27 to 31 people per square mile. By 1790 the southern towns averaged 40–53 people per square mile and the northern towns, 33–39. Bruce Daniels, *The Connecticut Town: Growth and Development, 1635–1790* (Middletown: Wesleyan University Press, 1979), 50–63.

36. Woodbury Probate District, Docket 2972; Newtown Probate District, Docket 1714; NTL, 1820; Account Book of Joseph and Simeon Curtiss of Southbury, 1783–1827 (YUL); and Account Book of David Stiles of Southbury, 1789–1815

(privately owned). Several inventories of joiners listed boards at the sawmill. Newtown Probate District, Docket 69; and FPR 14:160–63.

37. Diary of Charles Prindle of Woodbury, 1799–1802 (CHS). On the trade of cherry boards among merchants, see Account Book of Freegift Hawkins of Derby, 1770–1825 (LHS).

38. Account Book of Thomas Tousey of Newtown, 1716–1761 (NHS), 124; and Account Book of Matthew Minor of Woodbury, 1800–1820 (privately owned), 5.

39. In *With Hammer in Hand,* Hummel illustrates tenon-cutting bits, a scraper, a turning chisel, and keyhole saws that the Dominys had made from old tools.

40. Account Book of John Hubbell of Newtown, 1792–1793 (OSV); WPR 7:37, 10:158; Account Book of Shadrach Osborn of Southbury, 1783–1792 (YUL); Miscellaneous Receipts of Shadrach Osborn of Southbury (CSL); and DPR 9:319–25.

41. John Worrell uses the term *low technology* craft production in his discussion of Hervey Brooks, a potter in Goshen, Connecticut, during the early national period. "Ceramic Production in the Exchange Network of an Agricultural Neighborhood" (paper presented to the Society for Historical Archeology, Philadelphia, 1982).

Two

1. Robert Seybolt, *Apprenticeship and Apprenticeship Education in Colonial New England and New York* (New York: Columbia University Teachers College, 1917); Paul Douglas, *American Apprenticeship and Industrial Education* (New York: Columbia University Press, 1921); Ian Quimby, *Apprenticeship in Colonial Philadelphia* (New York: Garland Publishing, 1985); and William Rorabaugh, *The Craft Apprentice: From Franklin to the Machine Age in America* (New York: Oxford University Press, 1986).

2. Mutual obligations affected not only crafts training but the whole realm of social and economic activities. Philip Greven, *Four Generations: Population, Land, and Family in Colonial Andover, Massachusetts* (Ithaca, N.Y.: Cornell University Press, 1970); James Henretta, "Families and Farms: *Mentalité* in Pre-Industrial America," *William and Mary Quarterly* 35, no. 1 (1978): 3–32; and John Waters, "Patrimony, Succession, and Social Stability: Guilford, Connecticut, in the Eighteenth Century," *Perspectives in American History* 10 (1976): 131–60. On the role of apprentice woodworkers in the life cycles of their masters, see Edward Fix, "A Long Island Carpenter at Work: A Quantitative Inquiry into the Account Book of Jedediah Williamson," parts 1 and 2, *Chronicle of the Early American Industries Association* 32, no. 4 (1979): 61–63; 33, no. 1 (1980): 4–8; and Ann Dibble, "Major John Dunlap: The Craftsman and his Community," *Old-Time New England* 68, nos. 3–4 (1978): 50–58.

3. Apprenticeship agreement between Lazarus Prindle and Joseph Peck Jr., June 5, 1793 (privately owned).

4. The importance of observation, learning fundamental formulas, and internalizing a master's values is stressed by the master upholsterer Andrew Passeri, "My Life as an Upholsterer, 1927–1986," in Gerald Ward, ed., *Perspectives in American Furniture* (New York: W. W. Norton, 1988), 169–203. Philip Zimmerman points out the role of workmanship of habit in "Workmanship as Evidence: A Model for Object Study," *Winterthur Portfolio* 16, no. 4 (1981): 283–307.

5. Works that indicate how a craftsman broadened his performance include

George Sturt, *The Wheelwright's Shop* (1923; reprint, New York: Cambridge University Press, 1963); and R. Gerald Alvey, *Dulcimer Maker: The Craft of Homer Ledford* (Lexington: University Press of Kentucky, 1984). Pertinent works on American furnituremakers include John Bivins Jr., *The Furniture of Coastal North Carolina, 1700–1820* (Winston-Salem, N.C.: Museum of Early Southern Decorative Arts, 1988); William Hosley Jr., "Timothy Loomis and the Economy of Joinery in Windsor, Connecticut, 1740–1786," in Ward, *Perspectives*, 127–51; Brock Jobe, "Urban Craftsmen and Design," in Brock Jobe and Myrna Kaye, *New England Furniture: The Colonial Era* (Boston: Houghton Mifflin, 1984), 3–46; Robert Trent, *Hearts and Crowns* (New Haven: New Haven Colony Historical Society, 1977); and Philip Zea, "Furniture," in William Hosley Jr. and Gerald Ward, eds., *The Great River: Art and Society of the Connecticut Valley* (Hartford, Conn.: Wadsworth Atheneum, 1985), 185–91.

6. Edward S. Cooke Jr., "Craftsman-Client Relations in the Housatonic Valley, 1720–1800," *Antiques* 125, no. 1 (1984): 272–80; and Cooke, "The Work of Brewster Dayton and Ebenezer Hubbell of Stratford, Connecticut," *Connecticut Historical Society Bulletin* 51, no. 4 (1986): 196–224.

7. For the most recent published treatment of these shops, see Edward S. Cooke Jr., "The Social Economy of the Preindustrial Joiner in Western Connecticut, 1750–1800," in Luke Beckerdite, ed., *American Furniture 1995* (Milwaukee: Chipstone Foundation, 1995); and Gerald Ward, *American Case Furniture in the Mabel Brady Garvan and Other Collections at Yale University* (New Haven: Yale University Art Gallery, 1988), 142–44.

8. Account book of Joseph Shelton of Stratford, 1728–1789 (YUL), 22, 30; Account Book of Ephraim Curtiss of Stratford, 1743–1775 (CHS), 264; and FPR 14:520.

9. Information on woods was drawn from a survey of FPR 4 through FPR 20. On local economic activities, see Connecticut Archives: Industry and Connecticut Archives: Trade and Maritime Affairs (CSL). On the Stratford examples, see Account Book of John Brooks Jr. of Stratford, 1784–1824 (Bridgeport Museum of Art, Science, and Industry, Conn.); and Account Book of Lewis Burritt of Stratford, 1794–1838 (STHS). In Marblehead, joiners such as Joseph Lindsey (1714–1764) and cabinetmakers such as the Boston-trained Nathan Bowen (1752–1837) worked according to the maritime seasonal cycle: they fitted furnituremaking in-between work at sea or work on board coastal schooners in the warmer months, as well as during the months when the harbor was frozen in. Local economics also affected the materials used in these shops. The accounts of Lindsey's and Bowen's shops reveal that they had access to imported woods such as walnut from the mid-Atlantic colonies and mahogany from the West Indies as well as white pine from New Hampshire and what is now Maine. Lacking an abundant local supply of cabinet-grade wood, these craftsmen naturally relied on their network with coastal traders and fishermen for their raw materials. Account Book of Joseph Lindsey of Marblehead, 1739–1764 (WML); Jobe, "Urban Craftsmen," 12–13; Account Book of Nathan Bowen of Marblehead, 1775–1779 (WML); Philip Chadwick Smith, ed., *The Journals of Ashley Brown (1728–1813) of Marblehead* (Boston: Colonial Society of Massachusetts, 1973), 2:646; and Richard Randall Jr., "An Eighteenth Century Partnership," *Art Quarterly* 23, no. 2 (1960): 152–61.

10. These observations are based on readings of account books from western Connecticut in the collections of the BHS, CHS, CSL, FHS, LHS, MHS, NHHS, NHS, OSV Library, WML, and YUL. The best sources are the Account Book of John Durand of Milford, 1760–1783 (MHS) and the Account Book of Elisha Hawley of Ridgefield, 1786–1800 (CHS). Even as late as 1844, it was customary for cabinetmakers in Greenfield, Massachusetts, a community no longer dominated by farming, to work evenings from September to March. These extended winter hours allowed a shop to produce sufficient pieces and parts for much of the following year. Christopher Clark, "The Diary of an Apprentice Cabinetmaker: Edward Jenner Carpenter's 'Journal' 1844–45," *Proceedings of the American Antiquarian Society* 98, part 2 (1989), 325 and 359.

11. In addition to the account books cited in note 10, see Account Book of David and Abner Haven of Framingham, Massachusetts, 1786–1841 (WML); Benno Forman, "Delaware Valley 'Crookt Foot' and Slat-Back Chairs: The Fussell-Savery Connection," *Winterthur Portfolio* 15, no. 1 (1980): 41–64; and Bernard Cotton, *The English Regional Chair* (Woodbridge, Suffolk: Antique Collectors' Club, 1990), esp. 13–31.

12. The best summary of the distinctive aspects of case furniture is Ward, *American Case Furniture*, esp. 3–17. Few scholars have specifically addressed the production rhythms involved in case furniture, but see Jeanne Vibert Sloane, "John Cahoone and the Newport Furniture Industry," *Old-Time New England* 72 (1987): 88–122; and Margaretta Lovell, "'Such Furniture as Will Be Most Profitable': The Business of Cabinetmaking in Eighteenth-Century Newport," *Winterthur Portfolio* 26, no. 1 (1991): 27–62.

13. For a contemporary perspective on the efficiency and exactness possible from empirical knowledge and repetitive action, see Sam Maloof, *Sam Maloof: Woodworker* (New York: Kodansha International, 1983). Maloof maintains that he can cut dovetails for a piece of case furniture in less time than it would take him to set up and use a jig for a router or table saw.

14. On the view that templates were an urban characteristic, see Forman, "Delaware Vallye," esp. 51; and Philip Zimmerman, "Workmanship as Evidence: A Model for Object Study," *Winterthur Portfolio* 16, no. 4 (1981): 283–308. Estimates on the time necessary to make case furniture have been drawn from prices listed in William Hosley, "Timothy Loomis and the Economy of Joinery," 137–39, 150–51; and Account Book of Oliver Avery of Norwich, 1788–1839 (WML).

15. See, for example, appendixes A and B.

16. Douglas Harper uses the terms *nature of work* and *context of work* in *Working Knowledge: Skill and Community in a Small Shop* (Chicago: University of Chicago Press, 1987).

17. My understanding of the social basis of design and workmanship is derived from Clifford Geertz, *Local Knowledge: Further Essays in Interpretive Anthropology* (New York: Basic Books, 1983); Michael Jones, *The Hand Made Object and Its Maker* (Berkeley and Los Angeles: University of California Press, 1975); Henry Glassie, *Folk Housing in Middle Virginia* (Knoxville: University of Tennessee Press, 1975); Christian Norberg-Schulz, *Intentions in Architecture* (Cambridge: MIT Press, 1968); and Louis Chiaramonte, *Craftsman-Client Contracts: Interpersonal Relations in a New-*

foundland Fishing Community (St. John's: Memorial University of Newfoundland, 1970).

18. Barbara Ward explains the terms *learned techniques* and *chosen techniques* in "The Craftsman in a Changing Society: Boston Goldsmiths, 1690–1730" (Ph.D. diss., Boston University, 1983), 40–44, 100–104.

19. Edward S. Cooke Jr., "Craftsman-Client Relations"; Cooke, "Work of Brewster Dayton"; and Cooke, "New Netherlands' Influence on Furniture of the Housatonic Valley," in Joshua Lane, ed., *The Impact of the New Netherlands Upon the Colonial Long Island Basin* (New Haven, Conn., and Washington, D.C.: Yale-Smithsonian Seminar on Material Culture, 1993), 36–43.

20. Edward S. Cooke Jr., "The Selective Conservative Taste: Furniture in Stratford, Connecticut, 1740–1800" (M.A. thesis, University of Delaware, 1979); and Account Book of Lewis Burritt of Stratford, 1794–1838 (STHS).

21. Cooke, "Craftsman-Client Relations"; Dean Failey, *Long Island Is My Nation* (Setauket, N.Y.: Society for the Preservation of Long Island Antiquities, 1976); and Michael Podmaniczky, "Examination Report of Brewster Dayton High Chest 68.772" (MS, Winterthur Museum, 1989).

22. Cooke, "Work of Brewster Dayton"; and Fairfield County Court Records, 1768–1773 (CSL), 307.

23. Robert Trent, "The Colchester School of Cabinetmaking, 1750–1800," in Francis Puig and Michael Conforti, eds., *The American Craftsman and the European Tradition, 1620–1820* (Minneapolis: Minneapolis Institute of Arts, 1989), 112–35; and Trent, "New London County Joined Chairs: Legacy of a Provincial Elite," *Connecticut Historical Society Bulletin* 50, no. 4 (1985): 15–186.

24. On the legacy of woodworking skills in the seventeenth century, see Robert St. George, "Fathers, Sons, and Identity: Woodworking Artisans in Southeastern New England, 1620–1700," in Ian Quimby, ed., *The Craftsman in Early America* (New York: W. W. Norton, 1984), 89–125. The adaptive nature of New Englanders in the eighteenth century is best demonstrated by Christopher Jedrey, *The World of John Cleaveland* (New York: W. W. Norton, 1979); Douglas Jones, *Village and Seaport* (Hanover, N.H.: University Press of New England, 1981); and Fred Anderson, "A People's Army: Provincial Military Service in Massachusetts During the Seven Years' War," *William and Mary Quarterly* 40, no. 4 (1983): 499–527.

25. The traditional emphasis on the lineal family and its influence on adaptive strategies is discussed by Jedrey, *World of John Cleaveland*; Jones, *Village and Seaport*; Robert Gross, *The Minutemen and Their World* (New York: Hill and Wang, 1976); and Henretta, "Families and Farms," 3–32.

26. Benno Forman, "The Crown and York Chairs of Coastal Connecticut and the Work of the Durands of Milford," *Antiques* 105, no. 5 (1974): 1147–54; Cooke, "Selective Conservative Taste," 44; Account Book of John Brooks Jr. of Stratford, 1784–1824 (Bridgeport Museum of Art, Science, and Industry, Conn.), 20, 81; and Bridgeport Probate District, Docket 2232. See appendix A for information on the Prindle family. A similar pattern of craft families and traditionalism existed on eighteenth-century Long Island. Failey, *Long Island*, 191–200.

27. See appendixes A and B for information on the Booths, Fabriques, and Prindles. The Beardslees included Henry and Andrew of Stratford, John of Trum-

bull, John of Newtown, and John of Woodbury (who apprenticed with Bartimeus Fabrique). Account Book of John Brooks Jr. of Stratford, 1784–1824 (Bridgeport Museum of Art, Science, and Industry, Conn.), 31; Account Book of Henry Curtiss of Stratford, 1749–83 (SHS), 82; Account Book of Philo Curtiss of Stratford, 1795–1824 (Boothe Homestead, Stratford, Conn.), 6; Stratford Probate District, Docket 151; Newtown Probate District, Docket 69; and Account Book of Bartimeus Fabrique of Southbury, 1785–1820 (YUL), 31–35, 47.

28. Robert Trent, "New England Joinery and Turning Before 1700," in Robert Trent and Jonathan Fairbanks, eds., *New England Begins: The Seventeenth Century* (Boston: Museum of Fine Arts, 1982), 3:501–50; Robert St. George, "Style and Structure in the Joinery of Dedham and Medfield, Massachusetts, 1635–1685," *Winterthur Portfolio* 13 (1979): 1–46; and I. T. Frary, *Early Homes of Ohio* (1936; New York: Dover Publications, 1970), 90–95. *Plain and Elegant, Rich and Common* (Concord: New Hampshire Historical Society, 1979), a catalogue of documented New Hampshire furniture, implies that many joiners who migrated to that state retained the traditions of their training. This study, as well as William Hosley Jr.'s "Vermont Furniture, 1790–1830," *Old-Time New England* 72 (1987): 245–86, and Kenneth Zogry's "Vermont Furniture in the Bennington Museum," *Antiques* 144, no. 2 (1993): 190–201, point out that more work needs to be done on cultural transfer in New Hampshire and Vermont.

29. Newtown Probate District, Docket 970; H. Franklin Andrews, *The Hamlin Family* (Exira, Iowa: H. Franklin Andrews, 1902); Samuel Orcutt, *A History of the Old Town of Stratford and the City of Bridgeport, Connecticut* (New Haven: Tuttle, Morehouse & Taylor, 1886), 494; SLR 28:402–3, 411; and WLR, 32:138, 35:58.

30. Hobart Family Papers (FHS).

31. Account Books of Silas Cheney of Litchfield, 1799–1821 (LHS); and John Kenney, *The Hitchcock Chair* (New York: Clarkson N. Potter, 1971).

Three

1. In this study Woodbury is defined not by strict political bounds, but by dynamic cultural relationships. *Culture*, as used here, refers to the behavioral system of "shared meanings, attitudes and values, and the symbolic forms in which they are expressed or embodied" within a particular social formation. Such goals and values were communicated on many related levels, including economic relations, kinship structure, and religious ideology. By this definition Woodbury refers to an area the physical bounds of which were never fixed but rather remained fluid and dependent on the people who lived there.

Before 1740, culturally cohesive Woodbury included most of the original grant except for the northwestern part that became Judea. Not only was this area separated from the First Society meetinghouse by eight miles of rugged terrain but the majority of its inhabitants had stronger ties with the more accessible town of Litchfield. Settlers in the northeastern section of the original grant, what is now Bethlehem, shared similar difficulties in traveling to the center of Woodbury. They did not, however, assume their own cultural identity until the settlement of Joseph Bellamy as minister in 1742. Under the leadership of the forceful Bellamy, Bethlehem focused its attention inward on theological and agricultural matters.

The western region of the original grant, which became Roxbury, experienced mixed cultural ties with the First Society. Separated from the Woodbury center by several ridges running northerly and southerly and distinguished by the largest concentration of Anglicans within the area of the original land grant, this region achieved some cultural autonomy. At the same time, familial and economic connections made it part, albeit limited, of the Woodbury cultural region. For the purposes of this study, the Woodbury cultural region is not considered to include Roxbury.

Although the area to the south of Woodbury had become the separate religious society of Southbury in 1732, it remained a part of cultural Woodbury through the end of the eighteenth century and into the nineteenth. The bulk of this society's population lived in the Pomeraug Valley and thus enjoyed easy interchange with the First Society. Such communicative connections were underpinned by familial ties, convivial relations between ministers of similar theological perspectives, and deference to an interrelated social and economic elite. The Masonic Lodge, whose members tended to live in either the First Society or in Southbury, best symbolized such cultural cohesion.

Only when the Kettletown district developed in the early nineteenth century did part of Southbury begin to establish its own orientation, and this was limited to that southeastern district. The northern part of Southbury remained united with Woodbury center. Woodbury, as used in this study, refers to the area most easily described in geographic terms as the Pomeraug Valley. Peter Burke, *Popular Culture in Early Modern Europe* (New York: Harper Torchbooks, 1978), prologue; and William Cothren, *History of Ancient Woodbury* (Waterbury, Conn.: Bronson Brothers, 1854), 1:219–83, 292, 331–34.

2. Connecticut towns' soil types, productivity, and crop adaptability can be found in Bruce Daniels, *The Connecticut Town* (Middletown: Wesleyan University Press, 1979), 186–90. Additional information on geography and crops is in John Pease and John Miles, *A Gazetteer of the States of Connecticut and Rhode Island* (Hartford, Conn.: William S. Marsh, 1819), 132–33, 157–58, 183–84, 266–68; and Cothren, *History of Ancient Woodbury*, 1:19.

3. Although other undetected joiners, particularly journeymen and apprentices, surely worked in the two towns, the existing list of sixty-one joiners in Newtown and fifty-two in Woodbury are a valid sample derived from similar sources. The technique of collective biographies is derived from such works as Philip Greven, *Four Generations: Population, Land, and Family in Colonial Andover, Massachusetts* (Ithaca, N.Y.: Cornell University Press, 1970); and Barbara Ward, "The Craftsman in a Changing Society: Boston Goldsmiths, 1690–1730" (Ph.D. diss., Boston University, 1983).

4. Appendixes A and B provide additional information and pertinent sources for all specific life histories.

5. The turned chairs of the coastal communities provide particularly clear examples of this compatibility. Robert Trent, *Hearts and Crowns* (New Haven: New Haven Colony Historical Society, 1977).

6. In the eighteen years after 1756, Newtown's population grew from 1,253 to

2,229. Evarts Greene and Virginia Harrington, *American Population Before the Federal Census of 1790* (New York: Columbia University Press, 1932), 56.

7. Account Book of Thomas Tousey of Newtown, 1716–1761 (NHS), 16–17; and NLR 2:347.

8. A comparable form of patriarchal authority among yeomen families in New England has been noted by Greven, *Four Generations*; and John Waters in "Patrimony, Succession, and Social Stability: Guilford, Connecticut, in the Eighteenth Century," *Perspectives in American History* 10 (1976): 131–60.

9. Occupational and genealogical information on the Fairchilds is drawn from the Newtown tax assessments for 1797 and 1798 (privately owned); and BC.

10. Several joiners possessed no farmland at death because they had already deeded it or because it had been confiscated during the Revolution. Land records and detailed tax lists from the 1790s, which distinguish between different types of land, provided a means to circumvent this problem of landless inventories.

11. Greene and Harrington, *American Population*, 61, report that Woodbury's population grew from 2,911 to 5,313 between 1756 and 1774.

12. Donald Jacobus, *The Genealogy of the Booth Family* (Pleasant Hill, Mo.: Eden Booth, 1952), 18. A fourth son, Asahel, may have also been a woodworker. He bought a tenon saw from Shadrach Osborn and provided Osborn with twenty-four days of work. Account Book of Shadrach Osborn of Southbury, 1796–1806 (WML), 1.

13. Thomas Tousey drew up an indenture contract for Amos Sanford in March 1758, the time when Ebenezer IV would have begun his seven-year apprenticeship. Some connection between the two is suggested by Amos's departure from Newtown in 1765 when Ebenezer IV had finished his training. Account Book of Thomas Tousey of Newtown, 1716–1761 (NHS), 85; and NTL.

14. Jacobus, *Genealogy*, 46; and NLR 8:380.

15. NLR 8:266; WLR 16:78, 24:87; and Jacobus, *Genealogy*, 49–50.

16. The only account book reference to the work of Ebenezer Booth IV occurs in the ledger of Samuel Beers, a Newtown hatmaker for whom Ebenezer stocked and mended guns in 1788. Account Book of Samuel Beers of Newtown, 1776–1810 (privately owned), 40. For the location and valuation of Booth's shop, see NLR 8:380; and NTL.

17. NLR 10:158, 11:55, 204, 428, 435, 12:128–29, 142, 242, 13:148, 156, 362, 14:254. The importance of transmitting land to the next generation in an agricultural economy and the traditional, nonspeculative role of land are described in Alan Macfarlane's *The Family Life of Ralph Josselin* (New York: W. W. Norton, 1970), 57–67; and in Christopher Jedrey's *The World of John Cleaveland* (New York: W. W. Norton, 1979), 14–16, 68–70.

18. Danbury Probate District, Docket 861 (CSL). It is unclear who did the actual weaving. Some joiners such as Thomas Stilson also wove, while for others like John Boyer their wives carded, spun, and wove.

19. Danbury Probate District, Docket 861.

20. U.S. Bureau of the Census, *Heads of Families at the First Census of the United States Taken in the Year 1790—Connecticut* (Washington: Government Printing Office, 1908), 19; and *Farmer's Journal*, 1, no. 17 (1790): 3.

21. Danbury Probate District, Docket 861; Jacobus, *Genealogy*, 47; Jane Eliza

Johnson, ed., *Newtown's History and Historian, Ezra Levan Johnson* (Newtown: Jane Johnson, 1917), 125; and Account Book of Dr. Samuel Orton of Woodbury, 1788–1798 (Woodbury Town Hall).

22. Danbury Probate District, Dockets 861 and 866.

23. Danbury Probate District, Docket 866; and NTL, 1790. Biographical information on the various creditors for Joel Booth's estate was gleaned from BC; HC; and *Heads of Families 1790*.

24. Danbury Probate District, Docket 866.

25. The indenture was transcribed and printed in the *Newtown Bee*, Feb. 12, 1904, p. 3. The use of apprentices and journeymen as farmhands is mentioned in Ann Dibble's "Major John Dunlap: The Craftsman and His Community," *Old-Time New England* 68, nos. 3–4 (1978): 50–58.

26. Danbury Probate District, Dockets 862, 866, 1446; Jacobus, *Genealogy*, 47; NLR 21:372, 377–78, 384–85; SLR 2:278, 4:52, 7:377, 8:138; Account Book of Bartimeus Fabrique of Southbury, 1791–1810 (YUL), 14; Account Book of David Stiles of Southbury, 1789–1815 (privately owned), 129; W. C. Sharpe, *South Britain: Sketches and Records* (Seymour, Conn.: Record Print, 1898), 63; J. L. Rockey, ed., *History of New Haven County, Connecticut* (New York: W. W. Preston, 1892), 2:787; and Account Book of Charles Booth of Southbury, 1827–1838 (YUL). On the careers of other chairmakers at this period who produced parts, see John Kenney, *The Hitchcock Chair* (New York: Clarkson N. Potter, 1971); and Don Skemer, "David Alling's Chair Manufactory: Craft Industrialization in Newark, New Jersey, 1801–1854," *Winterthur Portfolio* 22, no. 1 (1987): 1–21.

27. Jacobus, *Genealogy*, 48; WLR 16:78, 178–79, 18:75; and WTL. David Booth continued to run a joiner's shop and sawmill in Roxbury. Account Book of Israel Minor of Roxbury, 1762–1800 (privately owned), 57–58; and Roxbury Land Records (Roxbury Town Hall), 2:13.

28. The indenture was transcribed and printed in the *Newtown Bee*, Oct. 27, 1967, sec. A, p. 1. Account Book of Shadrach Osborn of Southbury, 1777–1784 (CHS), 12; Account Book of Joseph and Simeon Curtiss of Southbury, 1783–1827 (YUL); Account Book of Bennet French of Southbury, 1793–1804 (privately owned), 32; Account Book of David Stiles of Southbury, 1789–1815 (privately owned), 40–41, 140–41; Account Book of Shadrach Osborn of Southbury, 1796–1806 (WML), 110, 252; Account Book of Bartimeus Fabrique of Southbury, 1791–1810 (YUL), 40, 43; Account Book of Lewis Beecher of Southbury, 1813–27 (YUL), 17; Woodbury Probate District, Docket 536; and Jacobus, *Genealogy*, 48–49.

29. Elijah Booth's land transactions involved unimproved land bought in the last decade of the eighteenth century. WLR 18:75; and SLR 1:49, 263, 3:280. Evidence of Booth buying quantities of foodstuffs can be found in the Account Book of Shadrach Osborn of Southbury, 1777–1815 (CHS), 10–11, 40–42, 50, 77, 86; and Account Book of Bartimeus Fabrique of Southbury, 1791–1810 (YUL), 13. On the fluctuating tax assessments, see WTL and STL. Even Elijah and Ebenezer V bought looking glasses from Osborn. Account Book of Shadrach Osborn, 1801–1803 (LHS).

30. Account Book of David Stiles of Southbury, 1789–1815 (privately owned), 10–11, 40–42, 50, 77, 86; Account Book of Bartimeus Fabrique of Southbury, 1791–

1810 (YUL), 13; and Account Book of Shadrach Osborn of Southbury, 1796–1806 (WML).

31. After 1800 Elijah purchased great quantities of hay and potatoes, the favored fodder in Woodbury. Account Book of David Stiles of Southbury, 1789–1815 (privately owned), 42, 50, 56–57, 86–87; and Account Book of Bartimeus Fabrique of Southbury, 1791–1810 (YUL), 13, 17, 23.

32. *Heads of Families 1790*, 73; Gary Teeples and Ronald Jackson, eds., *Connecticut 1800 Census* (Provo, Utah: Accelerated Indexing Systems, 1974), 87; and Account Book of Bartimeus Fabrique of Southbury, 1791–1810 (YUL), 40. For similar changes in other woodworking families, see Charles Hummel, *With Hammer in Hand* (Charlottesville: University Press of Virginia, 1968), 215–41; and *The Dunlaps and Their Furniture* (Manchester, N.H.: Currier Gallery of Art, 1970).

33. SLR 2:126, 137, 190, 252, 264, 4:193, 195, 212; and Southbury Probate District, Docket 537.

Four

1. On the centrality of agriculture in the lives of early Americans and the connection between values and behavioral patterns, see James Henretta, "Families and Farms: *Mentalité* in Pre-Industrial America," *William and Mary Quarterly* 35, no. 1 (1978): 3–32; Allan Kulikoff, "The Transition to Capitalism in Rural America," *William and Mary Quarterly* 46, no. 1 (1989): 120–44; and Christopher Clark, *The Roots of Rural Capitalism: Western Massachusetts, 1780–1860* (Ithaca, N.Y.: Cornell University Press, 1990).

2. Bruce Daniels, *The Connecticut Town* (Middletown, Conn.: Wesleyan University Press, 1979), 125; Jane Eliza Johnson, ed., *Newtown's History and Historian, Ezra Levan Johnson* (Newtown: Jane Johnson, 1917), 14–34, 215–16. In the gross persistence rate, the denominator is the number of taxpayers listed in the first time period, and the numerator is the number of taxpayers who continued to the following time period. I made an informed decision based on familiarity with the inhabitants to resolve any cases of name ambiguity. This crude rate is merely an indicator of patterns, not a measure of absolute mobility. If the immense task of reconstituting the families of the two towns for the sixty-year period were to be accomplished, it would be possible to determine the influence of mortality, the differences betwen native sons and immigrants, and the frequency of migration. But such analysis is not the purpose of this particular study. For the interpretation of the craftsmen and their products, simple persistence rates should suffice.

This methodology and comparative data have been drawn from Douglas Jones, *Village and Seaport* (Hanover, N.H.: University Press of New England, 1981), esp. 104–13. Newtown's low persistence rate of 50 percent for the 1780s is an aberration. This low rate can be attributed directly to the unusually large number of Loyalists in Newtown during the Revolution, who either fled to New York or Nova Scotia or merely relocated until after the war. Loyalists were not reindoctrinated into town affairs until 1784. Stephen McGrath, "Connecticut's Tory Towns: The Loyalty Struggle in Newtown, Redding, and Ridgefield, 1774–1783," *Connecticut Historical Society Bulletin* 44, no. 3 (1979): 88–96.

3. Edward M. Cook Jr., *The Fathers of the Towns: Leadership and Community Structure in Eighteenth-Century New England* (Baltimore: Johns Hopkins University Press, 1976), 37–42, 51–60, 96–98; and Daniels, *Connecticut Town*, 165–67, 200–201.

4. Account Book of Thomas Tousey of Newtown, 1716–1761 (NHS), 81, 133, 137, 140–42; Benno Forman, "The Crown and York Chairs of Coastal Connecticut and the Work of the Durands," *Antiques* 105, no. 5 (1974): 1147–54; FPR 13: 177; and Fairfield County Court Records (CSL).

5. On Danbury's increasing importance, see Daniels, *Connecticut Town*, 155–56. For a fuller explanation of the derivation and validity of the commercial index, see Cook, *Fathers of the Towns*, 78–80, 801–2; and Jones, *Village and Seaport*, 4–10.

6. The quotation is taken from the February 27, 1798, apprenticeship agreement between Zachariah Clark and his nephew Daniel (privately owned). Christopher Jedrey notes the same effects of communal values on the inhabitants of Chebacco Parish, Massachusetts, in *The World of John Cleaveland* (New York: W. W. Norton, 1979), 74–97.

7. For comparative information about crops and stock, see Robert Gross, "Culture and Cultivation: Agriculture and Society in Thoreau's Concord," *Journal of American History* 69, no. 1 (1982): 42–61; Susan Geib, "'Changing Works': Agriculture and Society in Brookfield, Massachusetts, 1785–1820" (Ph.D. diss., Boston University, 1981); Percy Bidwell, "Rural Economy in New England at the Beginning of the Nineteenth Century," *Connecticut Academy of Arts and Sciences Transactions* 20 (1916): 241–399; and Howard Russel, *A Long, Deep Furrow* (Hanover, N.H.: University Press of New England, 1976).

8. Account Book of Thomas Stilson of Newtown, 1772–1803 (NHS). The operation of the barter economy in a relatively self-sufficient community of equal household units is explored by Geib, "Changing Works," 115–20; and Michael Merrill, "Cash is Good to Eat: Self-Sufficiency and Exchange in the Rural Economy of the United States," *Radical History Review* 4, no. 1 (1977): 42–47.

9. McGrath, "Connecticut's Tory Towns," 88–96; and Newtown Town Records, 4:31–34. On the role of a minister in a noncommercial village during the Revolution, see Jedrey, *World of John Cleaveland*, 104–72.

10. On the advantages of corn, the shortcomings of wheat, and the importance of meat exports to New York and the West Indies, see Bidwell, "Rural Economy," 294–95, 304, 322–24.

11. These percentages are much higher than in eastern Massachusetts, where cider production and cloth production were specialized tasks undertaken by a restricted number of people. For the Massachusetts figures and additional details about the implications of these figures, see Carole Shammas, "How Self-Sufficient Was Early America?" *Journal of Interdisciplinary History* 13, no. 2 (1982): 255–60.

12. NPR 1:259–65; Account Book of Samuel Beers of Newtown, 1776–1810 (privately owned); Account Book of Samuel Beers of Newtown, 1794–1815 (privately owned); and Account Book of Samuel Beers of Newtown, 1782–1805 (privately owned). The economic advantages of outwork were noted in the 1820 manufacturing census. Phineas Miller, the Fairfield County reporter, wrote that the cordwainers of Norwalk, Wilton, and New Canaan "receive the Leather from New York cut out, make the Shoes for a stipulated price by the pair, and return them when

so made to the shoe-manufacturers in N. York without being at all interested in the purchase of Leather or the sale of the Shoes." *1820 Census of Manufactures—Connecticut Schedules* (National Archives Publications, Microcopy No. 279), 148.

13. Johnson, *Newtown's History*, 152–57.

14. On the shift toward dairy production, see Bidwell, "Rural Economy," 304; and Russel, *Long, Deep Furrow*, 249, 272, 283–85. The contemporary observation about the sporadic marketing of agricultural surpluses in Fairfield County can be found in the *1820 Census—Connecticut*, 148.

15. Account Book of Philo Beardslee of Newtown, 1804–1833 (LHS).

16. Account Book of John Hubbell of Newtown, 1792–1793 (OSV); Account Book of John Hubbell of Newtown, 1805–1823 (OSV); NPR 1:187–89.

17. Account Book of Eden Burchard of Newtown, 1799–1801 (privately owned); Account Book of Eden Burchard of Newtown, 1809–1815 (privately owned); and James Bailey, *History of Danbury, Connecticut, 1684–1896* (New York: Burr Printing House, 1896), 216, 241, 525–26. The importance of outwork to the shoemaking industry during the period of protoindustrialization was emphasized by Alan Dawley in his study of Lynn, Massachusetts, *Class and Community* (Cambridge: Harvard University Press, 1976), esp. 11–58.

18. Daniels, *Connecticut Town*, 14–20, 119–27; and William Cothren, *History of Ancient Woodbury* (Waterbury, Conn.: Bronson Brothers, 1854), 1:32–42, 46–57, 65–71, 145–47, 157.

19. This sketch of Woodbury's socioeconomic structure in the 1730s and 1740s is drawn from James Walsh's "The Great Awakening in the First Congregational Church of Woodbury, Connecticut," *William and Mary Quarterly* 28, no. 4 (1971): 543–62. On the settlement of northwestern Connecticut, see Daniels, *Connecticut Town*, 28–34; and Charles Grant, *Democracy in the Connecticut Frontier Town of Kent* (New York: Columbia University Press, 1961; W. W. Norton, 1972), 1–28.

20. WPR 11:22, 18:75, 7:27, 9:166–71, 155. See also the Account Book of Matthew Minor of Woodbury, 1802–1826 (privately owned). Land rental in Newtown was noted in inventories only after 1810.

21. WPR; WTL; and STL. See WPR 7:28 (Dulivan estate), 8:82 (Wilmot estate), 6:250–51 (Ferry estate), 7:37 (Moody estate). WPR 9:155, 10:75; Account Book of Matthew Minor of Woodbury, 1801–1810 (privately owned), 8, 34, 39.

22. Boston's gross persistence rate was 53 percent from 1687 to 1695 and 56 percent from 1780 to 1790. Windsor, Connecticut, on the edge of the seventeenth-century frontier had a 57 percent rate from 1676 to 1686. Rates never dropped below 50 percent in the eighteenth century. Jones, *Village and Seaport*, 106–7.

23. Cook, *Fathers of the Towns*, 37–42, 51–60, 96–98; and Daniels, *Connecticut Town*, 200–201.

24. The General Assembly had appointed Litchfield as shire town more for its geographic centrality than its regional prominence. Woodbury petitioned in 1768 and in 1791 to establish Woodbury County, but each time the petition was dismissed. Cothren, *History of Ancient Woodbury*, 1:153–55.

25. Bidwell discusses the relationship between large area, early settlement, and market opportunities in "Rural Economy," 271. Gary Nash, *The Urban Crucible* (Cambridge: Harvard University Press, 1979), 236, 317; Account Book of Truman

Hinman of Southbury, 1765 (YUL); Account Book of Freegift Hawkins of Derby, 1770–1825 (LHS); Chester Destler, *Connecticut: The Provisions State* (Chester, Conn.: Pequot Press, 1973), 11; Cothren, *History of Ancient Woodbury*, 1:352–53.

26. The average domestic needs are summarized by Shammas, "How Self-Sufficient Was Early America?" 251. The advantages of sheep raising and the unsuitability of mutton as an export meat are pointed out by Jedrey, *World of John Cleaveland*, 65. On the relationship between the farmer and the local merchant, see Robert Mutch, "Yeoman and Merchant in Pre-Industrial America: Eighteenth-Century Massachusetts as a Case Study," *Societas* 7, no. 4 (1977): 279–302.

27. Quotation cited in Helen Everston Smith, *Colonial Days and Ways* (New York: Century, 1901), 311. See also Account Book of Shadrach Osborn and Truman Hinman of Southbury, 1775–1781 (CHS); and Cothren, *History of Ancient Woodbury*, 1:192–94.

28. *Old Woodbury in the Revolution: The Five Parishes and Their Soldiers* (Woodbury: Woodbury Bicentennial Committee, 1976). The economic importance of mobilization for the Revolutionary War to productional organization and market incentives is drawn from Destler, *Connecticut;* James Walsh, *Connecticut Industry and the Revolution* (Chester, Conn.: Pequot Press, 1978); and James Henretta, "The War for Independence and American Economic Development," in Ronald Hoffman, ed., *The Economy of Early America: The Revolutionary Period* (Charlottesville: University Press of Virginia, 1988), 45–87. On the important effect of Revolutionary experiences on values, see Jedrey, *World of John Cleaveland*, 136–72.

29. Jacob Price, "Economic Function and the Growth of American Port Towns in the Eighteenth Century," *Perspectives in American History* 8 (1974), 23–88; Allen Pred, *Urban Growth and the Circulation of Information: The United States System of Cities, 1790–1840* (Cambridge: Harvard University Press, 1973); David Gilchrist, ed., *The Growth of the Seaport Cities, 1790–1825* (Charlottesville: University Press of Virginia, 1967); George Rogers Taylor, *The Transportation Revolution, 1815–1860* (New York: Rinehart, 1951); and Winifred Rothenberg, "The Market and Massachusetts Farmers, 1750–1855," *Journal of Economic History* 41, no. 2 (1981): 283–314.

30. Samuel Orcutt, *The History of the Old Town of Derby, Connecticut, 1642–1880* (Springfield, Mass.: Springfield Printing Co., 1880), 248–52; Account Book of Shadrach Osborn and Nathan Preston of Southbury, 1790–1796 (WML); Account Book of Shadrach Osborn of Southbury, 1796–1806 (WML).

31. Southbury Town Records, 1:31–32.

32. For comparative information, see Geib, "Changing Works," 41–52, 61–85; and Gross, "Culture and Cultivation," tables 2 and 4. Observations on the surviving architecture are based only on the author's familiarity with surviving structures; a systematic survey and analysis of the two towns' houses should be undertaken.

33. Account Book of Shadrach Osborn of Southbury, 1796–1806 (WML); and Account Book of Shadrach Osborn, 1801–1803 (LHS). The Osborn family papers at NHHS reveal that Erastus Osborn was the New Haven agent for Shadrach Osborn. The Account Book of Matthew Minor of Woodbury, 1802–1826 (privately owned) shows frequent trips to New Haven to take Matthew's ward, Josiah, to Yale. On the market orientation of farmers, see Azel Backus, *Bethlem in 1812* (1813; reprint, Hartford: Acorn Club of Connecticut, 1961), 9–11. A similar shift to market ex-

change in the upper Connecticut River Valley is analyzed by Christopher Clark in "Household Economy, Market Exchange, and the Rise of Capitalism in the Connecticut River Valley, 1800–1860," *Journal of Social History* 13, no. 2 (1979): 169–89.

34. Backus, *Bethlem in 1812*, 8–9; Geib, "Changing Works," 61–85; Gross, "Culture and Cultivation," 48–49; and Henretta, "Families and Farms," 16–17.

35. The manufactory opened in 1806. Timothy Dwight, *Travels in New England and New York* (London: Charles Wood, 1823), 3:374–78.

Five

1. Although only about two-thirds of Connecticut's probated estates contained inventories, and these principally represent the wealthier or older members of society, this does not invalidate inventory analysis. Rather we must remember that the documents provide information only for that particular segment of the population whose estates were appraised. The literature on probate inventories as a source for the study of historical material culture is extensive, but a good introduction is Peter Benes, ed., *Early American Probate Inventories* (Boston: Dublin Seminar for New England Folklife, 1987).

2. Many original probate dockets and microfilms of the original probate court record books are on file at the CSL. The following data were collected for each inventory in the seven groups: name, date, gross wealth, description and value of real estate, and description, value, and frequency of personal estate. Personal estate was divided into agricultural assets (livestock, crops, farm tools and implements, agricultural produce), secondary assets (agricultural storage equipment, agricultural processing equipment, artisanal equipment and materials, fishing equipment, store inventory, labor, cloth), financial assets, and consumer assets. Consumer assets were subdivided into furniture, bedding (including bedsteads), personal goods (clothing, books, weapons, watches, grooming aids), and household goods (cookware, eating equipment, table linens and towels, lighting and heating equipment, silver, clocks, looking glasses, carpets, pictures, and so on).

These categories and divisions were derived from Jack Michel, "'In a Manner and Fashion Suitable to Their Degree': A Preliminary Investigation of the Material Culture of Early Rural Pennsylvania," *Working Papers from the Regional Economic History Research Center* 5, no. 1 (Wilmington, Del.: Eleutherian Mills–Hagley Foundation, 1981); and from Alice Hanson Jones, *American Colonial Wealth* (New York: Arno Press, 1977).

To counter bias from the nature of the elderly's consumer assets—marked by possession of only land and financial assets or of only household goods—inventories were not included in the quantified analysis when consumer goods were less than 8 percent or more than 70 percent of the personal assets of that particular estate. Values of all the inventories were compared for the effects of inflation. Weighting by personal possessions or by real estate altered values in each period only minimally, so actual recorded values were left intact. To convert dollars into pounds, the consistent rate was one dollar to six shillings.

3. Recent historical works that examine inventories quantitatively or quali-

tatively include Jackson Turner Main, "The Distribution of Property in Colonial Connecticut," in James Kirby Martin, ed., *The Human Dimensions of Nation Making* (Madison: State Historical Society of Wisconsin, 1976), 54–104; Susan Prendergast Schoelwer, "Form, Function, and Meaning in the Use of Fabric Furnishings," *Winterthur Portfolio* 14, no. 1 (1979): 25–40; Michel, "In a Manner and Fashion Suitable to Their Degree"; Dell Upton, "Vernacular Domestic Architecture in Eighteenth-Century Virginia," *Winterthur Portfolio* 17, nos. 2/3 (1982): 95–119; Kevin Sweeney, "Furniture and the Domestic Environment in Wethersfield, Connecticut, 1639–1800," *Connecticut Antiquarian* 36, no. 2 (1984): 10–39; Lorna Wetherill, *Consumer Behavior and Material Culture in Britain, 1660–1760* (London: Routledge and Paul, 1988); Carole Shammas, *The Preindustrial Consumer in England and America* (Oxford: Clarendon Press, 1990); Paul Shackel, *Personal Discipline and Material Culture: An Archaeology of Annapolis, Maryland, 1695–1870* (Knoxville: University of Tennessee Press, 1993); and Lois Green Carr and Lorena Walsh, "Changing Lifestyles and Consumer Behavior in the Colonial Chesapeake," in Cary Carson, Ronald Hoffman, and Peter Albert, eds., *Of Consuming Interests: The Styles of Life in the Eighteenth Century* (Charlottesville: University Press of Virginia, 1994), 59–166.

4. For evidence on importation of ceramics, see the accounts of the Southbury merchant Shadrach Osborn. Although Ziba Blakeslee worked as a silversmith in Newtown beginning in 1791 and Elias Smith worked in Woodbury in 1794, the presence of silver in many inventories and the dearth of manuscript references to local silversmiths implies a dependence on imported plate, especially before 1790. For information on the towns' silversmiths, see Henry Flynt and Martha Fales, *The Heritage Foundation Collection of Silver* (Old Deerfield, Mass.: Heritage Foundation, 1968), 159, 161, 194, 325; Account Book of Ziba Blakeslee of Newtown, 1789–1822 (WML); and Account Book of Shadrach Osborn and Nathan Preston of Southbury, 1790–1796 (WML).

5. Robert Trent, *Hearts and Crowns* (New Haven: New Haven Colony Historical Society, 1977); and Edward S. Cooke Jr., "The Selective Conservative Taste: Furniture in Stratford, Connecticut, 1740–1800" (M.A. thesis, University of Delaware, 1979), 28–33.

6. DPR 3:225–28, 7:22–23.

7. Ibid., 6:119–20, 12:11–13. Matthew Minor of Woodbury was one such sawmill owner. He provided Nicholas Jebine with sixty chair bottoms of basswood plank. Account Book of Matthew Minor of Woodbury, 1801–1810 (privately owned), 12.

8. DPR 3:343–49, 8:140–41. On the cost of upholstery, see Brock Jobe, "The Boston Upholstery Trade, 1700–1775," in Edward S. Cooke, Jr., ed., *Upholstery in America and Europe from the Seventeenth Century to World War I* (New York: W. W. Norton, 1987), 65–90.

9. DPR 7:22–23, 331–32, 10:569–75.

10. Ibid., 6:12, 7:421–22, 293–94, 481–82, 8:83–85, 10:418–19, 569–73, 11:483–85, 12:619–21.

11. "Black chairs" and "red chairs" were ubiquitous throughout the inventories. Although Trent stated that *red chair* meant a specific type of chair, in the Newtown and Woodbury inventories the term was used more often in a generic sense to describe a chair's color rather than its form. Newtown inventories included "red

fiddleback chairs" (1774), "red straight back chairs" (1801), "black crown chairs" (1772), "black slat back chairs" (1801), "black fluted back chairs" (1806), and "black bannister chairs" (1811). Unfortunately the lack of room-by-room inventories from Newtown prevents an understanding of where the painted furniture was used and what other types of furniture appeared in the same room.

Washbon owned red chests, red chairs, and red tables at his death in 1782. Another Newtown inventory appraised two years later included white or unpainted chairs, six black chairs, six red chairs, and two white chests. DPR 3:135–40, 225–28, 5:74, 124–26, 7:544–46, 9:282–84, 10:528–32, 11:224–26. The estate of Stephen Burwell of Newtown listed "4 blue chairs 12/ blue chest 9/." Ibid., 9:82–84. The popularity of green painted furniture and the introduction of blue paint parallel the patterns in the Philadelphia region documented by Nancy Evans in "Unsophisticated Furniture Made and Used in Philadelphia and Environs, 1750–1800," in John Morse, ed., *Country Cabinetwork and Simple City Furniture* (Charlottesville: University Press of Virginia, 1970), 167–69, 174–75.

12. DPR 3:211–13, 7:22–23, 12:285–87. A particularly valuable discussion of cultural separations during the early nineteenth century is Russell Handsman, "Early Capitalism and the Center Village of Canaan, Connecticut: A Study of Transformations and Separations," *Artifacts* 9, no. 3 (1981):1–22.

13. Jane Eliza Johnson, ed., *Newtown's History and Historian, Ezra Levan Johnson* (Newtown: Jane Johnson, 1917), 43. The 1811 inventory of David Baldwin proves that an inhabitant of Newtown could purchase the most fashionable furniture. It also shows that through such furniture's local ownership, other townspeople could see it easily. The uniqueness of this furniture, however, attests to its conscious rejection by most. Baldwin's estate included "inlead tea table 3. cherry secretary and escrutoir 21. dining table inlaid 7. candlestand .60 tea stand 1.25." DPR 10:569–73.

14. The value categories were chosen after the accumulation of data and represent one arbitrary way to organize the inventories for analysis. These groupings were picked because they are the same ones used by Michel (see note 2) and thus allow comparison between earlier Pennsylvania and later Connecticut data.

15. DPR 7:468, 525.

16. Ibid., 5:102–3; NPR 1:191–93.

17. DPR 5:103–4, 292; NPR 1:77–8.

18. DPR 3:225–27, 6:12, 119–20, 12:11–13, 160.

19. Painted chair forms specified in Woodbury inventories included "red crown backt chairs" (1776), "red chairs one slat in the back" (1804), "black york chairs" (1775), "black bannister backs" (1798), and "black setting chairs" (1803). WPR 5:268–70, 10:156, 7:85–86, 9:278, 10:161–62, 11:117–19; and Account Book of Nathaniel Bacon of Woodbury, 1798–1849 (CHS).

20. WPR 6:184–87, 7:89–90, 10:256–64, 11:107, 12:41–42, 11:200–1. By 1810, most inventories used dollars rather than pounds.

21. Ibid., 10:63.

22. Ibid., 8:114, 11:41–42, 9:160–62.

23. Ibid., 13:31–33.

24. Ibid., 11:90–91, 109–10, 140–42, 12:6–7, 41–42, 110–13, 135–36, 165–66,

207–8. On the introduction of the Federal style to the upper Connecticut River valley, see Philip Zea, "The Emergence of Neoclassical Furnituremaking in Rural Western Massachusetts," *Antiques* 142, no. 6 (1992): 842–51.

25. WPR 12:31–33, 135–36; Woodbury Probate District, Docket 2021 (CSL).

26. Pertinent comments on the Federal style, new woodworking techniques introduced at the end of the eighteenth century, and the importance of the sideboard can be found in *The Work of Many Hands: Card Tables in Federal America, 1790–1820* (New Haven: Yale University Art Gallery, 1982); Jonathan Fairbanks and Elizabeth Bates, *American Furniture 1620 to the Present* (New York: Richard Marek, 1981), 235–37; and Michael Dunbar, *Federal Furniture* (Newtown: Taunton Press, 1987).

27. On the elaboration of dining in the early national period, see Barbara Carson, *Ambitious Appetites: Dining, Behaviors, and Patterns of Consumption in Federal Washington* (Washington, D.C.: American Institute of Architects Press, 1990). The importance of looking at constellations of goods of various media associated with specialized activity is stressed in Ann Smart Martin, "Makers, Buyers, and Users: Consumerism as a Material Culture Framework," *Winterthur Portfolio* 28, nos. 2/3 (1993): 153–54.

28. WPR 5:12–13, 6:184–87, 10:84, 11:21; and William Cothren, *History of Ancient Woodbury* (Waterbury, Conn.: Bronson Brothers, 1854), 1:322.

29. David Hall, "The World of Print and Collective Mentality in Seventeenth-Century New England," in John Higham and Paul Conkin, eds., *New Directions in American Intellectual History* (Baltimore: Johns Hopkins University Press, 1979), 166–80. On the separation of elite and popular culture, see Peter Burke, *Popular Culture in Early Modern Europe* (New York: Harper Torchbooks, 1978), 244–81.

30. James Hart, *The Popular Book: A History of America's Literary Taste* (New York: Oxford University Press, 1950), 3–50; Account Book of Shadrach Osborn of Southbury, 1786–1788 (WML); WPR 9:160–61, 13:31–33; and Woodbury Probate District, Docket 2021 (CSL).

31. On the commercial use of the desk-and-bookcase, see Jules Prown, "Mind in Matter: An Introduction to Material Culture Theory and Method," *Winterthur Portfolio* 17, no. 1 (1982): 11; and Leonee Ormond, *Writing* (London: Her Majesty's Stationery Office, 1981), 38.

32. WPR 11:41–42, 117–19, 140–42, 195–96, 240, 12:6–7, 13:8, 31–33; Woodbury Probate District, Dockets 2021, 2414, 2617 (CSL).

33. WPR 9:191, 248; and Gerald Ward, "'Avarice and Conviviality': Card Playing in Federal America," in *The Work of Many Hands*, 15–38. Ward downplayed the social function of card playing, but T. H. Breen's exploration of gambling's social and symbolic significance suggests otherwise. "Horses and Gentlemen: The Cultural Significance of Gambling Among the Gentry of Virginia," in *Puritans and Adventurers* (New York: Oxford University Press, 1980), 148–63.

34. WPR 3:158–59. On tea drinking and its relation to domesticity, see Shammas, *The Preindustrial Consumer*; and Rodris Roth, "Tea Drinking in 18th Century America: Its Etiquette and Equipage," *United States National Museum Bulletin* 225 (1961): 63–89.

35. The causes and characteristics of domesticity are well explained by Nancy

Cott in *The Bonds of Womanhood* (New Haven: Yale University Press, 1977), 63–100.

36. WPR 8:50, 10:256–64, 11:90–91, 140–42, 183–86, 12:6–7, 41–42, 101–3, 13:31–33. The importance of grooming among the genteel and cultivated is stressed by Richard and Claudia Bushman, "The Early History of Cleanliness in America," *Journal of American History* 74, no. 4 (1988): 1213–38.

37. WPR 7:15.

38. Ibid., 8:82, 10:52.

39. Ibid., 8:27, 13:285–86.

40. Ibid., 11:200–1, 12:33–34, 41–42; Woodbury Probate District, Docket 2021 (CSL).

Six

1. The discussion of the different qualities of the lumber and its relationship to sawing practices is informed by Bruce Hoadley, *Understanding Wood: A Craftsman's Guide to Wood Technology* (Newtown: Taunton Press, 1980), esp. 1–17, 207–15.

2. Edward S. Cooke Jr., "The Selective Conservative Taste: Furniture in Stratford, Connecticut, 1740–1800" (M.A. thesis, University of Delaware, 1979); Cooke, "Craftsman-Client Relations in the Housatonic Valley, 1720–1800," *Antiques* 125, no. 1 (1984): 272–80; Cooke, "The Social Economy of the Preindustrial Joiner in Western Connecticut, 1750–1800," in Luke Beckerdite, ed., *American Furniture 1995* (Milwaukee: Chipstone Foundation, 1995); and appendixes A and B.

3. Danbury Probate District, Docket 861 (CSL). *Horn chair* may refer to a flag-seated turned chair with pointed ears that flow up and out. Chairs with such horned crest rails have been found in Monroe, the town immediately to the east of Newtown. Robert Trent, *Hearts and Crowns* (New Haven: New Haven Colony Historical Society, 1977), figs. 76, 77. Another possibility may be flag-seated turned chairs with yoke-shaped crest rails pinned between the rear posts. Ibid., figs. 55–59.

4. Michael Ettema examines the economics of design, that is, the relationship between labor-intensive technology and stylistic design, in "Technological Innovation and Design Economics in Furniture Manufacture," *Winterthur Portfolio* 16, nos. 2/3 (1981): 197–223. Ettema states that the York chair was "the most chair for the price," but his argument can also be applied to the plain chair. In producing a plain chair, the craftsman gave more weight to cost and technology than to design.

5. DPR 3:519–21, 7:441–42. Benno Forman points out a similar meaning for white chairs in Philadelphia during the 1740s in "Delaware Valley 'Crookt Foot' and Slat-Back Chairs: The Fussell-Savery Connection," *Winterthur Portfolio* 15, no. 1 (1980): 42.

6. For similar Milford chairs, see Trent, *Hearts and Crowns*, 65, 72–73.

7. DPR 3:318–23. "Round backed chairs" were usually valued at two or three shillings each. "Round backt chairs" in Stratford inventories were valued at six or seven shillings each and probably referred to cherry crookedback chairs with yoke-shaped crest rails and flag seats. Cooke, "Selective Conservative Taste," 31.

8. This discussion of the traditional craftsman who breaks down old ideas into parts and then reorders them into a new structure is derived from Henry Glassie, "Folk Art," in Richard Dorson, ed., *Folklore and Folklife* (Chicago: University of

Chicago Press, 1972), 259–60. Discussions of urban-made chairs in the Georgian style and the less expensive urban and rural adaptations are in Forman, "Delaware Valley," 41–64; Trent, *Hearts and Crowns*, 60–63; and Ettema, "Technological Innovation," 199. A related great round-top chair made in Newtown is attributed to a Milford shop by Trent, *Hearts and Crowns*, fig. 46.

9. John Kirk, *Connecticut Furniture: Seventeenth and Eighteenth Centuries* (Hartford, Conn.: Wadsworth Atheneum, 1967), 116–7; Trent, *Hearts and Crowns*, figs. 22, 23, 26, 33, 43, 73; Forman, "Delaware Valley," 51; Ettema, "Technological Innovation," fig. 1.

10. Many past studies have identified any turned chair with a baluster-shaped banister as a fiddleback chair. Therefore York chairs and other different types have also been referred to as fiddlebacks. But eighteenth-century documents from the Housatonic River Valley region explicitly distinguish between York chairs and fiddleback chairs. Abner Curtiss of Stratford owned "6 York chairs £1.4.0" and "6 fiddle Backd Chairs £1.10.0" at his death in 1780. Furthermore, fiddlebacks did not appear in inventories or joiners' account books until the last three decades of the eighteenth century, well after the baluster-shaped banister had gained common acceptance. Thus it seems likely that the crest rail rather than the banister was the more important delimiting feature of a fiddleback chair. The swept crest rail would have gained some popularity in the Housatonic River Valley at about the time when fiddlebacks appear in the inventories. Cooke, "Selective Conservative Taste," 33–34; Account Book of Elisha Hawley of Ridgefield, 1786–1800 (CHS).

11. On the importance of front rounds in the identification of regional traditions and other details for shop distinction, see Bernard Cotton, *The English Regional Chair* (Woodbridge, Suffolk: Antique Collectors' Club, 1990); Benno Forman, *American Seating Furniture, 1630–1730* (New York: W. W. Norton, 1988), 335–38.

12. Another explanation for the elimination of the decorative termini may be the desire to make the juncture of the crest more like a joiner's chair, but that would be inconsistent with the other features of the chair.

13. The turned vocabulary on the front round, the double baluster turnings at the top of the front post, the ring on the front post just under the joint where the front round fastens to the post, chamfered bottoms on the rear posts, and the long quarter-round profile on the base of the splat link the Blackman chair with several other local chairs. Trent, *Hearts and Crowns*, figs. 34, 38–41, 44; Kirk, *Connecticut Furniture*, 116–17.

14. On Stratford examples, see Cooke, "Selective Conservative Taste," figs. 4–6; Trent, *Hearts and Crowns*, figs. 31–33. Stratford fiddlebacks have been identified with two types of crest rails: one with a central yoke and pointed ears and one with a three-bowed crest and rounded ears.

15. Jules Prown discusses the pervasive lightening of the neoclassical style in "Style as Evidence," *Winterthur Portfolio* 15, no. 3 (1980): 197–210.

16. An example of a Stratford crookedback chair is illustrated in Cooke, "Selective Conservative Taste," fig. 10.

17. Examples of related Connecticut desks-on-frames can be seen in Kirk, *Connecticut Furniture*, 68, 70. In a November 1994 conversation with me, the British

furniture historian Bill Cotton remarked that the Newtown desk type relates to examples found in the West Midlands of England.

18. On the drawers of the desk and the dressing table, the joiner laid out the dovetails in the following manner: each corner has a half pin at the upper edge, several thick pins below it, and a half pin at the lower edge. For similar Stratford case furniture, see Cooke, "Selective Conservative Taste," figs. 25–27, 30. The dressing table bears the chalk signature "E B" on the back of the backboard of the central carved drawer, which may refer to Ebenezer Booth IV (1743–1790).

19. The case of drawers was examined just prior to auction at a Richard W. Withington, Inc., Auction in Andover, Massachusetts, on January 9, 1982. The history of its ownership was typed on a piece of paper tacked to its backboards.

20. Characteristics of this second Newtown shop include drawer backs dovetailed to the drawer sides, half pins cut at both the top and bottom edges of the drawer front, use of a wide quarter-round and shallow fillet molding along the drawer edges, cornice moldings made entirely of cherry, a distinctive two-piece midmolding (part of which was nailed to the upper section and part to the lower section), a central support for the full-width drawer in the lower section and the central drawer underneath it (dovetailed into the drawer divider and tenoned into the backboard), a double-thickness skirt in the lower section (a ⅞-inch-thick piece of cherry with a 1-inch-thick yellow poplar board behind it), the consistent method of pegging tenons in the lower section, and use of an odd number of ribs in the decorative fan.

The midmolding consisted of two parts: a tall cyma with fillets at each end fastened along the base of the upper section and an overhanging cyma with rounded lower edge fastened along the upper part of the lower section. The second part of the midmolding is the important constructional feature. The uppermost front rail was tenoned into the front legs, and then a side rail was secured along the inside of each sideboard. Each side rail was lapped to the back edge of the front rail and was notched to fit around the upper part of the rear leg. A rose-headed nail, driven horizontally, fastened the back end of the side rail to the rear leg. On top of these rails the joiner nailed moldings that were mitred at the corners and featured shallow rabbets cut along the inside. The upper section of the case of drawers fit within the rabbet but still rested on the rabbeted surface of the molding. Another consistent constructional convention was the joiner's use of three tenons to secure the yellow poplar backboard to the rear legs. The craftsman secured the upper mortise and tenon joint with two pegs, the middle one with a single peg, and the lower one with two pegs.

The use of the same quarter-round molding plane accounts for the same moldings along the edges of the drawer fronts, while workmanship of habit explains the consistent use of an odd number of ribs. The joiner continued to lay out his design in the same manner regardless of the size of the piece. For a more decorative effect or for a customer willing to pay more money, he added a perimeter of lobes.

21. Kirk illustrates the case of drawers shown in figure 20 and reports the tradition of its ownership by Hannah Grant in *Connecticut Furniture*, 53. The term *crown case of drawers* appeared in the addenda to Henry Glover's inventory. Danbury Probate District, Docket 1965 (CSL).

22. Kirk, *Connecticut Furniture*, 56, 58–60; Minor Myers Jr. and Edgar Mayhew,

New London County Furniture, 1640–1840 (New London, Conn.: Lyman Allyn Museum, 1974), 43; Cooke, "Selective Conservative Taste," 129 and fig. 42; Joseph Downs, *American Furniture: Queen Anne and Chippendale Periods* (New York: Bonanza Books, 1952), figs. 149, 337.

23. Kirk, *Connecticut Furniture*, 53; DPR 1:258–62; Jane Eliza Johnson, ed., *Newtown's History and Historian, Ezra Levan Johnson* (Newtown: Jane Johnson, 1917), 193.

24. On blockfront chests, Newport joiners made use of a butterfly key to secure tops to carcasses for much the same reasons. Margaretta Lovell, "The Blockfront: Its Development in Boston, Newport and Connecticut," *Fine Woodworking* 23 (July 1980): 146.

25. The yellow poplar back of the dressing table in figure 23 is tenoned to the rear legs with three tenons, which are pegged with a sequence of two pins at the top, one in the middle tenon, and two at the bottom; the outer drawer supports are tenoned into the back and slant-tenoned to the back edge of the drawer blade or skirt; the central drawer supports for the full-width drawer and carved central drawer are tenoned into the back and dovetailed to the skirt; and the drawer sides are dovetailed to the fronts and the drawer backs to the sides.

26. The joiner responsible for the case furniture and tables in figures 18–21 always oriented the grain of the bottom boards in a consistent fashion. In full-width drawers, he placed the bottom so that its grain paralleled the drawer front. When fitting together narrower drawers, he placed the bottom so that its grain ran perpendicular to the drawer front. On all the drawer bottoms, the joiner used a panel plane to chamfer the underside of their fronts and sides. The chamfering allowed the bottoms to fit into grooves cut into the inside surfaces of the drawer fronts and sides. To secure the bottoms, this joiner then drove two or three rose-headed nails through the bottoms into the underside of the drawer backs.

The joiner who made the dressing table in figure 23 made his drawers in a significantly different way. Regardless of the drawer size, he oriented the bottom boards so that their grain paralleled the drawer front. Rather than chamfering the edges of the bottom, he ran a rabbeting plane along the side and front edges. The rabbeting plane produced tabs that fit into grooves cut into the fronts and sides (see fig. 5). The result was a better-fitting and stronger drawer bottom. This second joiner also secured drawer bottoms differently. He toed in the bottom by hammering a single nail on each side, approximately halfway between the front and the back, a convention that allowed the bottom board to expand and contract equally in either direction and limiting the amount of potential shrinkage.

For a discussion of the differences between the two shops, see John Herdeg, "A Lower Housatonic Valley Shop Tradition: An Analysis of Six Related Dressing Tables," *Connecticut Historical Society Bulletin* 56, nos. 1–2 (1991): 38–56. In western Connecticut furniture, the rabbeting (rather than the chamfering) of the drawer bottom into a groove on the drawer side appears to be a convention first used between 1790 and 1800.

27. The top of a case of drawers from the Sherman family is owned by the NHS. A privately owned example descended in the Glover family.

28. For a discussion of proportions on Housatonic Valley furniture, see Edward

S. Cooke Jr., "New Netherlands' Influence on Furniture of the Housatonic Valley," in Joshua Lane, ed., *The Impact of the New Netherlands Upon the Colonial Long Island Basin* (New Haven, Conn., and Washington, D.C.: Yale-Smithsonian Seminar on Material Culture, 1993), 39–42.

29. The antique dealer Ken Hammitt advertised two related tables that he found in the Newtown area: a rectangular-top table with a drawer that featured a scalloped skirt and a round-top version with a drawer that featured splayed legs. Both examples have a similar flattened ball with flanking rings that flow into flaring transition, as seen on the base and capital of the table in figure 25, but the tripartite turned vocabulary consists of a central flattened ball with flanking balusters. For illustrations of these tables, see *Antiques* 67, no. 2 (1955): 113; no. 6 (1955): 469.

30. In the desk shown in figure 27, instead of pinning the base molding to the outside of the carcass as in figure 26, the joiner nailed a frame-like structure to the bottom of the carcass and ran a molding plane along its protruding edge. The drawer construction of the Beers desk, which features half pins at the bottom of each corner of the drawer linings and a rabbeted edge on the drawer bottom, and the use of chalk half circles to mark the orientation of several boards used in the construction of the carcass and drawers suggest that the desk may have been made in the shop that also made the pieces shown in figures 23 and 24.

31. Trent, *Hearts and Crowns*.

32. Michael Owen Jones cautions against the static view of tradition in *The Hand Made Object and Its Maker* (Berkeley and Los Angeles: University of California Press, 1975), 68–74. A sensitive study of vernacular craftsmen is Dell Upton's "Vernacular Domestic Architecture in Eighteenth-Century Virginia," *Winterthur Portfolio* 17, nos. 2/3 (1982): 95–119. These insights and the following discussion of the workmanship of habit are drawn from Forman, "Delaware Valley," esp. 46–48; Barbara Ward, "The Craftsman in a Changing Society: Boston Goldsmiths, 1690–1730" (Ph.D. diss., Boston University, 1983), 100–106, 127–31; Philip Zimmerman, "Workmanship as Evidence: A Model for Object Study," *Winterthur Portfolio* 16, no. 4 (1981): 283–307.

33. Visible grooves for drawer blades, long and deep saw kerf in dovetail joints, and use of second-rate, knotty wood in an inconsistent fashion can be found on much Boston furniture, even the expensive bombé forms. Boston joiners also used mahogany and other primary woods in a very wasteful manner. In Newtown, joiners concealed the grooves, cut precise joints, and used yellow poplar or red oak consistently. Wallace Gusler was the first scholar to point out the relatively poor quality of the interior workmanship found on Boston-area case furniture. Gusler, "Variations in 18th-Century Casework," *Fine Woodworking* 23 (July 1980): 52.

Seven

1. On the Boston versions of banister-back turned chairs, see Benno Forman, *American Seating Furniture, 1630–1730* (New York: W. W. Norton, 1988), 281–317; and Robert Trent, "The Spencer Chairs and Regional Chair Making in the Connecticut River Valley, 1639–1863," *Connecticut Historical Society Bulletin* 49, no. 4 (1984): 175–93. The button-on-urn finial is seen on earlier Stratford and Milford crown

chairs and the reeded banisters and the compressed urn-over-baluster turning on the rear posts parallel similar features on painted chairs from Milford. Robert Trent, *Hearts and Crowns* (New Haven: New Haven Colony Historical Society, 1977), figs. 12–17, 19–24, 47–50; Edward S. Cooke Jr., "New Netherlands' Influence On Furniture of the Housatonic Valley," in Joshua Lane, ed., *The Impact of the New Netherlands Upon the Colonial Long Island Basin* (New Haven, Conn., and Washington, D.C.: Yale-Smithsonian Seminar on Material Culture, 1993), 36–43.

2. Trent, *Hearts and Crowns*, figs. 73–74, 77–78; Edward S. Cooke Jr., "The Selective Conservative Taste: Furniture in Stratford, Connecticut, 1740–1800" (M.A. thesis, University of Delaware, 1979), figs. 2–5. York chairs with the same crest rail, rear posts, and front rounds descended in the Stiles and Strong families of Woodbury.

3. WPR 5:243–45, 260–61. Only in the last decade of the century did an increasing number of other forms such as desks, desk-and-bookcases, other types of cases of drawers, and bureaus challenge the dominance of the case of drawers.

4. The case of drawers in figure 31 descended in the Sherman family of Woodbury. Visible constructional similarities between this chest and the one shown in figure 30 include contrasting carved fans in the lower and upper sections, single-piece midmoldings fitted flush with the perimeter of the lower section, exposed dovetail grooves where the drawer blades fit into the sides, and moldings along the drawer front edges which have a thin quarter-round and a high fillet. Interior structural features provide additional proof that the two cases of drawers in figures 30–31 were made in the same shop. All have vertical backboards in the upper section; a two-piece composite cornice molding assembled by nailing the uppermost, projecting sequence of moldings to the cove molding already attached to the carcass; and a full-depth top board in the lower section. Along the inside of the back, the joiner nailed a full-width rail of yellow poplar, which provides horizontal stability in the upper section and occasionally carries the back end of the drawer supports for the uppermost tier of drawers. Another example with a five-drawer cluster in the upper tier of drawers descended in the Warner family of Woodbury. Edward S. Cooke Jr., *Fiddlebacks and Crooked-backs: Elijah Booth and Other Joiners in Newtown and Woodbury, Connecticut, 1750–1820* (Waterbury, Conn.: Mattatuck Historical Society, 1982), fig. 27.

5. Edward S. Cooke Jr., "Craftsman-Client Relations in the Housatonic Valley, 1720–1800," *Antiques* 125, no. 1 (1984): 272–80; Cooke, "Selective Conservative Taste," 57–59 and figs. 22–25. The Stratford chest-on-chest is also illustrated in Joseph Downs, *American Furniture: Queen Anne and Chippendale Periods* (New York: Bonanza Books, 1952), fig. 179. Blocky, squarish knees and rather straight legs characterize most of the long crooked legs on cases of drawers in southwestern Connecticut. In contrast, most legs produced in the Connecticut River Valley have rounded, modeled knees, accentuated knee brackets, and a more sinuous curve.

6. Examples of New Haven cases of drawers can be found at the NHHS and at the parish house of the Center Church in New Haven. For Hartford area examples, see John Kirk, *Connecticut Furniture: Seventeenth and Eighteenth Centuries* (Hartford, Conn.: Wadsworth Atheneum, 1967), figs. 81, 94, 179.

7. For information on Silas Butler and the case of drawers he built, I am indebted to Frederick Chesson and William Hosley, Jr. See appendix B.

8. The following ratios apply to the lower sections of all the examples shown in figures 30–31: HW 7:8; WD 2:1; HD 7:4.

9. Solomon Fussel's shop in Philadelphia produced a similar range of chair types. Benno Forman, "Delaware Valley 'Crookt Foot' and Slat-Back Chairs," *Winterthur Portfolio* 15:1 (1980): 42–45. Fiddleback chairs were not specified in a Woodbury inventory until 1800 and appeared only a few times thereafter. WPR 10:63. Cherry chairs with values commensurate with those of specified crookedbacks appeared in the 1776 inventory of Reuben Mallory. At his death in 1793, Sherman Hinman owned "Crock back cherry chairs" valued at twenty-six shillings. WPR 7:89–90, 9:160–62.

10. Another crookedback, which descended in the Bacon family, features a back splat pierced in a manner that resembles a popular Boston pattern, as is also seen on the great chair in figure 36. The rear stiles of the Woodbury crookedback chairs possess a very distinctive chamfered plane along the front edge between the bottom of the shoe rail and the feet. This sawn faceting gives the legs a bowed profile without modeling from files or spoke shaves.

11. A pair of chairs similar to that shown in figure 37, part of a set of at least eight chairs owned in the Tomlinson family, are now owned by Christ Episcopal Church in Quaker Farms.

12. WPR 6:184–87. An 1810 inventory listed "4 cherry chairs with flag bottoms 2. 6 do with cushion bottoms 7.50." Jabez Bacon's "6 cherry chairs with plush bottoms 6." provides another contemporary term for the most expensive seat construction. Ibid., 11:107, 10:256–64. The 1793 inventory of Sherman Hinman contains the first reference to "Dining chairs." Their individual value of five shillings implies that they were crookedback cherry chairs with flag seats. Samuel Curtiss's "6 dining chairs 6.50" must have been joiner's chairs. Ibid., 9:160–62, 11:200–201. Robert Trent points out that with all the available joinerly chairs produced in New London County during the same period, a true joiner's chair with cushion bottom was "a pure demonstration of purchasing power." Trent, "Legacy of a Provincial Elite: New London County Joined Chairs, 1720–1790," *Connecticut Historical Society Bulletin* 50, no. 4 (1985): 29. On the high cost of upholstery during this period, see Brock Jobe, "The Boston Upholstery Trade, 1700–1775," in Edward S. Cooke Jr., *Upholstery in America and Europe from the Seventeenth Century to World War I* (New York: W. W. Norton, 1987), 65–90.

13. WPR 8:114, 10:119–20, 156, 256–64, 13:31–33; Dean Fales Jr., *American Painted Furniture, 1660–1880* (New York: E. P. Dutton, 1972), 84–91; Fales, *The Furniture of Historic Deerfield* (New York: E. P. Dutton, 1976), 83–89.

14. On three different occasions between 1802 and 1807, Josiah's father, Matthew Minor (1753–1835), purchased a set of six green chairs from Jebine. Since Matthew also had Jebine make a desk for Josiah in 1802, one of the three sets of Windsors may have been intended for Josiah. Account Book of Matthew Minor of Woodbury, 1800–1820 (privately owned), 11–12; appendix B.

15. For information on the regional characteristics of Windsor chairs, I am in-

debted to Nancy Goyne Evans, formerly of the Winterthur Museum, who is preparing a book on American Windsors. Triple-beaded bows can be seen in Fales, *Furniture of Historic Deerfield*, figs. 167, 172.

16. A chair from the Masonic Lodge is currently in the collection of the Museum of Our National Heritage and illustrated in their 1991 annual report. The Bellamy example is illustrated in *Litchfield County Furniture* (Litchfield, Conn.: Litchfield Historical Society, 1969), 104–5. According to Nancy Goyne Evans (see note 15), the turned vocabulary and seat shape of these examples resemble those features in documented New Haven work.

17. Similar tilt-top tables descended in the Stiles and Strong families; stands, in the Bull and Munson families. Common features seen in this shop's work include the fully arched underside of the leg, the stepped knee on the upper surface of the leg, and the distinctive turned vocabulary of the pillar, which can be described as reel/half-urn/incised line/ring/incised line/tapered column. Use of a pattern to trace the outline of the leg explains the first two similarities. Workmanship of habit and use of a turning stick to scribe the general proportions of the pillar account for the consistent turning on each pillar. On the importance of tables in domestic comforts and social relations, see David Barquist, *American Tables and Looking Glasses in the Mabel Brady Garvan and Other Collections at Yale University* (New Haven: Yale University Art Gallery, 1992), esp. 73–76, 232–38; Rodris Roth, "Tea Drinking in 18th-Century America: Its Etiquette and Equipage," *United States National Museum Bulletin* 225 (1961): 61–91; John Crowley, "Artificial Illumination in Early America and the Definition of Domestic Space and Time," in Barbara Karsky and Elise Marienstras, eds., *Travail et Loisir dans les Sociétés Pre-industrielles* (Nancy, France: University Presses of Nancy, 1991), 59–69; Richard Bushman, *The Refinement of America: Persons, Houses, Cities* (New York: Vintage Books, 1992), esp. 182–86.

18. WPR 9:160–62, 11:90–91, 107, 109–10, 117–19.

19. Examples of fall leaf tables identical to that in figure 41 have descended in the Hinman, Strong, and Stiles families.

20. On the case of drawers in figure 42, the joiner laid out the fan with an even number of ribs rather than an odd number (and carved a pair of contrasting fans in a manner reversed from that seen on figures 30–31). He ran a different molding plane for the drawer edges, producing a small quarter-round and pronounced fillet that contrasted with the wider quarter-round and shallower fillet on Newtown drawer edges (see fig. 5 detail). Structurally, the joiner used a series of horizontal boards for the back of the upper section rather than vertical boards and dovetailed the drawer sides to the fronts and backs rather than dovetailing the sides to the front and the back to the sides (see fig. 5).

21. Several constructional features define figures 42 and 43. The drawer edge moldings are characterized by a relatively thin and high quarter-round profile with a pronounced fillet. Drawer backs from this shop tended to measure ¾"–⅞". Drawer sides were considerably thinner, approximately ⁷⁄₁₆"–½". The joiner attached wide drawer supports in two ways. In one technique, which he favored in the case sections with quarter-columns or pilasters, he fit drawer supports into housed dovetail dados on the inside of carcass sides and tenoned them into the back of the drawer blades. In the sections with plain fronts, he simply nailed the supports to the sides. Often

the back ends of these supports were cut diagonally. Drawer guides to keep the drawers sliding smoothly without binding or sliding off square were nailed on top of the supports. In some cases the guides were notched where the nails were driven.

22. A related desk, from another branch of the Stiles family, has plain unmodeled legs without beading and a simpler sort of desk interior with stringing around the central prospect door. Cooke, *Fiddlebacks and Crooked-backs*, fig. 31. Wallace Gusler points out that Williamsburg cabinetmakers often planed an ogee shape into a long board, then sawed up pieces for bracket feet. Gusler, *Furniture of Williamsburg and Eastern Virginia, 1710–1790* (Richmond: Virginia Museum of Fine Arts, 1979), 53.

23. The Woodbury feet and knees are more modeled than those on Dayton examples. For illustrations of related Stratford feet, see Cooke, "Craftsman-Client Relations"; Cooke, "Selective Conservative Taste." At least four other types of related carved feet have been found on furniture associated with the Woodbury area. Cooke, *Fiddlebacks and Crooked-backs*, figs. 26–29. The combination of similar scrolled, bulbous knees and carved feet can also be seen on a desk-and-bookcase from the Danbury area. That desk-and-bookcase, advertised as the work of E. Booth of Woodbury by Israel Sack in 1935, was still attributed to Booth in a 1969 exhibition of Litchfield County furniture; however, a Danbury origin is more likely. Before 1935, it was part of the collection of Dr. J. Milton Coburn, who lived in Danbury at one time in his life, and an ink inscription on the back of a small drawer in the lower section reads, "George F. Ives Danbury, Conn. 1893–1896 / If this is for sale let me know." All the drawers feature a large half pin on the upper edge of each corner, a rabbet rather than a groove along the inside of the drawer front into which the drawer bottom is set and nailed, and drawer backs nailed to the sides. Another distinctive characteristic is the series of paired pins along the front corners of the drawer with the carved fan. Construction of the base also differs from Woodbury work. The Danbury joiner tenoned the feet into a notch cut into the bottom corner and then pinned a molding along the lower part of the case. Between the rear feet he ran a thin, white pine board, which was tenoned into both legs. For illustrations and discussion of this desk-and-bookcase, see *Antiques* 28, no. 1 (1935): frontispiece; *Litchfield County Furniture*, 68–69; and Ethel Bjerkoe, "The Booth Family of Newtown and Southbury, Connecticut," *Old-Time New England* 48:1 (1957): 10.

24. Kirk, *Connecticut Furniture*, 35, 40–41, 56–57, 60; Edward S. Cooke Jr., "The Social Economy of the Preindustrial Joiner in Western Connecticut, 1750–1800," in Luke Beckerdite, ed., *American Furniture 1995* (Milwaukee: Chipstone Foundation, 1995).

25. In crafting the chest of drawers in figure 44, the joiner turned the base, rope-twist column, and capital from a single timber rather than piecing together three different parts. To secure the quarter-columns in place, he glued and pinned them into a corner framed by sawing a notch along the front edge of the side and tenoning the ends of the drawer blades into a vertical stile. For an example of a mature craftsman's awkward attempt at quarter-columns, see Cooke, *Fiddlebacks and Crooked-backs*, fig. 26.

26. Kirk, *Connecticut Furniture*, 56–57, 69, 73–75; *George Dudley Seymour's Furniture Collection in the Connecticut Historical Society* (Hartford: Connecticut Historical

Society, 1958), 56–57. Examples of similar drops can be found in Minor Myers Jr. and Edgar Mayhew, *New London County Furniture, 1640–1840* (New London, Conn.: Lyman Allyn Museum, 1974), 46, 50, 52; Walter Whitehill et al., eds., *Boston Furniture of the Eighteenth Century* (Boston: Colonial Society of Massachusetts, 1974), 123, 194; Wallace Nutting, *Furniture Treasury* (New York: Macmillan, 1928), fig. 377. Another Woodbury chest of drawers with rope-twist quarter-columns but no pendent in the skirt is illustrated in *Connecticut Masters: The Fine Arts and Antiques Collections of the Hartford Steam Boiler Inspection and Insurance Company* (Hartford: Hartford Steam Boiler Inspection and Insurance Co., 1991), 212–13.

27. On the features of the bureau versus the chest of drawers, see Charles F. Montgomery, *American Furniture: The Federal Period* (New York: Viking Books, 1970).

28. Barry Greenlaw attributed this case of drawers to the Booth family and speculated that work by two members of the family could explain the slight differences in dovetail size and dimension of drawer linings between the upper and lower sections. Such an attribution to the Booths is unfounded because no documented furniture by any member of the family is presently known. Furthermore, the constructional differences are relatively minor and are more likely the result of a journeyman's or apprentice's work in the shop. A more cautious attribution would consider this case of drawers and other furniture related to it by construction and decoration to be the work of one Woodbury shop whose master is still unknown. *New England Furniture at Williamsburg* (Williamsburg, Va.: Colonial Williamsburg Foundation, 1974), 94–96.

29. As on figure 44, the drawer supports in the upper section of figure 46 are glued into housed dovetail grooves in the sides, nailed at the rear, and tenoned into the backside of the drawer blades. The drawer blades of the upper section are tenoned into the fluted pilasters, just as those on figure 44 are tenoned into a support stile for the rope-twist quarter-column. Drawer supports in the lower section were simply nailed to the side and bevel-tenoned to the backside of the drawer blade or skirt. Figure 46's ten-ribbed fan, use of a single piece of cherry cornice molding with triangular-sectioned scrap wood behind, horizontal backboards, and deep, unfinished front rail in the lower section link it to figure 42. A second crown top example—in which the joiner altered the skirt profile, added a second ten-ribbed fan to the lowermost drawer, eliminated the rosettes and stop-fluted pilasters in the upper section, removed the plain pilasters from the lower section, and carved plain pilasters in the upper section only—represents a slightly less expensive example, but still reveals a link with southeastern Connecticut work. The maker carved shell-like intaglio ribs in the plinth, which was an interpretation of the relief-carved shells applied to the plinths of crown case furniture from Colchester. *New England, Philadelphia and New York Cabinetwork* (New York: Park-Bernet Galleries, 1960), cat. no. 252. A similar crown top example, with a skirt profile exactly like the Williamsburg example, descended in the Stiles-Burpee family. *Maine Antique Digest* (Aug. 1992), 18D. The upper section of a case of drawers from this shop, complete with a crown top, carved plinth, carved fan with eight ribs, and fluted pilasters, can be seen on the married case of drawers—in which the top and lower sections, although both old, are not original to one another—illustrated in Dean Failey, *Long Island Is My Nation*

(Setauket, N.Y.: Society for the Preservation of Long Island Antiquities, 1976), 158–59.

30. For southeastern Connecticut examples, see Downs, *American Furniture*, figs. 191, 311; Fales, *Furniture of Historic Deerfield*, 212–14; Myers and Mayhew, *New London County Furniture*, 36–37, 42–43, 76–77; Kirk, *Connecticut Furniture*, 37–38; *The John Brown House Loan Exhibition of Rhode Island Furniture* (Providence: Rhode Island Historical Society, 1965), 82–83, 96–97, 108–9.

31. The career of William H. Peabody provides later evidence of the introduction of the Norwich-Colchester tradition to Woodbury. Although he moved to Woodbury from Stratford in 1804, he was originally from Norwich. See appendix B.

32. A desk-and-bookcase probably made in Derby and presently on display at the Tapping Reeve House in Litchfield provides another possible influence. The desk-and-bookcase has rope-twist quarter-columns like those on figure 47 on its lower section and a rope-twist quarter-round molding under its dentil and cornice. A related Woodbury example with a slightly different skirt profile was photographed by William Lamson Warren. The shop also made a flat-top version that stood upon a frame rather than having integral legs. Sotheby's Sale #6350 (Oct. 25, 1992), lot no. 388.

33. At least three related desk-and-bookcases have been identified: the illustrated example, which features a mariner's compass inlay on the front of the fielded panel doors and the fall-front writing surface, a plainer version without inlay, and an example from the Stiles-Burpee family that had glazed doors in the upper section. *Antiques* 90, no. 3 (1966): 275; *Maine Antique Digest* (Aug. 1992), 18D.

34. WPR 8:169, 174. The base of figure 49, in some respects, is simply an extension of the joiner's framed base without an applied base molding. In a manner more characteristic of the late eighteenth century, the joiner nailed a five-piece frame, mitred at the corners, to the bottom of the carcass; planed the protruding edge of the frame to make the base molding; and then glued and nailed three-piece corner blocks under each corner of the frame. Similar splayed bracket feet can be seen on documented furniture by Oliver Demming of New Haven, George Belden of Hartford, Erastus Grant, who trained in Hartford and worked in Westfield, Massachusetts, and Daniel Clay, who trained in Windham or Middletown, Connecticut, and worked in Greenfield, Massachusetts. Fales, *Furniture of Historic Deerfield*, 196; Kirk, *Connecticut Furniture*, 77; Decorative Arts Photographic Collection (Winterthur Museum); Phyllis Kihn, "Connecticut Cabinetmakers," *Connecticut Historical Society Bulletin* 32, no. 4 (1967): 97–144; 33, no. 1 (1968): 1–40.

35. Benjamin Hewitt, "Regional Characteristics of American Federal Period Card Tables," in *The Work of Many Hands: Card Tables in Federal America, 1790–1820* (New Haven: Yale University Art Gallery, 1982), 73–84.

36. The dimensions of the drawer backs and sides, drawer construction, mortising of drawer blades to the pilasters in both sections, molding profiles, and wedge-shaped core of the cornice molding all combine to document this chest-on-chest as the work of the same joiner. For examples of similar pattern inlays, see Montgomery, *American Furniture*. A second related chest-on-chest descended in the Stiles-Burpee family. *Maine Antique Digest* (Aug. 1992), 18D.

37. In terms of structural differences, the second joiner assembled his drawers

with more and thicker pins in the dovetailed corners, used a regular composite cornice molding without a wedge-shaped core, favored a heavier and more intricate cornice and midmolding, nailed vertical boards along the back of the upper case, inserted a full-depth dustboard under the first tier of drawers, tenoned all drawer supports through the backboards, and dovetailed the central drawer supports to the back side of the drawer blades. The maker carved his flutes with five channels rather than four and compressed six carved ribs into the plinth instead of four.

38. The ratios for the lower section in figure 51 were HW 9:11, WD 11:5, HD 9:5; for the upper section, 11:8, 20:9, and 3:1. By contrast the ratios for the lower section of figure 45 were HW 9:10, WD 2:1, HD 9:5; and for the upper section, 11:9, 2:1, and 22:9. An excellent discussion of proportions is Timothy Philbrick's "Tall Chests: The Art of Proportioning," in *Fine Woodworking* 9 (Winter 1977): 39–43.

39. A case of drawers with a carved fan closer in execution to that in figure 51, including the punch-decorated half circles at the end of the ribs, descended in the Ives family of Danbury. Kenneth Hammit, "A Connecticut Masterpiece," in *Bulletin of the Connecticut League of Historical Societies* 17, no. 3 (1965): 8–10.

40. On the importance of consistent layout and work when carving claw feet, see Gusler, *Furniture of Williamsburg and Eastern Virginia*, 103–5.

41. For examples of Philadelphia prototypes, see Downs, *American Furniture*, fig. 223; John Snyder, *Philadelphia Furniture and Its Makers* (New York: Main Street/ Universe Books, 1975), 150; Snyder, "John Shearer, Joiner of Martinsburgh," in *Journal of Early Southern Decorative Arts* 5, no. 1 (1979): 15–19.

42. Burnham and Chapin trained in Philadelphia and then set up shop in the important inland towns of Colchester and East Windsor. Kihn, "Connecticut Cabinetmakers," 111, 113–14. On Munson, see appendix B.

43. The joiner used the skew rabbet plane along the lower inside edges of the front and sides of a small desk drawer. By running a matching rabbet along three edges of the bottom board and sliding this bottom into place, he achieved a more easily made, stronger bottom construction than that used in earlier work. The older technique involved running a normal rabbet along the inside edges of the drawer front and sides and pegging the bottom within this rabbet.

44. For related studies that link stylistic and technical fluctuations to periods of significant market involvement and artisanal migration, see Barbara Ward, "The Craftsman in a Changing Society: Boston Goldsmiths, 1690–1730" (Ph.D. diss., Boston University, 1983); Robert Trent, "The Colchester School of Cabinetmaking, 1750–1800," in Francis J. Puig and Michael Conforti, eds., *The American Craftsman and the European Tradition, 1620–1820* (Minneapolis: Minneapolis Institute of Arts, 1989), 112–35.

Conclusion

1. For surveys about the changes of this period, see James Henretta, *The Evolution of American Society, 1700–1815: An Interdisciplinary Analysis* (Lexington, Mass.: D. C. Heath, 1973), 157–223; and Jack Larkin, *The Reshaping of Everyday Life, 1790–1840* (New York: Harper and Row, 1988).

2. Jane Eliza Johnson, ed., *Newtown's History and Historian, Ezra Levan Johnson* (Newtown: Jane Johnson, 1917), 180–88.

3. DPR 12:11–13, 60; appendix A; NPR 1:187–89; Account Book of John Hubbell of Newtown, 1792–1793 (OSV); Account Book of John Hubbell of Newtown, 1805–1823 (OSV); NLR 21:297, 387–88, 23:13, 266, 25:215, 32:553.

4. Appendix A; Johnson, *Newtown's History*, 288.

5. *Population Schedules of the Fourth Census of the United States—1820* (National Archives Microfilm Publications, microcopy no. 33), 1:213.

6. Johnson, *Newtown's History*, 248–60, 285–90.

7. An invaluable summary of the literature on the increased importance of household goods and the catalysts for consumerism in the colonial and early national periods is Ann Smart Martin, "Makers, Buyers, and Users: Consumerism as a Material Culture Framework," *Winterthur Portfolio* 28, nos. 2/2 (1993): 141–57.

8. T. H. Breen discusses the changes brought by the increased availability of English goods in "An Empire of Goods: The Anglicization of Colonial America, 1690–1776," *Journal of British Studies* 25, no. 4 (1986): 467–99. On the developments of urban marketing and the pressures they exerted upon local cabinetmakers, see Benjamin Hewitt, Patricia Kane, and Gerald Ward, *The Work of Many Hands: Card Tables in Federal America, 1790–1820* (New Haven: Yale University Art Gallery, 1982); Laura Fecych Sprague, "Patterns of Patronage in York and Cumberland Counties, 1784–1830," in Laura Fecych Sprague, ed., *Agreeable Situations: Society, Commerce, and Art in Southern Maine, 1780–1830* (Kennebunk, Maine: Brick Store Museum, 1987), 163–72; Nancy Goyne Evans, "American Painted Seating Furniture: Marketing the Product, 1750–1840," in Gerald Ward, ed., *Perspectives on American Furniture* (New York: W. W. Norton, 1988), 153–68; John Bivins Jr., *The Furniture of Coastal North Carolina, 1700–1820* (Winston-Salem, N.C.: Museum of Early Southern Decorative Arts, 1988), esp. 94–112; Jonathan Prown, "A Cultural Analysis of Furniture-Making in Petersburg, Virginia, 1760–1820," *Journal of Early Southern Decorative Arts* 18, no. 1 (1992): 1–172; Johanna McBrien, "Portsmouth Furniture Making, 1798–1837," in Brock Jobe et al., *Portsmouth Furniture: Masterworks from the New Hampshire Seacoast* (Boston: Society for the Preservation of New England Antiquities, 1993), 58–72.

9. For suggestive explorations of house joiners' rhythms in Woodbury, see William Warren, "The Oxford Meeting House," *Connecticut Antiquarian* 33, no. 1 (1981): 4–8; Warren, "The First Two Southbury Meetinghouses," *Connecticut Antiquarian* 33, no. 2 (1981): 22–32.

10. See appendix B. John Worrell finds a similar decline in the potteries of Goshen, Connecticut, during the same period. Worrell, "Ceramic Production in the Exchange Network of an Agricultural Neighborhood" (paper presented to the Society for Historical Archeology, Philadelphia, Pennsylvania, 1982).

11. *Population Schedules of the Fourth Census of the United States—1820*, 1:420, 3:38; *1820 Census of Manufacturers—Connecticut Schedules* (National Archives Microfilm Publications, microcopy no. 279), 146, 202–3; *1820 Census of Manufacturing* (Microfilm at National Archives and Records Service, Waltham, Mass.), 4:111, 337, 353, 437, 483.

12. For the standard literature on transportation and technological revolutions,

see George Rogers Taylor, *The Transportation Revolution, 1815–1860* (New York: Rinehart, 1951); Brooke Hindle, *Technology in Early America* (Chapel Hill: University of North Carolina Press, 1960); and Thomas Cochran, *Frontiers of Change: Early Industrialization in America* (New York: Oxford University Press, 1981).

13. Recent literature on the rise of English exports and its influence upon American purchases and production includes Neil McKendrick, John Brewer, and J. H. Plumb, *The Birth of Consumer Society: The Commercialization of Eighteenth-Century England* (Bloomington: Indiana University Press, 1982); John McCusker and Russell Menard, *The Economy of British America, 1607–1789* (Chapel Hill: University of North Carolina Press, 1985); John Brewer and Roy Porter, eds., *Consumption and the World of Goods* (New York: Routledge, 1993); Breen, "An Empire of Goods"; Martin, "Makers, Buyers, and Users."

14. Discussion of comparative data from Windsor and Colchester is drawn from William Hosley Jr. and Gerald Ward, eds., *The Great River: Art and Society in the Connecticut Valley, 1635–1820* (Hartford, Conn.: Wadsworth Atheneum, 1985); Robert F. Trent, "The Colchester School of Cabinetmaking, 1750–1800," in Francis Puig and Michael Conforti, eds., *The American Craftsman and the European Tradition, 1620–1820* (Minneapolis: Minneapolis Institute of Arts, 1989), 112–35; Trent, "New London County Joined Chairs: Legacy of a Provincial Elite," *Connecticut Historical Society Bulletin* 50, no. 4 (1985): 15–35.

15. It is noteworthy that Hosley and Ward's *Great River* contains few pieces of furniture made in gentry towns after 1800. Most of the post-1800 furniture was made in Hartford, new commercial centers, or yeoman hill towns. For one perspective on the demise of the gentry leaders, see Robert St. George, "Artifacts of Regional Consciousness in the Connecticut River Valley, 1700–1780," in *Great River,* 29–40.

16. J. L. Rockey, ed., *History of New Haven County, Connecticut* (New York: W. W. Preston, 1892), 783–88. For a discussion of mass or bulk production versus custom or batch, see Philip Scranton, "Diversity in Diversity: Flexible Production and American Industrialization, 1880–1930," *Business History Review* 65, no. 1 (1994): 27–90. Recent examples of the assumption that centers of commercial agriculture become centers of manufacturing are Gregory Nobles, "The Rise of Merchants in Rural Market Towns: A Case Study of Eighteenth-Century Northampton, Massachusetts," *Journal of Social History* 24, no. 1 (1990): 5–23; Don Skemer, "David Alling's Chair Manufactory: Craft Industrialization in Newark, New Jersey, 1801–1854," *Winterthur Portfolio* 22, no. 1 (1987): 1–21.

17. *Great River;* Donna Keith Baron, "Furniture Makers and Retailers in Worcester County, Massachusetts, working to 1850," *Antiques* 143, no. 5 (1993): 784–95; Merritt Roe Smith, *Harpers Ferry Armory and the New Technology* (Ithaca, N.Y.: Cornell University Press, 1977).

18. A study of the craftsman-initiated response to industrialization is Susan Hirsch's *Roots of the American Working Class: The Industrialization of Crafts in Newark, 1800–1860* (Philadelphia: University of Pennsylvania Press, 1978). The revisionist view that small shop or craft production remained dynamic and complemented, even supported, mass production, is made by Charles Sabel and Jonathan Zeitlin, "Historical Alternatives to Mass Production," *Past & Present* 108 (Aug. 1985): 133–76; and Jean Quataert, "A New View of Industrialization: 'Protoindustry' or the Role of

Small-Scale, Labor-Intensive Manufacture in the Capitalist Environment," *International Labor and Working Class History* 33 (Spring 1988): 3–22. On the various adaptations in Rhode Island, see Patrick Malone and Carolyn Cooper, "The Mechanical Woodworker in Early 19th-Century New England as a Spin-off from Textile Industrialization" (paper presented at Old Sturbridge Village, 1990).

Glossary of Furniture Terms

Throughout the book, period terms for furniture forms and parts have been used as often as possible. This glossary is for the reader unfamiliar with period terminology and current furniture nomenclature (see also figures 2–5).

Ball-and-claw foot: Elaborately carved foot, at the bottom of a leg, that represents an animal's paw or bird's claw grasping a ball.
Baluster: Vase shape of crookedback chair banisters or the turned decoration of a fiddleback chair's posts or front rounds.
Banister: Splat. Vertical back support of a chair which is tenoned into the crest and shoe rails of a turned chair or the rear seat rail of a joiner's chair.
Bureau: Chest of four drawers. The term was first used in the early national period and often denoted a chest of drawers about three feet six inches wide, with thin, flaring bracket feet, cock-beaded drawer edges, and inlaid decoration.
Case of drawers: Highboy; also called a high chest of drawers. Consisted of a lower case that resembled a dressing table surmounted by an upper case that resembled a chest of drawers. Tops were flat or pedimented; cases with the latter were called crown cases of drawers.
Cornice: Uppermost projecting molding or series of moldings on case furniture.
Crest rail: Horizontal element set atop the rear posts of a chair or tenoned between the tops of the rear posts. Often embellished with sinuous shaping and carved or modeled surfaces.
Crookedback chair: Type of flag-seated chair characterized by sawn-out rear legs, with a curved ogee or canted profile. Also featured baluster-shaped banisters, rounded crest rails, a turned front round, and front legs that were sawn out and decoratively turned.
Crooked leg: Cabriole leg. Modeled, curved leg that curves out at the knee and then inward toward the ankle. Common on joiner's chairs, dining tables, dressing tables, and cases of drawers.
Crown: Broken-scroll pediment that can top a case of drawers. Also used to identify a type of early eighteenth-century western Connecticut turned chair with an elaborate crest rail, the sawn-out profile of which resembled a broken-scroll pediment.

Cushion seat: Slip seat. Separate upholstered wooden frame, which was set into the rabbets on the inside edge of the seat rails of a joiner's chair.

Drawer blade: Horizontal rail that separates drawers from each other. Often let into a dado that was cut into the inside surface of the carcass side.

Drawer linings: Collective term for the sides and back of a drawer (see fig. 5).

Dressing table: Lowboy. Supported by crooked legs, it usually had four drawers and featured a large flat surface on which to lay out toiletries. Often made *en suite* with cases of drawers.

Drop: Turned pendant that ornamented the skirt of a dressing table or case of drawers.

Escutcheon: Brass plate that covered a keyhole or backed a bail, or pull.

Fall leaf table: Had hinged leaves that could fold out, supported by a fly rail.

Fiddleback: Flag-seated chair with turned posts, baluster-shaped banisters, rounded crest rails, and a turned front round. The turned rear legs most easily distinguish it from the crookedback.

Finial: Turned ornament at top of the rear post of a turned chair or a separate turned decorative element that embellished the corners or plinth of a crown case of drawers.

Flag: Rush-like plant (*Acorus calamus*), the leaves and stalks of which were twisted together and then woven to bottom the seats of turned chairs.

Fluting: Series of parallel shallow, concave grooves running vertically. Often found on quarter-columns or pilasters of case furniture or on the straight legs of tables or chairs.

Fly rail: Separate rail on a fall leaf table that swings out to support a leaf. Attached by a finger joint to the fixed rail and tenoned at the other end into the upper part of a leg.

Joiner's chair: Featured sawn-out frame elements, no turned elements or decoration, framed seats consisting of four rectangular rails tenoned into the legs, and upholstered cushion seats, which set within the framed seat.

List: Framing member of a flag seat that was tenoned into the legs. Flag was woven over the lists.

Midmolding: Molding or series of moldings that adorned the waist of a case of drawers or desk-and-bookcase. Often disguises the separation joint between the upper and lower sections of these forms.

Pegging: Wooden pins or treenails driven into holes to secure mortise and tenon joints.

Pilaster: Vertical architectural element, rectangular in section and adorned with fluting, that adorned the front corner faces of case furniture.

Post: Rear leg, or stile, of a turned chair.

Primary wood: Exterior, or show, wood of a piece of furniture.

Rabbet: Open-sided groove cut along only one edge of a board.

Round: Turned chair's stretcher, a framing member tenoned into the chair posts below the seat level to join and strengthen the legs of a chair. Also used on turned table frames.

Secondary wood: An interior or structural wood.

Shoe rail: Horizontal rail tenoned into the rear posts of a turned chair just above seat level. The banister was tenoned into the shoe rail.

Skirt: Horizontal board tenoned into the legs of a table, forming its frame, or into the legs of a piece of case furniture, forming its lowest carcass rail. Usually ornamented with sawn-out profile along its lower edge or with carving.

Slat: Horizontal back supports that were tenoned into the rear legs of a turned chair.

Spindle: Rounded rod, tapering slightly at each end, used for the back of a Windsor chair.

Stile: Another term for the legs of a turned chair.

Stretcher: Framing member, rectangular in section, tenoned into chair legs or other stretchers to join and strengthen the legs of a chair.

Turnings: Series of turned decorative elements.

York chair: Flag-seated chair with a round-shouldered, saddled crest rail, broad baluster-shaped banister, and a turned version of the popular crooked legs for the front legs. Resembled round-top chairs except for the York chair's substitution of pad-footed, bulging legs for regular turned front legs.

Windsor chair: Plank-seated chair with turned legs and rounds and with backs made mainly of shaved spindles. The chairs usually were painted to unify the various woods from which they were made.

Note on Sources and Methods

The study of eighteenth-century New England craftsmen and artisanal economies has languished far behind the study of the region's farmers and agricultural economies. While some social historians have focused on a variety of issues including social stratification, economic change over time, the interdependence of farms, networks of service transactions, and the transmission of cultural values, the role of the artisan has not been fully explored. Examples of such research are Christopher Clark, *The Roots of Rural Capitalism: Western Massachusetts, 1780–1860* (Ithaca, N.Y.: Cornell University Press, 1990); Robert Gross, *The Minutemen and Their World* (New York: Hill and Wang, 1976); James Henretta, "Families and Farms: *Mentalité* in Pre-Industrial America," *William and Mary Quarterly* 35, no. 1 (1978): 3–32; Christopher Jedrey, *The World of John Cleaveland* (New York: W. W. Norton, 1979); Bettye Pruit, "Self-Sufficiency and the Agricultural Economy of Eighteenth-Century Massachusetts," *William and Mary Quarterly* 41, no. 3 (1984): 333–64; and Steven Hahn and Jonathan Prude, eds., *The Countryside in the Age of Capitalist Transformation* (Chapel Hill: University of North Carolina Press, 1985).

Even labor historians who focus their analyses on the shop-floor dislocations of the mid nineteenth century merely refer to a homogeneous, roughly sketched past as a backdrop to or a contrast with the changes of industrialization. See, for example, Alan Dawley, *Class and Community* (Cambridge: Harvard University Press, 1976); Merritt Roe Smith, *Harpers Ferry Armory and the New Technology* (Ithaca, N.Y.: Cornell University Press, 1977); Thomas Dublin, *Women at Work* (New York: Columbia University Press, 1979); and Jonathan Prude, *The Coming of Industrial Order: Town and Factory Life in Rural Massachusetts, 1810–1860* (New York: Cambridge University Press, 1983). In any sort of discussion about craft activity, both agricultural historians and labor historians continue to rely on Rolla Tryon, *Household Manufactures in the United States, 1684–1860* (Chicago: University of Chicago Press, 1917), and Carl Bridenbaugh, *The Colonial Craftsman* (New York: New York University Press, 1950), both pioneering but broadly descriptive works.

For the most part, decorative arts scholars have abstained from the historical dialogue, remaining content to publish genealogical information on individual craftsmen and compile lists of a town's or region's craftsmen. Only within the past decade have material culture scholars begun to develop more rigorous analytical works on craftsmen. For a historiographical review of the craftsman literature, see Ian Quimby, ed., *The Craftsman in Early America* (New York: W. W. Norton, 1984); and Edward S. Cooke Jr., "Craftsmen," in Kenneth Ames and Gerald Ward, eds., *Decorative Arts and Household Furnishings in America, 1650–1920: An Annotated Bibliography* (Winterthur: Henry Francis du Pont Winterthur Museum, 1989), 333–42. More ambitious works that focus on furnituremakers include Gerald W. R. Ward and William Hosley, eds., *The Great River: Art and Society of the Connecticut Valley, 1635–1820* (Hartford: Wadsworth Atheneum, 1985); Robert Trent, "New London County Joined Chairs: Legacy of a Provincial Elite," *Connecticut Historical Society Bulletin* 50, no. 4 (1985): 15–35; Gerald W. R. Ward, *Perspectives on American Furniture* (New York: W. W. Norton, 1988); Robert Trent, "The Colchester School of Cabinetmaking, 1750–1800," in Francis Puig and Michael Conforti, eds., *The American Craftsman and the European Tradition, 1620–1820* (Minneapolis: Minneapolis Institute of Arts, 1989); and *American Furniture 1995* (Milwaukee: Chipstone Foundation, 1995). This book builds on such efforts to place the makers and their products within a specific context, but seeks to push the manuscript and artifactual data further in order to address those issues and questions that have concerned social historians.

The importance of contextual analysis in exploring and explaining changes in experiences or patterns of behavior underscores the need for more sophisticated documentary and artifactual linkage in the study of preindustrial craftsmen. Even though it is not possible to interview the artisans directly or to look at documentary photographs of their shops or of the homes of their patrons, one can reconstruct the craftsmen's world through careful, integrated use of a wide variety of primary documents and artifacts. For a thorough guide to the vast and varied sources used to analyze the Newtown and Woodbury joiners, their products, and their communities, see the chapter notes. Here follows a brief review of the major primary sources this study employs.

The most valuable manuscript sources were probate inventories of the period. The itemization of a person's real and personal estate offers quantitative and qualitative data about household possessions. By grouping together similar artifacts into larger categories, we can compare patterns of choice. People from different times or economic groups may have allocated different proportions of their estate to furniture, personal goods, household goods, and eating and drinking equipment. These choices often reflect the influence of social values or economic exchange systems. On the other hand, the language used in the inventories also deserves close attention. Types of ceramics or textiles often reflect the aspirations or wealth of their owner. Furthermore, contemporary terminology and classification systems reflected commonly held notions. Important items received more elaborate or more specific names and classification. For example, tea equipment gained more precise terms and descriptions as tea drinking assumed greater importance and popularity in the eighteenth century. Although inventories principally represent the older or wealthier members of society, such inherent shortcomings do not invalidate probate analysis. In the discussion of furnituremaking and fashion, it is appropriate to study this section of society through analysis of probate inventories.

Works that make effective use of inventory analysis to address household consumption include Susan Prendergast Schoelwer, "Form, Function, and Meaning in the Use of Fabric Furnishings," *Winterthur Portfolio* 14, no. 1 (1979): 25–40; Jack Michel, "'In a Manner and Fashion Suitable to Their Degree': A Preliminary Investigation of the Material Culture of Early Rural Pennsylvania," *Working Papers from the Regional Economic History Research Center* 5, no. 1 (Wilmington, Del.: Eleutherian Mills–Hagley Foundation, 1981); Kevin Sweeney, "Furniture and the Domestic Environment in Wethersfield, Connecticut, 1639–1800," *Connecticut Antiquarian* 36, no. 2 (1984): 10–39; Peter Benes, ed., *Early American Probate Inventories* (Boston: Dublin Seminar for New England Folklife, 1987); and Paul Shackel, *Personal Discipline and Material Culture: An Archaeology of Annapolis, Maryland, 1695–1870* (Knoxville: University of Tennessee Press, 1993).

Probate inventories provide further information about some of the craftsmen in the community. Appraisers of a craftsman's estate often listed a shop and its contents or an assemblage of tools that indicated artisanal activity. From these records the scholar can get explicit data on the identity of craftsmen, type of tools used, and type of work undertaken. Additional indirect information can be garnered about seasonal rhythms from the date of the appraisal and about artisanal traditions based on the bequest of tools, as well as about identities of additional craftsmen, since the appraisers of a craftsman's estate were often other craftsmen. Microfilms of the probate court record books from all Connecticut counties are on deposit at the Connecticut State Library in Hartford, Connecticut, as are individual estate dockets listed by name. Woodbury remained in the Woodbury Probate District throughout the period covered in this book, but Newtown began in the Danbury Probate District and then became part of its own Newtown Probate District in 1820. For this study all Newtown and Woodbury probate inventories filed between 1760 and 1825 were surveyed to establish a core list of joiners and woodworkers and to understand long-term or broad patterns of consumer behavior. Intense, systematic analysis that focused on seven five-year groups spaced ten years apart provided data about specific trends over time and between wealth groups.

Account books, many of which are in the collections of local historical societies, were the second most valuable documentary source for this study. Even if a farmer or nonjoiner kept the accounts, the double-entry accounting system of these books offers detailed information about production and exchange within that community. Therefore all available account books from Newtown, Woodbury, and neighboring towns were examined to gain familiarity with exchange patterns in the specie-poor economy, identify joiners and other craftsmen, document the types of furniture and their values, and examine the methods and time frame of payment. Notations in the account books often indicated the apprentices or journeymen who picked up or delivered items for their masters. The best public collections of account books from western Connecticut are those at the Connecticut Historical Society and those in the Manuscript and Archives Room, Sterling Library, Yale University. Many account books remain in private hands.

Tax lists for Newtown and Woodbury, some of which are located in their respective town halls and some at the Connecticut Historical Society in Hartford, supplied a third manuscript source. The assessments for faculties, or shops, provide the identity of some of the master craftsmen and the relative complexity of artisanal activities. The tax lists from the 1790s, which itemize the various types of lands, animals, grains, and so on (see table 12) are particularly useful in reconstructing the economy of that time period. Land deeds, census records, and wills also provided details about joiners active in the towns. Once the pool of craftsmen was established and fleshed out through these various means, the inventories, account books, and tax lists were used in a more rigorous and interconnected manner as the source material for a reconstruction of the joiners' social economy. For a detailed explication of this approach, see Edward S. Cooke Jr., "The Study of American Furniture from the Perspective of the Maker," in Ward, *Perspectives on American Furniture*, 113–26.

A craftsman's products as such provide the most important source material for craft scholars, yet one cannot "read" three-dimensional records easily. Given the importance of habit, patterns, and certain jigged tools in preindustrial furnituremaking, it follows that each joiner's products will demonstrate certain consistencies in design and workmanship. Common diagnostic traits attributable to composition and technique thus become a means of identifying shop traditions and authorship. Many studies have drawn upon such reasoning to identify regional traditions or individual hands based on aesthetic or formal links, but few have sought to explore the whys or hows of these correlations. It is a truism among decorative arts scholars that craft organizations and practices determined similarities among artifacts from the same region. See Charles Montgomery, "Regional Preferences and Characteristics in American Decorative Arts, 1750–1800," in Charles Montgomery and Patricia Kane, eds., *American Art, 1750–1800: Towards Independence* (Boston: New York Graphic Society, 1976); John Kirk, *American Chairs: Queen Anne and Chippendale* (New York: Knopf, 1970); and Michael Moses, *Master Craftsmen of Newport: The Townsends and Goddards* (Tenafly, N.J.: MMI Americana Press, 1984).

It is essential to examine a large-enough quantity of similar surviving forms or regional examples in order to distinguish regional characteristics, individual shop conventions, the gradual variation over a shop's career (also known as drift), the slow, selective accommodation of new techniques or decoration, and the distinction between occasional or anticipated deviation and significant deviation. Such scientific analysis separates common traits from rare ones, identifies significant characteristics and reveals the slight variations over time, and permits the recognition of a shop signature based on either certain exclusive traits or a particular combination of weaker traits that are insufficient or ambiguous alone. George Kubler first drew attention to the importance of drift in *The Shape of Time: Remarks on the History of Things* (New Haven: Yale University Press, 1962). Scholars analyzing turned chairs have made particular use of Kubler's work on seriation, invention, and replication. See Robert Trent, *Hearts and Crowns* (New Haven: New Haven Colony Historical Society, 1977); and Benno Forman, "Delaware Valley 'Crookt Foot' and Slat-back Chairs: The Fussell-Savery Connection," *Winterthur Portfolio* 15, no. 1 (1980): 41–64. For the importance of a large object pool, see Frederick Wiseman's review of Walter Backhofen's *Some Queen Anne Furniture from New Hampshire's Federal Period*, in *Maine Antique Digest* 18, no. 1 (1990): 10E–11E.

One must use the classification schemes produced by correlation analysis to generate additional questions or hypotheses about the behavior or performance of the makers. See Bernard Cotton, "Regional Furniture Studies in the Late 18th- and

19th-Century Traditions: An Introduction to Research Methods," *Regional Furniture* 1 (1987), esp. 17–18; Thomas Kugelman and Alice Kugelman, "The Hartford Case Furniture Survey," *Maine Antique Digest* 21, no. 1 (1993): 36A–38A; and Thomas Kugelman, Alice Kugelman, and Robert Lionetti, "The Chapin School of East Windsor," *Maine Antique Digest* 22, no. 1 (1994): 12D–14D.

Diagnostic features pertaining to form, construction, and ornament can all be derived from close qualitative and quantitative analysis of a large object pool of surviving furniture. The eighteenth-century joiner resolved certain formal considerations through an internalized sense of compositional logic and proportional relationships, as shown by recent studies on the proportions of case furniture and the structural logic of turned chairs. See Timothy Philbrick, "Tall Chests: The Art of Proportioning," *Fine Woodworking* 9 (Winter 1977): 39–43; Robert St. George, "Style and Structure in the Joinery of Dedham and Medfield, Massachusetts, 1635–1685," *Winterthur Portfolio* 13 (1979), esp. 20–22; Trent, *Hearts and Crowns*, 25–29; and Philip Zimmerman, "Workmanship as Evidence: A Model for Object Study," *Winterthur Portfolio* 16, no. 4 (1981): 283–307.

Furnituremakers building case furniture relied on proportional relationships among height, width, and depth of the overall form as well as geometric relationships between parts such as drawer openings and finial heights. Reliance on certain units of measurement and geometric relationships simplified the cutting of parts and subsequent assembly. Chairmakers also used certain given units of measurement to generate the lengths of legs, stretchers, and lists, and the size and placement of slats and positioning of stretchers. To make the compositional process more comprehensible and practical, furnituremakers used templates for bracket feet, crooked legs, crest rails, chair splats, and for shaped tops for chests or tables, or used jigged tools such as planes for moldings and strike poles to lay out turned elements and assembly marks on chairs. See Walter Backofen, *Some Queen Anne Furniture from New Hampshire's Federal Period* (East Plainfield, N.H.: Lord Timothy Dexter Press, 1988); John Bivins, *The Furniture of Coastal North Carolina, 1700–1820* (Winston-Salem: Museum of Early Southern Decorative Arts, 1988), esp. 185–206, 244–322; Bernard Cotton, *The English Regional Chair* (Woodbridge, Suffolk: Antique Collectors' Club, 1990), esp. 241–58; Benjamin Hewitt, "Regional Characteristics of American Federal-Period Card Tables," in *The Work of Many Hands: Card Tables in Federal America, 1790–1820* (New Haven: Yale University Art Gallery, 1982), 55–106; and Zimmerman, "Workmanship as Evidence."

Quantitative analysis of workmanship permits another level of insight. Workmanship can be broken down into large-scale features, which are closely related to compositional logic and often have a more regional coherence, and finer details, which often permit the identification of shop traditions (my own discussion of the choices evident in the workmanship is derived from the work of Zimmerman, Backofen, Hewitt, and Cotton). Large-scale features include formal type (chest with drawers, chest of four drawers, tall chest of six drawers, case for drawers, or chest-on-chest, to name a few storage examples); wood choice; placement of drawers in case furniture; the writing height and interior layout of desks; fasteners (nails, wooden pins, etc.); and finishes. Another level of workmanship consists of drawer construction (sequence, angle, and spacing of dovetails; the finish of the upper edge of the drawer sides; thickness of the linings; and the means of constructing and fastening the drawer bottom); carcass construction (sequence, spacing, and fastening of the joints used to frame the storage unit; finishes of the inner surfaces; indications of indexing marks; means of constructing and fastening the back and bottom; and the joints used to fit in drawer blades, columns, or pilasters); the sequence of turned vocabularies on the legs, stretchers, and arm supports of turned chairs; and the preparation and fitting of nonvisible structural elements such as drawer supports.

One should also assess the joints used to construct the furniture, both their appropriateness given possible choices of the period and the level of execution. Turning and cutting joints such as dovetails or mortise and tenons were two activities in which the joiner relied on habit and dexterity to save time and to ensure precision and uniformity. For chair parts, finials, and other turned elements, a craftsman consistently used the same vocabulary or combination of turned features since practice, a particular set of turning gouges, and repetition made certain turning techniques easier and more rhythmic. Similarly, a joiner laid out and cut joints in the same manner; he did not have to focus intently while cutting multiple series of pins and tails or mortises and tenons. The time and concentration required by an unfamiliar action would have made his work too time-consuming to produce given his time and his clients' expectations.

The techniques and workmanship of decoration offer slightly different information and should be examined carefully. Many decorative features represent the decision of the buyer rather than the training or habit of the joiner. The customer often chose the type and amount of decoration in relation to his aspirations and willingness to pay for extra work. Nevertheless the joiner executed the work with techniques he found familiar or comprehensible. For example, the customer might request a carved fan or fluted pilasters on a case of drawers. The joiner would then execute the desired ornament in his own manner of work. On the importance of consumer preference on decoration, see Zimmerman, "Workmanship as Evidence," 291, 293–95; and Hewitt, "Regional Characteristics," 99–101.

For this study, data was gathered on overall measurements, dimensions of individual parts, layout, evidence of patterns, wood usage, surface preparation, carcass construction, types of joints, workmanship evident at the joints, indexing marks such as awl lines or chalk marks, placement of pegs or nails, turned vocabulary, and drawer construction. The existence of only two pieces of furniture signed or labeled by joiners who worked in each of the two towns would seem to place certain restrictions upon this analysis. The paucity of such documented furniture precludes a sound foundation on which to base attributions to certain makers and thereby link a certain joiner's career with his production.

But a preoccupation with individual authorship can often be misleading if it is pursued as an end unto itself. Instead of building up attributions to known craftsmen, I found it necessary to establish regional characteristics and to distinguish between several anonymous shops in each town. First, all furniture with any specific or attributed association with Newtown or Woodbury was examined. This included objects with documented histories of ownership in local families, those still owned by descendants of eighteenth-century Newtown or Woodbury families, and those that antique dealers have attributed to the area. Related examples were then culled from books, periodicals, museum catalogues, and similar published sources. From a preliminary object pool of approximately three hundred objects, it was possible to winnow out certain objects and to group others by histories of ownership, constructional conventions, and stylistic similarities. The 1982 exhibition on the towns' furniture for which I was guest curator and several of my subsequent articles have helped to locate other related works.

In the end it was possible to identify about one hundred and fifty pieces of furniture made in Newtown or Woodbury. Although the identified examples do not include all the forms made in the late eighteenth century, they should not be dismissed on the basis of such incomplete survival. Any sort of survival offers important evidence about the past, and the examples discussed in this study do offer a broad selection of forms. See also Edward S. Cooke Jr., *Fiddlebacks and Crookedbacks: Elijah Booth and Other Joiners in Newtown and Woodbury, 1750–1820* (Waterbury, Conn.: Mattatuck Museum, 1982); Cooke, "Craftsman-Client Relations in the Housatonic Valley, 1720–1800," *Antiques* 125, no. 1 (1984): 272–80; and Cooke, "New Netherlands' Influence on Furniture of the Housatonic Valley," in Joshua Lane, ed., *The Impact of New Netherlands Upon the Colonial Long Island Basin* (New Haven, Conn., and Washington, D.C.: Yale-Smithsonian Seminar on Material Culture, 1993), 36–43. The relative importance of artifactual survival is discussed in Jules Prown, "Mind in Matter: An Introduction to Material Culture Theory and Method," *Winterthur Portfolio* 17, no. 1 (1982): 1–4; and James Deetz, *In Small Things Forgotten* (Garden City, N.J.: Anchor Press/Doubleday, 1977), 6–7, 93.

Index

Page references to illustrations are printed in italic type.

A. & G. Bradley furniture company, 192, 203
Adee, William, 29, 56, 57, 217
agricultural economy: and animal husbandry, 3, 69, 74–77, 79, 86–90; craftsmen's role in, 3–4, 6, 60–62, 76–78, 81–82, 202, 212, 217; and dairy farming, 12, 15, 66, 77, 88, 194, 199; decline of, 198–99; and manufacturing, 5, 195, 270n16; and market economy, 14, 44, 66, 71, 73, 75, 81, 85–90, 194, 197; of Newtown, 72–82, 96, 119, 125, 147, 191; percent of population in, 193, 195; products of, 49, 72–73, 77, 253n2; and social economy, 5, 30, 74, 150, 190–91; and values, 69, 249n1; war's effects on, 75, 86, 89, 92; of Woodbury, 73, 82, 83, 85–90, 119, 195, 199; and woodworking, 8, 14–15, 27, 88, 119. *See also* craftwork, and agriculture
Allen, Amos D., 195
Allin, Thomas, 201
Anglican church, 42, 45, 70, 75, 206, 221
Anglo-Dutch tradition, 36, 42–43, 143, 147, 152, *163*
apprenticeship, 28, 33–37, 41, 74, 182; and tradition, 51–52, 146, 182; uses of, 30, 157, 248n25; in Woodbury, 56–58
architectural woodwork, 8, 17, 58, 197, 226
Austin, E., 87

Bacon, Gary, 110–13
Bacon, Jabez, 57, 85, 115, 193, 225
Bacon, Nathaniel, 110, 221, 224–25, 229
Bacon, Seth, 217
Baldwin, Caleb, 203, 212–14
Baldwin, David, 102
Baldwin, Josiah, 218
Beach, John, 75, 108
Beardslee, David, 218
Beardslee, Henry, 37
Beardslee, John, 53–54, 57, 201, 222
Beardslee, Philo, 81, 213
Beardslee family, 40, 46, 54, 81, 201, 202, 218
bedsteads, 28, 203, 209, 213, 221, 224–25, 230; parts for, 16–17, 30–31, 208; timber for, 65, 209, 229, 231
Beecher, T., 87
Beecher, William, 87
Beeman, Reuben, 36
Beers, Samuel, 76, 80, 82, 211–13, 215

Beers family, 77–78, 125, 142, 148, 208–9, 213
Bellamy, Joseph, 159
Benedict, Noah, 152, *163*
Bennett, Ezekiel, 202
Bennett, Silas, 66, 218
Bethlehem, Connecticut, 14–15, 18, 31, 159, 227–28, 230
Bishop, Daniel, 14
Blackman family, 124
blacksmiths, 3, 31, 52, 79, 192, 195, 223
Bolt, George, 57, 218
Bolt, John, 218
bookcases. *See* desk-and-bookcases
books, 112–13, 230, 256n30
Booth, Asahel, 60, 64, 247n12
Booth, Charles, 64, 198
Booth, David, 59–60
Booth, Ebenezer III, 59–60, 65
Booth, Ebenezer IV, 59–60, 62, 65–68, 109, 121, 201–2, 205, 214, 247nn13&16, 259n18
Booth, Ebenezer V, 59, 62–64, 68, 218
Booth, Ebenezer VI, 58, 65, 67, 218
Booth, Elijah, 31, 57, 59, 64–68, 83, 206, 209, 219, 222, 230
Booth, Ezra, 101
Booth, Joel, 27, 29–31, 61–63, 67, 104, 195, 202
Booth, Noah Hinman, 58, 65, 67, 219
Booth, Olive Sanford, 59, 62
Booth family, 29–31, 46, 52, 59–68, 120
Boston, Massachusetts, 11, 41–42, 44; furniture styles from, 8, *132*, 147, 149, 152, 156, *180*, 185, 188
Botsford, Jerusha, 208
Botsford, John, 32
Bowne, Robert, 194, 228
Boyer, John, 53, 202, 210
Bradley, Abijah, 30, 54, 203
Bradley, Dennis, 31, 57–58, 219
Bradley, Eliphalet B., 203
Bradley, George, 30, 54, 203
Bradley family, 54–55, 59, 82, 87, 192, 203, 219

Bradley & Huggins company, 87
Branford, Connecticut, 51, 56–57, 222, 226
Bridenbaugh, Carl, 6, 7, 11
Bridgeport, Connecticut, 58, 80–81, 191, 195, 228
Bridgeport Turnpike, 81, 195
Brisco, Nathaniel, 204
Briscoe, James, Jr., 25, 53, 122, 202, 204–5
Briscoe, Mehitable, 53, 202
Briscoe family, 122, 204
Bristol, Joseph, 205
Bronson, Harvey, 198
Brookfield, Connecticut, 17–18, 87
Brookhaven, New York, 36
Brooks, John, 37, 43
Bryan, Alexander, 31, 120, 122–23, 205–6
Bryan, Ezra, 205
Bryan family, 122, 205
Buddington, Ozias, 123
Bull, Ebenezer, 57, 83, 219
Bunce, Isaac, 58, 220
Burchard, Eden, 82
bureaus, 47, 54; from Newtown, 100, 108, 192, 208; from Woodbury, 111, 116–17, *174*, 182, 184–85, 225–26, 229
Burnham, Benjamin, 44, 186, 197
Burrill, Samuel, 206
Burritt, Lewis, 37, 43, 242, 244
Butler, Silas, 154, *166*, 220

cabinetmakers, 66, 194, 208, 228; terms for, 18, 58, 63, 238n18. *See also* joiners
Canaan, Connecticut, 31, 36, 162
Candee, Naboth, 57, 220
Canfield, Burton, 198
carpenters, 23, 79–80; and other woodworkers, 8, 13–14, 18, 25, 27, 66, 194, 211; tools of, 17, 225, 229, 231
case furniture. *See* storage furniture
Catherine, New York, 53, 210, 218

ceramics, 85, 112, 159, 193, 254n4, 269n10
chairs: carving on, 98, 122, 126, 157; construction of, 18–19, 23–25, 28–29; from Newtown, 96–99, 102, 118, 120–26, *127*, *129–31*, 149, *167*, 192; nomenclature for, *20–21*, 121–22; ornamentation on, 98, 110, 121–24, 126, *127*, *129*, *131*, *167*; painted, 101, 158, 255n11; parts for, 38–39, 47, 61, 63, 125, 207–8, 217, 226; prices of, 110, 157; from Stratford, 42–43; trading of, 37–38, 64; and types of woodworkers, 14, 16–17, 54–55, 58, 66, 81, 202; from Woodbury, 65, 97, 110–12, 115–17, 152, 154–59, *163*, *167–69*, 188; wood for, 103, 119. *See also particular styles*
Chapin, Eliphalet, 186
Chapin family, 197
Chappell, William, 54, 192, 208
Charlestown, Massachusetts, 37
Cheney, Silas, 47
Cherevoy, Philemon, 220, 222, 229
Chester County, Pennsylvania, 184
chests, 17, 31; construction of, 19, 23, 39; from Newtown, 99–101, 142, 149; from Woodbury, 100, 153, *179*, 182, 184–85
chests of drawers, *133*, *134*; construction of, 19, 143; from Newtown, 99–101, 103, 142, 149, 161; ornamentation on, *135*, *139*, 145, *175*, *180*, 182–83; from Woodbury, 100, 152–53, 160–62, *164–66*, *172*, *174–76*, *180*, 182, 186
Clark, Christopher, 5
Clark, Zachariah, 74
Clark family, 86–87
Clinton, Simeon, 222
clocks, 30, 65, 78–79, 88, 105, 198
Colchester, Connecticut, 44, *175*, 183, 185–86, 197–98
Cole, Hezekiah, 31
Concord, Massachusetts, 87
Connecticut River Valley, 158, *164*, *166*, 184–85, 198

conservatism, 42–44, 123; in Booth family, 60–65; in Newtown, 74–75, 97, 104–5, 109; selective, 126, 149, 187; in Woodbury, 160–62
consumption patterns, 12, 69, 91, 110–12, 120, 142, 190, 199, 236n19; changes in, 10–11, 45, 48; for consumer goods, 79, 88, 105–8, 194, 197; and market economy, 193–94; in Newtown, 76–77, 92–96, 101, 109, 121, 147, 150, 197; and social economy, 5, 30, 191; variations in, 91–94, 96, 117, 190; in Woodbury, 85, 88, 93–96, 115, 117, 153, 188–89
coopers, 195, 225, 237n4; and other woodworkers, 8, 13–14, 194; property of, 79–80; tasks performed by, 15, 81, 87–88; in Woodbury, 15
Cornwall, Connecticut, 83
craftsmen. *See particular types*
craftwork, 6–8, 12, 37–38; and animal husbandry, 69, 78, 83, 194, 199, 221; community role of, 4–5, 57, 190. *See also particular types*
craftwork, and agriculture, 8, 40–41, 69, 199; in Newtown, 52–54, 75–78, 80, 96, 119, 147, 150; seasonal rhythms, 10, 14–15, 27–28, 37–38; in Woodbury, 194
Crammer, Amos, 221
Crofut, John, 108
crookedback chairs, 43–44, 97–99, 110–11, 116, 120, 126, *131*, 155–58, *167*, 188
cupboards, 17, 58, 112, 214, 230–31
Curtiss, Joseph, 14, 65–66
Curtiss, Josiah, 81
Curtiss, Samuel, 56, 120, 221
Curtiss, Sarah, 183
Curtiss family, 144–45, 221

Danbury, Connecticut, 64, 122; craftsmen from, 54, 82, 192, 208; importance of, 73, 75, 191, 250n5; trade with, 11, 61, 71, 78
Dayton, Brewster, 27, 36, 43, 153, 162
decoration. *See* ornamentation

Deforrest, William, 195, 221, 224
Derby, Connecticut, 25, 30–31, 70; craftsmen from, 18, 46, 50, 54, 203, 206, 223; trade with, 11, 64, 86–89, 193, 195
desk-and-bookcases, 100, 104, 223; examples of, *177–78*, *181*, 183–84, 186–87; from Newtown, 100, 104; from Woodbury, 110, 112–14, 116–17
desks, 40, 43; in Newtown, 61, 63, 99, 100, 103–5, 109, *132*, *140–41*, 142, 147–49; in Stratford, 36; in Woodbury, 65, 110, 112–14, 116–17, 161–62, *173–74*, *177–78*, *181*, 183–84, 186–87, 223
Dikeman, Ely, 78
Dominy family, 28, 240
Down, Joel, 116
Dulivan, John, 83
Dunlap, John, 28
Dunning, Benjamin, 15, 105
Durand, Andrew, 71, 205
Durand family, 40, 46
Dutchess County, New York, 206

East Hampton, Long Island, 28
East Windsor, Connecticut, 186, 197
Edgartown, Massachusetts, 51, 220
Edwards, John, 83
England: immigrants from, 42, 153; trade with, 44, 86, 193, 197
exports. *See* trade

Fabrique, Bartimeus, 46, 57–58, 67, 206, 220–23, 229–30
Fabrique, David, 18, 53, 147, 206, 221, 229
Fabrique family, 40, 46, 58, 120, 206, 220–22, 229
Fairchild, Clement, 192, 206
Fairchild, Ebenezer, 206
Fairchild, Edward, 206
Fairchild, Peter, 215
Fairchild family, 52–53, 202, 207
Fairfield, Connecticut, 11, 37, 73; craftsmen from, 25, 47, 50, 203, 215; furniture styles from, 122–23, 142
family: and agriculture, 4, 40, 76, 80, 88; and apprenticeship, 34–35, 63; attitudes toward, 47, 60–64, 66–67; and consumption, 45, 91–95, 105, 188, 191, 193–94, 197, 269n7; and craftwork, 10, 12, 40, 44, 46, 52–54, 56, 66–67; and inheritance, 46–47, 60; and market economy, 80–81, 199, 233n2; in Newtown, 70–71, 74, 92–93, 122–23, 150; production by, 16, 77, 85, 235n8; self-sufficiency of, 3, 5–6, 250n8; and stability, 4, 41, 45, 61, 75; in Woodbury, 57, 82–84, 87
Farmington, Connecticut, 51, 151, 217, 219, 227
Ferris, Joseph, 51, 207
Ferry, Joseph, 83
fiddleback chairs: in Newtown, 61, 97–98, 101, 103, 109, 120–26, *127*, *129–30*, 142, in Stratford, 43–44; in Woodbury, 110, 152, 155–58, *167*
finishes, 23–25, 27, 121, *131*, 239n23
fishing, 11, 37, 242, 253n2
Foot, Daniel, 52, 207
Foot, Edward, 52, 207
Foot, George, 52, 207
Foot, Joseph, 29, 52, 207
Foot family, 52, 207
Forbes & Henry company, 87
Ford, Ebenezer, 59, 98, 109
Ford, Sarah, 59
French, Bennet, 65, 225
French, Samuel, 42
furniture: and consumer patterns, 91–92, 95–96; in Newtown, 96–106, 108–9, 191; painted, 101, 103–4; significance of, 9–10, 33, 101, 112; by value, 106–9, 115–16; in Woodbury, 105, 107, 109–17. *See also particular forms and styles*
furnituremaking: attitudes toward, 47–48, 54–55; and market economy, 193–94, 197–98; and mixed economy, 53, 199; in Newtown, 50–

54; seasonal rhythms of, 28–29, 37–41; social aspects of, 41–42, 44, 151; in Woodbury, 51, 55–59, 193. *See also* shops

General Assembly, Connecticut, 70–71, 82, 84–85, 87
gentry class, 8, 12, 82–84, 94, 117, 151, 160, 197–98
George III (king of England), 75
Georgian style, 36, 42, 122, *127*, 152, 162, 258n8
Glastonbury, Connecticut, 144, 162
Glover, Charles, 16, 192, 207
Glover, Henry, 15, 213
Glover, Solomon, 125
Glover family, 17, 207–9, 213–14
Goodrich, Samuel, 3–4, 12
Goshen, Connecticut, 51, 56–57, 223
Gould, John Whitehead, 57, 222
Grant, Donald, 73, 144, 197
Grant, Hannah, 144–45
Grant family, 145–46
Gray, Nehemiah, 30
Great Awakening, 113
Green, Jesse, 83
Griffin, Samuel, 208
Guilford, Connecticut, 70, 96, 211
Guyre, William, 84

Hall, Eli, 57, 66–67, 222, 231
Hamilton & Brush company, 195
Hamlin, Arcillus, 46, 54, 82, 192, 208–9
Hann, Anna, 63
hardware, 31–32, 218, 222, 227
Hartford, Connecticut, 51, 56, 153, 162, 182, 184–85, 197
Hartford, New York, 213
Hawley, Elisha, 3–4, 12
Hawley, Ezekiel, 29
Hawley, Samuel, 28, 195
Hazard, Robert, 63
Hicock, Amos, 83
Hide, Chauncey, 113
Hill, Billious, 57, 223

Hine, Hezekiah, 58, 223
Hingham, Massachusetts, 70
Hinman, Curtis, 111, 113, 116, 237
Hinman, Edward, 65, 83
Hinman, Frances, 65
Hinman, Herman, 222–23
Hinman, Joel, 115, 183
Hinman, Justus, 116
Hinman, Sherman, 159, 221
Hinman, Timothy, 93, 112, 157
Hinman, Truman, 14, 85–86, 116
Hinman family, 83, 85, 112, 116–17, 156, 218, 222–23
Hitchcock, Lambert, 47
Hobart, Justin, Jr., 47
Hobart, Mary, 47
Housatonic Valley, 11, 25, 30, 49, 86–87; furniture styles in, 120, *127*, 152
household economy. *See* family
house joiners, 78–79, 88, 269n9; mobility of, 18, 52; and other woodworkers, 13–14, 17, 20, 23, 27–28, 58, 194, 237n13, 238nn14&15; tools of, 31, 201, 209, 211–12, 218–21, 227
How, Bates, 36
Hubbell, Ebenezer, 36, 43
Hubbell, John, 31, 81, 192, 211
Hubbell family, 36, 40, 43–44, 46, 81–82
Humphreysville, Connecticut, 90
Huntington, Connecticut, 17–18, 30, 51, 78, 218, 229
Huntington, Felix, 44
Huntington, Jabez, 198
Hurd, John, 223
Hurd, Lewis, 65
Hurd, Solomon, 224
Hurd, Zadok, Jr., 83
Hurd family, 223, 224
Hurlbut, Daniel, 58, 195, 221, 224
Hurlbut, Truman, 56, 110, 224
Hurlbut, William, 30, 58, 195, 221, 224
Hurlbut family, 58–59, 64, 160, *172*, 224

imports. *See* trade
industrialization, 4, 6, 12, 16, 30, 90, 190–94, 199; and agriculture, 5, 195, 270n16; and market economy, 16, 64, 69, 85, 191, 194, 198, 237n10
inheritance, 92, 99, 108; of craft identity, 46–47, 55–57, 62, 65, 67, 244n24; of land, 83, 204, 206; of tools, 46–47, 49, 52, 54–55, 62–63, 67, 203, 211, 227
interest, money on, 4, 78–79, 88
involution, 5, 10, 234n5
iron industry, 12, 30–31

Jackson, John, 47
James English company, 195
James Hurlbut & Company, 78
Jebine, Nicholas, 57, 66, 110, 158, *169*, 224
John Broome company, 32
Johnson, Ebenezer, 121
Johnson, Ichabod, 209
Johnson, Walter, 143
Johnson family, 144–47, 209, 214
joiners, 3–4, 45–47; and agriculture, 10, 39, 74, 96–97; nomenclature of, 20–21; and other woodworkers, 18, 237n13, 238nn15&18; social economy of, 11–12, 33–36, 38, 41; specialization of, 13–14, 17. *See also* house joiners; shops
joiner's chairs, *20*, 23–24, 43–44, 97–98, 110–12, 116, *127*, *129*, 154–57, *168*, 188, 198
Jordan, Philo M., 209
Jordan, Timothy, 120, 161, 209
Judson, Abner, 53, 57, 66, 68, 120, 147, 192, 208–9, 213
Judson, David, 98–99, 210
Judson, Simeon, 83, 116
Judson family, 68, 116, 161, 209–10, 214

Kasson, James, 15
Kent, Connecticut, 36, 162
Kent, William, 123
Kimberly, Thomas, 29, 225

King, Simeon, 55, 226, 230

labor, as power source, 29–30, 34–35, 51
land, 8, 11, 49, 194; attitudes toward, 67–69; and craftwork, 40–41, 46, 53–57; inheritance of, 83, 204, 206, 247n17; in Newtown, 70–71, 74, 78–81; rental of, 251n20; shortages of, 5, 45, 52; in Woodbury, 80, 82–84, 87, 246n1
Larkin, Edward, 37, 38
Latten, Benjamin, 123, 210
Leavenworth, Amos, 56, 226
Leavenworth, John, 15, 211–12, 226
Leavitt, Jacob, 25, 27
Lebanon, Connecticut, *166*, 220
Lenox, Massachusetts, 47, 57, 223
Lewis, Eli, 153
Lewis, Silas, 222
Lewis family, 87, 213
Lines, Abraham, 87, 226, 230–31
Linsley, Harvey J., 27, 58, 226
Litchfield, Connecticut, 46–47, 85, 213, 218–19, 221
Litchfield County, Connecticut, 11, 83–85, 87
Long Island, New York, 28, 36, 42, 78; furniture styles from, 43, 143, 147, 152, *163*, *164*
Loomis, Samuel, 44, 197
Loomis, Timothy III, 197
Loomis family, 197

Mallery, Curtis, 222
Mallery, Ebenezer, 53, 210
Mallery family, 210
Manchester, Connecticut, 47
Marblehead, Massachusetts, 37
market economy, 4–5, 8, 39, 44, 47, 69, 85, 87; and agriculture, 71, 75, 81, 85, 87, 194, 197, 251, 251n14; and animal husbandry, 14, 44, 66, 73, 81, 85–86, 88–90; and capitalism, 12, 96, 190, 197–99; and consumer patterns, 93–96, 115, 117,

193–94; and craftsmen, 14–15, 37, 64, 71, 78, 80, 90, 151, 188, 191, 194–95, 197, 199, 268n44; and furnituremaking, 10–11, 45, 58–59, 150–51, 188, 193–94, 197–98, 268n44, 269n8; and industrialization, 16, 64, 69, 85, 191, 194, 198, 237n10; in Newtown, 74, 78, 81–82, 88, 192–93, 197–99; and power sources, 30, 240n34; responses to, 37, 190–92; and Revolutionary War, 14, 16, 86, 151, 252n28; and social change, 48, 67, 80–81, 113, 199, 233n2; and social structure, 74–75, 193, 198; and tradition, 5, 67–68, 114; in urban areas, 10, 69, 86, 192; in Woodbury, 59, 64, 89–90, 190–91, 193–95, 197–99
Martin, Job, 115
material culture, 9, 43, 48, 109, 197, 253n1; and artifactual analysis, 3–4, 7, 10–12, 101, 118, 147; of Newtown, 99, 120, 126; of Woodbury, 117, 151
McCracken, Grant, 9, 235
Mechanick exercises (Moxon), 17
merchants, 6, 10, 14, 42, 44, 66, 193, 197–98; and agricultural products, 71, 85–86, 88; and craftsmen, 12, 31–32, 43, 57; mortgages held by, 55, 194, 228; property of, 79–80, 110–11, 114, 116; social status of, 44, 85, 90, 113
Middletown, Connecticut, 240, 246, 249, 267
Miles, David, 30, 56–57, 120, 152, 227
Milford, Connecticut, 56, 70–71, 120; craftsmen from, 50–51, 205, 227; furniture styles from, 122–24, 152–53, *163*
Minor, Josiah, 158
Minor, Matthew, 31, 84, 219, 221, 224–26, 229–30
Minor, Timothy, 227
Minor family, 83, 152, 158, *169*, 217, 224, 227, 229–30

Mitchel, David, 109
Mitchell, Reuben, 17, 230
Mitchell, Stephen, 144
Mitchell family, 230
mobility: of craftsmen, 18, 40–41, 46–47, 49, 68, 82, 185; and furniture styles, 117, 120; in Newtown, 50, 69–71; and persistence rates, 71, 93, 105, 249n2; in Woodbury, 51, 55–59, 70–71, 84, 87, 93, 96, 151, 187, 193
Monroe, Connecticut, 211–12
Moody, Samuel, 31, 83
Moody, Zimri, 56–57, 218, 227
Moody family, 227
Morris, Matthew, 83
mortgages, 55, 194–95, 203, 209, 228
Moxon, Joseph, 17, *26*
Munn, Benjamin, 55
Munn, Daniel, 55, 227
Munn, Patty, 55
Munn, Ruth, 55
Munn, Samuel, 55, 222, 227
Munn family, 84, 227
Munson, Ephraim, 58, 66, 186, 227
Munson family, 158, *169*, 227–28

neoclassical style, 43, 100, 126, *178*, 182–83, 192
New Haven, Connecticut, 195, 198; furniture styles from, 122, 153, *169*; and Woodbury, 87–89, 193
New London, Connecticut, 84, 197, 221; furniture styles from, 44, 154, 162, 182–83, 188
New Milford, Connecticut, 11–12, 15–16, 46, 80, 195
Newport, Rhode Island, 41, 44, 160, *171*, *180*
New Stratford, Connecticut, 78
Newtown, Connecticut, 12, 16, 30–31, 75; agriculture in, 72–82, 96, 119, 125, 147; animal husbandry in, 73–76, 81, 191; choice of woods in, 103–4, 119; compared to Woodbury, 151, 153, 155–56, 158, 183, 187–89,

195; conservatism in, 67–68, 74–75, 97, 104–5, 109; consumer patterns in, 76–77, 91–97, 101, 109, 121, 147, 150, 197; economy of, 32, 90, 237n10; furniture forms in, 61, 63, 100–101, 106, 109–12, 116–18; furniture styles in, 120–23, 125–26, 144, 146–47, 149–50, 264n20; material culture of, 99, 120, 126; mobility in, 50, 69–71; population of, 79–80, 92–93, 105; and Revolutionary War, 70, 75, 92; social economy of, 30, 68, 74, 125, 150, 190–91; social structure in, 69, 84; stability in, 45, 50–54
New York City: craftsmen of, 47; furniture from, 42, 44, 66, 123, 126, *135*, 144, 147, 152, 158–60, *170–71*, 188; trade with, 11, 14, 32, 49, 64, 85, 87, 193, 197
Nichols, Elijah, 197
Nichols, Lemuel, 109, 117, 192
Nichols family, 109
Norfolk, Connecticut, 31, 60
Northrop, Alanson, 53–54, 202
Northrop, Jonathan, 108, 116
Northrup, David, 211
Northrup, George, 108
Northrup, Oliver, 54, 211
Northrup, Samuel, 81
Norton, Nathaniel, 211
Norton family, 211
Norwalk, Connecticut, 29, 37, 51, 57, 71, 78, 96, 123, 125, 218
Norwich, Connecticut, 44, 47, 51, 58, 144, *175*, 182, 183, 185, 228

occupations, 79–80, 88, 193
Olmstead, David, 3
ornamentation, 7, 9–10, 35, 41, 118, 195; carving as, 8, 27, 38, 111, 143; on chairs, 98, 110, 121–24, 126, *127*, *129*, *131*, 157, *167*; on chests, *179*, 185; on chests of drawers, *135*, *139*, 145, *175*, *180*, 182–83; cost of, 23, 112; on desks, *173*, *177*, 184, 187;

inlaid, 23–24, 38, 43, 65, 104, 111–12, *177–79*, 183–85, 189; in Newtown, 143–44, 147, 148–50, 161, 191; on sideboards, 111; and social status, 8, 44, 193; styles of, 23, 33, 36–37, 42, 120, 143; on tables, *136–37*; techniques for, 23, 146, 226; tools for, 24–25, 208; in Woodbury, 117, 147, 151, 153–56, 158–60, 162, *176*, 182, 185–86, 188–89
Osborn, Barnum, 228
Osborn, Josiah, 228
Osborn, Shadrach, 65, 113–14, 194, 228; trading by, 14, 32, 66, 86, 88, 193, 222
Osborn family, 32, 87–89, 223, 228
Ovit, Luman, 17, 230
Oxford, Connecticut, 220, 223
Oxford meeting house, 221
Oxford Turnpike, 88, 90

Pardee, William, 87
Parmelee, Amos, 211
Parmelee, David, 81, 211
Parmelee, Nathaniel, 211
Parmelee family, 211, 212
Patterson, New York, 53, 215
Peabody, William H., 27, 47, 58, 194, 228–29
Pearce family, 83
Peck, Charles, 59, 195, 224
Peck, Daniel, 212
Peck, Joseph, Jr., 34–35, 212
Peck, Samuel, 205, 212
Peck family, 34–35, 59, 212
Peleg Wood company, 78
Perry, Daniel, 212
Perry, Nathaniel, 195
Perry family, 195, 212
Peter Parley stories, 3
Philadelphia, Pennsylvania, 43–44, *180*, 185–87
Platt, Moses, 122
Platt, Nathan, 213
political power, 4, 71, 84
population: density of, 11, 28–30, 46,

52, 55, 60, 240n35; growth of, 5, 10, 45, 52, 70, 74, 83, 85; mobility of, 4, 84, 93, 151; by occupation, 192–93, 195; persistence rates of, 71, 93, 105, 249n2
Porter, Hezekiah, 21, 29
Porter, Lemuel, 46
Poughkeepsie, New York, 18
Pray, Nehemiah, 17–18
Prentice, Joseph, 229
Preston, Nathan, 86, 210, 222, 227–28
Prindle, Arthur, 229
Prindle, Charles, 17–18, 25, 31, 58, 66, 215, 222–23, 229–30
Prindle, Cyrus, 27, 52–55, 212–13
Prindle, Enos, 52
Prindle, Ephraim, 52
Prindle, Joseph, 52, 54–55, 206, 213
Prindle, Lazarus, 34, 52, 55, 212–13
Prindle, Lewis, 27, 212–13
Prindle, Rivirius, 66, 192, 209, 212–13
Prindle family, 34–35, 40, 46, 52, 58, 206, 210, 214, 229–30
Providence, Rhode Island, 184–85

Queen Anne style, 122

Redding, Connecticut, 50, 53, 78, 214–15
Revolutionary War: economic effects of, 4, 44, 66, 113, 198; loyalists in, 51, 75, 206–7; and market economy, 14, 16, 86, 151, 252n28; and Newtown, 70, 75, 92; and Woodbury, 75, 86, 89, 94, 160
Ridgefield, Connecticut, 3–4, 12, 28, 195
Rogers & Murray company, 32
Romans, Bernard, 2, 195
Roots, David, 230
Roxbury, Connecticut, 12, 15, 246n1, 248n27

Salem, Massachusetts, 182
Salisbury, Connecticut, 83, 213
Salmon, Thomas, 42
Sanford, Amos, 51, 59, 214

Sanford, John, 64
Sanford, Stephen, 214
Sanford family, 51, 60, 207, 214
sawmills, 29–31, 39, 49, 52, 54–56, 60, 65–66, 80, 98, 119, 147, 202–3, 205, 209, 214–15, 221, 224, 227–28
Scudder, Isaac, 202, 210, 214
Seger, William, 105
Selah Conkling company, 78
Seven Years' War, 85
Sharon, Connecticut, 47, 50–51, 54, 192, 208, 214
Shepard, Susannah, 100
Sherman, Anna Curtiss, 185
Sherman, Cyrus, 230
Sherman, Elijah, 30, 214
Sherman family, *165*, 214, 230
Shipman & Denison company, 87
shops, 28, 40, 79–80, 197; in Newtown, 142–43, 146, 149, 198–99; organization of, 7, 27; traditions of particular, 35–37, 43–44, 124–25; in Woodbury, 56, 58, 88, 160, 185, 193
sideboards, 111–12
Skidmore, Elnathan, 215
Skidmore, John, 215
Skidmore, Nehemiah, 215
Skidmore, Thomas, 52, 215
Skidmore, Zardis, 53, 215
Skidmore family, 52, 215
Slason, Ezra, 25
Smith, Nathaniel, 186, 226, 230–31
Smith, Richard, 226, 230
Smith, William G., 192
Smith family, 221, 230
social economy, 5–9, 30, 33–36, 41–42, 45–48, 69, 80–81, 118; and artifacts, 9–10, 118, 121, 123, 152; and class, 69, 84, 112–15, 190; craftsmen's role in, 3–4, 6, 11, 41, 45–46, 49, 53, 55, 100, 149, 190; and cultural change, 42, 67, 88, 150–51, 188; local variations in, 11–12, 45, 102, 117, 190, 197, 199; of Newtown, 30, 68, 74, 125, 150, 190–91; of Woodbury, 156

social structure, 5, 7, 10, 12, 74, 82, 84–85, 112, 117, 197–98; and consumer patterns, 91, 93–94, 96; and furniture forms, 92, 105, 108–9, 112, 114–17, 151, 193; and furniture styles, 44, 159–60, *176*, 188–89; and social economy, 69, 84, 112–15, 190

South Britain, Connecticut, 198, 218, 228, 248

Southbury, Connecticut, 60, 78, 93; furniture from, 110, 125, 156, 158, 161, 184–85; and trade, 87, 90, 114, 210

Southford, Connecticut, 64

Spencer, Eldad, 56, 218, 220, 230

Spencer family, 197, 230, 261

Sperry, Stephen, 14

Squier, Joseph, 37

Stamford, Connecticut, 25

Stedman, Thomas, 15

Stiles, David, 31, 65–66, 223

Stiles family, 31, 87, 125, 161, 182, 223

Stilson, Israel, 215

Stilson, James, 215, 230

Stilson, Thomas, 74, 215

Stilson family, 74, 215

stockpiling of parts, 29, 38–39, 61, 142, 150

Stoddard, Nathan A., 230–31

Stonington, Connecticut, 63

storage furniture, 21, 39, 43, 91, 119, *133*; construction of, 18–19, 23–24, 38; from Newtown, 99–101, 103, 108, 142, 145, 147, 149, 161; nomenclature for, *19*; ornamentation on, 120, 143, 162, 266n29; from Woodbury, 100, 111–17, 152–54, 160, *174*, *175*, 182–83, 185, 187–88; wood for, 31, 118–19. *See also particular types*

Stratford, Connecticut, 42, 70, 82, 191, 258n10; furniture styles in, 44, 123, 125–26, 143–44, 152–53, 162, *164*–*65*; trade with, 11, 37, 71, 87

Strong family, 83

Sturdevant, John, 16

Summers, Jervis, 222, 231

tables, 30, 91; construction of, 18–19, 21, 23–24, 27; from Newtown, 54, 61, 63, 101–2, *132*, *134*, *136*–*37*, *140*, 142–47, 149; from Stratford, 42–43; from Woodbury, 65, 102, 114–15, 154, 159–60, *170*–*71*, 188

textiles: commercial manufacture of, 90, 198; and furnituremaking, 99, 110, *129*, 157, 193; household manufacture of, 6, 74, 76; in market economy, 85–86, 193; tools for making, 15–16, 64, 76–77; and water power, 30, 109, 192

Tomlinson, Samuel, 115

Tomlinson family, 195

tools: attitudes toward, 56; changes in, 187–88, 195; farming, 38; and furniture styles, 144, 146, 149, 188; hatmaking, 78; of housewrights, 201; inheritance of, 46–47, 49, 52, 54–55, 62–63, 67, 203, 211, 227; of joiners, 17, 20–21, 23–25, 27, 31–33, 39–41, 60–61; repair of, 58, 229; sources of, 7, 31–32, 81, 83, 85; and stockpiling, 29, 96; for textile manufacture, 15–16, 64, 76–77; value of, 192, 194; woodworking, 8, 13–16, 28

Tousey, Thomas, 31, 71, 158, 204–6, 208–9, 213–15

trade: in agricultural products, 76, 85, 89, 197, 199; coastal, 8, 11, 37, 45; within Connecticut, 11, 61, 64, 71, 78, 193, 195; in consumer goods, 94, 99, 113, 188; with England, 45, 86; with Europe, 85; in furniture, 6, 35, 38, 64, 66, 199; in meat, 85–90; in meat and dairy products, 15, 44, 77, 81; with New York, 11, 14, 32, 42, 49, 64, 85, 87, 193, 197; in wood, 43, 103, 119

Treadwell, Hezekiah, 71

Trent, Robert, 149

Trumbull, Connecticut, 18, 57
Tryon, Rolla, 6, 11
turned chairs, *129*, 149, 152, 154–56, 158, *163*, 192, 197, 211
turning, 15, 20, 27, 55, 205; of chair parts, 21, 24–25, 29, 38–39, 43, 61, 63, 96–99, 103, 108–111, 116, 119, 121–23, 126, *127*, *167*, *169;* of furniture parts, 17, 120; of ornamentation, 23, 124, 162; and stockpiling, 142, 150; of tables, *140*, 159; tools for, 16, 54, 125, 202–4, 208, 214, 217, 226, 231; and water power, 64
Tuttle, Newton, 184
Tuttle, Noah, 222
Tuttle, Ruth Pearce, 184
Tuttle family, 210, 228, 229

Ustick & Hartshorn company, 32

Wagner, Adam, 87
wagons, 15–16, 77, 81, 208
Wakeman, Ohio, 58
Wallingford, Connecticut, 51, 227
Washbon, Nathan, 101
Waterbury, Connecticut, 29–30, 46, 158, 198
water power, 29–30, 40, 55, 59–60, 64, 82, 109, 191–93
West & Hatch company, 47
West Indies, 11, 14, 37, 44, 85, 87
Western Reserve, 46
Weston, Connecticut, 18, 50–51, 53, 57, 202, 222
Wethersfield, Connecticut, 144
Wheeler, Abraham, 78
Wheeler, Andrew, 216
Wheeler family, 82, 216
wheelwrights, 15–17, 79–80; and other woodworkers, 8, 13–14, 237n9
Wilmot, William, 83
Windham, Connecticut, 195
Windsor chairs, 24, 47, 57, 97–98, 101, 108, 110–11, 116–17, 119, 152, 158–59, *169*, 192, 197, 203, 225
wood, 8–9, 13, 38; choices of, 43–44, 103–4, 122, 155, 159, 189; finishes for, 24, 101, *131;* sources of, 8, 30–31, 55, 61, 78, 80, 87; types of, 31, 38, 40, 54, 61, 103, 118–19
Wood, Elijah, 111, 115
Woodbury, Connecticut, 11–12, 88; agriculture in, 82–83, 85–88, 199; animal husbandry in, 87–90, 119, 195; compared to Newtown, 151, 153, 155–56, 158, 183, 187–89, 195; conservatism in, 160–62; consumer goods in, 91–97, 100, 102–5, 107, 113, 117; consumption patterns in, 85, 153, 188–89; furniture forms in, 109–12, 116, 118–19, 142, 153; furniture styles in, 31, 120, *131*, *139*, 144, 146–47, 151–52, 154, 161–62, *164–66*, *172–81*, 184–87; and market economy, 59, 64, 89–90, 190–91, 193–95, 197–99; political power in, 84; population of, 70–71, 83–84, 86, 93, 247n11; proprietary system in, 82–83, 87, 193; and Revolutionary War, 75, 86, 89, 94, 160; social economy of, 156; social structure of, 69, 82; trade in, 85, 87
woodworking: and agriculture, 8, 14–15, 27, 88, 119; specialization in, 14–15, 21, 57, 186, 194; techniques for, 20, 35–36, 39–40, 145–46, 149–50; tools for, 27, 81, 206, 210; types of, 13–16, 25, 31–32, 34, 54, 58, 215, 224
Worcester County, Massachusetts, 198, 270

Yale College, 42, 88
York chairs, 43, 96, 98, 123, 152, 237, 244, 250, 257–58, 262

Library of Congress Cataloging-in-Publication Data

Cooke, Edward S.
　Making furniture in preindustrial America : the social economy of Newtown and Woodbury, Connecticut / Edward S. Cooke.
　　p.　　cm.　—　(Studies in industry and society ; 10)
Includes bibliographical references and index.
ISBN 0-8018-5253-6 (alk. paper)
　　　1. Furniture making—Connecticut—Newtown—History—18th century.　2. Furniture making—Connecticut—Newtown—History—19th century.　3. Furniture making—Connecticut—Woodbury—History—18th century.　4. Furniture making—Connecticut—Woodbury—History—19th century.　5. Newtown (Conn.)—Economic conditions. 6. Woodbury (Conn.)—Economic conditions.　I. Title.　II. Series.
　　TT194.C495　1996
338.4′76841′009746109033—dc20　　　　　95-52689

www.ingramcontent.com/pod-product-compliance
Lightning Source LLC
Chambersburg PA
CBHW032221010526
44113CB00032B/207